THE NATURE OF INTELLIGENCE

Novartis Foundation Symposium 233

THE NATURE OF INTELLIGENCE

2000

JOHN WILEY & SONS, LTD

Chichester · New York · Weinheim · Brisbane · Singapore · Toronto

Other Wiley Editorial Offices

John Wiley & Sons, Inc., 605 Third Avenue,
New York, NY 10158-0012, USA

WILEY-VCH Verlag GmbH, Pappelallee 3,
D-69469 Weinheim, Germany

Jacaranda Wiley Ltd, 33 Park Road, Milton,
Queensland 4064, Australia

John Wiley & Sons (Asia) Pte Ltd, 2 Clementi Loop #02-01,
Jin Xing Distripark, Singapore 129809

John Wiley & Sons (Canada) Ltd, 22 Worcester Road,
Rexdale, Ontario M9W 1L1, Canada

Novartis Foundation Symposium 233
viii+300 pages, 24 figures, 24 tables

British Library Cataloguing in Publication Data

A catalogue record for this book is available from the British Library

ISBN 0 471 49434 8

Typeset in 10½ on 12½ pt Garamond by Dobbie Typesetting Limited, Tavistock, Devon.
Printed and bound in Great Britain by Biddles Ltd, Guildford and King's Lynn.
This book is printed on acid-free paper responsibly manufactured from sustainable forestry,
in which at least two trees are planted for each one used for paper production.

Contents

v

Participants

R. Anderson   Neurology (127), Birmingham VA Medical Center, 700 S 19th Street, Birmingham, AL 35233, USA

J. M. Bailey   Department of Psychology, Northwestern University, 2029 Sheridan Road, Evanston, IL 60208-2710, USA

N. Brody   Department of Psychology, Wesleyan University, Middletown, CT 06459, USA

I. J. Deary   Department of Psychology, University of Edinburgh, 7 George Square, Edinburgh EH8 9JZ, UK

D. K. Detterman   Department of Psychology, Case Western Reserve University, 10900 Euclid Avenue, Cleveland, OH 44106-7123, USA

R. Dunbar   School of Biological Sciences, Nicholson Building, University of Liverpool, Liverpool L69 3BX, UK

J. R. Flynn   Department of Political Studies, University of Otago, PO Box 56, Dunedin, New Zealand

S. Gangestad   Department of Psychology, University of New Mexico, Albuquerque, NM 87131, USA

S. Harnad   Department of Electronics and Computer Science, University of Southampton, Highfield, Southampton SO17 1BJ, UK

R. Hinde   St John's College, Cambridge CB2 1TP, UK

D. Houle   Department of Biological Science, Florida State University, Tallehassee, FL 32306-1100, USA

N. Humphrey   Centre for Philosophy of Natural and Social Science (CPNSS), Tymes Court Building, London School of Economics, Houghton Street, London WC2A 2AE, UK

A. R. Jensen   Graduate School of Education, University of California, Berkeley CA 94720-1670, USA

A. Karmiloff-Smith   Neurocognitive Development Unit, Institute of Child Health, 30 Guilford Street, London WC1N 1EH, UK

D. Lubinski   Department of Psychology and Human Development, Vanderbilt University, Nashville, TN 37203, USA

N. J. Mackintosh   Department of Experimental Psychology, University of Cambridge, Downing Street, Cambridge CB2 3EB, UK

J. Maynard Smith   School of Biological Sciences, Biology Building, University of Sussex, Falmer, Brighton BN1 9QG, UK

P. McGuffin   Social, Genetic and Developmental Psychiatry Research Centre, Institute of Psychiatry, King's College London, De Crespigny Park, Denmark Hill, London SE5 8AF, UK

G. Miller   Centre for Economic Learning and Social Evolution, University College London, Gower Street, London WC1E 6BT, UK

R. M. Nesse   Department of Psychiatry and Institute for Social Research, The University of Michigan, Ann Arbor, MI 48106-1248, USA

A. Pomiankowski   The Galton Laboratory, Department of Biology, University College London, London NW1 2HE, UK

M. Rutter (*Chair*)   Institute of Psychiatry, De Crespigny Park, Denmark Hill, London SE5 8AF, UK

T. Suddendorf (*Bursar*)   School of Psychology, University of Queensland, Brisbane, QLD 4072, Australia

A. Whiten   School of Psychology, University of St Andrews, St Andrews, Fife KY16 9AJ, UK

ntroduction

ichael Rutter

cial, Genetic and Developmental Psychiatry Research Centre, Institute of Psychiatry, *e Crespigny Park, Denmark Hill, London SE5 8AF, UK*

he main rationale put forward for this meeting was that there was an apparent ash between the expectations of evolutionary psychologists and the claims of haviour geneticists with respect to genetic influences on variations in telligence. Evolutionary psychologists, it was said, would expect that a trait so rongly adaptive as general intelligence would have been intensely shaped by atural selection and that, as a result, intelligence should show only weak genetic fects on individual variations within the population (Tooby & Cosmides 1990). y contrast, behaviour geneticists have argued that empirical research findings ave been consistent in showing a high heritability for intelligence. The upposed quandary was how to explain why the high intelligence that stinguishes us from other species, and which must have been under strong lection, nevertheless still shows large individual differences that are subject to rong genetic influences.

In trying, over the course of the next few days, to come up with some kind of solution of this apparent paradox, we will need to consider carefully the sumptions that underlie this proposition. The starting point, I suppose, is the eoretical expectation that traits under strong selection tend to have low eritability and that evolution by natural selection destroys the genetic variation n which it feeds (Dawkins 1999, citing Falconer 1960 and Lewontin 1979). robably, most of us will be inclined to accept this as a reasonable presumption om an understanding of how evolution operates, but questions may be raised n the extent to which the postulate is actually supported by empirical research ndings. Which multifactorial traits can be contrasted with respect to the kelihood that they were or were not subject to strong selection? Is it the case at the heritabilities of the former are consistently lower than those of the latter? intelligence truly a rather unusual exception to a well-validated, empirically pported, general rule, or is there a lack of research data on the issue?

The second assumption is that intelligence has been subject to strong selection. n the face of it, it would seem obvious that this must have been the case. In pport, Pinker (1997) pointed to the tripling in brain size during the time eriod between some 4 million years ago and some 100 000 years ago, and to the

1

fact that the cognitive skills of humans far exceed those of other species. Clearl
there are huge interspecies differences and it may be accepted that it is virtual
certain that there have been major increases in cognitive capacity over tim
What is not quite so self-evident is that it will have to have taken place as a resu
of evolutionary adaptation of a single cognitive trait — general intelligence.

Thornhill (1997) argued that a Darwinian adaptation was a feature of a
organism that had been functionally designed through the process of evolutic
operating by means of natural selection in the past. Note that the proposition
that the trait was adaptive in the past during the period when it evolved; it do
not necessarily have to be adaptive currently. Nevertheless, we may need
consider the extent to which intelligence is adaptive today. It has often be
assumed that it is obvious that it must be so on the grounds that measured I
correlates so consistently with measures of social success such as occupatio
earnings, and parenting and crime. Jensen (1969) presented data on occupatic
30 years ago, and Herrnstein & Murray (1994) outlined the findings mo
recently on a broader range of variables. There can be no doubt that IQ do
indeed correlate with most measures of social success but, apart from scholast
achievement, the correlations are mostly moderate rather than strong (see Cawle
et al 1997, on income, and Manolakes 1997, Rutter et al 1998, on crime). It
clear that IQ is only one of many factors, both in the individual and in societ
that predispose to social success. The findings on scholastic achievement do n
help much because IQ tests were designed to predict it. We may conclude th
the claims on the overriding importance of IQ have been overstated but, equall
it does have considerable predictive value.

These findings, however, are of very limited relevance to the question of t
adaptive value of IQ during the course of past evolution. Pinker (1997) posed t
question in terms of why it was humans (rather than other animals) who develop
high intelligence in the way that they did. He argued that vision, group livin
precision-grasp hands and hunting all played a part. All of these, like langua
(Pinker 1994), represent characteristics that are universally present, wi
individual differences of less importance. If these constitute the key adaptation
it may be that the current individual differences in intelligence are less of
paradox. Also, we need to note that the key features with respect to evolutiona
adaptation concern reproductive fitness and not social success.

That brings us to the next assumption, namely that intelligence constitutes
single trait that functions in a unitary fashion in adaptation. We will hear pape
that argue forcefully for the validity of the concept of 'g' — general intelligenc
There can be no doubt that there are very substantial intercorrelations amor
cognitive tests and that, as an abstraction, g has a greater predictive power tha
more specific cognitive tests (Carroll 1997). Whether that implies a biologic
unity, rather than a psychometric construct, is perhaps less certain. Also, to a

portant extent, different specific cognitive scales have somewhat different rrelates and functions. We may conclude that it is likely that the reality is that ere are both general and specific cognitive skills, with the former having a greater edictive power overall but the latter important in some connections. I am more eptical, however, as to whether the degree of modularity matters much with spect to the questions we are supposed to tackle.

Of possible relevance, however, is the assumption that higher IQ is always laptively better. If one asks whether, at an individual level, a low IQ is ever an vantage, the answer is probably that it is not. On the other hand, it is certainly ar that many human qualities other than IQ play key roles in adaptive success. lecting only on IQ would not be a good strategy. Also, bearing in mind that we e social animals, it is not self-evident that it would be desirable for everyone to ve the same high IQ with the same pattern. Successful adaptation in all societies lls on a range of skills (cognitive but also social, emotional and physical) and it is obably advantageous at a society level for there to be diversity.

We may also wish to ask how great individual differences in intelligence are. 'ithin industrialized societies, it matters hugely whether your IQ is 70 or 130. rom that perspective, the individual variation is very great. However, if mparisons are made across species, the difference among humans in the normal nge pale into insignificance beside the vastly greater differences among, say, umans, monkeys, dogs and mice. Perhaps, from an evolutionary perspective, e latter are more crucial than the former.

Up to this point I have used intelligence and IQ in a somewhat interchangeable shion and I have made the implicit assumption that intelligence has a biological asis. There must be a great deal of interest in the specifics of brain–mind terconnections, and it is all too obvious that our knowledge of them is dimentary, but it would seem very odd indeed not to assume that they must xist. We will hear more in this symposium about the empirical findings but I oubt that we will wish to query the basic assumption. The extent to which IQ sts measure intellectual performance has been subject to more dispute. It is ndoubtedly apparent that cognitive functioning in real life circumstances is far om synonymous with IQ test performance (Ceci et al 1994a,b) but, when all is id and done, IQ scores have at least as good empirically demonstrated validity as ny other measure of a behavioural trait. They are imperfect indices but they work markably well as measures of current cognitive performance. Of course, they do ot, and could not, measure innate potential (Rutter & Madge 1976).

What, then, of the claim that individual differences in intelligence are subject to rong genetic influence? We will hear summaries of findings from twin and doptee studies indicating a substantial broad heritability. Most reviewers have ut the figure somewhere in the 40–80% range (Hunt 1997, Waldman 1997) but, om both theoretical and practical perspectives, it matters little just where in that range it is. We are likely to conclude that genetic influences are of considerabl importance but, equally, non-genetic influences are also highly influential. Th importance of the rearing environment is probably most strikingly an convincingly demonstrated by the rise in IQ following removal from a high-ris home and adoption into a well-functioning one (Duyme et al 1999). It is relevai both that the extent of the rise is a function of the qualities of the adoptive hon and that the rise makes no difference to individual differences. It is also relevant th: nature and nurture are not as independent as they used to be thought to be. It obvious, for example, that individual differences in IQ are likely to result i differing school experiences and different patterns of social interaction. Genes ac in part, through their role in bringing about a shaping and selecting of experienc (Rutter et al 1997). Also, it may be that, as with other behavioural traits, genet influences operate through their impact on susceptibility to environmental factor We also need to remind ourselves that heritability estimates are population an environment-specific and are uninformative on the origins of differences betwee groups (Plomin et al 1997, Rowe et al 1999).

I expect, therefore, that we will conclude that both genetic and environment. factors influence cognitive performance and that some of the influence deriv from a synergistic interplay between the two (stemming from both gen environment correlations and interactions). The key question is whether th: applies differently to intelligence than to any other behavioural trait (Gangesta 1997). We are likely to conclude that it does not. The heritability of most traits in the 30–60% range, which is not that different from the estimates for IQ. The have been attempts to use heritabilities to draw inferences about the basis o dimensional traits (as, for example, in relation to concepts of temperament — s(Rutter 1994) but these have been unsuccessful because there is no clear demarcatio between traits with high and low heritability; most are in the mid-range.

That brings us back to our starting point. How does the bringing together c evolutionary and behaviour genetic perspectives help our understanding of th nature of intelligence? I hope to be persuaded that it will, but I begin th symposium from a somewhat sceptical position.

References

Carroll JB 1997 Theoretical and technical issues in identifying a factor of general intelligence. I Devlin B, Fienberg SE, Resnick DP, Roeder K (eds) Intelligence, genes, and success: scientis respond to the Bell Curve. Copernicus, New York, p 125–156

Cawley J, Conneely K, Heckman J, Vytlaeil E 1997 Cognitive ability, wages and meritocracy. I Devlin B, Fienberg SE, Resnick DP, Roeder K (eds) Intelligence, genes, and success: scientis respond to the Bell Curve. Copernicus, New York, p 179–192

Ceci S J, Bronfenbrenner U, Baker-Sennett JG 1994a Cognition in and out of context: a tale two paradigms. In: Rutter M, Hay D (eds) Development through life: a handbook fc clinicians. Blackwell Science, Oxford, p 239–259

ci SJ, Baker-Sennett JG, Bronfenbrenner U 1994b Psychometric and everyday intelligence: synonyms, antonyms and anonyms. In: Rutter M, Hay D (eds) Development through life: a handbook for clinicians. Blackwell Science, Oxford, p 260–283

awkins R 1999 The extended phenotype, 2nd edn. Oxford University Press, Oxford

uyme M, Dumaret A-C, Tomkiewicz S 1999 How can we boost IQs of 'dull children'?: a late adoption study. Proc Natl Acad Sci USA 96:8790–8794

lconer DS 1960 Introduction to quantitative genetics. Longman, London

angestad SW 1997 Evolutionary psychology and genetic variation: non-adaptive, fitness-related and adaptive. In: Characterizing human psychological adaptations. Wiley, Chichester (Ciba Found Symp 208) p 212–230

errnstein RJ, Murray C 1994 The bell curve: intelligence and class structure in American life. Free Press, New York

unt E 1997 Nature vs. nurture: the feeling of vuja dé. In: Sternberg RJ, Grigorenko E (eds) Intelligence, heredity and environment. Cambridge University Press, Cambridge, p 531–551

nsen AR 1969 How much can we boost IQ and scholastic achievement? Harv Educ Rev 39:1123

ewontin RC 1979 Sociobiology as an adaptionist program. Behav Sci 24:5–14

anolakes LA 1997 Cognitive ability, environmental factors and crime: predicting frequent criminal activity. In: Devlin B, Fienberg SE, Resnick DP, Roeder K (eds) Intelligence, genes and success: scientists respond to the Bell Curve. Copernicus, New York, p 235–255

nker S 1994 The language instinct. Harper Collins, New York

nker S 1997 How the mind works. Penguin, London

omin R, DeFries JC, McClearn GE, Rutter M 1997 Behavioral genetics, 3rd edn. WH Freeman, New York

owe DC, Jacobson KC, van den Ooord JCG 1999 Genetic and environmental influences on vocabulary IQ: parental education level as a moderator. Child Dev 70:1151–1162

utter M 1994 Temperament: changing concepts and implications. In: Carey WB, McDevitt SC (eds) Prevention and early intervention: individual differences as risk factors in the mental health of children. Brunner/Mazel, New York, p 23–34

utter M, Madge N 1976 Cycles of disadvantage: a review of research. Heinemann Educational, London

utter M, Dunn J, Plomin R et al 1997 Integrating nature and nurture: implications of person–environment correlations and interactions for developmental psychopathology. Dev Psychopathol 9:335–364

utter M, Giller H, Hagell A 1998 Antisocial behavior by young people. Cambridge University Press, New York

hornhill R 1997 The concept of an evolved adaptation. In: Characterizing human psychological adaptations. Wiley, Chichester (Ciba Found Symp 208) p 4–22

ooby J, Cosmides L 1990 On the universality of human nature and the uniqueness of the individual: the role of genetics and adaption. J Pers 58:17–67

aldman I 1997 Unresolved questions and future directions in behavior genetic studies of intelligence. In: Sternberg RJ, Grigorenko E (eds) Intelligence, heredity and environment. Cambridge University Press, Cambridge, p 552–570

Intelligence: success and fitness

David Lubinski

Department of Psychology and Human Development, Vanderbilt University, Nashville, TN 37203, USA

Abstract. This chapter presents the consensus among psychometricians regarding th construct of general intelligence ('*g*') and its measurement. More than any oth construct, *g* illustrates the scientific power of construct validation research. To date, *g* carried by more assessment vehicles and saturates more aspects of life than any oth dimension of human variation uncovered by psychological science. Phenomena mo vital to the core of *g*'s nomological network are reviewed (e.g. abstract learnin, information processing, and dealing with novelty). This is followed by coverage relevant but more peripheral phenomena (e.g. crime, health risk behaviour, ar income). Because *g* constitutes such a ubiquitous aspect of the human condition, i omission in social science research often results in underdetermined causal modellin, Frequently, this constitutes a longstanding error in inductive logic, namely, the Falla of the Neglected Aspect. Attending to Carnap's Total Evidence Rule can help to foresta neglected aspects in scientific reasoning.

2000 The nature of intelligence. Wiley, Chichester (Novartis Foundation Symposium 23. p 6–36

This symposium is about the nature of intelligence and its evolutionar significance. Some might find it surprising, then, that Sigmund Freud's famou remark that life consists of loving and working, *lieben* and *arbeiten*, sets the stag for my presentation. Yet, these two important domains are good starting points fc illustrating the scope of individual differences in general intelligence, which is th topic of my contribution. Assortative mating coefficients for general intelligenc (or '*g*') approximate 0.50 (Plomin & Bergeman 1991); and *g*'s predictive validity fc work performance surpasses this value as occupations become more fluid in term of their complexity and novelty—that is, as they become more conceptuall demanding (Schmidt & Hunter 1998). The evolutionary concept of fitnes however one chooses to define it, certainly would involve at least these tw major components: mating and resource acquisition. To be successful in the endeavours requires learning and, in particular, as industrialized cultures hav developed and evolved into the information age, learning demands hav concentrated on solving abstract problems. In his award-winning book, *Will u be smart enough?*, Hunt (1995) refers to people especially able at learning abstra relationships (and solving abstract problems) as 'symbol analyzers'. Historically, the psychology of individual differences has simply referred to them as intellectually gifted or talented (Benbow & Stanley 1996). The reason *g* accounts for more variance than any other personal characteristic in Freud's two chief realms of human endeavour is probably because, at least as much as anything else, *g* reflects individual differences in rate of learning abstract relationships (Carroll 1997).

Freud's statement identifies significant purviews of human activity. Functioning effectively within the dominant spheres of achievement and interpersonal relations is critical for general psychological well being, as well as for general biological survival. If cross-fertilization between differential psychology and evolutionary psychology has the potential to produce scientifically viable offspring, targeting psychological realms that both disciplines care about and are prominent features of the human condition will facilitate the process. In this regard, it is hard to imagine better arenas than mating and resource acquisition. None the less, the centrality of *g* is equally pervasive in many other facets of human life (Jensen 1998, Lubinski 2000). That needs to be emphasized.

For example, throughout this century, several personality theorists have pointed out that *g* constitutes an important dimension of psychological diversity relevant to molar behaviour (i.e. general personological functioning). When personality is viewed as a system of longitudinally stable behavioural tendencies that operate across situations, *g* clearly constitutes a substantively significant feature of the total personality (Lubinski 2000). Raymond B. Cattell (1950), arguably Spearman's most famous student, thought so; and Stark Hathaway, inventor of the most widely used personality inventory, the Minnesota Multiphasic Personality Inventory (MMPI; Hathaway & McKinley 1940), thought so as well. Hathaway was a brilliant diagnostician whose clinical acumen was legendary (Nichol & Marks 1992). As one of his students recalls, Hathaway would always tell his clinical advisees: 'We tend to think of general intelligence in isolation, as if it only operated in educational and vocational contexts; yet, it is a salient aspect of personality that saturates almost everything we do.' (P. E. Meehl, personal communication, July 1993.)

The preamble above serves as an important introduction to my discussion of general intelligence. It is intended to forestall concerns that we are discussing a molecular strand of human diversity (e.g. book learning). To the contrary, the nomological network of the *g* construct is broader and deeper than any other systematic source of individual differences uncovered by psychological science to date. Moreover, its conceptual underpinnings were embryonically embedded in differential psychology's origin. Given this, and because differential and evolutionary psychology germinated from common soil, it might be useful to review certain key antecedents to modern treatments of the *g* factor (Gottfredson 1997, Jensen 1998).

Some background

Early on, Francis Galton, the father of differential psychology, held that a *general* dimension was central to many academic achievements as well as subsequent developmental trajectories throughout life but especially in the world of work. He also appears to have believed that psychological assessment should focus on attributes that operate widely. In Galton's (1869/1961) words:

> In statesmanship, generalship, literature, science, poetry, art, just the same enormous differences are found between man and man; and numerous instances recorded in this book, will show in how small degree, eminence either in these or any other class of intellectual powers, can be considered a due to purely special powers. They are rather to be considered in those instances as the results of concentrated efforts, made by men who are widely gifted. People lay too much stress on apparent specialties, thinking over rashly that, because a man is devoted to a particular pursuit, he could not possibly have succeeded in anything else. They might just as well say that because a youth has fallen desperately in love with a brunette, he could not possibly have fallen in love with a blonde. (p 7)

In addition to postulating a general cognitive ability, Galton stressed that measures of intellective functions should forecast something important outside of assessment contexts. After examining, for example, Cattell's (1890) classic *Mental tests and measurements*, wherein the term 'mental test' was first introduced, Galton (1869/1961) appended two pages of profoundly influential remarks.

> One of the most important objects of measurement is hardly if at all alluded to here and should be emphasized. It is to obtain a general knowledge of the capacities ... by sinking shafts, as it were, at a few critical points. In order to ascertain the best points for the purpose, the sets of measures should be compared with an independent estimate. ... We thus may learn which of the measures are the most instructive. (p 380)

Looking back, these remarks set the stage for subsequent *construct validation research* (Cronbach & Meehl 1955): the phrase 'independent estimate' anticipated external validation, whereas 'most instructive' depicts an empirically based form of competitive support. To Galton (1890), like subsequent participants of the mental measurement movement, scientific measures were not all seen as equally important (Lubinski 1996). Importance was to be calibrated against the breadth

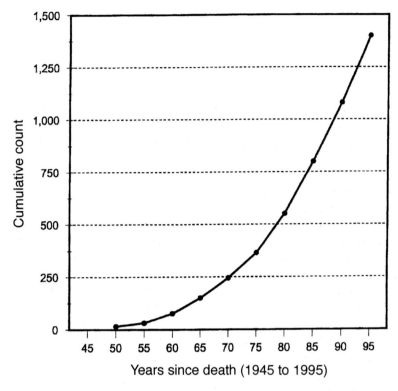

FIG. 1.   Spearman's cumulative citation count, plotted in five-year blocks, beginning with the year of his death 1945. (From Jensen 2000.)

and depth of external relationships achieved outside of assessment contexts. Furthermore, scientifically significant sources of human variation should manifest predictive validity over extended temporal gaps (Lubinski 2000, Schmidt & Hunter 1998). *Predictive* validity was seen as an important aspect of construct validity because, by generating impressive forecasts, the former helped confirm the latter. Evaluating the psychological character of individuals or groups involves assessing longitudinally stable attributes. Longitudinally stable attributes are the ones that lend themselves to *proximal selection* (*phenotypes* for securing mates and resources through social selection) and *ultimate selection* (*genotypes* for perpetuating adaptive characteristics through natural selection).

The *g* factor: instrumentation and measurement

Shortly after Galton's (1890) remarks, Spearman (1904) published one of the psychological landmarks of the twentieth century: " 'General intelligence,' objectively determined and measured", which supported Galton's view. Here, the concept of a general factor was spawned. At the phenotypic level, modern tests of general intelligence index essentially the same construct uncovered herein — albeit with much more efficiency and precision (Carroll 1993). We also know a great deal more about the correlates of g amassed from 95 years of research (Gottfredson 1997, Jensen 1998). That Spearman's thinking continues to influence modern thought is revealed by his cumulative citation count, compiled in five-year blocks, beginning with the 1945–1950 interval (Fig. 1). The positive acceleration of Spearman's current impact is remarkable for a psychologist who died in 1945.

Spearman–Brown prophesy formula

Important psychological constructs saturate multiple assessment vehicles because they operate in multiple aspects of life. Important constructs are ubiquitous. They are typically 'with us'. But because human behavioural determinants are both multilevel and multifaceted, evidence for even general psychological constructs needs to be secured through technical scientific instrumentation. This is not unique to psychological assessment, as E. O. Wilson (1998) observed in *Consilience*,

> Without the instruments and accumulated knowledge of the natural sciences — physics, chemistry, and biology — humans are trapped in a cognitive prison. They invent ingenious speculations and myths about the origin of the confining waters, of the sun and the sky and the stars above, and the meaning of their own existence. But they are wrong, always wrong, because the world is too remote from ordinary experience to be merely imagined. (p 45)

The discipline of psychometrics has developed instruments for dealing with psychological phenomena remote from personal experience. Psychological constructs are 'removed' from experience because they co-occur with other phenomena. Multiple behavioural episodes are necessary to detect them. Psychometric procedures sample responses to discrete performance opportunities (responses to items) and uncover dominant dimensions running through them (through aggregation). Each behavioural sample (test item) usually contains a tiny amount, say, 4% *construct-relevant* variance and, hence, a preponderance (96%) of *construct-irrelevant* variance. Most of any particular response is largely noise relative to signal. But Spearman's celebrated formula, discovered contemporaneously with Brown (hence, Spearman–Brown prophesy formula), interchanges these percentages (i.e. it interchanges the preponderance of noise to signal) through aggregation:

$$r_{tt} = (k)r_{xx}/[1 + (k - 1)r_{xx}]$$

where: r_{tt} = the proportion of common variance in a composite of items, k = the number of items, and r_{xx} = the average inter-item correlation.

Psychometric procedures like Spearman–Brown provide psychological windows on human variation akin to the microscope in biology and the telescope in astronomy. With an average inter-item correlation of 0.20, a mere 40 item scale can generate a composite whose common (reliable) variance is 91%. This is how psychometrics distils dimensions of common variance for submission to construct validation procedures.

Labelling scales

Once a reliable source of individual differences has been established (e.g. r_{xx} = 0.91) attention naturally turns to its psychological nature — or, construct validity. That the same construct may run through ostensibly distinct assessment vehicles and generate functionally equivalent external relationships is implicit in *convergent validity* (Campbell & Fiske 1959). Otherwise, construct validation would not work. Construct validity implies multiple vehicles (convergent validity) and heterogeneous criterion families (for establishing nomological networks).

To illustrate how the same construct may run through varying mediums, Table 1 presents three measures of verbal ability all assessed with different item types: reading comprehension, literary information and vocabulary. Yet, in the context of a heterogeneous collection of external criteria, they behave as functionally equivalent measures of the same underlying construct. They can be used interchangeably, yet, superficially, they appear to be measuring different qualities. Note also how these cognitive measures co-vary with distinct measures of mathematical and spatial ability as well as a variety of information tests. Careful sampling at this level of generality (technically, *systematic heterogeneity*) is how the construct of general intelligence is uncovered (Lubinski & Dawis 1992, Lubinski & Humphreys 1997).

Figure 2 illustrates how g is distilled by systematically aggregating content distinct groupings of ability mediums (quantitative–numerical, spatial–pictorial and verbal–linguistic). In this illustration, each of the three ability measures manifests 90% reliable variance (i.e. r_{xx} = 0.90). However, the preponderance of each scales reliable variance is specific (unshared with the other two). Yet, when all three are aggregated in a composite, the amount of specificity associated with each is attenuated, and the resulting amalgam primarily consists of what they have in common (viz., a general factor, 'g'). This is how psychometricians distil *general factors* from assessment vehicles whose reliable variance is primarily specific.

Probably the most impressive review of indicators of g is Carroll's (1993) book on the 20th century's factor analytic work (Fig. 3). This figure nicely illustrates the hierarchical aggregation developed here: items → scales → general constructs.

TABLE 1   Extrinsic convergent validation profiles across three measures having verbal content

	Literature	Vocabulary	Reading comprehension
Aptitude tests			
Mechanical reasoning	0.43	0.52	0.54
2-D visualization	0.25	0.32	0.35
3-D visualization	0.35	0.43	0.47
Abstract reasoning	0.45	0.53	0.61
Arithmetic reasoning	0.54	0.63	0.63
High-school maths	0.57	0.59	0.57
Advanced maths	0.42	0.43	0.39
Information tests			
Music	0.67	0.68	0.62
Social studies	0.74	0.74	0.71
Mathematics	0.62	0.63	0.57
Physical sciences	0.64	0.67	0.60
Biological sciences	0.57	0.61	0.56
Interest			
Physical sciences	0.24	0.25	0.22
Biological sciences	0.26	0.25	0.22
Public service	0.16	0.12	0.12
Literary-linguistic	0.37	0.32	0.32
Social service	0.07	0.06	0.07
Art	0.32	0.30	0.29
Music	0.23	0.20	0.20
Sports	0.12	0.12	0.13
Office work	−0.35	−0.29	−0.27
Labour	−0.08	−0.06	−0.06

These correlations were based only on female subjects (male profiles are parallel). $N = 39\,695$. Intercorrelations for the three measures were the following: literature/vocabulary $= 0.74$, literature/reading comprehension $= 0.71$ and vocabulary/reading comprehension $= 0.77$. (From Lubinski & Dawis 1992.)

Among the more important points illustrated here is the abstract nature of g. When heterogeneous collections of cognitive tests are aggregated, they form a general factor relatively free of any particular content or product, which accounts for approximately 50% of their common variance. This occurs when pictorial, quantitative and verbal item types are administered individually or in a group, orally or by paper and pencil. Because it is general, g can be assessed in many

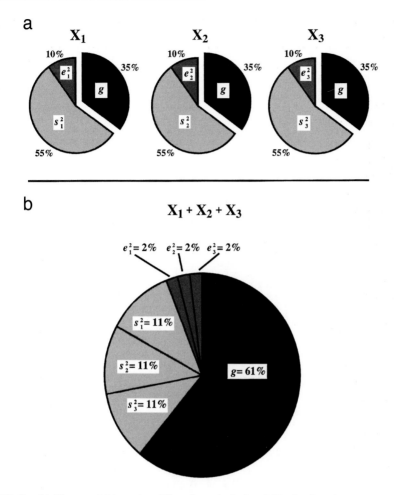

FIG. 2.   (a) Three variable variate. Three hypothetical variables having the same amount of common, specific and error variance. As individual components of a predictor variate, most of the variance of each component is specific variance. (b) Three variable composite. When the three components found in (a) are aggregated, most of the composite's variance is variance shared with a general factor common to each. Moreover, the influence of any one form of specificity is considerably reduced. (From Lubinski & Dawis 1992.)

different ways; for the same reason, g extends to many different kinds of life events. It is important to keep in mind, however, that multiple ways of assessing general intelligence typically converge on a common core, just as the verbal measures in Table 1 do. That is, ostensibly disparate assessment procedures can eventuate in functionally equivalent measuring operations.

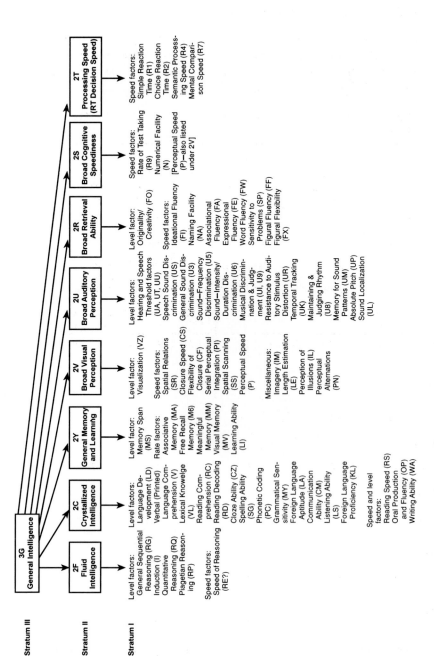

FIG. 3. The three-stratum structure of cognitive abilities. Reproduced from Carroll (1993).

Construct validity: *g*'s nomological network

The scientific meaning of constructs accrues from the role they play in nomological networks. Construct validation proceeds by establishing functional relationships between assessment vehicles and external criteria with the ultimate aim of tracing the causal directionality of these functions.

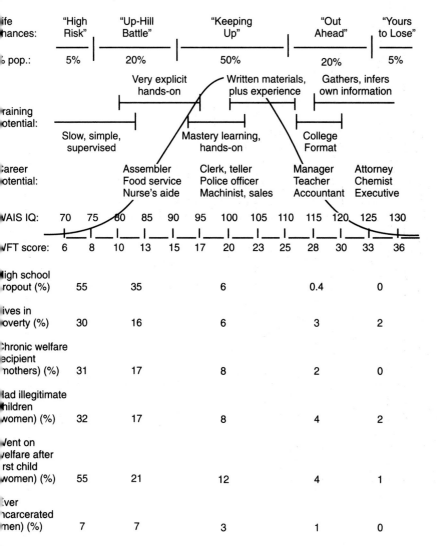

FIG. 4. Overall life chances at different ranges of IQ. WAIS IQ, intelligence quotients obtained from the Weschler Adult Intelligence Scale (Weschler 1981); WPT, Wonderlic Personnel Test, Inc. (1992). Reproduced from Gottfredson (1997) with permission.

That *g* displays functional relationships with many different kinds of importan outcomes and events is well known (Gottfredson 1997, Jensen 1998). Peopl identified on the bases of high levels of *g* and tracked longitudinally displa impressive arrays of socially desirable achievements and outcomes (Holohan & Sears 1995, Terman 1925–1959). On the other hand, individuals found at lowe tiers of the *g* spectrum evince extraordinary risks for medical, physical and socia psychological maladies (see Fig. 4). To be sure, people identified on the bases o intense socioeconomic status (SES) as environmentally privileged do abov average, too, but not nearly as well (Lubinski & Humphreys 1992, 1997 Herrnstein & Murray 1993, Murray 1998).

Some benchmarks pertaining to the scope of *g*'s nomological network ar outlined in the *Annual Review of Psychology* (Lubinski 2000, p 408), '[G]enera cognitive ability covaries 0.70–0.80 with academic achievement measures, 0.40 0.70 with military training assignments, 0.20–0.60 with work performanc (higher values reflect job complexity families), 0.30–0.40 with income, an around 0.20 with law abidingness....' Correlations between the SES level tha children were raised in and *g* are around 0.40, but correlations between achieve SES (i.e. their SES as adults) and *g* range between 0.50–0.70. A mor comprehensive detailing of the scope of *g*'s nomological network is found i Gottfredson (1997) and Jensen (1998). Two additional important publication are Snyderman & Rothman (1987) and Neisser et al (1996). This network ha served as the basis for some of psychology's broadest generalizations.

In educational and industrial psychology, for example, Snow (1989) an Campbell (1990) have, respectively, highlighted the real-word significance of *g* b featuring it in law-like empirical generalizations.[1]

Given new evidence and reconsideration of old evidence, [*g*] can indeed b interpreted as 'ability to learn' as long as it is clear that these terms refer t complex processes and skills and that a somewhat different mix of thes constituents may be required in different learning tasks and settings. The ol view that mental tests and learning tasks measure distinctly different abilitie should be discarded (Snow 1989, p 22).

General mental ability is a substantively significant determinant of individua differences in job performance for any job that includes information-processin tasks. If the measure of performance reflects the information processin components of the job and any of several well-developed standardize measures used to assess general mental ability, then the relationship will b found unless the sample restricts the variances in performance or mental abilit

---

[1]This review will be restricted to the behavioural manifestations of *g*. For reviews of the man biological correlates of *g*, see Jensen (1998, 2000, this volume) and Lubinski (2000).

to near zero. The exact size of the relationship will be a function of the range of talent in the sample and the degree to which the job requires information processing and verbal cognitive skills (Campbell 1990, p 56).

Because of the foregoing considerations, g has achieved the status of differential psychology's most central dimension. Clearly, other things matter; complex human behaviour is almost always multiply determined. In fact, differential psychology has uncovered a number of 'deep shafts' in the realm of human ability (group factors) distinct from g (Achter et al 1999, Humphreys et al 1993, Messick 1992). And in conceptually distinct domains, such as vocational interests and personality (proper), scientifically valuable dimensions of human variation also are prevalent and well known (Lubinski 1996, 2000); yet, their psychological significance pales when contrasted to that of general intelligence (Gottfredson 1997, Jensen 1998). Indeed, in the words of some of the most distinguished psychometricians of all time:

The general mental test stands today as the most important technical contribution psychology has made to the practical guidance of human affairs (Cronbach 1970, p 197).

[A general] intelligence test is the single most important test that can be administered for vocational guidance purposes (Humphreys 1985, p 211).

Almost all human performance (work competence) dispositions, if carefully studied, are saturated to some extent with the general intelligence factor g, which for psychodynamic and ideological reasons has been somewhat neglected in recent years but is due for a comeback (Meehl 1990, p 124).

[T]he great preponderance of the prediction that is possible from any set of cognitive tests is attributable to the general ability that they share. What I have called 'empirical g' is not merely an interesting psychometric phenomenon, but lies at the heart of the prediction of real-life performances. (Thorndike 1994).

For further support, readers are referred to the 25-point editorial in a special issue of *Intelligence* entitled 'Mainstream science on intelligence', which is signed by 52 academic scientists working in the general intelligence arena (Gottfredson 1997). Here, general intelligence was described as:

...a very general mental capability that, among other things, involved the ability to reason, plan, solve problems, think abstractly, comprehend complex

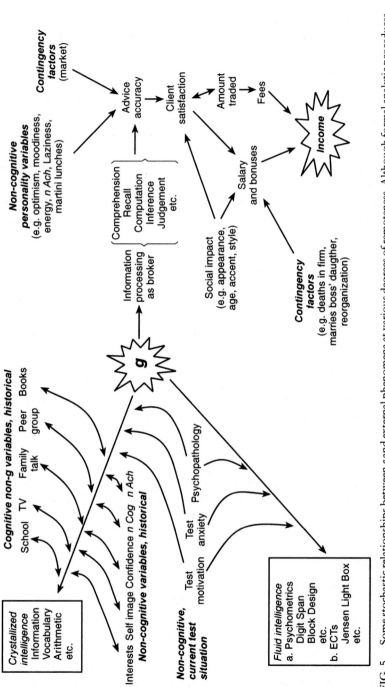

FIG. 5. Some stochastic relationships between g and external phenomena at various degrees of remoteness. Although formal analytic procedures for demarcating regions within theoretical networks are currently unavailable, near relationships are closer to the essence of constructs under analysis ('g') and construe what Carnan (1950) referred to as 'meaning postulates'. Reproduced with permission from P. E. Meehl (___ pers).

ideas, learn quickly and learn from experience. It is not merely book learning, a narrow academic skill, or test-taking smarts. Rather, it reflects a broader and deeper capability for comprehending our surroundings — 'catching on', 'making sense' of things, or 'figuring out' what to do. (p 13)

This is a reasonable statement. And it is consistent with Spearman's (1927) 'eduction of relations and correlates'. Yet as Meehl (1998) points out, verbal definitions (Sternberg & Detterman 1986) are always problematic because they lack consensus. A scientific understanding of a construct is achieved by placing measurement operations of purported attributes into nomological networks and examining their functional relationships with meaningful external criteria. Meehl (personal communication, 1999) has offered a sketch illustrating some core phenomena central to the 'meaning' of g as well as more remote phenomena (Fig. 5).

Notice how, moving from 'pure' information processing capability and abstract learning to more distal phenomena, the relationship between g and more remote phenomena breaks down. This is understandable, because large temporal gaps open up possibilities for many different kinds of intervening events (Humm 1946). This can be played out a bit more. Given our knowledge of the many different kinds of external and internal influences operating within the g nexus, an important consideration is how much covariation one should anticipate between vehicles assessing g and construct-relevant criteria. To the extent that investigators are disappointed by covariational patterns generated by this ability construct (or the g-factor 'take' on human ability), the implication is that ability should account for more variance; and hence, non-ability attributes should account for less. Nevertheless, the question should be asked. Upon examining the functional relationships in g's nomological network (and given the role that energy, health, interests, personality, psychopathology and chance factors, etc., play as determinants of complex behaviours and outcomes — to mention but a few non-ability attributes), 'Is this a reasonable amount of covariation for one variable to achieve?'

Is g a causal entity?

A concern about the above correlates is that they do not imply causation. Because g covaries with other purported causal determinants of social outcomes, for example SES, the causal antecedents of its correlates are equivocal. In Terman's (1925–1959) famous longitudinal study of intellectually gifted participants, for example, subjects were appreciably above the norm on several educational and vocational criteria. On various indices of physical and psychological health, they were also significantly better off than normative base rate expectations would lead one to

TABLE 2   Paired sibling sample comparisons

	Cognitive class				
	Very dull siblings (<10th %ile)	Dull siblings (10th–24th)	Normal reference group (25th–74th)	Bright siblings (75th–89th)	Very bright siblings (≥90th %ile)
IQ characteristics					
$\overline{X}$ IQ (SD)	74.5 (5.4)	85.9 (2.5)	99.1 (5.9)	114.0 (2.7)	125.1 (5.6)
$\overline{X}$ Difference	−11.2	−21.1	—	+11.8	+21.8
N	199	421	1074	326	128
Years of education					
$\overline{X}$ Difference	−1.6	−0.8	$\overline{X}=13.5$ SD=2.0	+1.3	+1.9
N	149	326	850	266	109
Occupational prestige					
$\overline{X}$ Difference	−18.0	−10.4	$\overline{X}=42.7$ SD=21.5	+4.1	+10.9
N	102	261	691	234	94
Earned income					
$\overline{X}$ Difference	−9462	−5792	$\overline{X}=23703$ SD=18606	+4407	+17786
Mdn Difference	−9750	−5000	Mdn=22000	+4000	+11500
N	128	295	779	257	99

From Murray (1998).

anticipate. Nevertheless, critics were quick to point out that they were more privileged in environmental circumstances and opportunity (SES); and thus launching causal inferences emanating from g were hazardous.

Isolating cognitive abilities from SES

Recently, Murray (1998) has offered a clever methodology for untangling SES from ability–performance and ability–outcome functions. This is an important study because, of all the competing interpretations attached to causal inferences assigned to the g-factor, the hypothesized causal significance of SES has been by far the most prevalent competitor. So much so that it even has a name: *the sociologist's fallacy*. (This fallacy occurs when causal inferences emanating from SES are ventured without considering other possible determinants, for example, endogenous personal attributes like g.) Here is how Murray cracked the IQ/SES conundrum.

TABLE 3   Paired sibling sample comparison

	Cognitive class				
	Very dull siblings *(< 10th % ile)*	*Dull siblings* *(10th–24th)*	*Normal reference group* *(25th–74th)*	*Bright siblings* *(75th–89th)*	*Very bright siblings* *(≥ 90th % ile)*
Bachelor's degrees					
For reference siblings without a BA					
Comparison siblings with a BA	1%	1%	(0%)	42%	59%
n	177	339	811	220	75
For reference siblings with a BA					
Comparison siblings with a BA	0%	18%	(100%)	76%	91%
n	19	55	198	78	46

From Murray (1998).

Murray (1998) analysed data from the National Longitudinal Survey of Youth (NLSY). NLSY consists of 12 686 subjects born between 1957–1964, with successive cohorts assessed, beginning in 1979, on the Armed Forces Qualifying Test (AFQT). AFQT was converted to IQ estimates normalized around a mean of 100 and a standard deviation of 15.[2]

Using NLYS 15-year longitudinal data, Murray (1998) studied outcome differences between biologically related siblings (reared together) but who differed in general intelligence (see Table 2). He compared various outcomes of 1074 sibling pairs. Each sibling-pair consisted of a member within the normal IQ range (25–74%) and a sibling in one of the following four IQ ranges: very dull (less than 10%), dull (10–24%), bright (75–89%), and very bright (greater than 89%). As ability differences between siblings increased, so did differences in socially valued outcomes. Table 2 illustrates only some of Murray's (1998) measured differences (years of education, occupational prestige and earned income), which mirror those in the general population at similar ability ranges.

Table 3 reports on the percentage of siblings who earned a Bachelor's degree, after blocking on the norm reference group (i.e. separating those who did and did

---

[2]For more detail on the NLSY, see Hernstein & Murray (1993).

not earn a Bachelor's degree). It is clear that cognitive ability is predominantl related to securing a BA, but there are other ways to analyse these data t highlight the relationship between cognitive ability and this educational outcome

For example, of the sibling pairs in Table 3, 228 pairs had different outcomes (i.e one got a BA, while the other did not); interestingly, of these 228 discordant siblin pairs, the BA went to the higher IQ sibling 88% of the time. This indicates th profound advantage that higher cognitive abilities bestow.

Eliminating social deprivation and poverty

Subsequently, Murray (1998) created a 'utopian sample' from NLSY for informing policy researchers aiming to evaluate social interventions. He deleted all subject who were either raised in the bottom quartile of income or in single-paren households. This gives researchers a purchase on the eventualities of eliminating poverty and single-parent homes on various social outcomes. Table 4 presents dat from the Full NLSY sample with the Utopian sample. With respect to outcom differences across contrasts involving educational attainment, employment and earned income, and the childbearing characteristics of women, the Full NLSY and Utopian samples are not all that different. The largest difference is betweer the Full NLSY and Utopian sample for the Bright category (50% and 57% respectively) for obtaining a BA.[3]

Collectively, when Murray's findings are teamed with recent advances from biometrically informative twin and adoption studies, the causal significance o SES, for most environments found in industrialized societies, become attenuated further. It also motivates the necessity of more general scientific tools.

Other tools for future research

In an early differential psychology text, Ellis (1928) introduced psychologists to th Fallacy of the Neglected Aspect:

> The logicians point out that a cause of much incorrect thinking is what is knowr as the fallacy of the neglected aspect. Early students of certain disease

---

[3]As important as Murray's (1998) study is, however, a component is missing: it would be fascinating to reverse this analysis. It would be informative to select groups of biologically unrelated subjects at comparable ability levels, who are raised in different homes, which systematically vary in SES. If these subjects were studied longitudinally, they would complement the power of Murray's (1998) design, which controls for SES, by controlling for ability analogously. Both analyses would independently converge on a precise estimate of the relative influence of reared-in SES and general intelligence on various outcomes. Naturally, the relative influence of reared-in SES and general intelligence on remote outcomes may change over the life span, which is why Murray's (1998) decision to study these relationships longitudinally is so compelling. Other useful methods for establishing controls between *g* and SES are found in Lubinski & Humphreys (1992) for physical health, and Waller (1971) for social mobility.

TABLE 4 Utopian sample comparisons

	Cognitive class									
	Very dull (<10th %ile)		Dull (10th–24th)		Normal (25th–74th)		Bright (75th–89th)		Very bright (≥90th %ile)	
Sample	Utopian	Full NLSY	Utopian	Full NLSY	Utopian	Full NLSY	Utopian	Full NLSY	Utopian	Full NLSY
Educational attainment										
X̄ years of education	11.4	10.9	12.3	11.9	13.4	13.2	15.2	15.0	16.5	16.5
% obtaining BA	1	1	4	3	19	16	57	50	80	77
Employment & earned income										
X̄ number of weeks worked	36	31	39	37	43	42	45	45	46	45
Mdn earned income (US$)	11000	7500	16000	13000	23000	21000	27000	27000	38000	36000
% with spouse with earned income	30	27	38	39	53	54	61	59	58	58
Mdn earned family income	17000	12000	25000	23400	37750	37000	47200	45000	53700	53000
Female childbearing characteristics										
Fertility to date	2.1	2.3	1.7	1.9	1.4	1.6	1.3	1.4	1.0	1.0
Mother's X̄ age at first birth	24.4	22.8	24.5	23.7	26.0	25.2	27.4	27.1	29.0	28.5
% children born out of wedlock	49	50	33	32	14	14	6	6	3	5

From Murray (1998).

considered them to be due to hot weather or excessive rain — neglecting th
activities of the fly or the mosquito in spreading the bacteria. Neglecting
aspects of problems often hides variable agencies that must be understood
before the problem can be solved. Experiment has often been the only way
out of this difficulty, and where experiment is not possible the problem may
remain unsolved. (p 8)

Subsequently, Carnap (1950) formalized this fallacy as the *Total Evidence Rule*. The
rule maintains that, when evaluating the plausibility of a particular hypothesis, or
the verisimilitude of a theory, it is imperative to take into account all of the relevant
information (Lubinski & Humphreys 1997). As commonsensical as this seems, it
frequently is not done.

For example, investigators readily assume that the covariation between parent
and child's general intelligence, verbal intelligence, personality, or vocational
interests is due to the kinds of environmental stimulation parents provide (cf
Thompson's [1995] review of Hart & Risley [1995]). Yet, biometrically informed
analyses reveal that covariation among the attributes studied by differential
psychologists (abilities, interests, and personality) approach zero as adulthood is
reached among biologically unrelated siblings reared together. As unrelated
individuals who were reared together grow older, they appear to 'grow up and
grow apart' (McCartney et al 1990), with respect to conventional dimensions of
individual differences. It appears that an inconspicuous cause, namely shared
genetic make-up, is responsible for the phenotypic covariation between
biologically related parents and children. Parents do, indeed, have an influence
on their children with respect to major dimensions of individual differences
however, this influence is transmitted through a different mechanism than many
initially presupposed. This is also supported by a variety of kinship correlates, such
as the intriguing finding that, on 'environmental measures' (e.g. HOME, cf
Plomin & Bergeman 1991), identical twins reared apart assess their reared-in
home environments as being as similar as fraternal twins reared together do
(Scarr 1996).

Now, to be sure, this is not to say that abusive environments are not detrimental
to optimal development. Of course they can be, and they frequently are. What these
studies do speak to, however, is that, in the large majority of environments, many
families are functionally equivalent in terms of fostering the development of major
sources of individual differences studied by differential psychologists (McGue &
Bouchard 1998). Yet, much of psychology appears to *neglect* these findings when
launching causal inferences about exogenous influences based on correlation
between biologically related individuals. In many social science domains, for
example, not considering g and incorporating general ability measures in
empirical studies amounts to errors of omission, and misspecified or

underdetermined causal models, which constitute Fallacies of Neglected Aspects and violations of Total Evidence (Lubinski & Humphreys 1997). But furthermore, at times, scientists who 'know better' appear to conscientiously avoid placing their favourite constructs in competition with general ability measures (Coleman 1990, Humphreys 1991). In such instances (cf. Scarr 1998, p 231), should scientific malpractice perhaps be used to characterize their behaviour?

In conclusion, the construct of general intelligence is a pivotal feature of the human condition. The best evidence suggests that the observed covariation between measures of g and abstract learning and work performance, as well as social and vocational outcomes, is primarily causal rather than merely associative. Future work in evolutionary psychology and the social sciences more generally would do well by exploiting this construct more routinely. To the extent that g is ignored in biosocial sciences aiming to better understand broad human behaviour patterns, the comprehensiveness of purported frameworks are virtually guaranteed to fall short. This is especially likely to be found in the most general and familiar aspects of the human condition, such as mating and resource acquisition, which, according to Freud, and many other acute observers of human biosocial phenomena, constitute the two most central aspects of life.

Acknowledgements

Earlier versions of this article profited from suggestions by Camilla P. Benbow, Daniel L. Shea and Rose Mary Webb. The article was supported by an anonymous funding agency, the Kennedy Center at the College of Education and Human Development, Vanderbilt University, and a Templeton Award for Positive Psychology.

References

Achter JA, Lubinski D, Benbow CP 1999 Assessing vocational preferences among gifted adolescents adds incremental validity to abilities: a discriminant analysis of educational outcomes over a 10-year interval. J Educ Psychol 91:777–786

Benbow CP, Stanley JC 1996 Inequity in equity: how 'equity' can lead to inequity for high-potential students. Psychol Pub Policy Law 2:249–292

Campbell DT, Fiske DW 1959 Convergent and discriminant validation by the multitrait-multimethod matrix. Psychol Bull 93:81–105

Campbell JP 1990 The role of theory in industrial and organizational psychology. In: Dunnette MD, Hough LM (eds) Handbook of industrial and organizational psychology, 2nd edn, vol 1. Consulting Psychology Press, Palo Alto, CA, p 39–74

Carnap R 1950 Logical foundations of probability. University of Chicago Press, Chicago, IL

Carroll JB 1993 Human cognitive abilities: a survey of the factor-analytic literature. Cambridge University Press, Cambridge

Carroll JB 1997 Psychometrics, intelligence, and public perception. Intelligence 24:25–52

Cattell JM 1890 Mental tests and measurements. Mind 15:373–380

Cattell RB 1950 Personality: a systematic theoretical and factual study. McGraw-Hill, New Yorl

Coleman JS 1990 The Sidney Hook Memorial Award address: on the self-suppression o academic freedom. Acad Quest 4:17–22

Cronbach LJ 1970 Essentials of psychological testing, 3rd edn. Harper and Row, New York

Cronbach LJ, Meehl PE 1955 Construct validity in psychological tests. Psychol Bull 52:281–30.

Ellis RS 1928 The psychology of individual differences. Appleton, New York

Galton F 1890 Remarks. Mind 15:380–381

Galton F 1961 Classification of men according to their natural gifts [Originally published ir 1869]. In: Jenkins JJ, Paterson DG (eds) Studies in individual differences. Appleton Century-Crofts, New York, p 1–16

Gottfredson LS 1997 Intelligence and social policy. Intelligence 24:1–320

Hart B, Risley TR 1995 Meaningful differences in the everyday experience of young Americat children. Brookes, Baltimore

Hathaway SR, McKinley JC 1940 The Minnesota multiphasic personality inventory manual Psychological Corporation, New York

Herrnstein RJ, Murray C 1994 The bell curve: Intelligence and class structure in American life Free Press, New York

Holahan CK, Sears RR 1995 The gifted group in later maturity. Stanford University Press Stanford, CA

Humm D 1946 Validation by remote criteria. J Appl Psych 30:333–339

Humphreys LG 1985 General intelligence: an integration of factor, test, and simplex theory. In Wolman BB (ed) Handbook of intelligence. Wiley, New York, p 201–224

Humphreys LG 1991 Limited vision in the social sciences. Am J Psychol 104:333–353

Humphreys LG, Lubinski D, Yao G 1993 Utility of predicting group membership and the rol(of spatial visualization in becoming an engineer, physical scientist, or artist. J Appl Psycho 78:250–261

Hunt E 1995 Will we be smart enough? A cognitive analysis of the coming workforce. Russel Sage Foundation, New York

Jensen AR 1998 The g factor: the science of mental ability. Praeger, Westport, CT

Jensen AR 2000 The g factor: psychometrics and biology. In: The nature of intelligence. Wiley Chichester (Novartis Found Symp 233) p 37–46

Jensen AR 2000 Charles Spearman: the discoverer of g. In: Kimble GA, Westheimer M (eds Portraits of pioneers in psychology. Vol IV. American Psychological Association Washington DC, and Erlbaum, NJ, in press

Lubinski D 1996 Applied individual differences research and its quantitative methods. Psycho Public Policy Law 2:187–203

Lubinski D 2000 Scientific and social significance of assessing individual differences in humat behavior. 'Sinking shafts at a few critical points'. Annu Rev Psychol 51:405–444

Lubinski D, Dawis RV 1992 Aptitudes, skills, and proficiencies. In: Dunnette MD, Hough LM (eds) Handbook of industrial and organizational psychology, 2nd edn, vol 3. Consulting Psychology Press, Palo Alto, CA, p 1–59

Lubinski D, Humphreys LG 1992 Some bodily and medical correlates of mathematica giftedness and commensurate levels of socioeconomic status. Intelligence 16:99–115

Lubinski D, Humphreys LG 1997 Incorporating general intelligence into epidemiology and th(social sciences. Intelligence 24:159–201

McCartney K, Harris MJ, Bernieri F 1990 Growing up and growing apart: a developmenta meta-analysis of twin studies. Psychol Bull 107:226–237

McGue M, Bouchard TJ 1998 Genetic and environmental influences on human behaviora differences. Annu Rev Neurosci 21:1–24

ehl PE 1990 Appraising and amending theories: the strategy of Lakatosian defense and two principles that warrant it. Psychol Inquiry 1:108–141

ehl PE 1998 The power of quantitative thinking. American Psychological Society, New York

essick S 1992 Multiple intelligences or multilevel intelligence? Selective emphasis on distinctive properties of hierarchy: on Gardner's Frames of Mind and Sternberg's Beyond IQ in the context of theory and research on the structure of human abilities. Psychol Inquiry 3:365–384

urray C 1998 Income, inequality, and IQ. American Enterprise Institute, Washington, DC

eisser U, Boodoo G, Bouchard TJ Jr et al 1996 Intelligence: knowns and unknowns. Am Psychol 51:77–101

omin R, Bergeman CS 1991 The nature of nuture: genetic influence on 'environmental' measures. Behav Brain Sci 14:373–427

arr S 1996 How people make their own environments: implications for parents and policy makers. Psychol Public Policy Law 2:204–228

arr S 1998 On Arthur Jensen's integrity. Intelligence 26:227–232

hmidt FL, Hunter JE 1998 The validity and utility of selection methods in personnel psychology: practical and theoretical implications of 85 years of research findings. Psychol Bull 124:262–274

ow RE 1989 Aptitude treatment interaction as a framework for research on individual differences in learning. In: Ackerman PE, Sternberg RJ, Glasser RG (eds) Learning and individual differences. WH Freeman, New York, p 13–59

yderman M, Rothman S 1987 Survey of expert opinion on intelligence and aptitude testing. Am Psychol 42:137–144

earman C 1904 'General intelligence,' objectively determined and measured. Am J Psychol 15:201–292

earman C 1927 The abilities of man: their nature and measurement. Macmillan, New York

ernberg RJ, Detterman DK 1986 What is intelligence? Contemporary viewpoints on its nature and definition. Ablex, Norwood, NJ

erman LM 1925–1959 Genetic studies of genius (I–V). Stanford University Press, Stanford

hompson T 1995 Children have more need of models than critics: early language experience and brain development. J Early Interven 19:264–272

horndike RL 1994 g (Editorial). Intelligence 19:145–155

aller JH 1971 Achievement and social mobility: relationships among IQ score, education, and occupation in two generations. Soc Biol 18:252–259

eschler D 1981 WAIS-R manual: Wechsler adult intelligence scale revised. Psychological Corporation, New York

ilson EO 1998 Consilience: the unity of knowledge. Knopf, New York

onderlic Personnel Test 1992 Wonderlic personnel test and scholastic level exam: user's manual. Wonderlic, Libertyville, IL

ISCUSSION

Harnad: I want to make a comment on causality, which will no doubt be a ecurring theme in these discussions. Causality is, in my opinion, the key cientific question in connection with intelligence and IQ. Suppose we had a attery of athletic skill measures: swimming, javelin throwing, long-distance unning and so on. Imagine that we then factor-analysed them and came up with factor, which turned out to be a *g* factor, involving a basis such as the ratio of slow

twitch to fast twitch muscle fibres. The question is, where would that ha
advanced us if we didn't know the causal mechanisms of muscle use, a
movement and motor patterns? The counterparts of this in cognition are t
cognitive mechanisms underlying cognitive capacity. To what extent does t
correlation pattern that g seems to exemplify help us understand the real cau
mechanisms underlying cognitive capacities? I'm inclined to say that g h
provided approximately zero benefit in helping us with cognitive modelling.

Lubinski: One thing I wanted to emphasize in my paper is that there is a lot mc
to differential psychology than g. There are group factors, interests and personali
and you can get at all of them through the Spearman–Brown formula (Lubins
1996, Lubinski & Humphreys 1997). In terms of how g can help us understa
low-order mechanisms, I think the jury is still out (but see Lubinski 200(
Science moves slowly sometimes. I think it can help us find and isolate differe
populations, look for genetic markers and look for individual differences in t
CNS that can provide clues to the underlying structure. To be clear, the
construct is not a 'thing'; it's an abstraction like horsepower. There are differe
components to horsepower, such as carburettors and cylinders, but still there's
general property. The overall functioning of this general property can be increas
by tinkering with the components individually, tinkering with the whole syste
or tinkering with fuel: there are a variety of different variables underlyi
'horsepower' as there undoubtedly are with g. It helps us to know where to loo
just as Skinner's principle of reinforcement helped us identify different areas of tl
brain for positive reinforcement centres and so on.

Detterman: To a large extent I agree with Stephen Harnad's comment: I think I
was exactly right until he said that g has made zero contribution to cogniti
modelling. We could think of g as being the gold standard that we need
compare cognitive models to: if we look at it that way then it is the cogniti
models that have let us down, not g.

Harnad: Wouldn't you say that the gold standard of cognitive models f
cognitive capacity is cognitive capacity itself?

Detterman: As related to g, since g is known to correlate with all these soci
variables.

Maynard Smith: I'm already baffled. I am not clear about what kind of claim
being made for g. Let's take the analogy of athletic performance that Steph
Harnad drew, which I think is quite a good one. One's athletic ability will I
influenced by factors such as heart volume, leg length, muscle development ar
motivation: if you were to measure each of these factors independently, yc
would be in quite a good position to predict how people might perform
athletic contests. You would probably find high heritabilities in these feature
But there isn't a thing called 'athletic ability': it is just a performance category.
you were then to analyse this you wouldn't necessarily expect to find th

everybody with a high athletic ability had one set of traits: you would expect to find these different components, such as heart, muscle and nerves, contributing to it. You wouldn't find one thing; you would find many contributors, just as you would if you analysed the horsepower of an engine. Are we required to think that there exists a 'thing' which will have a specific neurological component? Because, if not, let's not talk about it as if it were a 'thing'. It is just a correlate that statistically is quite good at predicting one's performance. That is fine. There is no reason why it shouldn't have a high heritability. But somehow the discussion about it seems not to be in those terms: it is discussed as if there were an object like a heart in there that we could identify.

Jensen: No one who has worked in this field has ever thought of *g* as an entity or thing. Spearman, who discovered *g*, actually said the very same thing that you're saying now, and Cyril Burt and Hans Eysenk said that also: just about everyone who has worked in this field has not been confused on that point.

Maynard Smith: From reading the abstracts of the papers in this meeting and listening to you, this is not the impression I got. I'm delighted to hear workers in the field do not think of *g* as a thing.

Detterman: There are some people who believe there may be a single underlying variable that explains *g*.

Deary: Can I comment on what you, David Lubinski, were saying about the McKeen Cattell paper from 1890 and Galton's (1890) response, because I think therein lies the reason for the situation we're in today. The phenotypes that ability tests seem to get at have proved relatively easy to measure and mental tests are predictively quite successful. The problem lies in understanding the causes of mental ability differences. The roots of this problem were already present in these early papers. McKeen Cattell didn't present any correlations, but simply described some tests off the top of his head. These tests were much less good than those he had developed under Wundt (Deary 1994). Galton's comments on the McKeen Cattell suggestions were twofold. One is that there was no theory driving the tests, which worried him, and second was the point that psychologists should strive to sink a few critically placed shafts into the brain. What he meant was just what has been raised here: we should try to identify a few key processing parameters that are actually the partial bases of mental ability differences. Galton was lamenting then something that we still don't have. I think that little interchange in 1890 is very much the same sort of thing we are going to see replayed here at this meeting. We can describe ability phenotypes and use test scores in prediction but we still don't know the cognitive or biological bases of human mental ability differences.

Flynn: David Lubinski, I picked up your comments on Murray. The sociologists have had a serious setback. Murray's utopian experiment simulated improving people in terms of SES plus other factors, and it looks like if we were to improve those environmental factors, people would not benefit as much as we would hope.

However, you could say that Murray's own thesis is subject to an even more devastating disappointment: we actually have made massive IQ gains over time, without any of the progress that he would anticipate from that. That is, during the period in which solo-mother homes have risen and crime has risen, there have been massive IQ gains. One could say, therefore, that his position has been subjected not merely to a simulated refutation, but to a devastating real-world refutation. There are ways out of that, of course: you can claim that the massive IQ gains over time are really just a result of test sophistication — that they are artefacts. There is strong evidence against that; I won't go into that now, but I will offer an alternative interpretation. It could well be that IQ gives enormous advantages within a group in which there is intragroup competition, particularly for the reason you've given — and that this results in a matching between genes for IQ and quality of environment. An intelligent kid with good genes makes a lot more out of a library than an unintelligent kid. Therefore, his genes get the credit for potent environmental factors: the latter are hidden behind a genetic mask in a competitive intragroup situation. When you look at IQ gains over time — there of course we think that there is effectively genetic parity between the generations — you see the potent force of the environment revealed in all of its naked power. There is no longer a covariance between genes and environment that hides the explosive force of environment. In sum, it could be argued against Murray that his hopes that raising IQ will bring progress are suspect. Let me give a simple analogy. It may be that self-seekingness is very profitable in competition at a particular place and time, in terms of getting you higher on the ladder. It's not at all clear that were the human race to become more self-seeking, that there would be group progress over time — that is, from one generation to another. In other words, a trait that pays enormous dividends within a competitive situation at a given place and time, doesn't necessarily solve social problems over time. At present, it looks like increases in IQ are totally feeble in this regard—perhaps even more feeble than SES.

Brody: Examine Table 3. If you look at the performance of normal siblings who have graduated college and those who have not, you see for the same range of IQ differences among siblings enormous differences in the probability of higher education. For example, the dull siblings of those siblings who did not graduate college have a 1% probability of graduating college, and the dull siblings of those normal siblings who did graduate college have an 18% probability of graduating college. This raises an interesting issue. As determinative as IQ is, there surely is a great deal of variation among children with equivalent IQ, and this must be some kind of a family influence.

Suddendorf: You ended your talk by stating that social sciences might commit the 'fallacy of neglected aspect'. How would you respond to the reverse criticism, raised by people like Robert Sternberg (1999), that psychometricians might be committing a 'confirmation bias' by restricting the range of participants, tasks and the situational context in which testing takes place?

Lubinski: I would say the opposite. Differential psychologists tend to be very sensitive to restriction of range and try hard to study the full range of human talent and, if not, they will correct for that. Sternberg studies Yale undergraduates.

Deary: That wasn't the point being made: the point was about the restricted range of tests that we use, not the attenuation of the sample variance. Sternberg (1999) makes the point that by looking at what he calls 'analytic reasoning' we are restricting the range of talents and abilities we examine. We don't look at what he would call 'creative and practical reasoning'.

Lubinski: That is the general factor that factors into a broader array of criteria that we're interested in predicting when we talk about the concept of intelligence. To my knowledge Sternberg's creative and practical tests haven't added any incremental validity to those predictions in the full range of talent in any study that I know.

Suddendorf: Isn't the point that he's making that there is no correlation between practical intelligence the way he has tried to measure it and *g*?

Brody: I'm going to address that in my paper. I will present data indicating that the correlation between creative intelligence as Sternberg assesses it and *g* is very high. Indeed, when Sternberg actually tries to measure something — not when he is being conceptual — the data show that *g* is a good predictor of the three kinds of intelligence that Sternberg postulates. I know of no data that show that Sternberg is able to measure components of intelligence that are independent of *g*.

Whiten: In relation to the worry raised by John Maynard Smith about whether *g* is being treated as a 'thing', I'm a bit concerned about your reference to 'construct validation'. Deriving a construct *g* as a statistical property describing the relationships amongst a battery of scores on tests thought appropriate for measuring intelligence is fine, but an effort to *validate* the construct could easily lead to reifying it as a natural 'thing' that equates with intelligence. The results of this could perhaps be presented as achieving a better definition of intelligence than the one existing before this research programme was undertaken — intelligence might be claimed to be better understood and measured. But both the internal correlations generating *g*, and the external, 'validating' correlations with external factors, obviously depend on what test results are used in the first place. If some important aspect of intelligence is not tested to begin with, one might still run through this whole research process and claim at the end to have validated the construct *g* — as a factor of general intelligence — because it correlates with certain outcomes one would expect to be associated with intelligence. But both the tests and the outcomes might be based on similar — and similarly limited — notions of intelligence, making the process somewhat circular, misleadingly appearing to justify those notions of intelligence as 'the real thing'.

One potential omission that naturally concerns me is social intelligence, that is the subject of my later paper. You talked of Sternberg's work. In one paper he and his colleagues actually went to railway stations and other public places and asked people what they thought 'intelligence' was, and what it meant to them (Sternberg et al 1981). When the study went into a second phase and asked people to rate these various notions in relation to everyday intelligence and academic intelligence, a factor analysis did indeed throw up a first factor that looked a bit like g — general problem solving. But the second factor was social intelligence, like tact and managing your social affairs. Such social intelligence could be one omission in the process that has been used to extract g and validate it. It's probably very difficult, if not impossible, to measure in quick tests — especially just using pen and paper — that then have predictive power.

So, two questions. First, what exactly is the 'construct validation' validating? Is it some claim about intelligence, and if so what? Second, is it possible the whole process could misleadingly appear to reify a notion of intelligence that is not in fact as rich or broad as that people apply in everyday life?

Lubinski: These are good questions, and Cronbach & Meehl's (1955) treatment of construct validation is still a must read for people interested in these topics (but see also Meehl's recent refinements [personal communication, 1999]). Construct validity seeks to validate measures of a postulated attribute. 'Horsepower' is a postulated attribute, you can't 'see' horsepower, but you can construct indicators that co-vary with meaningful criteria that reflect our concept of horsepower and make it a conceptually powerful and useful concept. Just as horsepower is an abstract property of complex combustion engines, g is an abstract property of complex biological systems. Moreover, constructs can be postulated intuitively, or inferred from families of empirical relationships, either is fine. In the final analysis what's important is, does the measure behave in accordance with our theoretical expectations about the postulated attribute it purports to assess? Perhaps it would be helpful to review how Cronbach & Meehl (1955) illustrated how construct validation works for psychological measures.

When Cronbach & Meehl (1955) introduced the logic of the construct validation process, they exemplified the process by systematically compiling a heterogeneous collection of empirical phenomena all related to the *psychopathic deviate* ('*Pd*') scale of the Minnesota Multiphasic Personality Inventory (MMPI). How, they asked, could a scale initially developed to isolate criminals and delinquents from the general population, also evince the following network of empirical relationships: elevated scores for Broadway actors, high school drop-outs, deer hunters who accidentally shoot people, police officers and nurses who were rated by their supervisors as not especially afraid of psychotic patients? (Note this was before wide use of psychoactive drugs, and patients commonly experienced florid psychotic episodes.) *Pd* also correlated negatively with peer itings of trustworthiness. What possible mechanism could possibly underlie this mily of empirical relationships? They reasoned that the communality (abstract roperty) cutting across all of these findings involved low anxiety.

Two years later, Lykken (1957) published support for a hypothesis that appears) have withstood the test of time. What these groups have in common is that, elative to the norm, they are fearless or in possession of a 'low anxiety IQ'. He ested this idea, using a Pavlovian conditioning paradigm, and showed that, as a roup, particularly hardened criminals (high Pd scorers), when contrasted with the eneral prison population, were 'retarded' when it came to developing conditioned esponses to neutral stimuli paired with an unconditioned aversive stimulus, 1ock. Replicated now in a number of laboratories, a differential sensitivity to the evelopment of conditioned responses to aversive stimuli seems to be a robust arameter of individual differences. This fits with all of the aforementioned mpirical findings. (It also fits with the idea that low anxiety can be an asset or a ability, depending on the constellation of other personal attributes that a person ossesses, and the purview one is operating in.) Hence, here, construct validity has larified and helped us to better understand this measure, and to generate valid iferences (about the internal make up, for example, of spies, paratroopers, oliticians, deep sea divers, stunt men, astronauts, etc., as well as a host of other henomena) about events, people, and outcomes that have not been studied mpirically.

Like the Pd scale of the MMPI, Binet's initial test was designed to ('simply') olate a particular group of people ('educable' children) from the general opulation. But the validity of this measure soon generalized to school erformance, amount of education, work performance and occupational roupings, and a variety of other domains involving abstract learning, iformation processing and responding to novel abstract problems in effective /ays (Gottfredson 1997). What seems to be operating here is rate of learning bstract material, which is what conventional g measures assess. (This is why :aders in a variety of information-dense occupations rich with novelty manifest igh levels of g. This also is why I quoted Galton's earlier on $general$ ability.) But,) be clear, there is more to the intellectual repertoire than this. For example, the nportance of mathematical, spatial and verbal abilities has actually been ocumented in some of my own work and that of others, which underscores why is important to assess abilities beyond g (Achter et al 1999, Humphreys et al 1993, ubinski & Dawis 1992); all differential psychologists agree that there is more to ognitive abilities than g. (I do not know of any exceptions.)

Your mentioning of social intelligence is, of course, not new; a number of early ifferential psychologists discussed social intelligence, practical intelligence and bstract intelligence (essentially g) early in the 20th century. People interested in 1e multitude of psychometric measure that have been developed to get at these (and other) unique aspects of cognitive functioning should consult Messick (1992) excellent review (and see Lubinski & Benbow 1995). But the problem with social intelligence is that no one appears to have developed a valid measur that adds incremental validity to measures of g or verbal ability; nothing new ha been developed (to my knowledge) over and above what conventional measures c g and verbal ability already give us. Although many measures have been propose (Messick 1992), and the concept of social intelligence is clearly attractive an intuitively appealing, we have not yet been able to derive an assessmer procedure to measure individual differences in this purported attribute.

Actually, this happens all of the time in psychology, a measure is proposed tha sounds appealing and 'validated' without ever considering whether it add anything to what we already have. A well-known measure of moral reasonin for example, generated hundreds of studies and at least three books. But it wz never evaluated in competition with general and verbal ability measures. Whil the Defining Issues Test (DIT) was correlated with conventional abilit measures, it was never evaluated for its unique predictive properties (increment: validity) in the context of relevant external criteria, over and above convention: measures of g and verbal ability. When the appropriate analysis was done (Sande et al 1995), all of the DIT's validity was absorbed by verbal ability and, moreove: verbal ability typically accounted for a great deal more criterion variance. Yet, thr decades of research with this instrument never involved this simple analysis, an research continues to appear as if the Sanders et al (1995) study didn't exis (Contemporary work on 'emotional intelligence' is encountering simil: problems [Davies et al 1998].) It is fine to theorize about new constructs and t build new assessment tools but, to make a scientific advance, innovativ procedures need to provide us with something new.

Finally, it is not scientifically problematic when postulated inferences abou constructs under analysis change through empirical research (construc validation). How constructs are conceptualized typically changes as a result c empirical research; indeed, if this did not happen, there would be little need fc empirical research. Measurement operations also evolve as empirical evidenc accrues. Developing scientific tools is an ongoing process, and material change in theoretical concepts and their measures are always to some extent evolvin (e.g. see Tellegen 1985). But this is to be expected, for example: with respect t the measures discussed here, modern research has indicated that Lykken's (1957 initially rough idea (low 'anxiety IQ') has been refined (and split) into tw components: physical anxiety and social anxiety (Lykken & Katzenmeyer 1973 Similarly, Binet's initially rough concept of mental age is essentially the core dominant-dimension in Carroll's (1993) hierarchy of cognitive abilities (Fig. 3 These refinements are important advances in the field of differential psychology and they enable us to speak more precisely about anxiety-proneness (and th omponents of anxiety-provoking situations) and cognitive abilities (and different inds of intellectual demands).

Hinde: One has to be awfully careful to make clear what we mean by adaptation. n my view, we must not talk about social success as being an adaptation: that will ead us right up the wrong path.

The dependent variables used in these studies are variables that you would xpect to show this pattern in an intensely competitive society such as the JSA. We should bear in mind that it is at least possible that different sorts f results would be obtained in a collectivist society such as East Asian ocieties. These variables could be rather culture-specific. This issue impacts n what James Flynn raised about changing the cultural environment over ime, and even the question of social intelligence. Do you agree that many f these data may be very much culture bound? The USA is a very peculiar ociety.

Lubinski: It's even more clear-cut than that I think. Anyone who just speaks one anguage is culture bound to being tested using that medium, if you're going to use language-based vehicle. This is why a lot of cross-cultural research uses things ike the Raven matrices, which are just pictorial.

Detterman: There is strong evidence that *g* applies cross-culturally.

Hinde: But are the measures that you are taking of social success as consequences f the economic success comparable with similar measures in other societies?

Detterman: There have been studies in Warsaw, Poland, which was destroyed fter World War II and reconstituted under a Communist regime. People were nore-or-less randomly assigned to neighbourhoods. They looked at academic chievement in relation to IQ, and found the same relationship as was found in lemocratic societies (Firkowska et al 1978).

Hinde: Supposing the test was done with a hunter–gatherer society, where social uccess depended in part on hunting success: would you get the same answer?

Detterman: Yes, you would get the same answer.

References

Achter JA, Lubinski D, Benbow CP, Eftekhari-Sanjani H 1999 Assessing vocational preferences among gifted adolescents adds incremental validity to abilities: a discriminant analysis of educational outcomes over a 10-year interval. J Educ Psychol 91:777–786

Carroll JB 1993 Human cognitive abilities: a survey of the factor-analytic literature. Cambridge University Press, Cambridge

Cronbach LJ, Meehl PE 1955 Construct validity in psychological tests. Psych Bull 52:281–302

Davies M, Stankov L, Roberts RD 1998 Emotional intelligence: In search of an illusive construct. J Pers Soc Psych 75:989–1015

Deary IJ 1994 Sensory discrimination and intelligence: postmortem or resurrection? Am J Psychol 107:95–115

Firkowska A, Ostrowska A, Sokolowska M, Stein ZA, Susser M, Wald I 1978 Cognitive development and social policy: the contribution of parental occupation and education to mental performance in 11 year olds in Warsaw. Science 200:1357–1362

Galton F 1890 Remarks on 'Mental tests and measurements' by J. McK. Cattell. Mind 15:380–381

Gottfredson LS 1997 Intelligence and social policy. Intelligence 24:1–320

Humphreys LG, Lubinski D, Yao G 1993 Utility of predicting group membership: Exemplified by the role of spatial visualization for becoming an engineer, physical scientist, or artist. Appl Psych 78:250–261

Lubinski D 1996 Applied individual differences research and its quantitative methods. Psychol Public Policy Law 2:187–203

Lubinski D 2000 Assessing individual differences in human behavior: 'Sinking shafts at a few critical points'. Annu Rev Psychol 51:405–444

Lubinski D, Benbow CP 1995 An opportunity for empiricism: Review of Howard Gardner's *Multiple intelligences: the theory in practice*. Contemp Psych 40:935–938

Lubinski D, Dawis RV 1992 Aptitudes, skills, and proficiencies. In: Dunnette MD, Hough LM (eds) The handbook of industrial/organizational psychology, 2nd ed. Consulting Psychologists Press, Palo Alto, p 1–59

Lubinski D, Humphreys LG 1997 Incorporating general intelligence into epidemiology and the social sciences. Intelligence 24:159–201

Lykken DT 1957 A study of anxiety in the sociopathic personality. J Abnorm Soc Psych 55:6–10

Lykken DT, Katzenmeyer C 1973 Manual for the activity preference questionnaire (APQ). In: Psychiatric research reports. University of Minnesota Press, Minneapolis, MN

McKeen Cattell J 1890 Mental tests and measurements. Mind 15:373–380

Messick S 1992 Multiple intelligences or multilevel intelligence? Selective emphasis on distinctive properties of hierarchy: On Gardner's *Frames of mind* and Sternberg's *Beyond IQ* in the context of theory and research on the structure of human abilities. Psych Inquir 3:365–384

Sanders CE, Lubinski D, Benbow CP 1995 Does the defining issues test measure psychological phenomena distinct from verbal ability? An examination of Lykken's query. J Pers Soc Psych 69:498–504

Sternberg RJ 1999 Successful intelligence: finding a balance. Trends Cognit Sci 3:436–442

Sternberg RJ, Conway BE, Ketron JL, Bernstein M 1981 People's conceptions of intelligence. J Pers Soc Psychol 41:37–55

Tellegen A 1985 Structures of mood and personality and their relevance to assessing anxiety, with an emphasis on self-report. In: Tuma AH, Maser JD (eds) Anxiety and the anxiety disorders. Lawrence Erlbaum, Hillsdale, NJ, p 681–706

The *g* factor: psychometrics and biology

Arthur R. Jensen

Graduate School of Education, University of California, Berkeley, CA 94720-1670, USA

Abstract. General ability, defined as psychometric *g*, arises from the empirical fact that scores on various cognitive tests are positively correlated in the population. The *g* factor is highly stable across different factor analytic algorithms, across different test batteries and across different populations. Because all cognitive tests, from the simplest to the most complex, regardless of their informational content, are *g*-loaded to varying degrees, *g* cannot be described in terms of the tests' content, or even in psychological terms. It is actually a property of the brain. The loadings of various tests on *g*, from tests of sensory discrimination and reaction time to those of highly complex problem solving, predict those tests' degree of correlation with a number of non-psychometric variables: the test's heritability, inbreeding depression, coefficient of assortative mating, brain size, reaction time, brain nerve conduction velocity, brain glucose metabolic rate and features of brain evoked potentials. Although some of the brain's cognitive functions are modular, the *g* factor reflects the all-positive correlations among virtually all cognitive functions that show individual differences. I hypothesize that the brain contains no module for general problem solving. Correlations between individuals' performances in various cognitive tasks result from quantitative individual differences in physiological conditions that do not constitute the brain's modular and other neural design features but do influence their speed and efficiency of information processing.

2000 The nature of intelligence. Wiley, Chichester (Novartis Foundation Symposium 233) p 37–57

The *g* factor: psychometrics and biology

The concept of general mental ability was first hypothesized in a scientific context by Sir Francis Galton (1869). It was later empirically investigated by Charles Spearman (1904, 1927), who invented factor analysis as a method for identifying general ability by analysis of the correlations among a number of tests of diverse mental abilities in any group of individuals whose test scores range widely. Spearman labelled this general factor simply as *g*. In discussing individual differences in mental ability, he eschewed the term 'intelligence', regarding it as a generic term for the many aspects of cognition, such as stimulus apprehension, attention, perception, discrimination, generalization, conditioning, learning,

short-term and long-term memory, language, thinking, reasoning, relation
eduction, inference and problem solving. A virtually unlimited variety of task
or tests involving one or more of these cognitive functions can be devised to
assess individual differences in level of performance.

It is an empirical fact that individual differences in performance on virtually all
such cognitive tests, however diverse the abilities they tap, are positively correlated
to some degree. The exceptions are due to statistical artefacts that affect test
intercorrelations: measurement error, sampling error and restriction of the range
of-talent. The all-positive correlations among tests mean that individuals who
score above the population mean on any given test tend, on average, to score
above the mean on all of the other tests, and those who score below average on
any given test tend to score, on average, below the mean on all of the others. The
existence of the g factor depends on this condition and reflects it quantitatively for
any collection of diverse mental tests administered to a representative sample of the
population.

Psychometric variance

Consider a test composed of n elements (i.e. items or subtests), i, j, etc. administered
to a number of individuals. The total variance (V_T) of all the individuals' scores on
this test consists of the sum of all the separate item variances (ΣV_i) plus twice the
sum of all the item covariances ($2\Sigma r_{ij}\sqrt{(V_i V_j)}$, that is,

$$V_T = \Sigma V_i + 2\Sigma r_{ij}\sqrt{(V_i V_j)} \tag{1}$$

Because the number of correlations among the n elements is $n(n-1)/2$, the sum of
the item covariances increases more rapidly as a function of n than the sum of the
item variances. In standard test batteries, such as the Wechsler, the Stanford–Binet
and the British IQ scales, which have large numbers of items, the item covariances
account for about 90% of the total variance. Hence most of a typical test's variance
attributable to individual differences in performance results from the correlations,
or common variance, among its various elements.

It is also possible mathematically, by means of factor analysis, to express these
elements' common variance, not in terms of the various elements themselves, but
in terms of one or more linearly independent (i.e. uncorrelated) hypothetical
sources of variance (Carroll 1993, 1997, Jensen 1998).

Factor analysis

Factor analysis comprises several closely related algorithms for transforming a
matrix of correlations among a number of observed variables into a matrix of

atent (i.e. hypothetical) variables, called *common factors*, each of which represents a
linearly independent source of variance that is common to at least three or more of
the variables in the analysis. A factor matrix shows the correlations of each of the
observed variables with each of the latent variables, or factors. These correlations
are called the *factor loadings*. The number of significant factors is typically much
smaller than the number of variables. Yet an algorithm applied to the factor
loadings can usually reproduce the original correlation matrix within some
negligible margin of error. In terms of factor analysis, then, the total variance
(V_T) of scores on a test is composed of the variance contributed by the *g* factor
that is common to all of the observed variables + the variance associated with
group factors F1, F2, etc. (so-called because each one is common only to certain
groups of variables that share some variance independent of *g*), + all the variance
components [*s*] that are specific to each observed variable, + the variance due to
measurement error [*e*], thus:

$$V_T = Vg + V_{F1} + V_{F2} + \ldots V_{Fn} + V_s + V_e \qquad (2)$$

The V_T in Equation 1 is identical to V_T in equation 2. The second term in equation
1 is equal to the sum of all the common factor variances in equation 2, while the first
term in equation 1 is equal to the sum of V_s and V_e in equation 2. From this we see
that the second term in equation 1 (which constitutes the test's so-called 'true-
score' variance) comprises different sources of common variance, which the
orthogonalized hierarchical factor-analytic model divides up into *g*, and a
number of other common factors independent of *g* and of each other. Factor
analysis is usually performed on the standardized covariances (i.e. Pearson
correlation coefficients) rather than on the raw covariances. This type of
hierarchical analysis is shown graphically in Fig. 1. Table 1 is the corresponding
factor matrix showing the loadings of each variable on each of the orthogonal (i.e.
uncorrelated) factors. This represents only one of several different algorithms or
factor models for estimating *g* (and other factors) in a given correlation matrix.
Provided the mental tests in the analysis are numerous and diverse in the kinds of
knowledge and cognitive skills they call for, the obtained *g* factors are highly
congruent (i.e. correlations > 0.95) across the different methods of analysis
(Jensen & Weng 1994). Estimates of *g* are also highly similar across different
batteries of numerous and diverse tests, and tests' *g*-loadings remain virtually the
same whether extracted from the tests' intercorrelations obtained entirely within
families (thereby excluding the effects of all of the shared 'family background'
variables) or from unrelated individuals in the general population (Jensen 1998,
p 170). In a wide range of different test batteries, depending on the cognitive
diversity of their subtests and the range-of-talent in the subject sample, the *g*
factor generally accounts for anywhere from about 30–60% of the total variance

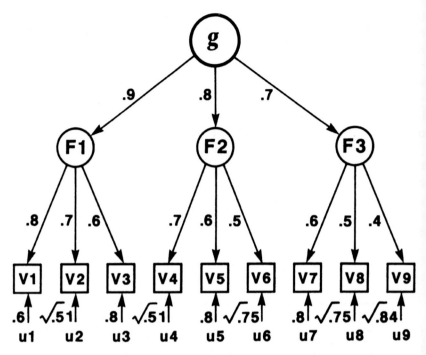

FIG. 1.   A hierarchical factor model in which the group factors (**F**) are correlated, giving rise to the higher-order factor *g*. Variables (**V**) are correlated with *g* only via their correlations with the group factors. The correlation coefficients are shown alongside the arrows. The **u** is a variable's 'uniqueness', i.e. its correlation with whatever it does not have in common (i.e. specificity + error) with any of the other eight variables in the analysis. Reproduced from Jensen & Weng (1994) with permission.

in test scores. Most psychometric tests have higher loadings on *g* than on any independent group factors.

Unlike the group factors, which can usually be described in terms of the types of tests (e.g. verbal, spatial, numerical, memory) most highly loaded on them, the higher-order *g* on which virtually all objectively scored cognitive tests are loaded cannot be described in terms of the test's visible characteristics or even the hypothesized mental operations called for by the test. Extremely dissimilar tests requiring very different cognitive skills can have identical *g* loadings. It appears that *g* itself is not really an ability but rather something in the brain that causes all cognitive abilities, however diverse, to be positively correlated to some degree. The *g*-loadings of various tests is a perfectly continuous variable ranging from about +0.10 to about +0.90.

TABLE 1   An orthogonalized hierarchical factor matrix

| | Factor loadings | | | |
| | Second order | First order | | |
Variable	g	F_1	F_2	F_3
V_1	0.72	0.35		
V_2	0.63	0.31		
V_3	0.54	0.26		
V_4	0.56		0.42	
V_5	0.48		0.36	
V_6	0.40		0.30	
V_7	0.42			0.43
V_8	0.35			0.36
V_9	0.28			0.29
% variance[a]	25.4	3.1	4.4	4.4

[a] Per cent of total variance accounted for by each factor.
Besides g, which is common to all of the variables, there are three distinct classes of variables here (group factors F_1, F_2, F_3), e.g. verbal, quantitative and spatial reasoning. The original correlation matrix can be reconstituted (usually within a small margin of error) by adding the products of their factor loadings, e.g., the correlation between V_1 and V_2 is $(0.72 \times 0.63) + (0.35 \times 0.31) = 0.56$. Altogether 37.3% of the total variance in all nine variables is accounted for by common factors, of which g is the largest, accounting for 25.4% of the total variance and 68% of the common factor variance. The remaining 62.7% of the total variance (consisting of specificity and error) is unique to each of the variables so does not contribute to their intercorrelations.

Non-psychometric correlates of g

Although the g factor is necessarily revealed by psychometric methods, it is not exclusively a psychometric construct, nor is it a methodological artefact of the way psychometric tests are constructed or of the particular factor-analytic algorithms used to extract g. The extra-psychometric reality of g is indicated by the many significant correlations that g has with a wide variety of variables, both physical and behavioural, that have no intrinsic or conceptual relationship to psychometrics or factor analysis. In this respect, g seems to differ from other psychometric factors (Jensen 1993, 1994).

The method of correlated vectors

Because every psychometric test reflects, besides g, its specificity and usually at least one group factor, the correlation between any single psychometric test and some non-psychometric variable is not informative as to precisely which source of

TABLE 2   Example of the method of correlated vectors based on the evoked potential habituation index (EPHI) and the *g* factor loadings of the Wechsler Adult Intelligence Scale (WAIS)

| | *g factor loadings* | | | | *subtest × EPHI correlations* | | | |
| | *uncorrected* | | *corrected*[a] | | *uncorrected* | | *corrected*[a] | |
WAIS subtest	*g*	*Rank*	*g'*	*Rank'*	*r*	*Rank*	*r'*	*Rank'*
Information	0.71	10	0.74	10	0.41	8	0.43	7
Comprehension	0.49	5	0.55	5	0.39	7	0.44	8
Arithmetic	0.57	7	0.64	7.5	0.32	5	0.37	4
Similarities	0.59	9	0.64	7.5	0.50	11	0.53	10
Digit span	0.32	2	0.38	2	0.03	1	0.04	1
Vocabulary	0.77	11	0.80	11	0.45	10	0.46	9
Digit symbol	0.26	1	0.27	1	0.17	2	0.18	2
Picture completion	0.46	3.5	0.50	3	0.21	3	0.23	3
Block design	0.50	6	0.54	4	0.38	6	0.41	6
Picture arrangement	0.58	8	0.71	9	0.44	9	0.54	11
Object assembly	0.46	3.5	0.57	6	0.31	4	0.38	5

[a] Corrected for attenuation (unreliability).
From Jensen (1998, p 590).

variance these two measurements may have in common. An efficient, practicable and statistically rigorous way to discover whether a given variable is importantly related to psychometric *g* is the method of correlated vectors, which can show whether the relative sizes of a set of diverse tests' *g*-loadings predicts the degree to which those tests are correlated with some external variable. The method is most easily explained by an example. Schafer (1984, 1985) measured the habituation of the amplitude of brain potentials (EP) evoked by repeated auditory stimuli (50 'clicks' at short random intervals averaging 2 sec) in 50 young adults with IQs ranging from 98 to 142. The index of habituation of the evoked potential (EPHI) is the average amplitude of the EP over the first set of 25 clicks minus the average EP amplitude over the second set of 25 clicks. The EPHI correlated +0.59 with Full Scale IQ on the Wechsler Adult Intelligence Scale (WAIS). But what is the locus of this correlation in the factor structure of the WAIS? The method of correlated vectors, illustrated in Table 2, indicates that the column vector of the WAIS subtests' *g*-loadings is positively and significantly correlated with the column vector of the subtests' correlations with the EPHI, as shown in the scatter diagram in Fig. 2. The *g*-loadings and

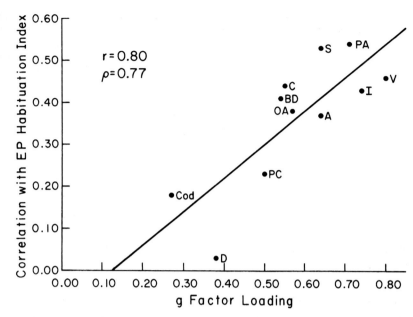

FIG. 2.   Scatter diagram showing the Pearson correlation (r) and the Spearman rank-order correlation (ρ) between the correlations of each of the 11 subtests of the Wechsler Adult Intelligence Scale with the evoked potential (EP) habituation index (on the vertical axis) and the subtests' loadings on the *g* factor. The subtests are: A, arithmetic; BD, block designs; C, comprehension; Cod, coding; D, digit span; I, information; OA, object assembly; PA, picture arrangement; PC, picture completion; S, similarities; V, vocabulary. Reproduced from Jensen (1998) with permission.

correlations are corrected for attenuation to rule out any correlation between the vectors because of correlated errors of measurement. Spearman's rank-order correlation, which minimizes the effects of outliers, is used to test the statistical significance of the correlation between the vectors. (For the statistical rationale and variations of this method, see Jensen 1998, p 589.) Finally, when *g* is statistically partialled out of the WAIS subtests' correlations with the EPHI, all of the partialled correlations diminish to near-zero, as does the overall correlation between the Full Scale IQ and EPHI.

The same method of correlated vectors based on the *g*-loadings of many different psychometric tests has revealed the predominant relationship of *g* to various non-psychometric variables in studies from different laboratories around the world (all of them referenced in Jensen 1998). Typical vector correlations are shown in parentheses:

- Scholastic performance (0.80).
- Occupational level (0.75).

- Assortative mating correlation between spouses' test scores (0.95).
- The genetic heritability of test scores (0.70).
- Inbreeding depression of test scores in offspring of cousin mating (0.80).
- Heterosis — outbreeding elevation of test scores in the offspring of interracial mating (0.50).
- Reaction time on various elementary cognitive tasks (ECTs) (0.80).
- Intra-individual variability in RT on ECTs (0.75).
- Head size as a correlated proxy for brain size (0.65).
- Habituation of the amplitude of brain evoked potentials (0.80).
- Complexity of waveform of brain evoked potentials (0.95).
- Brain intracellular pH level; lower acidity $\rightarrow$ higher g (0.63).
- Cortical glucose metabolic rate during mental activity (-0.79).

In addition, there are numerous studies that have shown significant and substantial correlations of certain sensory and brain variables simply with IQ, which is always highly g-loaded but may also contain other factors: visual, auditory and tactile discrimination; brain volume measured *in vivo* by magnetic resonance imaging (MRI); EEG coherence; event related desynchronization of brain waves; frontal lobe alpha brain wave frequency; and many other physical variables less obviously related to brain functions (Jensen & Sinha 1993). Hypothesizing that the physiological basis of g results in part from individual differences in nerve conduction velocity (NCV), Reed & Jensen (1992) demonstrated a relationship between non-verbal IQ (Raven's matrices) and NCV in a brain tract from the retina to the visual cortex. The result, shown in Fig. 3, was recently replicated (A. Andres-Pueyo, R. M. Boastre & A. Rodrigues-Fornells, unpublished paper, 9th Biennial Convention of the International Society for the Study of Individual Differences, 6 July 1999). Of course, to serve as reliable clues for developing a physical theory of g, the results for all of the physical variables listed above require replications.

Toward a theory of g

Although the present findings provide clues for possibly explaining the physical basis of g, we are still far from having a full-fledged theory of g, which must consist of more than just a collection of correlations. Understanding and explaining these correlations beyond psychometrics, that is, at a causal level, calls for the involvement of molecular genetics, the brain sciences (including animal models) and evolutionary psychology.

The task ahead may seem less daunting if we keep in mind the conceptual distinction between intelligence and g (or other psychometric factors). Intelligence involves the brain's neural structures or design features, circuitry

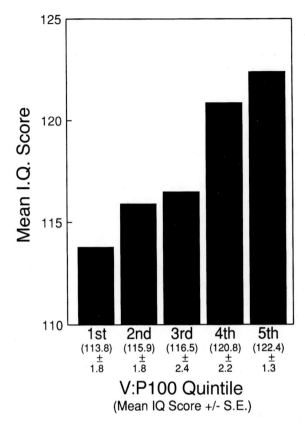

FIG. 3.   IQ means (in parentheses)±standard errors of each quintile of the distribution of
nerve conduction velocity (NCV) measured in the visual tract in 147 male college students.
This sample comprises only the top one-third of the IQ distribution in the general population.
Individual values of velocity (V:P100) were based on the P100 latency of the visual evoked
potential. The measures of NCV in this sample range from the slowest at 1.75 m/s to the fastest
at 2.22 m/s. The Pearson *r* between NCV and IQ is 0.26 ($P<0.002$); corrected for restriction of
IQ range in this college sample, $_{c}r=0.37$. Reproduced from Reed & Jensen (1992) with
permission.

and specialized modules that enable various behavioural capacities that are
common to all biologically normal members of a given species — capacities such
as learning, memory, language and reasoning in humans. The *g* factor results from
some condition(s) of the brain that causes correlation between individual
differences in the speed and efficiency of operation of these diverse capacities and
probably governs the asymptote of their growth or development under optimal
environmental conditions. These two conceptually distinct aspects of brain

function most likely have different physiological bases. Considering the great anatomical similarities between primate brains in their non-quantitative structural features, it seems unlikely that there are individual differences in the design features and operating principles of biologically normal brains within the same species. It seems more likely that the source of individual differences, hence *g*, lies in some quantitative features of the brain that affect many of its diverse cognitive processing mechanisms in common (Jensen 1997). A crude analogy would be like comparing different makes of cars that differ in quantitative performance indices such as horsepower, top speed and fuel efficiency. All the autos have internal combustion engines (i.e. the same operating principles), but these can differ quantitatively in number of cylinders and different cubic capacities, running on gas of different octane grades, and these variables are all positively correlated across the different cars — hence individual differences in overall performance.

Why is *g* related to brain size? This relationship *per se* is well established and may account for as much as 20% of the *g* variance, but its basis is still conjectural. Is it total number of neurons in those cortical regions that serve cognitive functions? Amount of dendritic arborization? Degree of myelination of axons, which affects nerve conduction velocity? Number of glial cells, which nutritionally support the myelin? Why is *g* inversely related to glucose metabolic rate in the active brain? Does the implied efficiency involve differences in brain chemistry, such as different concentrations of neurotransmitters (e.g. acetylcholine, glutamate, aspartate) or inhibitors that commonly affect chemical receptors in various cognitive neural systems or modules? Why do *g* factor scores show a curvilinear (inverted U) relationship to testosterone levels in males (Nyborg & Jensen 1999)? Do other hormones also affect *g*?

The first steps in the reductionist study of the basis of *g* call for securing beyond question the physical correlates of *g* already mentioned as well as other possible correlates yet to be discovered. The next steps will necessarily measure as many of these brain variables as possible in the same group of individuals. Analysis of the correlations among individual differences in these variables might be able to identify the one variable, or the few variables, that account for most of the heritable variance in *g*.

Is it all too fantastic to predict that there will be found a general factor in the correlations among some small number of brain variables — histological, biochemical, physiological — and that this general factor will prove to be coincident with psychometric *g*? I am betting on it. Such an outcome would be a major advance toward the kind of theory of *g* originally envisaged by Spearman (1927), who wrote that the final understanding of *g* '... must come from the most profound and detailed direct study of the human brain in its purely physical and chemical aspects' (p 403).

References

Carroll JB 1993 Human cognitive abilities: a survey of factor-analytic studies. Cambridge University Press, New York

Carroll JB 1997 Theoretical and technical issues in identifying a factor of general intelligence. In: Devlin B, Fienberg SE, Resnick DP, Roeder K (eds) Intelligence, genes, & success. Springer-Verlag, New York, p 125–156

Galton F 1869 Hereditary genius: an inquiry into its laws and consequences. Macmillan, London

Jensen AR 1993 Spearman's *g*: links between psychometrics and biology. Ann NY Acad Sci 702:103–129

Jensen AR 1994 Phlogiston, animal magnetism, and intelligence. In: Detterman DK (ed) Current topics in human intelligence, vol 4: Theories of intelligence. Ablex, Norwood, NJ, p 257–284

Jensen AR 1997 The neurophysiology of *g*. In: Cooper C, Varma V (eds) Processes in individual differences. Routledge, London, p 108–125

Jensen AR 1998 The *g* factor: the science of mental ability. Praeger, Westport, CT

Jensen AR, Sinha SN 1993 Physical correlates of human intelligence. In: Vernon PA (ed) Biological approaches to the study of human intelligence. Ablex, Norwood, NJ, p 139–242

Jensen AR, Weng LJ 1994 What is a good *g*? Intelligence 18:231–258

Nyborg H, Jensen AR 1999 Testosterine levels as modifiers of psychometric *g*. Pers Individ Differ 28:601–607

Reed TE, Jensen AR 1992 Conduction velocity in a brain nerve pathway of normal adults correlates with intelligence level. Intelligence 16:259–272

Schafer EWP 1984 Habituation of evoked cortical potentials correlates with intelligence. Psychophysiol 21:597

Schafer EWP 1985 Neural adaptability: a biological determinant of behavioral intelligence. Behav Brain Sci 8:240–241

Spearman CE 1904 'General intelligence' objectively determined and measured. Am J Psychol 15:201–293

Spearman CE 1927 The abilities of man: their nature and measurement. Macmillan, London

DISCUSSION

Hinde: I wanted to ask a question about causation. You showed that assortative mating was correlated with the *g* factor, and you said that people were choosing partners with similar genes. I understand that there's also a strong correlation between the length of the ear lobe between partners, implying perhaps that partners choose each other on the lengths of their ear lobes! What does one conclude from all this? Is the ear lobe part of *g*?

Jensen: On some of these physical features connected with IQ or *g* you can't find any causal connections, but you can be interested in what might be called the cultural anthropology or sociology of some of these correlations. For example, IQ is correlated with a host of physical variables that certainly have no causal connection with IQ, such as height. Height is positively correlated about 0.2 with an IQ in the population. This can be shown not to be a functional correlation, but it comes about through assortative mating. Both height and IQ are valued in our society, and these are both selected together in mate choice.

Therefore the genes for both of them show up in the progeny of people who are tall and intelligent, but they're not functionally related. You can show this by the fact that within families there's no correlation between height and intelligence, whereas the correlation is 0.2 in the population. If you take the taller siblings in families, the average IQ of those siblings will be the same as that of the shorter siblings. Now this isn't true of some traits, such as myopia. If you take the more myopic children in a family they will have higher IQs than the non-myopes in the same family. This is a kind of pleiotropic relationship rather than just a simple genetic correlation. There are other examples: the ability to curl the tongue is correlated with IQ. A single gene makes this possible. No one knows why that should be correlated with IQ. I wrote a whole chapter (Jensen & Sinha 1993) on physical correlates of IQs — it is a rather amazing collection of characteristics. Some of them are functionally related and some are not. Brain size is one that is functionally related, and shows up within families as well as between families: there's a correlation of about 0.4 between brain size and IQ.

Harnad: I am a tremendous admirer of your work, and so what I am about to say, although it is critical, is only about its limits rather than its limitations. You made an excellent description of the extraction of *g*, but what was left out of the description is how *g* is interpreted. There is a huge hermeneutic component to psychometric analysis. The empirical part is the calculation of the correlations in the extraction of the factors; the hermeneutic part is in interpreting the factors, figuring out what on earth they may mean. Of course, all you have to go by is patterns of correlation. Yet, I think one of the themes of this symposium is causation, and causation with dimension. I want to suggest that in the extension of the psychometric paradigm, which is a correlation-plus-hermeneutics paradigm, you get your factors and then you try to look back at the clusters of things that load on factors and guess what might be behind them — that's where the inference comes in. Do we get beyond hermeneutics when we add to the psychometric battery, a biometric battery? I want to suggest you don't: you are still stuck in the same paradigm. It is not just *psycho*metric anymore to be sure, but you're still in the business of looking at correlations and trying to guess hermeneutically what might be behind them, whereas what you really want is to find the underlying causal mechanism. To find this, you have to break out of the hermeneutic circle, because it won't be given to you by the loadings on *g*.

Jensen: The loadings of these physiological variables on *g* affords better clues than sheer guesswork as to where to look for causal mechanisms. For example, you can do a preliminary analysis to see whether some relationship is functional or not, looking to see whether you get within- or just between-family correlations, or both between and within. If you don't get any within-family correlations between two variables, they're not functionally related, so you can dismiss them. However, it may still be of interest to the cultural anthropologists and sociologists as to how those things got together, as in the case of height and intelligence.

Flynn: Are you saying that if you take a group of people who are one standard deviation above the mean in g, their degree of assortative mating will be greater than people one standard deviation below the mean in g? That is, the actual correlation between the spouses' IQ rises as g rises. Is this your point?

Jensen: That's not what I'm saying, but it happens to be true. There is a higher degree of assortative mating above the mean in the bell curve that there is below. The bell curve is not a perfectly normal Gaussian curve: it has a bump at the low end for types of mental defect and also an excess at the upper end. One explanation for this deviation at the upper end is that there is a higher degree of assortative mating in the upper half of the curve, which increases the genetic variance and pushes more offspring into the upper end of the curve.

Flynn: That is very interesting, because it seems to be another case of high IQ seeking out an enriched environment. After all, one's spouse is a great part of one's intellectual environment. Apparently, the higher you go up the IQ scale the greater the match with your spouse's IQ.

Jensen: Society itself helps a lot with that in the educational system, because graduate students don't often marry high school dropouts — they hardly ever meet them.

Flynn: Ulrich Neisser, in his review of your book *The g factor*, points out that when you compare reaction times in people with higher and lower IQs, the maximum responses are very similar — it tends to be more the variance that separates the two. Is that correct, and if so what do you make of it?

Jensen: Yes that's correct. Even comparing Berkeley students with mentally retarded people in institutions, their fastest reaction times do not differ all that much, but the retarded people produce many more slower reaction times. A more important correlate of g than reaction time is the intra-individual variance in reaction time: brighter people show less variation from trial-to-trial of a reaction time test than less bright people.

Flynn: Do you have any physiological explanation of that?

Jensen: No, but there are hypotheses, such as the theory that there's simply more noise in the nervous systems of lower IQ people, and that this variation from trial-to-trial in reaction time tests reflects neural noise, whatever that may mean. This should be investigated, because it's a more striking correlate of IQ than is reaction time itself.

Humphrey: I want to come back to the question of correlation and causation. It's tempting of course to assume that a relation between two variables is causal when we can see how it would work, but to assume it's a mere correlation when we can't see it. So, when we find that IQ correlates with brain size or head size, we think that's probably because large brains do indeed cause high IQ. But when we find IQ correlates with height or ear lobe size we don't think the relationship is causal — instead we postulate, for example, that bright men want to marry tall girls. But w should be careful. Because even in the case of IQ and brain size, the relationshi may not be what we think it is. In fact there is very good reason to suppose tha brain size really can't be the cause of IQ — at least in any straightforward way. Joh Skoyles (1999) in a recent paper has drawn attention to the fact that people wit brains as small as 800–900 cm^3 can have more or less normal IQ.

Jensen: That will always happen when there is a correlation as low as 0.4. In fac one of my former graduate students has been studying midgets. He wa interested in the brain size-intelligence correlation, so he's gone to Ecuado where there are true midgets who are perfectly proportioned and have hea sizes similar to a three-year-old child. He has collected some 80 of thes individuals, and they have perfectly normal intelligence when given IQ test (Kranzler et al 1998). This shows that variation in head size itself is not crucial factor in intelligence: it's neither necessary nor sufficient to have a larg head for above average IQ.

Humphrey: This has evolutionary implications. It suggests that our *Homo erectu* ancestors, who had brains of about 750–800 cm^3, may well have had the capacit for an IQ or *g* equivalent to that of modern humans. We should perhaps therefor be thinking of explanations of the doubling of brain size since then, other than tha it was just needed to increase general cognitive abilities.

Jensen: If you read some of my writings on this, I claim that the correlatio between brain size and IQ is still a mystery: we don't know what there is abou brain size that makes it correlated with IQ, but it certainly is — you can't deny correlation of 0.4. Many different studies have been done on this now. It is a interesting scientific question as to whether there is a causal relationship or not. may be a sociological kind of correlation, or it may actually be functional one. would suspect a functional explanation in the case of brain size, because a large brain size is not evolutionarily a good thing in its own right, unless it confer advantages such as increased behavioural capacity.

Humphrey: Among other things it confers strong resistance to dementia: if yo are in the lower quintile for brain size you have three times the risk of Alzheimer' disease (Schofield et al 1997).

Deary: Would that affect fitness? Alzheimer's disease usually occurs so long afte the age of reproductive activity that I can't imagine it having a fitness effect.

Humphrey: Fitness effects can occur after reproductive age. Grandmothers, fo example, are increasingly being seen as important for the fitness of thei grandchildren and perhaps even their great-grandchildren. For that matter, me can remain reproductive well into the age when they are beginning to suffer fron all sorts of brain deterioration of the kind for which larger brain size provide protection.

Deary: Was the average lifespan of people during the time this would have been ective getting to the age where Alzheimer's is common?

Humphrey: I don't think we can be sure of that at all. I have discussed the issue in a cent paper (Humphrey 1999).

Houle: I'm interested in the point you've made about within- versus between-mily correlations because it seems to me that you are drawing an incorrect nclusion. Assortative mating involving pairs of traits, such as height or brain :e, for example, even if they are not causally related to each other at all, will use genetic associations between these traits through linkage disequilibrium. his effect will be stronger for loci that are closely linked to each other. This will use within-family correlation. The conclusion I would draw when you have sortative mating and find a lack of within-family correlation, is that the sortative mating is actually not on the genetic component of the traits being nsidered, but on the environmental deviations from the breeding value.

Jensen: That's possible, but I have been told by geneticists that the linkage sequilibrium would not account for within-family correlations beyond the first :neration. This is something that washes out very quickly. In the general)pulation, if you have a large sample and look for these correlations, very little ' it would be caused by linkage. It would be more pleiotropic, meaning that one :ne has two or more apparently unrelated effects.

Houle: It depends on the assumptions you make. If you assume very simple :netics — for example, one gene influencing each trait — they are very unlikely • be closely linked. This would, to a large extent, get rid of this effect, but not itirely. Since traits such as brain function and height are the product of many :nes some loci are bound to be closely linked, so any association would decay owly for these loci; it's very unlikely that you would be able to wash that out)mpletely. The thing about assortative mating is that it occurs every generation) those correlations are constantly being reinforced: they won't be large, perhaps, it they won't be zero either. So if you can confidently say there's no within-family)rrelation, you're actually making a strong statement about the genetic lationship of genes to those traits.

Jensen: That's a good point.

Whiten: It was interesting that the hierarchical factor structures that you came up ith can apparently be accommodated within just three levels, or even sometimes wer. This becomes interesting if it represents a finding about the natural world 1at we might not have predicted in advance. You seem to be saying that it is not 1erely a mathematical or statistical feature of factor analysis. This leads to two 1oughts. First, could this be an answer to the question Stevan Harnad originally :ked, about what this tells us about cognition? If this is a discovery about the 1tural world — that this hierarchical structure exists — this could be one answer) Stevan's question. Second, if this is a finding about the natural world, is it about *intellect* in particular? Is there any other set of biological data that has been looked by this factor analytic approach, which actually produces more than three level Or is there just something about biological data of this kind that they naturally fa into this very economic number of levels?

Jensen: I don't know the answer to that. I know that there have been fact analyses of up to 50 different body measurements, but I can't recall t hierarchical analysis. There is a general factor in body measurements. The measurements still exist: the British garment industry has collected about body measurements on 10 000 women, and the correlation matrix exists. Wher took a course on factor analysis, our final exam project was to factor analyse th huge correlation matrix which in those days took a 40 hour week to do on a des calculator! There was a big general factor and about four or five other factors th were large enough to be significant.

Rutter: I'd like to return to the topic that John Maynard Smith posed at t beginning, in terms of the biological significance of *g*. It is still not clear to n what postulate either David Lubinski or Arthur Jensen is putting forward. T workings of the mind have to be based on the functioning of the brain. But it not obvious what more one can conclude. If one takes James Flynn's findings the rise in IQ over time, that rise was paralleled by a rise in head size. Similarly, our own study of adoptees from very deprived Romanian institutions (Rutter et 1998), their head size at the time of entering this country was well below U norms, as was their developmental quotient, but two years later both had ris greatly. There are good reasons for inferring that the initial deficits were due institutional deprivation and that the rise was a function of the much bett rearing conditions in the adoptive homes (O'Connor et al 2000). Obviously, t improved cognition must reflect the functioning of the brain but where does th get us? You are saying that *g* is not a 'thing', so what use it is?

Jensen: It is not a 'thing', but *g* is instead the total action of this number of thing Brain size may be correlated with intelligence because there are more brain cells more intelligent people, so this is something that can be investigated. You woul be one step further ahead if you found that to be the case, or even if you found it n to be the case. Then the next thing that you could look at may be the amount myelin in the brain: myelin controls the speed of neural conduction, and we kno that cognitive capabilities increase with age and myelination increases with age; w demyelinate as we get old and cognitive functions begin to decline, and so on. O can simply go through these correlates of *g* and investigate them empirically. M view is that the only place to go with this kind of research on *g* and mental abilities into the brain itself. We have to figure out strategies for zeroing in on those aspec of brain function that can be said to be causal of the *g* factor.

Rutter: Isn't there a danger of unwarranted biological determinism? F example, in studies of individuals with obsessive disorders there are differences

PET scan findings, and treatment changes that. But psychological treatments cause the same changes as do pharmacological ones (Baxter et al 1992). The abnormal behaviour and the brain functioning are meaningfully associated, but it doesn't necessarily follow that the behaviour is being driven by something that is biologically more basic.

Jensen: That is true, but I don't think we can give up the enterprise of trying to get a neurological or brain account of the kinds of phenomena that I've shown here. We are at the frontier of this research on the Galtonian paradigm. I can't see anywhere else left to go.

Maynard Smith: Your talk cleared up many of my difficulties. But the thing that became quite clear from the last part of your paper is that although you expect differences in cognitive ability to be reflected in differences between brains (it would be bloody weird if that were not the case), you are not looking for a single kind of difference between brains. In other words, you really rather expect all sorts of quite different anatomical and physiological measures on brains to have some effect upon your measurements of *g*. You are therefore looking for a multicausal, multifactorial basis for differences in cognitive ability. This is entirely reasonable, but in a sense you are not really looking for something like ethanol. The point about your ethanol example is that this is one factor.

Jensen: Every analogy only goes so far.

Maynard Smith: I liked the analogy, but you weren't implying, were you, when you used that analogy that you are really looking for one thing?

Jensen: This one thing is just a component of variance, not necessarily one brain process.

Brody: I have a very simple methodological question, which derives from the comment about the role of linkage. What about analyses using genetic covariance approaches in which you contrast correlations among monozygotic (MZ) and dizygotic (DZ) twins, with an effort to see whether or not the genes that are contributing to intelligence are co-varying in that way? For example, some studies suggest that assortative mating is not genetically covariant, even though it has a high correlation with your *g* factor. The correlation between MZ twin spouses in intelligence is no higher than the correlation of DZ twin spouses. This seems to come about solely because of social homogamy effects: people just get tossed together who are somewhat equal in IQ in social settings. The data on head size are ambiguous or undecided with respect to whether or not IQ and head size are genetically covariant. On the other hand, if you found that there are genetically covariant relations underlying these correlates, is that design sufficient to move you a step forward in the way that a comparison of between- and within-family correlations may not be?

Rutter: That is an interesting finding: can you say more about the studies that is based on?

Brody: This is a general and interesting phenomenon. It is something that people in evolutionary biology might tell someone like me a lot more about. Lykken & Tellegen (1993) looked at correlations between the spouses of MZ twins and DZ twins. We know that MZ twins are more alike primarily for genetic reasons, and that if people select spouses who are genetically similar to themselves you would expect the spouses of MZ twins to be similar in a way that the spouses of DZ twins are not. It turns out that across a large range of characteristics this is not the case. They argue that attraction to others is a kind of evolutionary mechanism to create genetic diversity, and people are simply attracted to people who are not necessarily genetically similar. People who study relationships often point out that it's very hard to know why people are initially attracted. You can sometimes predict whether people will stay together or break up, by differences in political attitudes, for example. But the initial attraction seems almost like a random phenomenon.

Hinde: There is a vast literature on the attractiveness of attitude similarity. This is presumably not very much genetically determined.

Miller: The biological correlates of *g* come back to Stevan Harnad's question about the hermeneutic interpretation of what *g* means. The last 10 years of work on the biological correlates keeps us from jumping to a cognitivist interpretation of *g* that would have been popular 20 years ago, when people tended to interpret *g* as meaning that perhaps there is some sort of general purpose processing device in the human brain, or some general purpose learning device. The explanation of *g* tended to be at the psychological level, and the biological correlations expand the possibilities for interpreting what *g* really is. It is not necessarily a psychological phenomenon at all: you can measure it psychometrically, but that doesn't mean that it taps into a unitary cognitive ability, for example.

Nesse: I would like to address this question of how we can account for the correlations that we're finding between measured intelligence and various other things. When one finds intelligence as a strongly heritable trait, correlating with another strongly heritable trait such as myopia, for instance, it is tempting to assume that the association must be a pleiotropic effect or some other explanation based on genetics. On the other hand, there are other possibilities. In the case of myopia, there's a very plausible explanation for the correlation aside from genetic pleiotropy: people who are more intelligent are more likely to read earlier in life because they're capable of it or more interested in it. It is clear that reading early in life is a precursor to myopia in those who are genetically predisposed. Thus we have an alternative mechanism that goes via intelligence to a preference for a behaviour, to a pathological state. The association turns out not to be genetic.

Jensen: Most researchers studying myopia have already dismissed that as an explanation for myopia. They find that retarded children who never take to reading or any other kind of near work have the same frequency of myopia.

Nesse: It would take us off topic to go too far into this, but the study I like the best is the one on Inuits, where on a population basis the rate of myopia was very low prior to institution of schooling, but increased rapidly afterwards (Norn 1997). It is very hard to imagine how severe myopia could be compatible with any high reproductive success on the African savannah.

Jensen: The latest opinion on this among myopia researchers is that it is caused by an interaction between some genetic predisposition and these other factors.

Nesse: Since we are on this subject, let me take the opposite point of view for a moment and turn to mechanisms. It appears that what's going on in myopia is that the eye grows to the right distance so that things focus. It is not pre-programmed, but based on feedback mechanisms. Blurry images cause the eyeball to grow until the image is in focus again, much like an automatic slide projector, but much better. And it appears that there's a strong genetic difference in how fast that happens, or whether the process stops at a certain point or not. I could imagine that in those people in whom the eyeball grew faster, or in whom that mechanism was programmed quite differently, this is related to some other brain function that could conceivably account for IQ. Another theme here is trying to see the specific mechanisms responsible for these correlations.

Houle: I'm concerned with the assumption that figuring out mechanisms is what this meeting is all about, or should be about. There are several overlapping questions here. How does the brain work and what's the relationship of brain function to *g*? What's the practical validity and the predictive usefulness of *g*? How does *g* evolve? Finally, we can ask what causes variation in *g*? These are very different questions; they're overlapping but not entirely the same.

I think that the next step forward in understanding variation in *g* is clearly not resting with any of us in this room — it is resting with the people who are going to map the genes responsible for variation in *g*. This will offer a clear explanation of what causes variation in *g*, but it's not necessarily going to tell us much about how the brain works. By the same token, evolutionary questions may or may not depend on the genetic details of what's going on here. Darwin invented the whole field of evolution before anyone worked out the mechanism of inheritance. There is more to this work than simply tracing everything down to causal mechanisms.

Rutter: In terms of causal mechanisms we need to come back to James Flynn's point, that the explanation for individual differences may or may not be the same as the explanation for changes over time. This is an empirical question. It's easy to think of examples where the causes are quite different. There are other examples where they probably are very similar.

Deary: The genetics of apolipoprotein E (ApoE4) have shown us that the individual differences in mental ability might have different causes at different ages (MacLullich et al 1998). If one has the ε4 allele of this gene one is more liable to get dementia. This raises the possibility, firstly, of giving us a clue as to where to start looking for mechanism once we get a gene–ability association and, secondly warning about the fact that that the genetics of intelligence might differ across time as well. Any one gene–ability association clue is liable to give us a small amount of the variance in a mental ability and it could just be the beginning of a very long series of causal mechanisms, possibly disappearing in so many biochemical processes that it is impossible to link genes to behaviours.

Rutter: At first, some investigators seemed to imply that ApoE4 might cause Alzheimer's disease directly despite the evidence that the association was only probabilistic. Individuals with the ε4 allele did not necessarily develop Alzheimer's disease and those with other alleles also developed Alzheimer's disease, although they did so less frequently. It is now apparent that, in addition, ApoE4 also predicts response to head injury (Teasdale et al 1997) and to cerebrovascular accidents (McCarron et al 1998). The implication is that the genetic effect may concern brain responses to a range of environmental hazards and not just predisposition to a single disease, Alzheimer's disease. But it is not known whether the effects involve one or several different causal mechanisms.

Gangestad: It seems that one of David Houle's points is that the factors that give rise to the genetic variance in *g* may have little to do with the brain mechanisms that underlie the cognitive abilities that are captured by *g*. For instance, it's possible that mutations across the whole genome contribute to that variation, but contribute to variation in lots of other traits as well. The genes may have little to do with the actual brain mechanisms.

Deary: Spearman addressed the problem of how the brain works in general in one book, and the individual differences in another. His 1923 book was called *The nature of intelligence and the principles of cognition*. The 'nature of intelligence' isn't what the differentialists are telling us about here. It wasn't about the individual differences in mental abilities: it was actually the ordinary, average (modal) function of the brain. Unfortunately, Spearman did that from the armchair, using a philosophical approach. In contrast, his 1927 book is full of data, and it's all about the individual differences in human mental abilities. He did, though, try to tie the two of them together: the modal function and the differences. He realized as early as the 1920s that one might or might not need to know the average function of the brain before one could account for the individual differences. These issues have been laid out long and wearily, and we are admitting that we still don't seem to know the answer today. Certainly, those of us who are studying individual differences haven't waited for the biological or cognitive architecture to arrive pre-packaged: we've gone on anyway with the crumbs from the cognitivist's and biologist's tables and seen whether their parameters are any good in predicting individual differences (Deary & Caryl 1997). As I will tell you after lunch, they are not particularly good.

References

Baxter LR, Schwartz JM, Bergman KS et al 1992 Caudate glucose metabolic rate changes with both drug and behavior therapy for obsessive-compulsive disorder. Arch Gen Psychiatry 49:681–689

Deary IJ, Caryl PG 1997 Neuroscience and human intelligence differences. Trends Neurosci 20:365–371

Humphrey N 1999 Why human grandmothers may need large brains: commentary on Skoyles on brain-expertise. Psycoloquy 10:024

Jensen AR, Sinha SN 1993 Physical correlates of human intelligence. In: Vernon PA (ed) Biological approaches to the study of human intelligence. Ablex, Norwood, NJ, p 139–242

Kranzler JH, Rosenbloom AL, Martinez V, Guevara-Aguire J 1998 Normal intelligence with severe insulin-like growth factor I deficiency due to growth hormone receptor deficiency: a controlled study in a genetically homogeneous population. J Clin Endocrinol Metab 83:1953–1958

Lykken DT, Tellegen A 1993 Is human mating adventitious or the result of lawful choice? A twin study of mate selection. J Pers Soc Psychol 65:56–68

MacLullich AMJ, Seckl JR, Starr JM, Deary IJ 1998 The biology of intelligence: from association to mechanism. Intelligence 26:63–73

McCarron MO, Muir KW, Weir CJ et al 1998 The apolipoprotein E ε4 allele and outcome in cerebrovascular disease. Stroke 29:1882–1887

Norn M 1997 Myopia among the Inuit population of East Greenland. Longitudinal study 1950–1994. Acta Ophthalmol Scand 75:723–725

O'Connor T, Rutter M, Beckett C, Keaveney L, Kreppner J, the English & Romanian Adoptees (ERA) Study Team 2000 The effects of global severe privation on cognitive competence: extension and longitudinal follow-up. Child Dev 71:376–390

Rutter M, the English & Romanian Adoptees (ERA) Study Team 1998 Developmental catch-up, and deficit, following adoption after severe global early privation. J Child Psychol Psychiatry 39:465–476

Schofield PW, Logroscino G, Andrews HF, Albert S, Stern Y 1997 An association between head circumference and Alzheimer's disease in a population-based study of ageing and dementia. Neurology 49:30–37

Skoyles JR 1999 Human evolution expanded brains to increase expertise capacity, not IQ. Psycoloquy 10:002

Spearman C 1923 The nature of intelligence and the principles of cognition. Macmillan, London

Spearman C 1927 The abilities of man. Macmillan, London

Teasdale GM, Nicoll JAR, Murray G, Fiddes M 1997 Association of apolipoprotein E polymorphism with outcome after head injury. Lancet 350:1069–1071

Psychometric intelligence differences and brain function

Ian J. Deary

Department of Psychology, University of Edinburgh, 7 George Square, Edinburgh EH8 9JZ UK

Abstract. Psychometric intelligence attracts a converging consensus about its phenotypi structure. Mental ability test scores have proven predictive validity. However, althoug individual differences in mental abilities can be measured, they are not understood. A long-standing aim of the 'London School' of British psychologists, since Galton an Spearman, is to understand the origins of psychometric intelligence differences in term of individual differences in brain processes. The history of this research is described, as the rise in interest since the 1970s. The first problem, met since antiquity, is to discover th relevant levels of brain function. Thus, aspects of brain function that 'explain psychometric intelligence differences are sought at psychometric, cognitive, psycho physical, physiological, neurochemical and genetic levels. The growing points and dead ends within each of these levels are identified. Special attention is given to research tha crosses levels of description of brain function. Two types of multi-level brain functio research are discussed, 'correlational' and 'circumstantial/experimental,' and examples o each are described. Illustrating both approaches, there is a detailed account of research o inspection time that discusses how psychometric intelligence–brain process correlation at one level (psychophysical) may be expanded using event-related potentials psychopharmacology and functional magnetic resonance imaging.

2000 The nature of intelligence. Wiley, Chichester (Novartis Foundation Symposium 233 p 58–78

Background

To ask about the nature of intelligence is to pose at least two questions. First, it i the question about the species-typical infrastructure that, for the healthy adult affords successful interaction with a complex world (the cognitive psychologist' 'nature' of intelligence). Second, it is the question about the nature and origins o individual differences in mental abilities (the differential psychologist's 'nature' o intelligence). In our present state of ignorance we don't know whether the firs must be known in order to answer the second. Spearman (1923) thought th cognitive question should be answered first. His *The nature of intelligence and th rinciples of cognition* was arguably the first cognitive psychology book, and was his ttempt to provide what he called a 'mental cytology.' This phrase is still pregnant vith accusation for differential psychologists. Compare our plight with the ιhysiologist interested in, say, differences in renal function. He has a ready-rticulated functional unit, the nephron, which has understood subunits glomerulus, loop of Henle, and so forth) and each of the subunits has specialized :ells with characteristic functions aided by specific cellular membrane molecules.

Spearman's solution to the 'principles of cognition' was the famous trilogy of he apprehension of experience, the eduction of relations and the eduction of orrelates. This was his economical, elementary account of how all cognition ιroceeds. It made little contact with the biology of the brain, and might as easily ιe seen as a work in artificial intelligence that showed, in a way that is comparable to he SOAR architecture's model of 'general intelligence' (Laird et al 1987), how :omplex cognition was possible with a few basic principles. The work owed nore to philosophy and introspective psychology than to brain science and was a vork in the tradition of Hobbes (1651) and Wolff (1732) who also sat in their ιrmchairs and tried to work out the nature of human intelligence. All three, too, ried to account for human ability differences in terms of cognitive-level elements ιf the nature of intelligence.

While not losing sight of the possibility that psychometric intelligence lifferences may be traced more or less to cognitive architecture variation, we can ιtill ask whether aspects of brain structure and function relate to individual lifferences in mental abilities. Because much of the functional architecture of the ιrain is a mystery it is inevitable that this type of research carries hazards. First, the ιrain indices examined are necessarily those accessible to measurement. Thus, they ιre examined because they can be, rather than because they derive from some heory of cognitive function. Second, the functional constructs contained within :he brain indices that are accessible to measurement are often obscure. Third, neasures of brain function cross many levels of reduction. Thus, especially for :hose at higher levels, it is not clear whether the indices are elementary. The first :omprehensive review of the brain bases of human ability differences was provided ιy Huarte in 1575. In this astonishing book, without significant progenitors, Huarte addressed the origins, number and nature and applications of mental ιbility differences. He addressed issues of brain function in his chapter 3: 'What part of the body ought to be well tempered, that a yoong man have abilitie'. And here is the introduction, that could serve well alongside the research considered here,

For there is none of these philosophers [especially, he meant, Hippocrates and Plato] that doubteth, but that the braine is the instrument ordained by nature, to the end that man might become wise and skilfull, it sufficeth only to declare with

what conditions this part ought to be endewed, so as we may affirme, that it i
duly instrumentalized, and that a yong man in this behalfe may possesse a goo
wit and habilitie. (p 24)

Huarte did not stop en route from 'wit' to brain to invent intermediate-leve
constructs, as Spearman (1923) did. He indicated those constructs of the brain'
make-up that are the sources of individual differences in mental abilities,

> Foure conditions the braine ought to enjoy, to the end the reasonable soul ma
> therewith commodiously perform the workes which appertaine to under
> standing and wisdome. The first, good composition; the second, that his part
> be well united; the third, that the heat exceed not the cold, nor the moist the drie
> the fourth, that his substance be made of parts subtle and verie delicate.
>
> In the good composition, are contained other foure things: the first is, goo
> figure: the second, quantitie sufficient: the third, that in the braine the four
> ventricles be distinct and severed, each duly bestowed in his seat and place: th
> fourth, that the capableness of these be neither greater nor lesse than i
> convenient for their workings. (p 24–25)

The state of play

Research relating human ability differences to brain function has never been
concerted. Even today, reports relating psychometric intelligence to miscellaneous
aspects of the brain appear willy-nilly, rarely accumulating enough supporting
evidence for agreement (Deary & Caryl 1997). The techniques and constructs of
cognitive psychology and broadly-defined psychophysiology since the 1960s have
been borrowed by investigators curious to discover whether there might be
parameters accounting for variance in ability test scores. The most obvious
aspect of the research that relates brain function to mental ability differences as
measured by psychometric tests is the range of levels at which putative brain
functions are measured. Briefly, they are as follows.

Psychometric

Psychometric tests have been 'decomposed' using various regression modelling
techniques, protocol analysis and computer modelling to discover the menta
processing elements that operate and combine to effect successful performance.
Thus Sternberg (1977) found mental 'components' of 'encoding', 'inference',
'mapping' and 'application' in analogical and other reasoning tasks. More recently,
different approaches have more consistently alighted on 'working memory' and
'control processes/goal management' as key brain functions providing the

source(s) of ability differences (e.g. Carpenter et al 1990, Embretson 1995, Duncan et al 1996).

Cognitive/experimental

Individual difference measures are derived from various reaction time procedures (Hick's, S. Sternberg's and Posner's), and these correlate significantly with ability test scores (for a review see Neubauer 1997).

Psychophysical

There are individual differences in the efficiency of the early stages of visual and auditory processing that correlate significantly with mental ability test scores (for reviews see Deary & Stough 1996, Deary 1999).

Psychophysiological

Over a hundred studies examined aspects of the electroencephalogram and event-related potentials and there exist some modest associations between the brain's electrical responses and mental ability test scores (for reviews see Deary & Caryl 1993, 1997).

Physiological/anatomical

Size of the brain is among the better established biological correlates of mental test scores, with a moderate effect size. There is some evidence for a small correlation between nerve conduction velocity and psychometric intelligence, and some preliminary work relating aspects of brain metabolism to mental abilities. These areas are reviewed by Deary & Caryl (1997).

Table 1 raises some of the issues that concern these types of study. The effect sizes are small to medium at best. In some cases significant effects are poorly established, especially for event-related potential measures. Beyond establishing a correlation, there are more profound issues. The first concerns the constructs being assessed by the brain function measure, the theoretical tractability. In several cases this is unclear. Table 2, for example demonstrates how little is understood about the correlation between brain size and ability test scores. In this field, more generally, there is a tendency for researchers to invoke constructs such as 'neural efficiency,' 'mental speed,' 'information processing speed/efficiency/capacity' and so forth to account for these correlations. These terms serve as poor camouflages for ignorance. Table 1 indicates that some measures of brain function might be consequences rather than causes of high ability levels. Not covered in Table 1 is the problem that some measures of 'brain function' that correlate with ability test

TABLE 1   An assessment of some biological/information processing approaches to intelligence

Measure	Correlation with psychometric intelligence	Theoretical tractability	Cause or consequence of psychometric test scores?	Comments
Brain size	0.4 to 0.5	Poor: several vague, proposed constructs	Probably cause	
Nerve conduction velocity	0.2 or less	Good: simple biological measure	Probably cause	Too few studies to date
ERP 'string length'	Contradictory	Poor[a]	Ambiguous[b]	One of many ERP measures
Hick reaction time	<0.25 for single parameters	Poor: not well understood[c]	Ambiguous[d]	R2 improved when several parameters combined
Inspection time	0.4 to 0.5 for non-verbal abilities	Problematic	Probably cause, but disputed	

[a] The parameters that govern variance are speculative.
[b] Could be response characteristic secondary to intelligence level.
[c] 'Rate of gain of information,' the supposed construct assessed by the Hick slope measure, has not proved to be a robust correlate of psychometric intelligence.
[d] Slope could be due to learning.
Adapted from Caryl et al (1999).

scores might, in fact, owe their variance to higher-level factors such as motivation, attention, personality, strategy formation and so forth.

In summary, the attempt to associate aspects of the brain with mental ability differences has produced a modest pool of confirmed findings. But the meaning of these associations is no straightforward matter. In the rest of this paper there are some indications of how different approaches can help to combine some of these levels of description.

Chains of correlation

If brain function measures that correlate with ability test scores occur at different levels of description then it is of interest to discover whether constructs from more than one level share variance that relates to ability test scores. Three examples of this approach follow. All three discuss ways in which the correlation between inspection times and psychometric intelligence may be investigated further.

TABLE 2 Suggestions for constructs to account for the correlation between brain size and psychometric ability test scores

Author	Suggested mechanisms of association
Huarte (1575)	'Galen said, that a little head in any man is ever faultie, because that it wanteth braine; notwithstanding, I avouch that if his having a great head, proceedeth from abundance of matter, and ill tempered, at such time as the same was shaped by nature, it is an evill token, for the same consists of bones and flesh, and contains a smal quantitie of braine, as it befals in very big orenges, which opened, are found scarce of juice, and hard of rinde.' (p 25)
Willerman et al (1991)	'... larger size might reflect more cortical columns available for analyzing high-noise or low-redundancy signals, thus enabling more efficient information processing pertinent to IQ test performance.' '... a greater number of stem cells, an increased number of mitotic divisions producing more descendant neurons, or different rates of neuronal death.' (p 227)
Andreasen et al (1993)	'... aspects of brain structure that reflect "quality" rather than "quantity" of brain tissue: complexity of circuitry, dendritic expansion, number of synapses, thickness of myelin, metabolic efficiency, or efficiency of neurotransmitter production, release, and reuptake. Factors such as these would facilitate the speed and efficiency of information transfer within the brain as well as expand its capacity, so that multiple tasks of multiple kinds could be performed simultaneously.' 'The greater volume of grey matter can be postulated to reflect a greater number of nerve cell bodies and dendritic expansion; a greater number of neuronal connections presumably enhances the efficiency of computational processing in the brain.'
Raz et al (1993)	'... leftward volume asymmetry may reflect either a greater number of processing elements or more extensive connectivity in the left hemisphere. Gross hemispheric asymmetries are likely to arise from differences in the number of neurons rather than from altered dendritic arborization or cell packing density ... the volume advantage is likely to reflect the excess of processing modules (cortical columns)'
Wickett et al (1994)	'The brain size–IQ correlation of $r=0.395$ clearly indicates that either there are many more variables to be introduced in an attempt to explain intelligence, or that the measure of brain size is itself only a proxy, and an imperfect one, to some aspect of the brain (e.g. neuronal quantity or myelinization) that is relevant to cognitive ability.' (p 837)
Egan et al (1994)	'... it at [sic] seems plausible that small differences in brain volume translate into millions of excess neurones for some individuals, accounting for their higher IQ.'

Inspection time, event-related potentials and psychometric intelligence

One method of progressing beyond raw correlation is to ask whether there are lower-level brain function correlates shared by psychometric intelligence and an index of information processing. For example, a group of studies has inquired whether there are individual differences in event-related potentials that are related to inspection time differences and mental ability test scores. Figure 1 summarizes these studies. Panel A shows the time-onset sequence of a typical inspection time trial. Panel B shows the association between stimulus duration and probability of a correct response for two experienced observers in an inspection time task. Panel C shows the average event-related potentials during the performance of an inspection time task (the response is time-locked to the onset of the inspection time stimuli) for two groups of subjects, one 'good' at the task and one 'poor.' Panel D shows that, in three of the studies, individual differences in the slope of the evoked potential excursion between the negative trough at about 140 ms post-stimulus onset (N1) and the positive peak at 200 ms (P2) relates to individual differences in inspection times and psychometric intelligence. This type of triangulation means that those constructs assessed by the relevant segment of the brain's electrical response (in this case the early stages of stimulus classification and decision making) may be considered as candidates for conceptually tying together psychometric intelligence and inspection times.

Functional anatomy of inspection time: preliminary findings

An additional level of investigation is to examine the brain's metabolic activity as a result of psychometric intelligence and its correlates. As a prelude to that we have examined brain activity during inspection time performance. Inspection time procedures pose challenges for the study of the functional anatomy with functional magnetic resonance imaging (fMRI), because of the short duration of the stimuli presented to the subject. We ran a pilot study to assess the feasibility of examining the brain activation–deactivation patterns on a 2T MRI clinical scanner (Elscint, Israel) at the Western General Hospital, Edinburgh. Subjects (seven adult, healthy volunteers) were presented standard inspection time stimuli on a custom built light-emitting diode (LED) array and were requested to locate the longer of two vertical bars presented, for a brief period of time, and then backward masked, on the LED array. Visual cues preceded the stimuli. We used a simple block mode design with three blocks: a reference task, which was a cue followed by mask only with no vertical line stimulus to be discriminated; and two levels of the discrimination task, one for a very short period of presentation of the vertical bars (40 ms) and the other one for a longer presentation (200 ms). Subjects were instructed to discriminate mentally, without reporting their decisions. Each

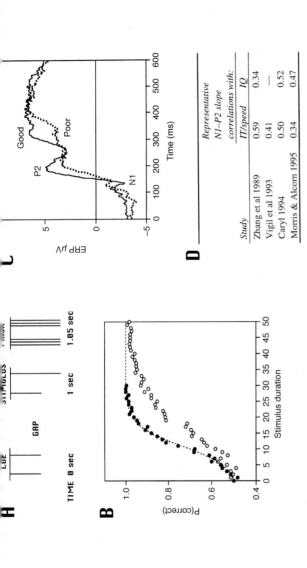

FIG. 1. (A) Cue, stimulus and mask used in inspection time assessment. The long line of the stimulus appears randomly on the right or left. The stimulus is shown for a variable, brief duration and the subject's accuracy in reporting the location of the longer line is recorded. (B) The relationship between stimulus duration and the probability of a correct response in the inspection time task (shown in A). Single data are shown from two subjects. Closed circles represent 600 trials per duration and open circles 800. These two subjects undertook 38 400 and 51 200 trials, respectively. (C) ERPs gathered while subjects perform the IT task (see A). The continuous line is the average from a group with good inspection time ability and the dotted line is the average ERP of a group with poorer IT ability. Note the difference in the steepness of the N1–P2 excursion between the two groups. (D) Reports of significant associations between the N1–P2 slope (illustrated in C) and inspection time ability or psychometric intelligence test scores.

block lasted 30 seconds and was repeated four times in an ABCABC... fashion During each block multiple discriminations (in random order and at a fixed rate of a decision every two seconds) were requested from the subjects. We used SPM99b (Wellcome Department of Cognitive Neurology, London) to analyse the data. FMRI data were first processed for reduction of movement artefact and then normalized to stereotactic space (defined by the ICBM, NIH P-20 project) for reporting of the results in a common standard space. All the seven subjects showed significant activations during the performance of the task. We performed both fixed effect analysis and a conjunction analysis to find 'typical' active areas for the population from which our group was sampled. Our preliminary results (Fig. 2) show that a complex network circuit involving frontal, temporal and limbic lobe is activated during the task. In conclusion, we have demonstrated the feasibility of further pursuing inspection time performance in an fMRI setting and we have gained some preliminary evidence regarding the functional anatomy of the inspection time task. Future work will include both the extension of the study to a wider pool of subjects varying in ability level and age. Repetition of the experiment will employ an event-related design instead of the block mode currently in use.

Age, inspection time and psychometric intelligence

A further technique that may be used to establish whether there is some explanatory substance to the correlation between a putative index of information processing and psychometric intelligence is to test the processing measure's power to account for developmental changes in psychometric intelligence. Using competing structural equation models and a cross-lagged panel design, Dear (1995) argued that auditory information processing had some causal influence on non-verbal and verbal ability levels as children developed from age 12 to age 14 years. More recently, 'speed of processing' has been nominated as a prime cause underlying much of the ageing effects in diverse cognitive functions. Salthouse (1996) amassed evidence that: (a) cognitive abilities do not age independently and (b) that measures of speed of processing account for a large proportion of the age-related variance in mental ability test scores. One partial objection to this interpretation is that the measures of processing speed are often coding tasks such as the Digit Symbol test from the Wechsler battery. This is a psychometric task and may hardly be considered a lower-level measure, one that can tap elementary brain functions in a tractable way. Other studies employ reaction times at various levels of complexity. Nettelbeck & Rabbitt (1992) found that inspection time could account for much of the age-related change in cognitive function in a sample of old people, with an exception for some aspects of memory. Their analyses were carried out using regression models and factor

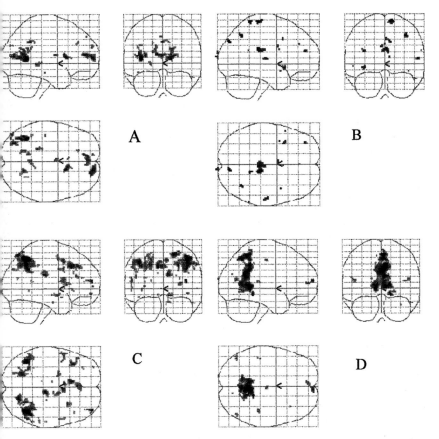

FIG. 2. (A) Maximum intensity projections of the statistical map for the comparison between the less difficult vs. the most difficult version of the task from the conjunction analysis of seven subjects. (B) Maximum intensity projections of the statistical map for the comparison between the most difficult vs. the less difficult version of the task from the conjunction analysis of seven subjects. (C) Comparison of the hard task condition vs. the control task. (D) Comparison of the control task vs. the hard task.

analyses. However, their and Salthouse's hypothesis, that speed of processing mediates the age–cognitive function association, can be put to a more severe test. They provided details of 98 subjects from their 1992 paper who had full data on age, three 'speed of processing' measures at different levels (inspection time, reaction time and coding) and three tests from the Performance subtests of the Wechsler Adult Intelligence Scale Revised (WAIS-R; block design, picture arrangement, picture completion). The model in Fig. 3 was tested and fitted the data well (see caption). The model formalizes the hypotheses that: (a) the three performance IQ subtests form single factor of psychometric intelligence; (b) the three processing speed tasks form a single latent trait; and (c) that the speed later trait mediates the effects of age on the psychometric intelligence trait. Though thi provides some insight into the nature of age changes in cognition, furthe information is needed about the underlying brain changes that lead to difference in the speed of processing trait.

Circumstantial evidence

Constructs linked by correlations can be investigated for their relative sensitivitie to experimental interventions. Thus, Stough and colleagues (1994, 1995a,b) foun that Raven's Matrices scores, reaction times, inspection times and event-relate potential indices all were improved by nicotine administration. This offer circumstantial evidence that all these variables might contribute to the ongoin level of cognitive ability. Were some index unaffected, causal integration migh be queried more closely. Hypoglycaemia of moderate severity temporaril deranges performance on mental ability tests (Deary 1998, reviews this area This arises because, although the brain accounts for about 2% of body mass in humans, it accounts for 20% of the metabolic activity and may use only glucose as fuel. Reaction times and aspects of visual information processing also show decrements during experimentally induced hypoglycaemia in humans (Dear 1998, McCrimmon et al 1996). In a new study we examined whether putativ indices of 'information processing' from different levels of function were affected by moderately severe hypoglycaemia. Thus, 16 healthy young subjects (8 male underwent, in a counterbalanced experiment, two hyperinsulinaemic glucose clamp procedures. During one clamp they were kept normoglycaemic and

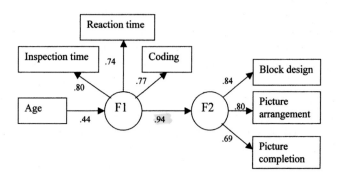

FIG. 3.   Structural equation model of data re-analysed from Nettelbeck & Rabbitt (1992 $n=98$). A latent 'speed of processing' factor mediates the effect of age on Performance IC subtests. Fit statistics are as follows: average off-diagonal standardized residuals$=0.02$; ch square$=15.7$ ($df=13$), $P=0.26$; Bentler–Bonett normed fit index$=0.95$; Bentler–Bonett non normed fit index$=0.99$; comparative fit index$=0.99$; all parameters are significant.

during the other their blood glucose was lowered for an hour to a target level of 2.5 mmol/l. In both conditions they undertook tests of information processing at four levels:

- Psychometric — WAIS-R Digit Symbol and British Ability Scales (BAS) Information Processing subtests
- Cognitive/experimental — a full Hick-type reaction time procedure
- Psychophysical — inspection time
- Physiological — median and peroneal nerve conduction velocities.

The results appear in Table 3. Each outcome measure was assessed at baseline on the two study days as well as during the study condition. Order of condition (euglycaemia–hypoglycaemia versus hypoglycaemia–euglycaemia) was used as a between-subjects factor and was non-significant for all outcomes. Study condition (euglycaemia versus hypoglycaemia) and time (baseline versus test) were employed as within-subjects factors. The main outcome, and the P values for this are shown in Table 3, was the interaction between condition and time; i.e. this informs whether hypoglycaemia significantly affected the information processing measure. The two psychometric measures of information processing (WAIS-R Digit Symbol and BAS Speed of Information Processing), decision time and movement time from the Hick reaction time procedure, and inspection time all showed significant decrements. Neither peripheral nerve showed slowed conduction velocity.

If indices of brain function are associated with prevailing levels of psychometric intelligence one might expect them to become impaired when mental test scores are affected by prevailing blood glucose levels. In the case of reaction time (decision time and movement time) and inspection time indices this occurs, but not for nerve conduction velocity. The Hick reaction time results are now considered in more detail. Forty trials were completed at each of four levels of stimulus uncertainty (1, 2, 4 and 8 alternative stimuli). Subjects completed 20 trials at each level, progressing from 1 to 8 stimulus lights, and then undertook 20 stimuli at each level in the opposite direction (8 through to 1 stimulus lights). Decision times and movement times were computed at each level. Figure 4 shows the effect of hypoglycaemia on each level of stimulus uncertainty. As expected, there is a straight line association between decision times and the base 2 logarithm of the number of alternative stimulus lights. The line for movement time is much flatter. Hypoglycaemia increases decision and movement times at each level of stimulus uncertainty. The original interest in the Hick procedure for intelligence researchers was the slope measure (Jensen 1987). High ability subjects were reckoned to have flatter slopes in the Hick test because their 'rate of gain of information' was better. Reviews of research on the Hick procedure and

TABLE 3 The effects of hypoglycaemia on different levels of 'speed of information processing'

	Baseline	Euglycaemia	Baseline	Hypoglycaemia	P value
WAIS-R Digit symbol (No. correct)	72.5 (10.8)	77.2 (10.2)	72.5 (10.7)	67.0 (13.1)	0.009
BAS information processing (secs)	69.7 (12.3)	65.6 (13.0)	72.5 (18.4)	83.6 (20.8)	0.003
4-choice decision time (ms)	300.9 (22.1)	298.5 (20.8)	304.4 (30.1)	328.9 (46.5)	0.019
4-choice movement time (ms)	115.1 (26.5)	109.2 (24.4)	117.4 (24.5)	128.9 (34.3)	0.008
Inspection time (ms)	47.6 (19.1)	47.3 (16.9)	50.2 (20.3)	63.4 (24.1)	0.001
Nerve conduction velocity (peroneal) (m/s)	49.3 (3.5)	48.9 (3.8)	46.9 (3.6)	45.9 (5.9)	NS
Nerve conduction velocity (median) (m/s)	55.4 (5.4)	54.0 (4.9)	56.6 (5.4)	55.7 (5.3)	NS

NS, not significant.
BAS, British Ability Scales; WAIS-R, Wechsler Adult Intelligence Scale Revised.

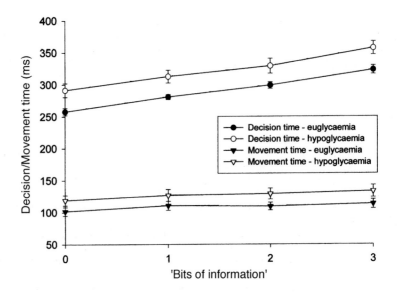

FIG. 4. Effect of moderate hypoglycaemia (2.6 mmol/l blood glucose) versus euglycaemia (5 mmol/l blood glucose) on decision and movement times at different levels of stimulus uncertainty in a Hick-type reaction time task. The 0, 1, 2 and 3 'bits of information' conditions refer to reaction times under 1, 2, 4 and 8 choice conditions, respectively.

psychometric intelligence offer little support for a special place for the Hick slope; mean reaction times and reaction time variabilities correlate better with mental test scores (Jensen 1987). In the present data (Fig. 4), as psychometric ability deteriorates, and reaction times and inspection times are impaired, the Hick slope appears steady, indicating no deterioration in the ability to cope with response uncertainty during moderate hypoglycaemia.

Conclusions

The effort to understand those brain functions that account for variance in psychometric intelligence produced a set of replicated correlations with indices at different levels of explanation. Future work will add to these associations and should devote more effort to explaining these correlations. A part of this explanatory toil must come from linking individual differences at different levels of description. Some contributions toward that end were offered, including statistical modelling, pharmacological intervention, functional brain imaging and event related potential studies.

Acknowledgements

Enrico Simonotto, Alan Marshall, Ian Marshall, Nigel Goddard and Heba Lakhani collaborated in the fMRI study. The research was supported by SHEFC. Mark Strachan, Fiona Ewing, Stuart Ferguson, Matthew Young and Brian Frier collaborated in the hypoglycaemia study. The research was supported by Eli Lilly Ltd and Novo Nordisk Pharmaceuticals Ltd. Ted Nettelbeck and Patrick Rabbitt generously provided data to examine age, inspection time and mental ability.

References

Andreasen N, Flaum M, Swayze V II et al 1993 Intelligence and brain structure in normal individuals. Am J Psychiatry 150:130–134

Carpenter PA, Just MA, Shell P 1990 What one intelligence test measures: a theoretical account of processing in the Raven's Progressive Matrices Test. Psychol Rev 97:404–431

Caryl PG 1994 Early event-related potentials correlate with inspection time and intelligence. Intelligence 18:15–46

Caryl PG, Deary IJ, Jensen AR, Neubauer AC, Vickers D 1999 Information processing approaches to intelligence: progress and prospects. In: Mervielde I, Deary IJ, de Fruyt F, Ostendorf F (eds) Personality psychology in Europe, vol 7. Tilburg University Press, Tilburg, p 181–219

Deary IJ 1995 Auditory inspection time and intelligence: what is the direction of causation? Dev Psychol 31:237–250

Deary IJ 1998 The effects of diabetes on cognitive function. Diabetes Annu 11:97–118

Deary IJ 1999 Intelligence and visual and auditory information processing. In: Ackerman PL, Kyllonen PC, Roberts RD (eds) Learning and individual differences: process, trait, and content determinants. American Psychological Association, Washington, DC, p 111–133

Deary IJ, Caryl PG 1993 Intelligence, EEG, and evoked potentials. In Vernon PA (ed) Biological approaches to the study of human intelligence. Ablex, Norwood, NJ, p 259–315

Deary IJ, Caryl PG 1997 Neuroscience and human intelligence differences. Trends Neurosc 20:365–371

Deary IJ, Stough C 1996 Intelligence and inspection time: achievements, prospects and problems. Am Psychol 51:599–608

Duncan J, Emslie H, Williams P, Johnson R, Freer C 1996 Intelligence and the frontal lobe: the organization of goal-directed behavior. Cognit Psychol 30:257–303

Egan V, Chiswick A, Santosh C, Naidu K, Rimmington JE, Best JJK 1994 Size isn't everything a study of brain volume, intelligence and auditory evoked potentials. Pers Individ Diffe 17:357–367

Embretson SE 1995 The role of working memory capacity and general control processes in intelligence. Intelligence 20:169–189

Hobbes T 1651 Leviathan. Routledge, London

Huarte J de San Juan 1575 Examen de Ingenios. Da Capo Press, Amsterdam Theatrum Orbi Terrarum (Engl transl 1594 The examination of mens wits. [transl R Carew] Richard Watkins London)

Jensen AR 1987 Individual differences in the Hick paradigm. In: Vernon PA (ed) Speed of information processing and intelligence. Ablex, Norwood, NJ, p 101–175

Laird JE, Newell A, Rosenbloom PS 1987 SOAR: an architecture for general intelligence. Arti Intell 33:1–64

McCrimmon RJ, Deary IJ, Huntly BJP, MacLeod KJ, Frier BM 1996 Visual information processing during controlled hypoglycaemia in humans. Brain 119:1277–1287

Morris GL, Alcorn MB 1995 Raven's progressive matrices and inspection time: P200 slope correlates. Pers Individ Differ 18:81–87

Nettelbeck T, Rabbitt PMA 1992 Age, intelligence, and speed. Intelligence 16:189–205

Neubauer AC 1997 The mental speed approach to the assessment of intelligence. In: Kingma J Tomic W (eds) Advances in cognition and educational practice: reflections on the concept o intelligence. JAI Press, Greenwich, CT, p 149–174

Raz N, Torres IT, Spencer WD, Baertschi JC, Millman D, Sarpel G 1993 Neuroanatomical correlates of age-sensitive and age-invariant cognitive abilities: an *in vivo* MRI investigation Intelligence 17:407–422

Salthouse TA 1996 The processing-speed theory of adult age differences in cognition. Psychol Rev 103:403–428

Spearman C 1923 The nature of intelligence and the principles of cognition. Macmillan, London

Sternberg RJ 1977 Component processing in analogical reasoning. Psychol Rev 84:353–378

Stough C, Mangan GL, Bates TC, Pellett OL 1994 Smoking and Raven IQ. Psychopharmacology (Berl) 116:382–384

Stough C, Bates TC, Mangan GL, Pellett OL 1995a Smoking, string length and intelligence Pers Individ Differ 18:75–79

Stough C, Mangan GL, Bates TC, Frank N, Kerkin B, Pellett OL 1995b Effects of nicotine on perceptual speed. Psychopharmacology (Berl) 119:305–310

Vigil Colet A, Piera PJFI, Pueyo AA 1993 Initial stages of information processing and inspection time: electrophysiological correlates. Pers Individ Differ 14:733–738

Wickett JC, Vernon PA, Lee DH 1994 *In vivo* brain size, head perimeter, and intelligence in a sample of healthy adult females. Pers Individ Differ 16:831–838

Willerman L, Schultz R, Rutledge JN, Bigler ED 1991 *In vivo* brain size and intelligence Intelligence 15:223–228

Wolff C 1732 Psychologia Empirica (1968 J. Ecole [ed]) Georg Olms, Hildesheim

Zhang Y, Caryl P, Deary IJ 1989 Evoked potentials, inspection time and intelligence. Pers Individ Differ 10:1079–1094

DISCUSSION

Rutter: I don't quite understand what you mean by your statement about brain size 'causing' intelligence. It seems to me that you are pitting two alternatives against each other, when a third is much more likely. Let's take a different structure–function relationship, and look at muscle bulk and strength, where 'strength' is in some way the equivalent to *g*. Does muscle bulk cause strength, or does strength cause muscle bulk? Of course, if you exercise, both go up. In a sense they are both dependent variables, and both are reflecting the same function, so talking about one 'causing' the other is misleading. In the same sort of way it ignores bi-directional relationships. Thus, with respect to testosterone and dominance, it is now clear from experimental findings that testosterone has effects on dominance. But it is also evident that changes in dominance influence testosterone levels. This has been shown in humans by studies of chess and tennis players (Mazur et al 1992, Mazur & Lamb 1980), and it has been evident in animal experiments (Rose et al 1971). Surely, we are not thinking about it in the right way if we are assuming one is an independent variable and one is a dependent variable. The argument that, for example, genetic factors drive both intelligence and brain size is fine, but so do experiential factors. The Romanian adoptees study (Rutter et al 1998) provides an example of that kind. Improved rearing circumstances (both nutritional and experiential) were followed by marked gains in both head size and IQ. It is not that the increased head size caused the rise in IQ — rather, they were both being driven by the improved environmental conditions.

Deary: That is a fair comment. Not a lot should hang on the direction with respect to brain size. It's more the reversal of the old saw that correlation doesn't imply causation: correlations have causes. There must be something or somethings about the differences in brain sizes that relate to ability difference and my guess is that those are biological level constructs. On the other hand, the directionality of causation is more moot with respect to reaction time and inspection time research, where one must investigate the tenable possibilities that their associations with mental test scores could be caused by 'higher' and/or 'lower' order factors. Neubauer (1997) provides a thorough discussion of this issue and I addressed this with respect to auditory processing (Deary 1995).

Suddendorf: Many of the correlates discussed appear not to have a priori theoretical relevance. For example, the *variance* in inspection time has been found to have the strongest correlation with intelligence. This has nothing to do with speed of processing. This correlation reminds me of research on another type of elemental cognitive paradigm: coincidence timing. These tasks involve a target stimulus moving across a screen and participants are asked to hit a button when the stimulus crosses a certain area. There is no information processing speed involved in this kind of task; what you need is reliability. Glen Smith and others

(Smith & Stanley 1983, Smith & McPhee 1987, Wright et al 2000) have found correlations with intelligence for both accuracy and variance of performance. These correlations are of comparable magnitude to the associations discussed here. What do you think of these findings?

Deary: A nice general point which you made at the beginning of your comment was about the a priori nature of these things. Among other things, I'm interested in how people began to study some of these parameters, because they are a ragbag. They don't look like a co-ordinated psychological research programme. They are often picked up by chance and then developed. With the coincidence timing and the inspection time, it is easy to be trapped into choosing some sort of verbal epithet just to describe what the task does, and then behaving as if one understands the brain processes giving rise to task performance. This latter part really is the work of decades of research, i.e. unpacking the mechanism of the correlation. It is always tempting to force the pace a bit faster, and make plausible-sounding guesses at mechanisms, but I think the work of people like Rabbitt & Maylor (1991) and Raz et al (1987) have shown that these measures that are speeded at the phenotypic level can easily be accounted for by things which have got nothing to do with speed at levels under that — it could be reliability, it could be fidelity or some other parameter. And if you instantiate it in, say, a neural network understanding, there could be many different parameters of a neural network that could offer phenotypic speed. I'm just asking for recognition of the well-established correlations, but then caution in terms of what they might represent with regard to an *understanding* of their association. There are many other tasks which I didn't mention, but I tried to pick the ones with the largest empirical base. What gets one rather upset about in this area, is that you'll get somebody who publishes a single study relating some cognitive variable to a psychometric test score, and say that this is the basis of psychometric intelligence. Now that is rather nauseating, because it never gets replicated and people fly off on a straw in the wind.

Detterman: I was interested in the functional magnetic resonance imaging (fMRI) study. Could you tell us what areas light up and why?

Deary: Particularly during the hard task, we are finding from looking at both the group level and at the individual level, that there is widespread activation and deactivation. It is premature to say more. I did insist that this was a pilot study. The next thing we plan to do is, having got it working, to bring people of different levels of ability and different ages in to see whether there are different activation/deactivation patterns.

Detterman: Were the areas reliable?

Deary: I think we have more analyses to do.

Karmiloff-Smith: I would like to make a comment which goes back to this morning, and our discussion of abnormal phenotypes. It seems to me that in the debate so far there has been a great deal of focus on where correlations do occur, and not enough exploration of where they don't. For argument's sake, let's imagine that there's a correlation between IQ and synaptic density but not IQ and neuronal density. Shouldn't one be exploring why some correlations do not occur? With respect to the particular issue of inspection time, with Mike Anderson of the University of Western Australia, I have been looking at this very task with different groups of abnormal patients. We have matched different syndromes on IQ measures and found very great differences in the inspection time measures that we take, suggesting that in the abnormal case IQ and inspection time are not correlated as they are in the normal case (Anderson 1992).

Deary: Your point about *not* finding correlations is very important. In your other point, it depends what sort of psychometric measure is used and what abnormality we are dealing with. A lot of the original work on inspection time was done in what was called 'mental retardation', and the correlations there were even stronger. This is what led some people to wonder about whether the correlation existed in the normal distribution, because any study that included people with handicaps inflated the correlation. Non-correlation is extremely important because, as I attempted to show with the ageing study, if you don't look for a targeted non-correlation, you can actually be trapped into thinking a specific hypothesis holds. In one study we were trying to see whether inspection time relates to psychometric ability because of some quirk of inspection time, not processing speed, but some strategy you can use in the task (Deary et al 1997). I took inspection time together with Phillips' visual change detection task and another task. They all seemed to be testing the same limitation, but phenotypically they all looked like very different tasks. I extracted a latent trait from the three of them, and saw whether that was the only component that related to psychometric ability. It was. I went a stage further to answer your question and included contrast sensitivity, which is a hard visual task that has all sorts of limitations shared by inspection time, except the time pressure. This neither related to the other visual tasks, nor to the psychometric test. I think you're right: the strength of that study was not in the three tasks that did relate to psychometric intelligence, but it was in the one that didn't. Going back to the abnormality, I would be very excited to hear more on that, because instances of non-correlation can be informative as well.

Karmiloff-Smith: People with autism have shorter inspection times than controls matched on IQ. People with Williams syndrome take significantly longer. Those with Down's syndrome fall between the two. This left me with questions about what the task was measuring.

Rutter: Annette Karmiloff-Smith, do you think that your findings have implications for the importance of *g*? That is, there seems to be a difference in the cognitive pattern seen in the general population (where intercorrelations among different cognitive skills are substantial) and the pattern found in unusual groups (in which special cognitive skills and deficits that are relatively independent of overall IQ are found). Does this mean that individuals with autism or Williams syndrome need to be thought of in terms of a different set of explanations to those that apply in the general population or do the cognitive patterns in such individuals have implications for cognitive functioning within the normal range?

Karmiloff-Smith: I think they have implications for the normal range. Where you find very uneven profiles of the kind that we have been looking at, it questions whether *g* is actually permeating all these different types of ability. The question challenges what is being measured when one finds the correlations. The abnormal phenotype questions some of the conclusions formed about the normal population. The atypical case cannot be treated as completely separate (Paterson et al 1999).

Houle: This gets back to the naïve observer's puzzlement over the unitariness of *g*. On the one hand you're saying that *g* is not unitary, and then on the other you're all puzzled that you can't find any one thing that seems to underlie it. This sort of difference from study to study or measure to measure of speed is only puzzling if you assume that *g* is unitary, and that therefore you should be able to go and find further unitary things that underlie it. If I, as a biologist, ask why a particular organism has low fitness — why does it fail? — I don't expect there to be one answer.

Deary: I took the focus off *g* to start with. The principal association between inspection time and mental ability is not with *g* (Crawford et al 1998).

Miller: Evolutionary psychologists often talk about the energetic costs of large brains. This was a theme that arose in the papers by both Arthur Jensen and Ian Deary concerning glucose. Arthur Jensen mentioned that the marginal glucose costs of doing a particular task are lower for high IQ people than for low IQ people. Ian Deary, you showed that you could reduce cognitive functioning by experimentally inducing hypoglycaemia. We also have this correlation of brain size and IQ. Is there any evidence that the larger brains of people with higher IQ are running with a lower net glucose cost than the smaller brains of people with lower IQ?

Deary: First of all, I wouldn't put the hypoglycaemia work together with the positron emission tomography (PET) work based on the ^{18}F-labelled deoxyglucose. The work looking at PET and mental ability has been done in two groups. Chase et al (1984) have done it in groups with dementia and cognitive ageing, and have shown that psychometric performance goes along with higher metabolic rates, and that looks like a phenomenon of brain deterioration. The second type of study includes work done by people like Haier (1993) on students, who are individuals high in ability. But some of these studies were done on fewer than 10 individuals, which is why I haven't dwelt on them: there just simply isn't enough work to put the results on the statute book. To look at correlations in groups of about $n=7$ is silly. I know it costs thousands of dollars to do each of these scans, but that doesn't make it work that's more than a straw in the wind.

Then to imply from the lower glucose metabolic rate of the people doing better on psychometric tests that there's a kind of phenomenon called 'neural efficiency', seems just to add salt to the wound. Let's wait until the empirical evidence is in before we start talking about running brains at different levels.

Brody: We are perhaps jumping ahead of the data in assuming that there isn't a limited general core ability that is involved in intelligence. If we were to do a large-scale factor analysis over a wide range of cognitive tasks that on the surface seem to have very different processing domains, we might find that there are a limited number of general cognitive abilities that might relate to brain processes. We might then find some kind of congruence. In other words, if g is general at the psychometric level, the proper approach to test the hypothesis of whether or not g is general at the cognitive processing level is to use the same strategy that defines the existence of g. You may do that, and it may turn out to be that there are no core abilities that cross different kinds of information processing tasks that are related to g. Then again, Ian Deary has some data which at least in a rather preliminary way suggest that there are some core abilities, that have a fairly substantial relationship with at least some ways of defining g.

Deary: That is one hypothesis from that kind of result. But the other hypothesis is a general one that takes you in the opposite direction. When E. L. Thorndike and colleagues (1909) and Spearman (1904) were arguing in 1909 about what it meant to discover that there was a correlation between sensory discrimination and psychometric abilities, such as could be measured at that time, Spearman went for the hypothesis (which he later changed himself) that sensory discrimination was the psychological basis of mental ability. This is what Galton (1883) had originally thought: he had found that piano tuners were all men, he 'knew' that men were cleverer than women, and therefore he concluded that sensory discrimination was the basis of intelligence. On the other hand, Thorndike said that this was all caused by some vague, general kind of motivational factor, and did not have to do with sensory discrimination being a core element of human mental ability. You have got to entertain these two hypotheses and recognize that the second one (to do with general factors like motivation and strategies) is much harder to test. It is not always one that I have sympathy with, but as long as it is on the table you have to address it. Both ideas are still open, 90 years after Thorndike and Spearman.

Brody: I agree they're open. If we had psychometric investigations of elementary processing tasks we would be in a much better position to answer that. As far as I can see, the problem is not theoretical or conceptual, but practical. It takes time to get elementary processing measures and if you really wanted to have a large battery, combined with a large battery of psychometric tests to try to see whether there are some latent traits that cut across these domains, it would be a very difficult study for practical reasons.

References

Anderson M 1992 Intelligence and development: a cognitive theory. Blackwell, Oxford

Chase TN, Fedio P, Foster NL, Brooks R, Di Chiro G, Mansi L 1984 Wechsler Adult Intelligence Scale performance: cortical localisation by fluorodeoxyglucose F 18-positron emission tomography. Arch Neurol 41:1244–1247

Crawford JR, Deary IJ, Allan KM, Gustafsson J-E 1998 Evaluating competing models of the relationship between inspection time and psychometric intelligence. Intelligence 26:27–42

Deary IJ 1995 Auditory inspection time and intelligence: what is the direction of causation? Dev Psychol 31:237–250

Deary IJ, McCrimmon RJ, Bradshaw J 1997 Visual information processing and intelligence. Intelligence 24:461–479

Galton F 1883 Inquiries into human faculty. Dent, London

Haier R 1993 Cerebral glucose metabolism and intelligence. In: Vernon PA (ed) Biological approaches to the study of human intelligence. Ablex, Norwood, NJ, p 317–332

Mazur A, Lamb TA 1980 Testosterone, status, and mood in human males. Horm Behav 14:236–246

Mazur A, Booth A, Dabbs JM 1992 Testosterone and chess competition. Soc Psychol Q 55:70–77

Neubauer AC 1997 The mental speed approach to the assessment of intelligence. In: Kingma J, Tomic W (eds) Advances in cognition and education: reflections on the concept of intelligence. JAI Press, Greenwich, CT, p 149–174

Patterson SJ, Brown JH, Gsödl MK, Johnson MH, Karmiloff-Smith A 1999 Cognitive modularity and genetic disorders. Science 286:2355–2358

Rabbitt PMA, Maylor EA 1991 Investigating models of human performance. Brit J Psychol 82:259–290

Raz N, Willerman L, Yama M 1987 On sense and senses: intelligence and auditory information processing. Pers Individ Differ 8:201–210

Rose RM, Holaday JW, Bernstein IS 1971 Plasma testosterone, dominance risk and aggressive behaviour in male rhesus monkeys. Nature 231:366–368

Rutter M, the English & Romanian Adoptees (ERA) Study Team 1998 Developmental catch-up, and deficit, following adoption after severe global early privation. J Child Psychol Psychiatry 39:465–476

Smith GE, McPhee KA 1987 Performance on a coincidence timing task correlates with intelligence. Intelligence 11:161–167

Smith GA, Stanley G 1983 Clocking g: relating intelligence and measures of timed performance. Intelligence 7:353–368

Spearman C 1904 'General intelligence' objectively determined and measured. Am J Psychol 15:201–293

Thorndike EL, Lay W, Dean PR 1909 The relation of accuracy in sensory discrimination to intelligence. Am J Psychol 20:364–369

Wright MJ, Smith GA, Geffen GM, Geffen CB, Martin NG 2000 Genetic influence on the variance in coincidence timing and its covariance with IQ: a twin study. Intelligence, in press

The *g* factor in non-human animals

Britt Anderson

Neurology (127), Birmingham VA Medical Center, 700 S. 19th Street, Birmingham, AL 35233, USA

Abstract. Animals possess the attributes we label as 'intelligent' in humans. 'Insight' and 'reasoning' have been demonstrated in chimpanzees, monkeys, racoons, rats, mice, ravens and pigeons. In the rat, the animal species best characterized psychologically and neuroanatomically, reasoning ability correlates with other cognitive capacities and brain size. Other learning task paradigms tested on mice and rats have confirmed consistent individual differences, indicated a neuroanatomical network for learning, and shown the presence of genetic influences for cognitive ability. Animals offer an opportunity to test ideas about intelligence that cannot be performed on humans. Methylazoxymethanol (MAM) administered prenatally can arrest cortical cell division and produce a 'mentally retarded' microcephalic rat. This intellectual deficiency can be ameliorated by postnatal induction of dendritic arborization and synapse formation with naltrexone, suggesting the relevance of neuronal and synapse number for behavioural variation in rat *g*. Inbred mice lines differ in brain size and behaviour, permitting, through the use of recombinant inbred strains, the determination of genetic loci with quantitative effects on structure and function. Lastly, genetic contributions to *g* can be directly tested by modifying gene expression and determining the anatomical, physiological, and behavioural benefits.

2000 The nature of intelligence. Wiley, Chichester (Novartis Foundation Symposium 233) p 79–95

The concept of a *g* factor originated from the positive intercorrelations observed between tests of mental abilities in humans. *g* relates to intelligence through the imputation of a general factor which generally influences cognitive ability; this factor may be under genetic control and may be neural rather than psychological (Anderson 1995, Jensen 1998). Given the relevance of intellectual ability for socioeconomic and educational performance, an understanding of the basis of human *g* is important.

Animals can contribute to this research in the same ways that they contribute to scientific research in general, by providing an opportunity for invasive manipulative research that would be technically or ethically problematic with humans. However, animals can only be useful for research on human *g* or intelligence if animals are 'intelligent' in some analogous way to humans.

After discussing the definition of intelligence, data will be reviewed showing that animals, especially mammals and birds, meet this definition. Relevant for the analogy to humans, and implying an animal *g*, rats and mice will be shown to have consistent individual differences that span a variety of learning and behavioural tasks. Further data from rats demonstrate a distributed neural systems involved in rat learning generally and also that individual differences in ability relate to variability in brain size, as has been shown for humans. Having made the suggestion that animals are 'intelligent' to a degree that makes them suitable experimental surrogates, examples of their application to intelligence research will be shown by reviewing experiments that manipulate brain and genetic variables and assess behavioural outcomes.

What is animal intelligence?

'First, we all — as speakers of English, rather than as psychologists — know what "intelligence" means ...' writes Macphail (1987). Macphail is correct. In their classic work, Sternberg et al (1981) showed that people generally agree on what marks the intelligent person. These authors assessed the ratings of lay people and professionals for how typical specific characteristics were for an intelligent person. Two main categories of responses were observed: verbal and problem solving (reasons logically and well, applies knowledge to the problem at hand). Important is that the typical attributions of intelligence were consistent across professionals and lay persons. We do know what intelligence means and it encompasses reasoning. However, to apply this cultural description to non-human animals we must operationalize the definition. Reasoning[1] is the ability to combine disparate experiences into a novel solution for a novel problem. Animals possess this skill.

Animal reasoning and insight

The origin of the study of animal reasoning is found in Wolfgang Köhler's *The mentality of apes* (Köhler 1925). Chimpanzees were observed to solve novel problems after exposure to the individual elements necessary for a solution. For example, exposure to boxes, and learning that one could pile them and stand on them, was later used to reach a suspended banana though the chimpanzee had never been taught to pile boxes as a way to reach food. An early recognition of individual

---

[1] In animal behaviour the terms reasoning and insight are synonymous and refer to a specific category of behavioural performance.

ifferences in animal reasoning can also be found in this work[2]. From this eginning, Köhler's Einsicht has been shown for many species (Maier & chneirla 1935).

Epstein et al (1984) demonstrated a perfect parody of the chimpanzee in the igeon. Trained to peck a banana simulacrum and separately trained to push a ox, the pigeons could, when confronted with an out-of-reach banana, push an vailable box under the banana, stand on it, and peck for reward. The pigeons ad never been trained to stand on the box or push it in the presence of the anana. Pigeons trained on only one or the other component of the task never olved it. Reasoning in animals is demonstrated when they are shown to be able o combine non-contiguously learned behaviours into a solution for a novel roblem.

N. R. F. Maier was a student of Köhler's who continued Köhler's work with the heaper and smaller white rat[3]. Maier used a variety of tasks of which the one most ommonly still employed is the 'Three Table Problem.' A variation of this problem as been the basis of my own work on animal reasoning.

I adapted Maier's reasoning task to the eight-arm radial maze (Olton & amuelson 1976, see Fig. 1). Rats are permitted to explore the maze for several ninutes in the absence of food. Next, they are fed in one of the arms but are not llowed access to the rest of the maze. Subsequently, for the test trial, the animal is laced in a distant start arm after the target arm has been rebaited. To 'reason' the at must unite his knowledge of the location of the goal arm with his separately earned knowledge of the relative location of his start position to chart a direct nd accurate course to food. Rats that are given only one or the other exposure o not solve the problem accurately (see Fig. 2), although with trial and error hey do reach the goal (Anderson 1992). Another component of insight and easoning problems is the sudden nature of the solution ('Aha!'). It is not radually moulded but comes about abruptly and then is fixed. Figure 3 shows he learning curve of one rat run on the eight-arm version of the reasoning task nd visually depicts this transition.

Maier (1932) examined the cortical contributions to reasoning performance but ailed to find specific important cortical regions. His three-table version of the roblem is still in modern use though and Poucet (1990) and colleagues have hown that the rat medial frontal cortex (the approximate analogue of human lorsal-lateral frontal cortex; Kolb & Tees 1990) is essential for the combining of

---

'...the chimpanzee has a wide range of individual variation...Rana's stupidity is onspicuous...' (Köhler 1925).

'My defense is also a defense of the white rats. They at least, have made a worthy contribution to ur science and should be given a just hearing.' (Maier 1935).

A.

B.

C.

D.

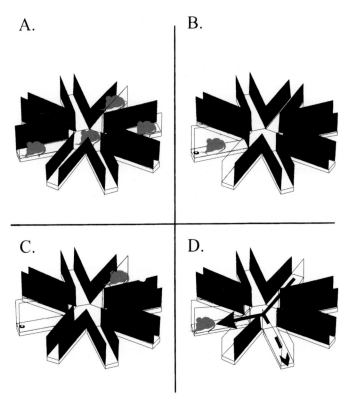

FIG. 1. The four stages of a rat reasoning task are shown. First (A), the rat is given an exploratory experience in which it has the run of the maze in the absence of any food reinforcement. Second (B), the rat is fed in one of the arms and is prevented from re-entering the rest of the maze. In the test component the rat is removed to a separate start arm and the target arm rebaited (C). The rat can then combine his two prior experiences to chart a direct accurate course to the reward (solid line in D) or may enter another arm, which is scored as an error (dashed line in D).

the basic experiences to achieve the novel solution, but is not critical for spatial learning *per se*. It would obviously not be possible in humans to lesion specific pre-frontal fields and assess their effect on IQ. While frontal lesions in humans do not affect crystallized intelligence, they do affect reasoning and problem solving (Duncan et al 1995).

Reasoning is a behavioural capability shared by more than pigeons, rats and chimpanzees. Foxes, dogs, monkeys, racoons and ravens have also been demonstrated to 'reason' (Maier & Schneirla 1935). Other animal classes have not been extensively studied. For our purposes, we are not so much interested in the comparative ability of which animal species are smarter, but whether any

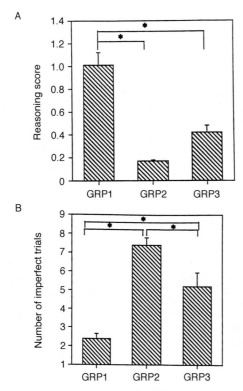

FIG. 2. The performance of rats given both of the preparatory experiences (Group 1) is compared to rats only allowed the prefeeding experience (Group 2) or exploratory experience (Group 3). (A) shows the total time to acquire the reward over 8 days summed as reciprocals. In (B), the comparison is for the number of trials on which the animals committed at least one error. All results are plotted as the mean + 1 standard error of the mean. Asterisks designate groups differing at the $P < 0.05$ level by Scheffé's *post hoc* test.

species possess the skills that permit them to be experimental models for human intelligence[4].

Generalized learning

As with so much of psychology, the seed of a modern idea seems to have germinated with Donald Hebb. In his studies of models of animal intelligence,

---

[4] 'So often it is implied that reasoning ability resides only in human beings. Since human beings make this claim, we may question its objectivity. I do not believe psychological terms should be restricted to a certain species. Rather a psychological term should designate a process and different processes should be designated by different terms.' (Maier 1937).

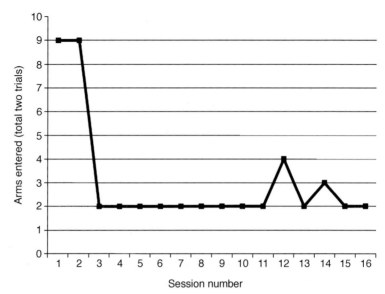

FIG. 3.   The performance of one rat is shown across a total of 16 trials on a reasoning task (Anderson 1992). Each session was conducted on a separate day and two trials for each start arm and goal arm configuration were performed each session. Each arm was the goal twice, and no start arm–goal arm combination was repeated over the 16 sessions. The number of arms entered per session is shown. Perfect performance would be two, one correct entry each trial. The pattern shows that after two trial and error sessions, the rat suddenly solves the problem with near perfect performance over the remaining sessions. This sudden conversion from random performance to correct performance is characteristic of 'reasoning' tasks and differs from a typical stimulus–response learning curve.

Hebb generated a technique for measuring generalized learning ability (Hebb & Williams 1946). In the Hebb–Williams maze task an animal is confronted with a common apparatus and motivation and is then given numerous variations of detour problems. By varying the problem frequently the animal must learn each new solution, but must also give up on previous, now incorrect, solutions. The presence of a generalized learning ability and consistent performance across problems of the Hebb–Williams maze has been shown for disparate species, including the cow (Kilgour 1981).

A more modern slant on this approach has been to argue that for a generalized learning system to be truly 'general' it should transfer across motivations, apparatus and sensory capacities. Using this definition Thompson et al (1990) standardized a series of 'problems' for the rat that involved different motivations (hunger versus thirst), apparatuses and sensory capacities (kinaesthetic versus visual) to see if specific brain areas were critical for learning. When rats developed a 'generalized' learning impairment after a brain lesion the deficit in performance could not be ascribed to a single motivation or apparatus factor. The authors found that a small number of brain structures, out of 50 tested, were components of a generalized learning system. These structures included: caudato–putamen, globus pallidus, ventrolateral thalamus, substantia nigra, ventrolateral tegmental area, superior colliculus, median raphe and pontine reticular formation. The importance of their work for models of human intelligence is that rats also possess a generalized learning system dependent on a restricted set of brain structures and, as will be shown below, this results in an individual consistency of performance.

Animal *g*

Animal behaviours meet the commonly accepted characteristics of human 'intelligence'. Do they possess other characteristics of human intelligence? A consistent finding in human intelligence research has been the *g* factor, a general factor observable in the correlation matrices of multiple cognitive tests (Jensen 1998). If intelligent animal behaviour relies on brain operations similar to humans, we would predict the presence of consistent individual differences.

Crinella did not find individual consistency in sham-operated white rats (a rather dull and homogeneous strain—despite Maier's defence) from their study (Thompson et al 1990). However, when all 424 rats were analysed together, including the 348 animals with lesions to one of 50 different brain sites, the correlations across the six categories of tasks were positive, frequently significant, and a general factor contributing to performance across all tasks was found.

In a group of unlesioned Long–Evans hooded rats, I (Anderson 1992) showed a consistent relationship between reasoning performance and attention to novelty (time measure: $r=0.58$ [$df=15$, $P=0.02$], error measure: $r=-0.485$ [$df=15$, $P=0.06$][5]). Attention to novelty for the rat refers to the tendency to explore an unfamiliar object placed within an open field. Attention to novelty in human infants, measured with looking time, has been shown to correlate to later life IQ (Fagan & Montie 1988). The intercorrelations for another 22 Long–Evans rats (some of which had been treated with the neurotoxin methylazoxymethanol [MAM]) across performance on a reasoning task, attention for novelty task, and response flexibility task (Anderson 1991) were all positive and ranged from 0.13 to 0.51 (Anderson 1994), even though all three tasks used different apparatus, were tested at different times, and differed in motivation. The linear regression on brain

---

[5] The time measure was plotted as a reciprocal so that a higher number was faster and to prevent skewing of the data by a single very slow performance. Thus, both a quicker performance and fewer errors correlated to more time exploring a novel object.

weight for the first factor extracted from this correlation matrix by a principal components analysis was significant (F $(1/18) = 5.3$, $P = 0.03$). More recently, Locurto & Scanlon (1998) looked at individual differences in unleisoned mice tested on a variety of spatial and non-spatial tasks and found consistent positive correlations demonstrating consistent inter-individual variation in problem-solving performance.

Benefits of animals for intelligence research

The reviewed data demonstrate that animals show consistent inter-individual variability and engage in behaviours that, in people, would be characterized as intelligent. In one study, this general factor correlated to brain weight, as has been repeatedly reported for IQ and brain size in humans (Flashman et al 1997). How can we use these facts to advance our understanding of human intelligence?

What are the brain structures or processes where variability accounts for variation in IQ? If genetic contributions to inter-individual variation in IQ are in the order of 50% (Devlin et al 1997), which genes are important and what do they control? Despite our expanding ability to non-invasively analyse the human brain we cannot count neurons or measure individual myelin sheath thickness. To do this requires studies of clinical populations coming to brain biopsy or autopsy. Work on these populations is slow, expensive, and subject to criticisms of the patient populations or variability due to uncontrollable post-mortem delay effects (Witelson & McCulloch 1991). Animals do not have these difficulties. Further, unlike correlative inferential human studies, animal studies can attempt to be causal by actually manipulating the variables of interest.

Is neuron number important for intelligence? Neuron number varies widely across human subjects (Pakkenberg & Gundersen 1997), and is a large determinant of brain size (Haug 1987), which correlates with IQ (Flashman et al 1997). No study of total neuron number and IQ has been done in humans and we cannot manipulate neuron number in humans, but we can in animals. MAM is a toxin that, if given to a pregnant rat, can induce a cortical hypoplasia characterized by fewer cortical neurons, but not gross morphological abnormalities (Haddad et al 1969). MAM-exposed rats show behavioural abnormalities (Rabe & Haddad 1972). In one study of low dose MAM, I (Anderson 1994) demonstrated no effect on early life reflexive development (see Fig. 4), but did show slower performance on a reasoning task, decreased attention to novelty, poor habituation, and more errors on the response flexibility task (see Fig. 5). This suggests that a decrease in neuron number below the normal range effects rat reasoning and implies a relationship between neuron number and intelligence for humans. The experimental ability to induce a range of neuron number offers the prospect of precisely defining a relationship for neuron number and cognitive ability in the rat.

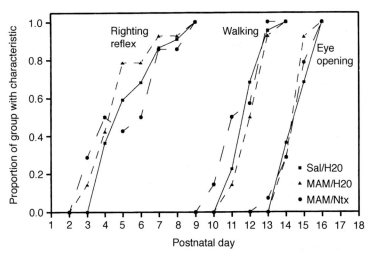

FIG. 4. The reflex acquisition of rats exposed to saline or MAM (14 mg/kg) prenatally with saline or naltrexone (50 mg/kg) given postnatally is shown. All groups acquired basic motoric skills at the same rate. Early-life motor performance, such as measured with the Bayley scales, is a poor predictor of late-life IQ in humans.

Is dendritic arborization and synapse number important for variability in cognitive ability (Anderson & Donaldson 1995)? Zagon has reported that postnatal administration of naltrexone, an opiate receptor antagonist, augments rat brain size and increases cortical neuron dendritic arborization (Hauser et al 1989, Zagon & McLaughlin 1984). In MAM-treated rats, I showed that postnatal treatment with naltrexone could ameliorate the behavioural deficit for attention to novelty, habituation performance and response flexibility (see Fig. 5) with intermediate effects on time to perform a reasoning task.

Animals offer the opportunity to alter brain structure and directly examine the behavioural effects. As we have defined tasks appropriate for 'animal intelligence', we can begin to define brain–behaviour relationships by testing specific hypotheses.

Genetic influences are an area of significant interest in the human intelligence literature. Examinations for quantitative trait loci in humans are slow due to the poorer characterization of the human genome and the lack of genetically homogeneous populations reared in common environmental conditions. Animals bypass many of these limitations.

In a preliminary study, I (B. Anderson, unpublished data) examined a small number of C57BL and DBA inbred mice and confirmed that mice can perform the reasoning task developed for rats. In addition, these inbred mice lines differ in their attention to novelty (time in centre square over two unique exposures: C57 mean = 20.02 seconds [SD = 12.88] versus DBA mean = 2.89 seconds

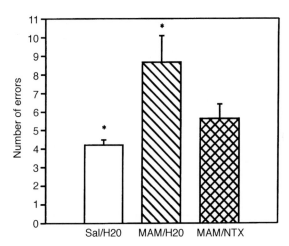

FIG. 5. The number of errors on an inclined plane response flexibility problem (Thompson e al 1990) is shown for the same groups of animals as seen in Fig. 4. Saline-treated controls mad the fewest errors. Animals exposed to the neurotoxin MAM were slower to abandon a previousl learned solution to try new routes to food. However, animals treated postnatally with naltrexone, an opiate receptor antagonist reported to induce dendritic arborization and spine formation, showed performance similar to controls. Decreases in neuron number, such as seer with MAM exposure prenatally, have adverse effects on tests of rat intelligence. Treatments tha induce dendritic arborization and synapse formation can ameliorate these deficits. The ability to modify brain structure permits direct testing of the causal role of variation in brain structure and behavioural performance.

[SD$=4.87$], $t=2.78$, $df=5$, $P=0.04$) and exploratory ability (squares entered over four days 230.4 [15.63] vs. 176.8 [37.5], $P=0.03$) with the bigger brained C57 (391 mg) being more active than the DBA (346 mg, $P=0.003$) mice.

This suggests that these two inbred mice strains differ in their rodent cognitive behaviour and that this may relate to their neurological variability. The C57 and DBA are the origin lines for the BXD recombinant inbred lines. The BXD line have been genotyped so that running the full set of BXD strains on the relevant behavioural tasks and measuring brain structure would permit analyses of genetic traits with quantitative effects on behaviour and structure (Belknap et al 1992) Computer programs for quantitative trait loci analysis are readily available Knowing the genetic loci linked to the brain and behavioural variability would indicate candidate genetic loci that might affect human brain structure and intelligence.

The best demonstration of the power of animal research for demonstrating the genetic effects on intelligence was published by Tang et al (1999). They produced a transgenic mouse that over-expressed the gene for NR2B, a component of the NMDA glutamate receptor. These mice were shown, by the study of cells in ulture, to have enhanced long term potentiation and behaviourally were superior n a novelty task, in learning a spatial learning task, and in the active relearning of a ontextual fear task. By varying the expression of a single gene, Tang et al (1999) roduced a 'smarter' mouse.

Conclusions

Animals possess the behavioural skills that in humans we label as 'intelligent'. These skills are not unique to one species, but are present in many mammals and irds, and could be present in other classes. Outbred members of these species how a consistent individual performance across cognitive tasks, as do humans, mplying an animal *g* factor. Animals bring to intelligence research the same dvantages they have for scientific research generally: they permit us to move eyond correlative research to testing specific neural and genetic hypotheses. A nild decrease in neuron number in the rat affects cognitive performance and this an be ameliorated by postnatal treatment with a drug to increase dendritic rborization. Inbred mice lines differ in brain structure and on mice 'intelligence' ests. Alterations of specific genes in mice can make a 'smarter' mouse. This esearch returns to human relevance by suggesting which investigations should e the highest priority for the labour intensive and expensive human correlative tudies.

References

Anderson B 1991 Open-field and response-flexibility measures in the rat. Psychobiology 19:355–358

Anderson B 1992 Rat reasoning: a reliability and validity study. Psychobiology 20:238–242

Anderson B 1994 Naltrexone (NTX) ameliorates the behavioral consequences of methylazoxy-methanol (MAM)-induced microcephaly. Neurology 44:A412

Anderson B 1995 G explained. Med Hypotheses 45:602–604

Anderson B, Donaldson S 1995 The backpropagation algorithm: implications for the biological bases of individual differences in intelligence. Intelligence 21:327–345

Belknap JK, Phillips TJ, O'Toole LA 1992 Quantitative trait loci associated with brain weight in the BXD/Ty recombinant inbred mouse strains. Brain Res Bull 29:337–344

Devlin B, Daniels M, Reeder K 1997 The heritability of IQ. Nature 388:468–471

Duncan J, Burgess P, Emslie H 1995 Fluid intelligence after frontal lobe lesions. Neuropsychologia 33:261–268

Epstein R, Kirshnit CE, Lanza RP, Rubin LC 1984 'Insight' in the pigeon: antecedents and determinants of an intelligent performance. Nature 308:61–62

Fagan JF, Montie JE 1988 Behavioral assessment of cognitive well-being in the infant. In: Kavanagh J (ed) Understanding mental retardation: research accomplishments and new frontiers. Paul H Brooks, Baltimore, MD, p 207–221

Flashman LA, Andreasen NC, Flaum M, Swayze VW II 1997 Intelligence and regional brain volumes in normal controls. Intelligence 25:149–160

Haddad RK, Rabe A, Laqueur GL, Spatz M, Valsamis MP 1969 Intellectual deficit associate with transplacentally induced microcephaly in the rat. Science 163:88–90

Haug H 1987 Brain sizes, surfaces, and neuronal sizes of the cortex cerebri: a stereologic investigation of man and his variability and a comparison with some mammals (primate whales, marsupials, insectivores, and one elephant). Am J Anat 180:126–142

Hauser KF, McLaughlin PJ, Zagon IS 1989 Endogenous opioid systems and the regulation dendritic growth and spine formation. J Comp Neurol 281:13–22

Hebb DO, Williams K 1946 A method of rating animal intelligence. J Gen Psychol 34:59–65

Jensen AR 1998 The g factor: the science of mental ability. Praeger, Westport

Kilgour R 1981 Use of the Hebb–Williams closed-field test to study learning ability of Jerse cows. Anim Behav 29:850–860

Köhler W 1925 The mentality of apes. Routledge Kegan Paul, London

Kolb B, Tees RC 1990 The cerebral cortex of the rat. MIT Press, Cambridge, MA

Locurto C, Scanlon C 1998 Individual differences and a spatial learning factor in two strains mice (Mus musculus). J Comp Psychol 112:344–352

Macphail EM 1987 The comparative psychology of intelligence. Behav Brain Sci 10:645–656

Maier NRF 1932 The effect of cerebral destruction on reasoning and learning in rats. J Com Neurol 54:45–75

Maier NRF 1935 In defense of reasoning in rats: a reply. J Comp Psychol 19:197–206

Maier NRF 1937 Reasoning in rats and human beings. Psychol Rev 44:365–377

Maier NRF, Schneirla TC 1935 Principles of animal psychology. McGraw-Hill, New York

Olton DS, Samuelson RJ 1976 Remembrance of places passed: spatial memory in rats. J Ex Psychol Anim Behav Process 2:97–116

Pakkenberg B, Gundersen HJG 1997 Neocortical neuron number in humans: effect of sex ar age. J Comp Neurol 384:312–320

Poucet B 1990 A further characterization of the spatial problem-solving deficit induced b lesions of the medial frontal cortex in the rat. Behav Brain Res 41:229–237

Rabe A, Haddad RK 1972 Methylazoxymethanol-induced microencephaly in rats: behavior studies. Fed Proc 31:1536–1539

Sternberg RJ, Conway BE, Ketron JL, Bernstein M 1981 People's conception of intelligence. Pers Soc Psychol 41:37–55

Tang Y-P, Shimizu E, Dube GR et al 1999 Genetic enhancement of learning and memory mice. Nature 401:63–69

Thompson R, Crinella FM, Yu J 1990 Brain mechanisms in problem solving and intelligence: lesion survey of the rat brain. Plenum Press, New York

Witelson SF, McCulloch PB 1991 Premortem and postmortem measurement to study structu with function: a human brain collection. Schizophr Bull 17:583–591

Zagon IS, McLaughlin PJ 1984 Naltrexone modulates body and brain development in rats: role for endogenous opiod systems in growth. Life Sci 35:2057–2064

DISCUSSION

Houle: Have you have thought about what the common ancestor of a rodent an primate would have looked like in terms of cognitive ability? If that was a stupi animal, does that change the relevance of this? Or is there only one way to make brain?

Anderson: I don't think that there is only one way to make a brain. My own vie is that there may be certain genes that determine brain structure and which a beneficial for whatever that part of the brain is doing. Whatever the task, it may be an advantage to have certain neural circuits built in certain ways. There may be many such genes affecting many different aspects of brain structure. Then, for whatever reason, e.g. assortative mating, there may be co-inheritance. Since we are affecting brains in general, we sort of 'psychometrically measure' genes: all our tasks' scores can correlate, but we can also damage an area of the brain, and dissociate functions in individual cases, that on a population basis seem to go together. Thus, I predict, we will find lots of things on the genetic side that relate to many things on the structural side, which then in turn relate to lots of things on the psychological side. Some things are good for brain function whatever the brain is supposed to be doing. This might make an animal a better reasoner in my task, and be relevant to whatever is adaptively significant in the natural environment.

Jensen: Do you think that the kind of research programme that you're displaying here today would be enhanced by looking at animals that have been bred for different abilities? Is it possible to breed rats for maze learning ability, for example?

Anderson: Efforts to breed animals for performance on particular tasks have not been particularly good at producing animals that are better *across* tasks. People looking for quantitative trait loci in humans have selected high performing populations and low performing populations on what we consider to be intelligence measures. If you could agree on a battery of tests in rodents of sufficient breadth, and you could somehow select for this, then that would probably be useful for the same reasons we think it's useful in people.

Rutter: Is the finding that breeding tends to have effects that are relatively task-specific have implications for the notion of *g*, which implies that individual skills ought to derive out of *g*? Surely on the basis of the hypothesis that *g* is 'driving' the individual skills, you would expect that the breeding would actually have a more general effect than it does, wouldn't you?

Jensen: It does have a somewhat general effect. If you go on selecting generation after generation on the one trait, you're combating the regression on the other tasks that you're not selecting for. Therefore, at the same time you are breeding out the other traits in which the animals may have been higher to begin with. Interestingly, when rats are bred for maze learning ability, there are concurrent increases in brain size and body size that are not being selected for at all. It is as if the increased maze learning ability required a somewhat larger brain and the body is a power-pack for the increased size of the brain and therefore has to increase also.

Anderson: In the breeding project there are many practical difficulties. One thing I noticed is that some rats will freeze in the maze. One might think that this sort of emotionality would be independent from maze learning. You could easily breed for rats that simply froze in the maze and would have poor 'maze learning scores' which were actually unrelated to what we really wanted to get at.

Mackintosh: Your line of research raises in a particularly acute form the question whether the *g* factor extracted from one battery of tests in one population has any resemblance at all to the *g* factor extracted from a quite different battery of tests, in this case in a quite different population. You may find intercorrelations between your rats' performance on different tests, so you've got a general factor, but how do we know this has anything to do with a general factor of human intelligence?

Anderson: At present we can't say that we know that. If you develop a mouse model of alcoholism, where the mouse prefers the alcohol solution, how do you know that this involves the same mechanisms as human alcoholism? Your criticism is not particularly unique to what I've talked about here. At some level it does rely on individual intuition and judgement in terms of the similarity of the tasks and behaviours. I am increasingly pessimistic about using animals as the surrogate for describing the biological correlates of intelligence. I now see them more as experimental surrogates for testing hypotheses of the nature of structure-function relationships derived from correlative studies of humans.

Mackintosh: Part of what worried me is the terminology you used. You described the Maier tests as 'reasoning', but one could question whether this is in any sense similar to the reasoning that we study in IQ tests? The more plausible account of what you're studying is that it is speed of learning and ability to generalize learning from one situation to a marginally different one. This is not quite the same as the sorts of things most IQ tests examine.

Anderson: If you say we're looking at generalized learning characteristics of rodents — and I think this does bear some similarity to some tests that are used to assess humans — I'd be able to accept that and abandon the word 'reasoning', which I appreciate is somewhat inflammatory.

Suddendorf: Perhaps you should do some reaction time or inspection time tests.

Anderson: I've actually thought about that — this could be done in rats — but I have not done it.

Whiten: Thinking about this issue the other way round, would it help to satisfy Nick Mackintosh's concern about comparability if you did the same tests in other species, particularly primates, including humans? For example, you could put children in similar testing situations and compare their responses with conventional IQ test results.

Anderson: Maier actually did similar studies in children.

Detterman: I find this work quite impressive. Both you and Thompson (Thompson et al 1990) have used rats where the variability was essentially bred out. Biologists who use these rats mostly don't like variability in their research. So, if you compare these rats to wild rats, many of them are highly unvariable and to be able to find this level of effects seems to me quite impressive.

Miller: I was surprised that you made such a tight link between intelligence in the sense of insight and reasoning, and intelligence in the sense of the *g* factor. One ould imagine species that don't show any particular insight or reasoning abilities hat might still show the *g* factor in the psychometric sense of positive ntercorrelations between the behavioural capacities that they do have. Perhaps ne could also imagine species that show insight but not necessarily the *g* factor. Do you really think there's an intrinsic link there? Is it worth teasing these things ut, saying that the *g* factor might extend much further back phylogenetically than he evolution of insight? It may be that insight is a highly *g*-loaded skill in a lot of nimals, but that doesn't mean that it is equivalent to the *g* factor.

Anderson: I agree. I don't think that insight is a necessary concomitant of having *g* factor. For many reasons it could be interesting to look for species that do or on't possess that capacity.

Deary: I have a comment on something you said about human studies. You numerated some of the new scanning techniques we have in humans, and I was eminded that the *Proceedings of the Royal Society* recently published a study showing hat pH of the brain in humans correlates with psychometric ability test scores (Rae : al 1996). The next study failed to replicate it (Anderson et al 1998). Then, more ecently, they published something with magnetic resonance spectroscopy nowing that N-acetyl aspartate correlated with psychometric test scores (Jung et . 1999). Now this seems to me a kind of degenerate way of going about science: to ave a new technique, and to do a quick in-and-out poorly-powered study which nds something and then is usually not replicated. We have these little studies very so often as a new technique comes out. There is a better way to do this cience, but why isn't it happening? Why is there no larger scale research in this rea?

Anderson: I didn't do the magnetic resonance spectroscopy study, but in their efence I'm not sure that it was a total fishing expedition. N-acetyl aspartate is nown to be a component of neural membranes. We now have a way to assess hat that we didn't have before. People have talked about its role in neurons, and he role of neuronal arborizations to intelligence, so it was plausible to use this new ool to ask a question which has some reasonable rationale behind it. As to why here aren't more large-scale studies in this field, if I write a proposal saying that I m looking for biological correlates of intelligence, the response of the funding gencies is not overwhelming! This is one reason that many of these studies are eing spun-off from others. Andreasen and Flashman (Andreasen et al 1993, lashman et al 1997) looked at a large number of magnetic resonance imaging MRI) scans in a study of brain volume and IQ, but this was basically a chizophrenia study, where control groups are being used for that purpose. The udy of brain pH you mentioned was a control group of boys 10 years old and nder for a study of brain metabolism in Duchenne's muscular dystrophy. My iled replication of this study involved going over to my epileptologist and nalysing their data.

Deary: Compared with the effort that is thrown at cognitive science an neuroscience, the individual differences work does live off the back of othe studies quite often.

Hinde: It is worth reminding ourselves of the importance of what Nic Humphrey said earlier about correlation and causation. As I understood i Arthur Jensen said that selection for maze brightness in rats led to bigger brai size and bigger body size. It seems to me possible that bigger body size was th thing being selected for because it might be much easier for a rat if its whiske touched both sides of the maze, and that brain size is a correlate of body size.

Jensen: That is an interesting thought. This was a doctoral dissertation done a Berkeley, and I don't think anyone on the committee thought of that particula hypothesis.

Gangestad: One issue that some of us are interested in is what accounts for th genetic variation from an evolutionary viewpoint. In life history theor building both a bigger body and a bigger brain is somatic investment. It investment in the future because it costs the organism energy to do so now and only over time may the organism reap the benefits of the investmer reproductively. It is possible that there is genetic variation in somati investment more generally, in a sense variation across individuals in the willingness to bet that there's enough of a future to make somatic investmer worthwhile. It is not clear that the genetic variation has anything to do wit building a better brain *per se*: it could simply be genes that code essentially fc somatic investment.

Jensen: Are there empirical studies that have demonstrated this investmer theory that you're talking about?

Gangestad: Not with regard to the genetic variance, but more broadly wit respect to the theory, yes. In evolutionary biology, life history theory is fundamental framework for thinking about problems of selection. Th adaptiveness of an organism's activities is thought of in terms of trade-offs. On basic trade-off is that between current and future reproduction. Again, developin a bigger brain is an investment in the future at the expense of reproduction in th short term, which the energy used to build the bigger brain could have bee allocated to. But investment in the long-term future does not always pa particularly if the long-term future cannot be counted upon. We think of lo intelligence as being bad, but it's quite possible that the brain size of everyone optimal given their condition and their phenotype, which is some function of the genotype. For instance, suppose there is genetic variation in disease susceptibilit such that some individuals have the misfortune of not resisting the prevailin pathogens. From a life history standpoint, we might expect that selection wou have designed organisms, whether humans or rats, to invest less in the future whe they find themselves having that misfortune.

Jensen: There is a good deal of sheer anatomical commonality between rat brains and human brains.

Humphrey: Steve Gangestad is suggesting that the development of IQ might be affected by life expectancy. Now, one thing that an infant might take to be quite a good indicator of life expectancy would be the condition of its mother. And there's been a tantalizing study just reported (Ikle et al 1999) on the effects of extracorporeal membrane oxygenation on newborn infants, showing that babies who receive hyperoxygenation of their brain turn out at the age of five to have above average performance IQ. This suggests, perhaps, that these babies have been given a false idea of the maternal background they come from: the extra oxygen may be acting as a signal to them that things are well, their mother is well fed and their environment is fine. They then prepare for a life in which they can support a larger brain and have a higher IQ.

References

Anderson B, Elgavish GA, Chu W-J et al 1998 Temporal lobe pH$_i$ and IQ: no consistent correlation. Intelligence 26:75–79

Andreasen NC, Flaum M, Swayze VW II et al 1993 Intelligence and brain structure in normal individuals. Am J Psychol 150:130–134

Flashman LA, Andreasen NC, Flaum M, Swayze VW II 1997 Intelligence and regional brain volumes in normal controls. Intelligence 25:149–160

Ikle L, Ikle DN, Moreland SG, Fashaw LM, Waas N, Rosenberg AR 1999 Survivors of neonatal extracorporeal membrane oxygenation at school age: unusual findings on intelligence testing. Dev Med Child Neurol 41:307–310

Jung RE, Yeo RA, Chiulli SJ et al 1999 Biochemical markers of cognition: a proton MR spectroscopy study of normal human brain. NeuroReport 10:1–5

Rae C, Scott RB, Thompson CH et al 1996 Is pH a biochemical marker of IQ. Proc R Soc Lond Ser B Biol Sci 263:1061–1064

Thompson R, Crinella FM, Yu J 1990 Brain mechanisms in problem solving and intelligence: a lesion study of the rat brain. Plenum Press, New York

Natural selection, mental modules and intelligence

Randolph M. Nesse

Department of Psychiatry and Institute for Social Research, The University of Michigan, Ann Arbor, MI 48106-1248, USA

Abstract. The question of whether intelligence is one trait or many has exercised several generations of researchers, but no consensus is in sight. Evolutionary psychology, with its emphasis on domain-specific mental modules, seems to offer hope for advancing understanding of this question. We know that the mind has been shaped by natural selection to maximize reproductive success. This tells us what the mind must do — it must solve the adaptive problems that the organism confronts. However, whether this functional capacity is manifest in congruent anatomic, physiological, genetic, cognitive or psychometric structures is another matter. Examination of how natural selection shaped other mechanisms suggests that knowing functional demands provides only modest guidance as to the structure of mechanisms. None the less, it remains simultaneously clear that these mechanisms are not entirely general, but have been shaped to cope with specific challenges. Our metaphors for the mind, whether as a digital computer or a Swiss army knife, are misleading because computers and tools are products of intelligent design. In contrast, minds are products of natural selection whose intertwined components are products of incorporated genetic mutations whose effects are widespread and constrained by historical precedents. Our tendencies to describe the structure of the mind in terms of discrete components make it difficult for us to comprehend the mind as a mind. One antidote may be to minimize metaphorical descriptions of postulated structures of mind and focus instead on its function.

2000 The nature of intelligence. Wiley, Chichester (Novartis Foundation Symposium 233) p 96–115

Research on intelligence was born of practical necessity and developed in concert with mathematical techniques for interpreting masses of data, yet it remains embroiled in controversies about many basic questions. Questions about how to measure intelligence are now mainly about possible cultural bias in intelligence tests. The question of what selective forces so rapidly shaped high levels of human cognitive intelligence remains unresolved, as does the related question of why there is substantial variation in a trait with presumed major fitness benefits. The data explaining individual differences in intelligence test scores are now fairly clear, but remain controversial mainly because of their perceived political implications. Perhaps the largest and deepest question, however, is what intelligence really is — in particular, if it is one trait or many (Sternberg 1999). Much of the work on this problem has focused on the '*g*' factor that emerges from the consistently high correlations among scores on measures of diverse kinds of intellectual ability. The existence of the *g* factor is not an issue, but its significance remains problematic. An emphasis on general intelligence has been opposed by those who insist that *g* is an epiphenomenon of the correlations of specific components of mental ability, or at least that it is less important than these components. This debate has had a prominent political tinge, in which those advocating for discrete differentiated intelligences see themselves as advocates for people who are bright in ways different from those measured by traditional intelligence tests. The historical legacy of political and ethical issues, and the prominent role intelligence tests now play in providing access to privilege and wealth, make these questions intensely controversial (APA Task Force 1996).

Not all of the controversy is political, however. Psychologists continue to propose specific kinds of intelligence, and to argue about how best to distinguish them, and how they do or do not relate to a general factor. The diversity of such perspectives is an important fact in and of itself. Thurstone offered his seven intelligences in opposition to a general factor (Thurstone 1938). More recently, there has been much discussion of Gardner's seven proposed kinds of intelligence — linguistic, logical–mathematical, musical, body–kinaesthetic, spatial, interpersonal and intrapersonal (Gardner 1983). Both proposals include factors for verbal, spatial and mathematical ability, but beyond that they differ considerably. Guilford first proposed 120 factors, derived from five operations, four kinds of content and six products, then expanded his list to 150 (Guilford & Hoepfner 1971). There has also been much comment on emotional intelligence, social intelligence, creativity and other abilities (Goleman 1995). In opposition to these proposals, other intelligence researchers emphasize the *g* factor, and downplay the importance of subtypes of ability (Jensen 1998). This discussion has been going on for decades and shows no signs of an emerging consensus. The difficulty does not seem to arise from lack of data. Although political factors and personal reputations are involved, they too do not seem to account for the difficulty. Thus, it is worth considering the possibility that the question is framed incorrectly, or that it may have no answer.

Can evolutionary psychology help?

Evolutionary psychology has developed rapidly in the past decade, in the wake of fundamental advances in understanding the evolution of behaviour regulation mechanisms. These advances have been successfully applied to classic problems

in animal behaviour (Buss 1999). The strong commitment of evolutionar
psychology to a search for domain-specific mental modules suggests that it ma
offer assistance in the problem of multiple intelligences. Modules are shaped b
natural selection to cope with specific adaptive problems that arise in specifi
domains. Different intelligences are proposed to reflect an individual's ability t
adapt to some aspect of the environment. These similarities offer a hint that a
evolutionary approach might provide a solid foundation for decisions about how
to understand the structure of the mind.

The emphasis on domain-specific modules has come most strongly from
Cosmides and Tooby, but other leaders in the field, especially David Buss and
Steve Pinker, are also strong advocates of the importance of modules (Cosmide
& Tooby 1992a, Buss 1995, Pinker 1997). Cosmides and Tooby state:

> From an evolutionary perspective, the human cognitive architecture is far more
> likely to resemble a confederation of hundreds or thousands of functionall
> dedicated computers, dedicated to solving problems endemic to the
> Pleistocene, than it is to resemble a single general-purpose computer equipped
> with a small number of general purpose procedures such as association
> formation, categorization, or production-rule formation. (Cosmides & Tooby
> 1995, p 1189)

The logic of the argument for domain-specific modules seems compelling. The
only force that can account for order in living systems is natural selection
Natural selection shapes phenotypes that increase the frequency of the genes tha
make them. Brains, therefore, must be shaped to maximize inclusive fitness — or
the average in the natural environment, of course. When an individual confronts a
adaptive problem — whether a hungry tiger, an angry group leader, a fruit high up
in a tree or a child in danger — the brain needs to be able to solve the problem. Pu
more accurately, individuals with brains that successfully solve such problems have
a selective advantage. As put by Pinker, 'The mind is a system of organs o
computation, designed by natural selection to solve the kinds of problems ou
ancestors faced in their foraging way of life' (Pinker 1997, p 21).

There are good examples of such modules. The ability to learn language is the
best. The famous debates between Chomsky and Skinner about whether a genera
learning mechanism could account for language learning is now settled — there is
special module for learning and using language (Pinker 1994). Furthermore, we
have long known that these capacities are localized to specific brain locations
mainly in the left temporal lobe. A universal grammar is recognized to underlie
all language. Children absorb language and learn words and a specific grammar a
a fantastic rate. In everyday life, the special nature of this learning is perhaps made
obvious when adults try to learn a foreign language.

Students of animal behaviour long ago abandoned attempts to explain behaviour using only general learning models. Once the work of Seligman and Garcia broke the taboo, it soon became clear that most behaviour of most animals can be fully explained only if specialized mechanisms are acknowledged (Garcia & Ervin 1968, Seligman 1970, Staddon 1983). In Gazzaniga's text *The cognitive neurosciences*, Ganistel reviews eating regulation, navigation, foraging and other domain-specific mechanisms (Ganistel 1995). Textbooks of animal behaviour now take the specialized nature of behaviour control mechanisms for granted (Alcock 1993).

In an extensively studied human example, Cosmides and Tooby have emphasized the benefits of specialized processing machinery to detect cheaters in social exchanges (Cosmides & Tooby 1992b). Using different versions of the Wason selection task, they have demonstrated that people are considerably superior at tasks framed as detecting rule violation compared to the same task framed in a domain non-specific way. While their method has been criticized, the notion that the mind has been shaped to cope with certain social situations is becoming widely accepted. A number of other examples have been well studied. Face recognition seems to depend on specialized algorithms localized in specific brain regions, and people have specialized abilities to do natural physics and to recognize natural kinds, and to absorb and use culture (Gazzaniga 1992, Sperber 1996, Atran 1998).

Moving away from the usual examples for a moment, consider the adaptive task of choosing food. Examination of this challenge offers insight into what natural selection shapes. This system seems not to be controlled by one module, but by many capacities. First there are taste and smell, with visual information augmenting them. Taste and smell are general capacities, but they are especially able to detect chemical cues related to the quality of food. Simple reinforcement learning is important but is not a general mechanism even in and of itself, since reinforcement is initiated first and foremost by food. As Garcia showed, a strange taste is avoided after it has been paired even once with sickness, a one-time learning of the most crucial sort (Garcia & Ervin 1968). Then there is social learning of food preferences, and the remarkable persistence of those preferences throughout life. Finally, cognitive learning can, at least in some people with strong will-power, increase consumption of healthy foods. If one wanted to consider all of these capacities together as a module one could, but they seem to be related mainly in that they all contribute to getting the job done. Most are somewhat general mechanisms that have specialized aspects for coping with the particular task of assessing food choices. Specific adaptive challenges do not necessarily shape specific structures in the mind. Specialization of behaviour control mechanisms for particular domains or problems does not imply a modular mental structure.

TABLE 1   The social emotions

Emotions and the Prisoner's Dilemma	Other cooperates	Other defects
Self cooperates	Friendship Trust	Suspicion (before) Anger (after)
Self defects	Anxiety (before) Guilt (after)	Dislike Rejection

The emotions are exemplars of domain-specific modules. Emotions are specia states shaped by natural selection to cope effectively with the adaptive challenge that arise in a situation that has recurred in the course of evolution (Frijda 1986). Ar emotion adjusts many aspects of the organism in synchrony — physiology cognition, behaviour and motivation — to cope well with that situation (Ness 1990, Tooby & Cosmides 1990). Panic offers a particularly fine example (Ness 1987). In the face of threat to life, people experience physiological arousal that makes escape more likely, they are motivated to flee, and they think about nothing except how to escape. Furthermore, this response is mediated by the locus coeruleus, a tiny cluster of cells in the pons where 80% of the brain's noradrenergic neurons originate. Electrical stimulation of the locus coeruleus causes every aspect of a panic attack. This makes a very nice package — congruence between an anatomic locus, a neurochemical system, a wel recognized syndrome and a very specific kind of adaptive challenge.

Conditioned fear offers a view of the subtlety of design. Monkeys have no innate fear of snakes or flowers, but life-long fear is conditioned by a single observation o other monkeys expressing fear of snakes. There is no such similar prepared fear o flowers (Mineka et al 1980).

Are all emotions so modular? Consider the emotions that mediate socia exchange in comparison to those that mediate goal pursuit. While detection o cheaters is important, several other situations have recurred often in the course o social exchange as modelled by the familiar Prisoner's Dilemma. Each situation has been so important in the course of evolution that it may well have shaped a particular emotion. Indeed, we can readily match recognized emotions to these domain-specific situations (Table 1).

The emotions that regulate goal pursuit offer an instructive contrast. They are about as domain general as anything could be. The organism faces the adaptive challenges of deciding what goal to pursue, how best to pursue it and when to give up the pursuit of goals that are not reachable. A set of emotions seems to match these situations remarkably well (Table 2).

TABLE 2   Emotions that regulate goal pursuit

Situation	Before	After (expected outcome)	After (unexpected outcome)
Opportunity/Gain			
Physical	Desire	Pleasure	Frustration
Social	Hope	Happiness	Disappointment
Threat/Loss			
Physical	Fear	Pain	Relief
Social	Anxiety	Sadness	Relaxation

To return to modules studied by evolutionary psychologists, a very general mechanism for intuiting the motives and dispositions of others has been proposed by Leslie and tested by Baron-Cohen, using evidence from autistic individuals who seem to lack this capacity (Baron-Cohen 1995). This module for 'theory of mind' is mainly supported by evidence from autistic individuals who seem to lack it. Other people seem to have it to a sufficient and similar enough degree that variations are not noticed. Thus, theory of mind may be, like ability to balance upright, more of a normal capacity than an intelligence. One could, of course, develop measures to array people on a scale that measures their ability to project themselves into the situations of others. Perhaps then it would be an intelligence.

Are modules intelligences?

This example segues into the relationship between evolved modules and types of intelligence. We all have language ability but relative language ability varies considerably. Thus, even a crude verbal intelligence scale can give consistent differences between individuals that predict functioning on many kinds of verbal (and other) behaviour. So, in this case the evolved module corresponds to a recognized subtype of intelligence. When we look at the theory of mind module, however, it is not so clear that there is interesting variation except that revealed when the system fails completely. As noted above, someone should look. When we consider cheater detection, it is also not clear if this module includes interesting variations in ability. The difficulty here is the one Cronbach warned about in 1957 — separating the study of individual differences from the study of functional capacities leads to confusion (Cronbach 1957). The general conclusion must be that some modules are congruent with intelligences but some are not. Some intelligences are modules, but some are not. And then there is the matter, discussed above, that considerable specialization of general mechanisms is likely even in the absence of a modules. An evolutionary approach that seemed to offer a simple solution turns out to reveal the depth of the problem. At stake here is nothing less than how we view the structure of the mind.

Structures and metaphors of the mind

The underlying problem is how we describe the structure of the mind. Components of mind can be constructed based on several kinds of criteria:

- Observed capacities such as perception, cognition, memory, etc.
- Distinct abilities such as verbal fluency or spatial judgement.
- Predicted adaptive modules such as cheater detection.
- Inferred functional structures such as ego and id.
- Anatomic loci such as Broca's area.
- Neurochemical systems such as serotonin.
- Effects of specific genes such as DA receptor 4.

How are we to choose which factor to follow? Which should we rely on to define the structure of the mind? As we parse the mind into components, we seem unable to proceed without resorting to metaphors. The current vogue is to make analogies to digital computers, with many resulting debates about what corresponds to hardware or software, and whether the software is object-oriented or not. Evolutionary psychologists have countered with the metaphor of the mind as a Swiss army knife. But the mind is not a machine designed by any intelligent planner. Consider how an existing nervous system is shaped by natural selection. A mutation that changes the system in a way that results in higher average reproduction will tend to increase in frequency. That mutation may influence only one system, or it may influence many. The cumulative effect of incorporating new alleles in this way over millions of years seems likely to blur any boundaries between any pre-existing components of the mind/brain. And, of course, any changes must be incremental modifications of existing structures. In short, consideration of the process by which natural selection shaped the mind/ brain suggests that sharply defined modules of mind may not even exist. The system works, but its structure only dimly reflects its functions. There are, of course, anatomic localization specific functions, such as language in the left parietal and frontal lobes. Instead of expecting such localization, however, we should try to explain it. Why aren't brain/mind structures blurred irretrievably by mutations that influence multiple structures? For one thing, all structure must emerge from previous structures, so phylogenetic continuity maintains some order. Also, however, genes that are essential to multiple systems are relatively resistant to change for the simple reason that alterations are very likely to be fatal.

Thus, intermediate metabolism is relatively consistent from individual to individual. But in systems that must change, such as behavioural control systems, a system that depends on the expression of a gene that is also important to many other systems is fragile on two counts. First, the system is rigid because any changes will have effects that are likely to be deleterious elsewhere. Second, and conversely, a mutation that gives major benefits in other systems may result in major pleiotropic costs to the system in question. Thus, systems are most robust if they rely on a combination of genes that are essential to all systems and thus secure, and genes that are expressed mostly in association with a particular system. The point is that this sequence offers a force that selects for somewhat distinct functional structures in opposition to the tendency for natural selection to blur all sharp divisions. The matter of defining such systems is admittedly a major problem. It may be that traits shaped in recent millennia to carry out new tasks, such as language, are more likely to be somewhat localized and autonomous than traits that go far back in phylogeny, such as choosing a mate. Emerging techniques that allow study of which genes are expressed in which tissues may prove instrumental, by revealing clusters of associated expressed genes that could provide an objective basis for defining functional mental structures. Specifically, one could use data about which genes are expressed in each of scores of brain tissues and loci and use latent class analysis to seek functional associations. One could also use techniques analogous to evolutionary systematics to look for possible phylogenetic associations among brain tissues that might be anatomically distant.

While it would be ideal to study the mind without metaphors, that may prove as difficult as using intuition to do quantum mechanics. Thus, consider a metaphor that is appropriate for the flesh and blood brain/mind—a computer program created by a genetic algorithm (Holland 1992, Vose 1999). Such programs are products of selection. Minor variations occur in every generation on some desired characteristic—accuracy in recognizing a shape, for instance. Programs that do well on this task have their information transmitted preferentially to the next generation. Over time, the program gets better and better at its task. When the programmer looks at how the program has solved the problem, it is often extremely difficult to discern how it did it. It is even more difficult to describe the components of the program, beyond those that are intrinsic to the program.

The mind is like a computer program shaped by a genetic algorithm. It works, and works well, but it is hard to say how, and even harder to find out what its components are, to the extent that they exist at all. This may help to explain why psychology has, so far, not been a cumulative science, and why our attempts to discover the structure of the mind, and the structure of intelligence, are so difficult. If this is correct, an evolutionary approach, even though it may not lead us to discrete mental modules, may provide the key to understanding the mind's functional structure, and the neural mechanisms that mediate those functions.

References

Alcock J 1993 Animal behavior. Sinauer Associates, Sunderland, MA

APA Task Force 1996 Intelligence: knowns and unknowns. American Psychological Association, Washington, DC

Atran S 1998 Folk biology and the anthropology of science: cognitive universals and cultural particulars. Behav Brain Sci 21:547–609

Baron-Cohen S 1995 Mindblindness: an essay on autism and theory of mind. MIT Press, Cambridge, MA

Buss DM 1995 Evolutionary psychology: a new paradigm for psychological science. Psychol Inquiry 6:1–30

Buss DM 1999 Evolutionary psychology: the new science of the mind. Allyn & Bacon, Boston, MA

Cosmides L, Tooby J 1992a Introduction: evolutionary psychology and conceptual integration. In: Barkow JH, Cosmides L, Tooby J (eds) The adapted mind: evolutionary psychology and the generation of culture. Oxford University Press, New York, p 1–18

Cosmides L, Tooby J 1992b Cognitive adaptations for social exchange. In: Barkow JH, Cosmides L, Tooby J (eds) The adapted mind: evolutionary psychology and the generation of culture. Oxford University Press, New York, p 163–229

Cosmides L, Tooby J 1995 Mapping the evolved functional organization of mind and brain. In: Gazzaniga MS (ed) The cognitive neurosciences. MIT Press, Cambridge, MA, p 1185–1197

Cronbach LJ 1957 The two disciplines of scientific psychology. Amer Psychol 12:671–684

Frijda NH 1986 The emotions. Cambridge University Press, Cambridge

Ganistel CR 1995 The replacement of general-purpose theories with adaptive specializations. In: Gazzaniga MS (ed) The cognitive neurosciences. MIT Press, Cambridge, MA, p 1255–1267

Garcia J, Ervin F 1968 Gustatory-visceral and telereceptor-cutaneous conditioning: adaptation in internal and external milieus. Commun Behav Biol A 1:389–414

Gardner H 1983 Frames of mind: the theory of multiple intelligences. Basic Books, New York

Gazzaniga MS 1992 Nature's mind. Basic Books, New York

Goleman D 1995 Emotional intelligence. Bantam Books, New York

Guilford JP, Hoepfner R 1971 The analysis of intelligence. McGraw-Hill, New York

Holland JH 1992 Adaptation in natural and artificial systems: an introductory analysis with applications to biology, control, and artificial intelligence. MIT Press, Cambridge, MA

Jensen AR 1998 The g factor: the science of mental ability. Praeger, Westport, CT

Mineka S, Keir R, Price V 1980 Fear of snakes in wild- and laboratory-reared rhesus monkeys (Macaca mulatta). Anim Learn Behav 8:653–663

Nesse RM 1987 An evolutionary perspective on panic disorder and agoraphobia. Ethol Sociobiol 8:73S–83S

Nesse RM 1990 Evolutionary explanations of emotions. Hum Nat 1:261–289

Pinker S 1994 The language instinct. Morrow, New York

Pinker S 1997 How the mind works. Norton, New York

Seligman M 1970 On the generality of the laws of learning. Psychol Rev 77:406–418

Sperber D 1996 Explaining culture: a naturalistic approach. Blackwell, Oxford

Staddon JER 1983 Adaptive behavior and learning. Cambridge University Press, New York

Sternberg RJ 1999 Successful intelligence. Trends Cognit Sci 3:436–442

Thurstone LL 1938 Primary mental abilities. University of Chicago Press, Chicago, IL

Tooby J, Cosmides L 1990 The past explains the present: emotional adaptations and the structure of ancestral environments. Ethol Sociobiol 11:375–424

Vose MD 1999 The simple genetic algorithm: foundations and theory. MIT Press, Cambridge, MA

DISCUSSION

Suddendorf: I am very much in agreement with your position and I am glad to see you articulate an alternative to the new orthodoxy in evolutionary psychology. In support of your analysis I want to add that evolution tends to tinker with what already exists, rather than to invent modules *de novo*. The fact that there is only a minute difference in genetic make-up between chimpanzees and humans is difficult to reconcile with the idea that we evolved many sophisticated, domain-specific and genetically determined modules in response to peculiar selective pressures in the Pleistocene (Corballis 2000). On the face of it, it does not make a lot of sense that a multitude of new modules would have been simply added without great underlying genetic modifications.

Nesse: What you say leads to a fairly specific and interesting prediction. That is, if a species confronts a task that it has never confronted before in its phylogeny, then it is much more likely to shape a specific module to deal with that. But if the task is a slight derivative of one that's happened before, such as allocating effort or mate choice, you would expect it to be a minor modification of something that already exists, and is probably blended more with other structures. I expect that one could look at this in other species, too. Species change their niches, they change their prey and they change their reproductive strategy — if there was some major transition then you would be more likely to see specific brain structures that are designed to do that.

Karmiloff-Smith: I liked the distinction you made between module and mechanism. To make it more precise, Simon Baron-Cohen (1998) and Alan Leslie (1992) have talked about an innately specified cognitive module for theory of mind that is domain-specific. I prefer to think in terms of domain-relevant mechanisms which only *become* domain-specific as a function of development (Karmiloff-Smith 1992, 1998). Another point missing from the discussion so far is that the basis of evolutionary psychology is adult psychology, very often adult neuropsychology. Evolutionary psychologists leap from the adult endstate directly to evolution, and ontogeny is not taken into account at all. Take the case of a purported face-processing module, but let us look at ontogeny. There is work showing that from early infancy, both the temporal specialization in terms of the wave-form, and the localization in terms of position in the brain, takes a very long time over the first months of life (Johnson 1993). There is a long process of ontogenetic development until the emergence of the kind of specialization that you see in adults. But evolutionary psychologists base their argumentation on the adult endstate. We also have data from abnormal development in the face-processing area, showing that you can get very specialized behaviour with a different temporal pattern at a different location in the brain (Karmiloff-Smith 1998). Understanding the process of ontogeny is crucial.

Suddendorf: Changes to ontogeny may, in fact, be a neat way around the problem of small genetic differences between chimpanzees and humans. Little genetic change may be needed to alter growth patterns. Changes to brain development may allow (what Annette Karmiloff-Smith calls) domain-relevant mechanisms to be shaped by environmental input into module-like structures. Development and the plasticity of our brain may be the keys to understanding how little genetic change resulted into the phenotypic distinctiveness of humans' cognitive apparatus.

Nesse: With respect to pathology, we have to make the point even more strongly. If you destroy a large portion of the left temporal parietal area, people still develop language if you do it at the right time of life. I don't know how to explain that.

Hinde: I would make the same point as Professor Karmiloff-Smith with regard to Cosmides and Tooby's social contract ideas. Mothers are saying to babies from the very start 'if you do this, then that'. Cosmides and Tooby pay no respect to ontogeny.

Humphrey: I have a general point about whether or not we should seek a Darwinian adaptive explanation for everything. Michael Gazzaniga, so Nesse says, starts every lecture on the brain with the reminder that the brain's main function is to enhance its owner's reproductive success. But while this may be true of the human brain it is not necessarily nearly so true of the human mind. Indeed the human mind may have been shaped — and be being shaped — by cultural forces that have, as it were, their own evolutionary agenda.

Nesse: My favourite example of a cultural creation that people have tried to propose evolutionary explanations for is religion. I'm in the midst of editing a book about this, called *The evolution of subjective commitment*. It seems plausible to me that natural selection has created in us, because of its selective advantage, the capacity to make irrational subjective commitments to ideologies as well as to other people. Once we have this capacity, it creates social structures. Once those social structures exist, they create new selective forces. There is co-evolution, not just of language and the like, but of social selective forces and brain mechanisms, that leads us to a wonderful complexity.

Houle: I would like to offer an empirical confirmation of your basic point that things should look like a big mess when we try to reverse-engineer the brain. Developmental genetics has progressed to the point that we can test a lot of the simple predictions that are made on the basis of common sense, the same basis as the prediction of the modularity of mind. It would make sense for parts of the body that work together, such as the two jaws which developed separately, to be independent of the rest of development. This is not really the case (J. Mezey, personal communication). You might predict that early development would be less malleable evolutionarily than late development, and this is not true (Raff

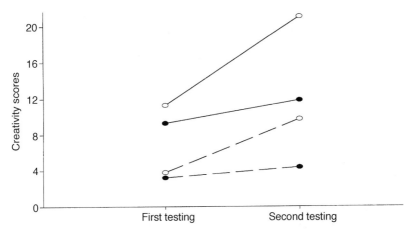

FIG. 1. Creativity scores (fluency ——; uniqueness − − −) at first and second testing for children who passed theory of mind tasks at the second testing (○) and children who continued to fail these tasks (●).

1996). You might predict that genes that are expressed in one role would tend not to be expressed in a very different role: again, that's not true (Lawrence 1992). It all suggests massive tinkering, where the criterion for success is not simplicity or elegance. This general view of evolution is amply confirmed already in other fields.

Suddendorf: I can add further developmental data. Social cognition, in particular 'theory of mind', is often cited as a prime example of the modularity of mind, since children with autism, for example, appear to be selectively impaired in social cognition. However, in a recent study (Suddendorf & Fletcher-Flinn 1999) on preschoolers we found that non-social skills improve in tandem with children's capacity to pass false-belief tasks (a classic measure of theory of mind). Children's ability to pass theory of mind tasks was significantly correlated with verbal intelligence as measured by the British picture vocabulary scale (BPVS) (Dunn et al 1982) and with non-verbal intelligence as measured by the Geometric Design subtest of the Wechsler preschool and primary scale of intelligence—revised (WPPSI-R) (Wechsler 1989). We also observed a significant correlation with measures of divergent thinking, replicating an earlier finding (Suddendorf & Fletcher-Flinn 1997). In the divergent thinking task children are asked to produce solutions to simple problems (e.g., 'tell me all the things that you can think of that are round') which do not involve any social cognition. Numbers of appropriate responses (fluency) and of unique responses (uniqueness) were correlated with theory of mind with coefficients of about 0.5. Three months later, I conducted a follow-up study, testing 20 children who had failed all false-belief tasks. Some of them now passed the theory of mind tasks and these children also improved in their creativity scores (see Fig. 1). We calculated the difference between scores at first testing and at the testing three months later, and found an association between intra-individual creativity improvement and theory of mind, even when controlling for the effects of age, verbal and non-verbal ability.

These results indicate that once children pass false-belief tasks they also improve in their ability to search their own mind for appropriate problem solutions. In addition to correlations with creativity, verbal and non-verbal intelligence, other studies have found further associations with non-social abilities such as working memory (Davis & Pratt 1995), pantomime (Suddendorf et al 1999, Taylor & Carlson 1997) and causal reasoning (Frye et al 1998). These findings fly in the face of the claim that there is an *encapsulated* theory of mind module. Indeed, the very idea that the human mind is characterized by new, independent, domain-specific modules seems to contradict the observation that the human mind is flexible and generative in its thoughts, actions and words (Corballis 2000). In regards to theory of mind, for example, we are quite happy to use the intentional stance beyond the social sphere (e.g., when we use mental terms to explain the actions of animals, plants and even machines).

Miller: I appreciate Randy Nesse's point about genetic algorithms and evolution generally operating through tinkering. It has often been difficult to understand the products of evolution. But things can't be that messy, because we do have bodies composed of relatively spatially distinct organs. I think the real messiness comes in with things like mutational damage. The effect of mutations is likely to be considerably messier than the natural adaptive structure of either the body or the mind. I'll be arguing in my paper that the *g* factor might to some extent reflect the messiness that arises through a certain mutation load that affects a lot of cognitive capacities. There is also probably a lot of messiness in development. Here I disagree with Annette Karmiloff-Smith: the reason why evolutionary psychologists focus on adult cognitive architecture is presumably that it is under a lot stronger selection than the particular developmental time-course that happened to evolve to grow the adult cognitive architecture. This is especially true if you believe that parental care insulates human infants and toddlers from selection pressures. If that is the case, then you expect development to be messy and you expect the effects of mutation to be messy, but not necessarily the adult cognitive architecture itself.

Nesse: Would you expect a difference between the amount of structure in physical structures, like the abdominal organs, versus general cognitive processing mechanisms?

Miller: We need several people to think much harder about that. There are spatial constraints on the operation of physiological organs that might create selection pressures.

Nesse: They can't blend into each other, in the same way that mental structures could interdigitate with each other.

Gangestad: I'll buy your point that you shouldn't expect to find discrete modules with membranes and so on. But functionally, we might still expect that we find some modularity, or special purposiveness, and that at a functional level cognitive architecture is not particularly messy. If organisms evolved genetic algorithms to solve problems, the way you described, we might expect the organism to be able to solve those problems pretty well. Because of constraints that happen to emerge through the evolution of the algorithms, however, the organism may not solve all problems extremely well, and if the constraints are sufficiently severe, performance might be severely compromised. This is Stephen Jay Gould's point about the importance of historical contingencies. Through blind tinkering, selection creates not only adaptation but also genetic and developmental constraints, which affect subsequent adaptation. As Gould has emphasized, an organism that has evolved through tinkering may not be readily reverse-engineered; the architecture of features may be too messy for us to be able to tell what problems they were designed to solve. Yet the adaptationist perspective to understanding animal behaviour has been a success story in the last 20 years. It appears that organisms have evolved to solve adaptive problems fairly well. One way to read the success of the adaptationist approach is that typically there are not overwhelming genetic and developmental constraints.

Nesse: I agree: the functional approach is the way to go, but I think we shoot ourselves in the foot by insisting that there must be discrete components that make it work, although there probably are some.

Gangestad: To second Geoffrey Miller's point, we do have to be careful about the criteria we use to say that things are not modular, as well as that they are modular. If we find that two aspects of performance are correlated, we should not necessarily conclude that they rely on common computational features. In a sense, the software used to perform the two tasks may be distinct, with the correlation due to the fact that there is common hardware.

Suddendorf: But what grounds do we have to suppose there are 'hardware' modules?

Gangestad: Independent of content you find this general *g* factor. It could be that there is a common component of neuronal integrity that affects how well anything works in the brain.

Suddendorf: One problem in all these debates is the lack of agreement about a clear definition of the term 'module'. Ever since Fodor (1983), people have associated with modules such properties as being (a) innately specified, (b) informationally encapsulated, (c) fast, (d) hardwired, (e) not assembled and (f) autonomous. Yet, Fodor (1983) only saw these characteristics as *typical* of modules; they are *not* necessary for a system to be a module. In his recent article, Coltheart (1999) reminds us that Fodor (1983) did not define modules. This point has been widely misunderstood not only by opponents (as Coltheart discussed) but also by proponents of modularity. Misconstruing typical characteristics as necessary characteristics can lead, and has led, to false conclusions from empirical data and from theoretical considerations. Proving that a particular system is not innately specified or autonomous does not mean that one has shown that the system is not a module. Nor does it follow that, when we have reason to believe that a system is hardwired and informationally encapsulated, we can conclude that the system must also be fast and innately specified. As Coltheart points out, each of these characteristics has to be tested empirically — we cannot reason from one to the other. Modules may or may not have any of these properties. But what then defines a module? Based on Fodor's arguments Coltheart proposes that one can define a cognitive system as a module when, and only when, it is domain-specific. This definition raises the question of what we mean by domain-specific. Coltheart (1999) explains: 'I mean that a cognitive system is domain-specific if it only responds to stimuli of a particular class: thus, to say that there is a domain-specific face-recognition module is to say that there is a cognitive system that responds when its input is a face, but does not respond when its input is, say, a written word, or a visually-presented object, or someone's voice' (p 118). If we accept this definition of modules, then whatever system underpins theory of mind or the intentional stance would not qualify as a social module, as it can also respond to non-social stimuli (e.g. to a computer). The possibility that modules might be learned, not informationally encapsulated, slow and assembled, creates an entirely different picture of modularity than the rigid structures that some evolutionary psychologists suggest to be our cognitive adaptations.

Rutter: Steve Gangestad, what are you postulating in terms of modules? Are you saying that the evidence that Randy Nesse is presenting doesn't necessarily mean there aren't modules? Your definition of 'modular' and your criteria for a module are not clear to me.

Gangestad: I confess I can't provide a precise definition for a module. I prefer to think in terms of 'special purposiveness': the notion that the brain is engineered to do certain things with certain information and other things with other information, and that what it does with information depends partly on its content. This view does not imply that we'll find modules with membranes. It also does not imply that specialized algorithms cannot be used for tasks other than the ones they were designed to solve. Discrete emotions may be good examples. It strikes me that they represent specialized functions and hence that special purpose processing supports them. But that is not to say that their underpinnings are encapsulated neurally or even cognitively.

Rutter: As I understand it, you're saying that there exist specialized functions, but adding the word 'module' is adding a baggage that does not get you very far.

Gangestad: I agree, which is why I don't typically introduce the term into a discussion myself. But I find talking in terms of specializations, sitting loose with regard to neural or cognitive underpinnings, useful.

Nesse: This is getting quite interesting. I think there are modules, and there are specialized things that are modular and those that are not modular. There are also general-purpose mechanisms. One shouldn't have to choose amongst them or pledge loyalty to any of them in order to do evolutionary psychology. I would actually go back to support what Steve Gangestad said about behavioural ecology. I did an interesting exercise with my critical reading seminar at Michigan, where everyone had to bring in their very best example of why knowing that the mind was evolved told us something about how it works. And about half of the people brought in examples about specialization. The others said that this is one thing you can get from evolutionary perspective, but the larger thing you get is a behavioural ecological perspective on why organisms do what they do in general — how to parse their behavioural patterns in ways differently than has been done before. One of the things I'm looking at clinically is how people allocate their effort: what proportion of effort is this person putting into mating effort, parenting effort, somatic effort, to defensive effort and so on. This turns out to illuminate certain psychiatric cases quite brightly. It is not a perspective you think of, unless you take this broader evolutionary view.

Rutter: Would you like to give us a definition of what is extra about the concept of a module and what criteria you would apply to that?

Nesse: My best answer is the slide where I showed the six different criteria by which one could define structures of the brain modules. I don't think we have any automatic way of choosing one in preference to others. I would say, however, that if an organism encounters a new adaptive challenge that is unprecedented in its phylogenetic history, then in that circumstance you might expect a fairly discrete mechanism, anatomically and physiologically, to be shaped.

Whiten: The 'Swiss Army knife' model of the mind is being promoted by a small but high profile set of people who are identifying it with evolutionary psychology in the USA (e.g. Cosmides & Tooby 1999). I agree with the point you just made, that in fact an evolutionary perspective should not of itself lead us to choose between the possibility of tightly defined modules, specializations, and/or some general intelligence.

Part of the problem in defining modules is that people have used different criteria. Fodor (1983) used nine necessary criteria, but then Baron-Cohen (1994) required only six. You've essentially honed it down in this last discussion to one: the notion of a 'skin'. So we are back with another metaphor — a module is a specialization with a skin round it. What is that metaphor really getting at? If you have something which could have been a module with a skin around it, and you cut the skin away, what does that specialization then do that the module wouldn't?

Nesse: Humans are almost unable to communicate with each other without metaphors. In this case, the membrane could represent the anatomical divisions or it could represent the information boundary.

Karmiloff-Smith: One of the differences that I've found useful is that when people use the notion of a module, they mean that the environment is merely a trigger. By contrast the notion of domain-relevant mechanisms means that the child's processing of the environment actually contributes to the structure of the resulting module. To an extent, infants and children structure their own brains. You can have the notion of a module in a fully developed organism, but it's the result of a process of increasing modularization or specialization, so the environment actually plays a structural role.

Nesse: I'd like to bring us back to *g* for just a moment. There is a notion that there may be a mechanism in the brain specifically designed to facilitate goal pursuit, such as long-term goals that require pursuit of several levels of hierarchies of subgoals. For a long time I said that humans aren't that different from animals, but as soon as I started talking about goal pursuit, I realized that our behavioural regulation is considerably different from animals. Although animals do things that have several layers of goals, if it doesn't work, they have to go back to the first layer. They don't have the flexibility that we do to figure different ways of getting to a goal. I think this is one plausible notion for selective forces shaping a rapid development of increased intelligence. Goal pursuit may require different kinds of cognition. It also offers a selective force that could shape a generalized intelligence factor, in contrast to specific intelligence factors, if in fact this is the key to reproductive success.

Humphrey: But is foresight only available to humans? Surely some of the evidence of chimpanzees apparently hatching plans for mounting political coups would suggest that they know what they want to do in three weeks' time.

Whiten: From my experience — and I don't know of any published findings to the contrary — I wouldn't think that the horizon for chimps is *that* far ahead.

Suddendorf: Neither would I. I wrote a review of apes' capacity to think ahead (Suddendorf 1994, Suddendorf & Corballis 1997). From what I could find, there was no credible evidence that apes, or any other animal for that matter, could flexibly anticipate the remote future. The survey was consistent with the so-called Bischof–Köhler hypothesis which states that animals may not be able to anticipate future motivational states and are thus limited to a present that is defined by the current state of drive or need. So the ability to imagine future motivational states (perhaps akin to the ability to attribute such states to others — i.e., theory of mind) and the consequential impetus to concern oneself with the remote future, may have

een a rather recent evolutionary advance. An advance that I think would have
een crucial in catapulting humans to the position we are in today.

Miller: If you are right that long-term goal planning is fairly evolutionarily
cent, and that evolutionarily recent things that don't have much phylogenetic
recedent are going to depend on a lot of new genes coming into play, then
lanning ability seems like it should have relatively few correlations with other
nental capacities; it should have a relatively low g-loading. It seems important to
istinguish what we're calling general purpose intelligence from the g factor.

Mackintosh: I would have thought that on the contrary there's rather good
vidence that at least short-term planning is highly g-loaded. The ability to solve
ings like the Tower of Hanoi problem depends on working through the
onsequences of one's choices and then selecting the initial move that results in
ne attainment of the next subgoal. This is very highly g-loaded (Carpenter et al
990). It may have a long history, but if planning is a module, it is yet another
xample of your central message: that a module actually consists of many
ifferent mechanisms. There isn't a single 'planning mechanism': it depends on
ll sorts of different things. It depends on thinking about states of affairs that
ren't immediately present; it depends on holding a lot of things in working
nemory in order to solve subgoals, and then holding these subgoal solutions in
nind in order to put them together to solve longer-term goals.

Deary: This may be using the same word with a different meaning. Goal
ormation and implementation is some people's favourite explanation for g. I'm
hinking of John Duncan and his task (Duncan et al 1996), and Susan Embretson
1995) and her cognitive components. But the point I wanted to come to concerns
hat very evocative list you had of the possibilities for module division. At one
xtreme they look like sort of common-sense phrenological guesses, but on the
ther hand you mentioned things like a factor analysis of mRNA from the genes.
Ve recently heard Karl Friston in Edinburgh talk about doing functional magnetic
esonance imaging (fMRI) but using factor analysis-type examinations of the
ctivation/deactivation patterns, and going beyond that to sequential depend-
ncy of activation/deactivation patterns using neural networks (i.e. non-linear
nodelling). This is quite exciting: in these kinds of small slices of consciousness,
eeing which functional units are sequentially dependent on other metabolic units.
Dne candidate for temporary (!) modularity may be the metabolic patterns that are
equentially dependent on other metabolic patterns as we solve problems.

Rutter: Annette Karmiloff-Smith, do you want to say more about what you
nean by a module being something that is inbuilt and not affected by experience?
take it what you mean by this is not that experience can't shape its degree or its
ourse, but rather that its existence is independent of any specific experience, and
imilarly that its pattern is independent of any specific experience. Is that what
ou're saying?

Karmiloff-Smith: Theoretically, yes. I don't agree with the position held by people like Chomsky, Pinker and others. If they carry the notion through to its logical end, it must mean that a module is ready to operate once the relevant data come in, but that it's not affected by anything to do with the structure of that data. So it isn't just a mechanism relevant to processing certain types of information: it has representational content from the outset, like Chomsky's Universal Grammar. I have thought about this mainly with respect to language, but I think it also holds for discussions of face processing. Those who hold that there is a face-processing module will argue that the module simply requires faces for it to start operating, but that it's not affected by the progressive learning about faces during ontogeny. think ontogeny is very important, particularly for higher-level cognition. Our capacity to learn in infancy seems much greater than that of other species. Perhaps modular descriptions are suitable for those species' behaviour which are relatively inflexible and operate at birth, like the spider's web.

Harnad: I would like to make a historical comment about modularity. Historically, the mother of all modules is Chomsky's 'autonomy of syntax'. That is where it started. It wasn't one of the criteria for modularity. The only criterion that was needed was its functional autonomy — the fact that it could be treated in MIT linguistics by MIT linguists without having to worry about memory, storage capacity, speed and so on. It could be understood on its own terms. This is the only non-arbitrary criterion for modularity that there is: the rest of it is things we've tacked on.

Karmiloff-Smith: I actually found Fodor's criteria useful in order to understand what is being claimed when theorists talk of the modularity of the adult brain. He listed a number of criteria that are actually quite useful theoretically to sort the discussions out, even if one disagrees. Other discussions of modularity can be rather imprecise in comparison.

Harnad: I would say that Chomsky's notion of modularity was really data-driven. It was an observation that he made about syntactic competence and the mechanism it turned out to require in order to account for it (Universal Grammar). Fodor's were armchair-generated, and Chomsky prominently doesn't recognize them at all, I believe.

Karmiloff-Smith: Fodor's views have influenced developmental psychology enormously. Much of the work that we have heard cited here stems from taking his views very seriously.

References

Baron-Cohen S 1994 How to build a baby that can read minds: cognitive mechanisms in mindreading. Cah Psychol Cognit 13:513–552

Baron-Cohen S 1998 Modularity in developmental cognitive neuropsychology: evidence from autism and Gilles de la Tourette syndrome. In: Burack JA, Hodapp RM, Zigler E (eds)

Handbook of mental retardation and development. Cambridge University Press, Cambridge, p 334–348

arpenter PA, Just MA, Schell P 1990 What one intelligence test measures: a theoretical account of the processing in the Raven Progressive Matrices Test. Psychol Rev 97:404–431

oltheart M 1999 Modularity and cognition. Trends Cognit Sci 3:115–120

orballis MC 2000 Evolution of the generative mind. In: Sternberg RW (ed) The evolution of intelligence. In press

osmides L, Tooby J 1999 Evolutionary psychology. In: Wilson R, Keil F (eds) MIT encyclopedia of the cognitive sciences. MIT Press, Cambridge, MA, p 295–298

avis HL, Pratt C 1995 The development of children's theory of mind: the working memory explanation. Aust J Psychol 47:25–31

uncan J, Emslie H, Williams P 1996 Intelligence and the frontal lobe: the organisation of goal-directed behavior. Cognit Psychol 30:257–303

unn LM, Dunn L, Whetton C, Pintillie D 1982 British picture vocabulary scale. NFER-Nelson, London

mbretson SE 1995 The role of working memory capacity and general control processes in intelligence. Intelligence 20:169–189

odor JA 1983 The modularity of mind. MIT Press, Cambridge, MA

rye D, Zelazo PD, Burack JA 1998 Cognitive complexity and control: I. Theory of mind in typical and atypical development. Curr Dir Psychol Sci 7:116–121

ohnson MH 1993 Brain development and cognition. Blackwell, Oxford

armiloff-Smith A 1992 Beyond modularity: a developmental perspective on cognitive science. MIT Press, Cambridge, MA

armiloff-Smith A 1998 Development itself is the key to understanding developmental disorders. Trends Cognit Sci 2:389–398

awrence PA 1992 The making of a fly. Blackwell Scientific, London

eslie AM 1992 Pretence, autism and the theory-of-mind module. Curr Dir Psych Sci 1:18–21

aff RA 1996 The shape of life: genes, development and the evolution of animal form. University of Chicago Press, Chicago, IL

uddendorf T 1994 Discovery of the fourth dimension: mental time travel and human evolution. MSocSci thesis, University of Waikato, Hamilton, New Zealand

uddendorf T, Corballis MC 1997 Mental time travel and the evolution of the human mind. Genet Soc Gen Psych Monogr 123:133–167

uddendorf T, Fletcher-Flinn CM 1997 Theory of mind and the origins of divergent thinking. J Creat Behav 31:169–179

uddendorf T, Fletcher-Flinn CM 1999 Children's divergent thinking improves when they understand false beliefs. Creativ Res J 12:115–128

uddendorf T, Fletcher-Flinn CM, Johnston L 1999 Pantomime and theory of mind. J Genet Psych 160:31–45

aylor M, Carlson SM 1997 The relation between individual differences in fantasy and theory of mind. Child Dev 68:436–455

Vechsler D 1989 Wechsler preschool and primary scale of intelligence — revised. Harcourt Brace Jovanovich, San Antonio, CA

General discussion I

Rutter: In this final session we have the opportunity to go back over the whole day. Are there issues people would want to reintroduce or feel should be followed through?

Jensen: I would like to suggest a thinking exercise. Let us try to think about intelligence in terms that completely exclude the notions of variance, correlation and individual differences. If there is only one person in the universe, what could be discovered about intelligence from that one person? There would still be modules that could be detected in an individual, because some things may be learned so much more easily than other things that seem to have the same degree of complexity. You could still study learning and see improvement with practice. Then, if you are going to talk about *g*, you have got to hypothesize a number of people, so you can get at variance, correlations and factors. Then you will have to deal with other questions, as to the causes of these differences. They may have very little in common with these things that you've studied in the single individual. I think there's a big division in this field, that has to be kept in mind and to keep them separate, and I keep hearing these things becoming confused and mixed up throughout all the discussions.

Harnad: I'm curious what you would draw from that point as regards your own work. Is that distinction so important? If there was really only one person, you could get a complete understanding: you could reverse-engineer his or her intellect completely. What other questions are added on by having lots of people and having them vary? It is a brilliant point, but I don't understand why you don't consider that to be damning *g*.

Jensen: I don't think it is damning for *g*, because *g* is still an empirical phenomenon that needs to be explained, and it's a phenomenon related to these individual differences.

Harnad: Supposing we had one last athlete. We completely reverse-engineer his motor capacities. Then we say, 'Well we need more athletes if we are to understand what the *g* factor in athleticism is.' What would really be added by that? Supposing it all turned out to be muscle-belly size: we would need some variance in the muscle-belly size in order to get *g*.

Jensen: The most conspicuous thing about intelligence is the individual differences in intelligence.

Harnad: From the perspective of artificial intelligence, the most conspicuous thing about intelligence is all the remarkable things it can do. The variation in what it can do is just the fine tuning.

Nesse: The slide I showed of Cronbach's 1957 plea to combine studies of function with those of variation is about just this.

Harnad: We're not making a distinction. Let's just call it cognitive capacity. Cognitive capacity is remarkable for the capacity that it is — all that you can do. The variation in it is like the variation in muscle-belly — that's interesting too, and if we can cast some light on it through correlational and factor analytic studies, we should do so. But the primary goal is still to explain cognitive capacity itself, and not just how it differs from person to person.

Jensen: If muscle building and athleticism had the same social importance that intelligence does, there would be a lot of interest in individual differences in these things. There probably is in the field of athletics and sports. There can lie the difference between a person making a million dollars a year or a person who can't even get into the school football team.

Nesse: What I think is so interesting about *g* is that it doesn't have to be that way. In fact, from an evolutionary point of view you might expect there to be trade-offs — you might expect that those minds that are really good at numbers are not so good at verbal things, or those who are really good at quick response time are not as good at thinking through problems. Guess what: that's not true!

Jensen: But it is a popular notion. If you ask a lay person, they will say that Einstein might have been a great mathematical genius but he was probably an idiot at everything else.

Nesse: So it didn't have to come out this way and therefore there's something to explain. I did an quick study just before coming here. I went onto the web, and found in Australia all the decathalon results from 1987: this included the individual results for 27 different people on 10 different tasks. I then ran a factor analysis, and discovered a *g* factor, with just one exception of the 400 m race. The second factor seems to be an upper body factor, and the third and fourth factors have to do with speed and jumping.

Jensen: It is all uniqueness or specificity; you haven't got anything else in there that takes care of aerobic capacity, but if you had a few other things that required a lot of aerobic capacity they would form a common factor too.

Flynn: Arthur Jensen, your suggestion that we imagine an isolated individual, so as to grasp that intelligence measures differences *between* individuals, you actually published this notion years ago. In an article in 1976, you posited a Robinson Crusoe situation. In this you imagined a person isolated on an island, and you said that person would have the concept of memory because they would remember things. He or she would also have the concept of learning things. But only when Man Friday arrived, and you found that Friday was learning things a lot faster than you did, would the concept of intelligence be born. I noticed that intelligence has crept back into your vocabulary, despite having been banished in favour of *g*. I think it would be very hard to talk about that Robinson Crusoe situation without a synonym for intelligence. I think you're right that the concept of intelligence arises out of individual differences. Explaining how people learn or remember might not hold the key to individual differences while *g* would be highly relevant. On the other hand, understanding what causes individual differences between people may not provide a total solution as to what causes a rise in group intelligence. That could pose a very different problem.

Brody: I don't think it's a question of legitimacy. There are differing areas of research and people ask different questions. Some people study variations between individuals, some people want to study different processes. The interesting scientific issue is to what extent is the general knowledge of the mind which we construct connected to individual differences? If you go back to the 1970s, Hunt et al (1975) published one of the first studies that revived the notion that you can study individual differences in intelligence by looking at individual differences in fundamental cognitive processes. They looked at differences between the time taken to decide that capital 'A' and small 'a' is the same semantic as opposed to physical identity. They assumed that this difference is related to intelligence, as indeed it was. They were looking at a cognitive parameter that was of interest to cognitive psychologists studying verbal processing. But if you go back and look at the data, what predicts intelligence best is not the parameter that is of interest to the cognitive experimental psychologists, but instead the average time taken to judge, irrespective of whether the judgement is a physical or a name judgement. This is a much better predictor of verbal ability. And I think this is paradigmatic of a fundamental problem that has emerged in the field. Namely, those parameters that are of greatest interest to the cognitive experimental psychologists trying to understand intelligence, turned out not to be the parameters that are most predictive from the point of view of individual differences. When we have a better understanding of the functions of the mind, will those theories help us to understand individual differences and vice versa? Or are these fields in some way going to exist on somewhat different tracks?

Harnad: I agree with the way you put it. Is the understanding of language capacity going to cast some light on individual differences in verbal performance? And a more vexed question: are individual differences in verbal performance going to cast any light on the nature of language capacity? I want to pick one prominent example. With Universal Grammar, we all have our own prejudices: let's set them aside, and pretend that the consensus in linguistics is correct. Universal Grammar is an organ that has been sculpted out theoretically by MIT linguists. It is something that we all have, we all share, and it doesn't vary appreciably. It is our 'grammatical competence'. If the autonomy of syntax is the mother of all modularity, then competence' (in the original competence–performance distinction) is the mother of all cognitive capacities. There is a case in which a completely unvarying capacity was understood on its own terms. Is there a sense in which if it had varied — if there were people who had higher or lower Universal Grammar capacity — we would have had some light cast on the enterprise? I don't see it, theoretically. The case is analogous with this hypothetical entity *g*.

Flynn: To get back to the analogy Arthur Jensen drew, if you imagine an individual, that individual could have a concept of wealth. But there could be no concept of socioeconomic status without a second individual. Moreover, unravelling what allows one individual to get ahead of another in terms of socioeconomic status would not necessarily tell you what would raise the communal wealth, unless of course you believe in the invisible hand. If you believe in the invisible hand, then what was good for the individual would be eventually good for the community, but that may not be true.

Miller: It seems that there are two distinct ways that the study of individual differences could inform the study of the species-typical cognitive architecture. First, it's probably impossible to understand even one individual's mechanisms of social judgement and social inference without having an idea of the dimensions of variation between people with respect to which any individual has to make judgements. If we want to choose a sexual partner or trading partner, or discriminate in hiring an employee, we need a rich set of cognitive inference procedures which are presumably going to be tuned to the typical distributions and covariances that exist within our species with respect to mental, physical and social traits. I don't think we will be able to understand the social judgement mechanisms without studying individual differences in psychology. A second tack is to say that we have the *g* factor, and we have a bunch of group factors (verbal, spatial, etc.): do those group factors now fall into any aspects of the cognitive architecture? There, I am not so sure that there is a very close fit.

Houle: As an evolutionary biologist, I think there is an explicit connection between variation and the state of a population. Variation is how you got where you are now. You can't think about evolution without thinking about variation. This is a separate issue from Geoffrey's point, which is saying that making inferences about variation is part of what mental architecture must be about.

Harnad: Variation and individual differences are not quite the same thing. They can swing together and they can swing apart. Variation is a much more general concept than individual differences. Individual differences are a particular kind of variation. It would of course be heretical and absurd to deny variation in evolutionary biology, but we are now talking about *current* individual variance in traits.

Houle: I don't see what you are getting at.

Harnad: The original variance on a particular fixed trait could have vanished, a in the case of Universal Grammar, where it has been fixed and there is no more variation. Variation is essential for evolution, but current Gaussian distribution in traits are not the only example of variation. Is this point obscure to people?

Rutter: You've certainly lost some of us. You are saying variation is different from individual differences, because individual differences are levels on a trait What is variation then?

Harnad: David Houle made an appeal to the importance of the consequent variation for any evolutionary thinking. I didn't deny that. What I said was that in a particular case of variation, namely, *current* individual differences in traits, my points about the relevance of that current variation to the understanding of the trait itself are not a reflection of the importance or non-importance of ancestral variation in evolution.

Rutter: Is this a difference in time frame or content? Evolution has to be in relation to what happened in the past.

Harnad: In the case of Universal Grammar, for example, if the story is true, something happened in the past based presumably on genetic variation in grammatical capacity that advantaged those who had it and disadvantaged those who lacked it. But today it is as invariant as bipedality in our species.

Hinde: Based on individual differences in the past.

Harnad: Based on variation at some point.

Hinde: But what is the difference from saying individual differences?

Harnad: Don't we also have founder effects in which we have some mutation and then the thing gets fixed? It is not that you are dealing with a Gaussian distribution.

Hinde: It is a founder effect because of individual differences.

Harnad: Historical individual differences versus extant individual differences.

Houle: If it is true, as Randy Nesse has been saying, that the only way you can understand the function of the brain is by understanding the evolution of the brain, variation becomes absolutely essential for understanding the nature of the brain.

Nesse: I'm not sure this will help, but recently I found it helpful to realize that natural selection is mostly keeping things the same: it's constantly weeding out things that keep you away from that modal spot, which is very helpful. Likewise, many people have a misunderstanding that we have to show variance in a trait to show that it is a product of natural selection. There are many traits that are narrowly bounded because they're functionally so important.

Harnad: I can put it as a much simpler methodological point, about current, extant creatures. You have an ability, and you have the causal mechanism that underlies it. Then you have current variation in that, on the basis of which you can do this individual difference testing, analyse the correlations, and come up with a g factor, some of it genetic and some non-genetic. The methodological question is, is that current variation casting any functional light on the nature of the underlying causal mechanism entity in question—light that wouldn't be cast if you only had one example (as in Arthur Jensen's hypothetical example)?

Reference

Hunt E, Lunneborg C, Lewis J 1975 What does it mean to be high verbal? Cognit Psychol 7:194–227

g and the one–many problem: is one enough?

Nathan Brody

Department of Psychology, Wesleyan University, Middletown, CT 06459, USA

Abstract. No one believes that *g* is the only construct needed to describe individual differences in intelligence. Many believe that *g* is a dispensable construct. Others object to what they construe as its hegemonic position in the domain of intelligence. In this paper I defend the hegemonic status of *g* by a brief consideration of diverse criticisms of the construct. I argue that *g* is a heritable component of intelligence that accounts for approximately 50% of the covariance among diverse measures of intelligence. It derives from a core information processing ability and it influences a diverse set of social outcomes. The covariances between *g* and information processing ability and social outcomes are, in large measure, attributable to common genetic influences.

2000 The nature of intelligence. Wiley, Chichester (Novartis Foundation Symposium 233, p 122–135

Psychometric and measurement issues

The *g* construct has been criticized by researchers who are committed to the multivariate analysis of psychometric indices and by researchers who believe that existing psychometric indices fail to encompass important dimensions of intelligence. I shall briefly consider both kinds of criticisms.

Factor analytic issues

Carroll's (1993) comprehensive reanalysis of the psychometric literature led to the development of a three-stratum hierarchical model in which *g* occupies a singular stratum at the apex of the hierarchy accounting for approximately 50% of the covariance among diverse measures of intellect. Carroll's synthesis of the factor analytic literature is subject to two related criticisms. Horn (2000) noted that the *g* factor is not invariant in several different studies and thus cannot constitute a well-defined theoretical construct. Gustafsson (1999) noted that Carroll used exploratory rather than confirmatory factor analyses. Gustafsson's confirmatory factor analyses led to the conclusion that *g* is identical with fluid ability (*gf*) and that there is no need to hypothesize an independent *g* factor.

Carroll and his critics agree that *gf* is a well-defined second stratum ability that ccounts for more of the covariance in the matrix of abilities than any other neasure. There are several sources of evidence that support Carroll's dentification of a separate *g* factor. *gf* is not independent of other higher-order bilities. *gf* and crystallized ability (*gc*), the second stratum ability that is most learly identified, are usually found to have correlations in excess of 0.5, upporting the idea of some common component, *g*, that is related to both of hese components. Carroll (1997) performed confirmatory factor analyses of hree of the correlation matrices included in the corpus of studies he subjected to xploratory factor analyses. In each instance his analysis led to a satisfactory fit for a nodel that postulated an independent *g* factor. Omission of *g* in each instance led to ess satisfactory fit to the data. In addition, in one of his analyses he found a test vhose loading was solely on *g* and in another analysis he found tests that loaded on he *gf* factor whose loading on the orthogonalized *g* factor was higher than their oading on the *gf* factor. These analyses indicate that Carroll's model is supported oy appropriate confirmatory analyses.

Sternberg's triarchic theory

Sternberg (1988) proposes to replace *g* with a triarchic theory of intelligence that issumes that there are three independent forms of intelligence — analytic ability, creative ability and practical ability. He argues that current tests focus on analytic ibility and do not measure the other two triarchic abilities.

Sternberg designed a triarchic abilities test (STAT). Sternberg et al (1996) idministered STAT to a sample of high school students chosen to participate in a program for gifted students who took a summer school college level psychology course. Sternberg assumes that the triarchic abilities are independent of each other ind that *g* relates primarily to analytic ability. Sternberg and colleagues obtained correlations between a briefly administered test of *g*, the Cattell Culture Fair test of ntelligence, and the three triarchic abilities of 0.50 for analytic intelligence, 0.55 for creative intelligence and 0.32 for practical intelligence. Neither the Cattell test nor he STAT are highly reliable. Correcting the obtained correlations for unreliability yields correlations between the Cattell and the STAT measures of 0.74, 0.85 and).56 for the analytic, creative and practical measures, respectively. These corrected disattenuated correlations underestimate the true relationship existing among these measures. The sample from which the correlations derive probably includes few, if any, individuals whose IQs are below the mean. The restriction in range of talent of the students taking the STAT would reduce the value of the disattenuated correlations.

The STAT measures are related to each other. The correlations among these measures range from 0.38–0.49, and the disattenuated correlations range from

0.64–0.78. Thus triarchic abilities are not independent of each other. And, a indicated above, corrections for range of talent would increase the value of thes disattenuated correlations.

Sternberg and colleagues assessed analytic, creative, and practical academi achievements. The measures of academic achievements were positively correlate with each other (average $r=0.72$, disattenuated average $r=0.84$). They found tha different facets of ability measured by STAT were not differentially predictive o academic achievements. They also found that analytic ability correlated with a overall index of performance 0.42 (disattenuated $r=0.56$) indicating that analyti ability is related to academic achievement even when that achievement is defined i terms of the expanded repertoire postulated by Sternberg's triarchic theory.

The Sternberg et al study provides little or no evidence suggesting that g i predominantly a measure of analytic ability that does not encompass creative an practical ability.

Elementary information processing

There is a large literature relating psychometric indices of g to relatively simpl information processing tasks. These data may be interpreted in tw contradictory ways. (1) There is a singular basic ability to process informatio that is related to g. (2) g arises from the interaction of several distinct elementar information processing abilities (see e.g. Detterman 1994, 1999). Studies of infan information processing abilities and some recent multivariate analyses provid support for the former interpretation.

Infant research

Sensory discrimination abilities manifest in the first year of life are related to th development of intelligence. Colombo (1993) summarized the literature relating measures of habituation and novelty preference to later intellectual abilities. Fixation times in habituation paradigms may be interpreted as an index of th speed of encoding features of the stimulus array (see Colombo 1993, Sokolo 1969). Fixation duration measures obtained from infants varying in age from newborn to six months have been correlated with IQ test scores for these children when they varied in age from 4 to 8 years. The correlations ranged from -0.29 to -0.63 (see Colombo 1993, Table 2.4). One study reported a correlation o -0.50 from an assessment of infant fixation times at age 11 months that wa correlated with IQ at age 11 years (Rose & Feldman 1995, J. F. Feldman, personal communication).

Infant performance on a test of novelty preference has also been related to late intellectual ability. In these studies attention to a novel visual stimulus is measure

1 paired comparison trials with a familiar stimulus. Measures of novelty preference btained between 3 and 7 months of age correlate with IQ obtained at ages varying etween 3 and 7 years, with values varying from 0.32 to 0.66 (see Colombo 1993, able 2.7).

Novelty preference and fixation duration have test–retest reliabilities of 0.46 and .54, respectively. The correlation between these measures in six different studies vas −0.46. This correlation has a disattenuated value of 0.92. The disattenuated orrelations between the infant measures and early childhood IQ are −0.77 (for the ixation time measure) and 0.83 (for the novelty preference measure). These lisattenuated correlations imply that the two infant measures are indices of the ame underlying processes and that these processes are substantially related to the ubsequent development of intelligence. There is continuity between the information processing abilities of infants and individual differences in intelligence.

What accounts for the relationships between infant measures and later IQ? Complex cognitive skills assessed by intelligence tests cannot be causally related o infant information processing abilities present in the first several months of ife. Short fixation times in a habituation study may be taken as an index of the apidity with which an individual is able to encode information about the timulus. Preference for novelty, an index that is highly related to duration of ixation time, may be dependent on the speed of encoding characteristics of a amiliar stimulus. Rapid encoding of the stimulus may contribute to the ability to pprehend the characteristics of a familiar stimulus and to discriminate between it nd a similar stimulus. Thus discrimination may be a byproduct of rapid encoding of stimuli. While it is impossible on the basis of current knowledge to construct a heory of the ways in which ability to rapidly encode features of stimuli might ontribute to the development of complex intellectual ability, there are some ninimal inferences that are plausible. The ability to encode stimulus information apidly leading to the ability to discriminate between stimuli might lead to the levelopment of more complex analogical abilities that are markers for gf. The mount of information possessed about a stimulus and its varied characteristics night relate to the ability to apprehend relationships between stimuli and to olve analogies based on relationships between stimuli. More complete encoding nd more accurate representations of the feature of stimuli might contribute to the levelopment of memory skills. Information about the characteristics of stimuli nay relate to the ability to relate one stimulus to another permitting the superior ecall of information that is organized into coherent units.

Sensory discrimination and g

Inspection time measures are thresholds for the minimal amount of time required o discriminate between two stimuli that differ on a single dimension, such as line length. Inspection time measures are inversely related to measures of intelligence (Deary & Stough 1996). Deary and colleagues administered tests of intelligence and three tests of the ability to discriminate between stimuli to their subjects (Deary 1999, Deary et al 1997). In addition to a visual inspection time task they presented subjects with a stimulus containing an array of 49 rectangles in a 10×10 matrix. After a variable inspection time for the array, a new rectangle is added and subjects are required to indicate which of the rectangles was the new one. In a second version of this task one of the original 49 rectangles changes its location. The subject is required to note the rectangle that changed. A threshold is obtained for the minimal stimulus onset asynchrony (SOA) required to accurately judge the rectangle that was added or the rectangle that moved. Deary used a latent trait model fitting analysis to ascertain the relationship between the visual discrimination tasks and measures of intelligence. He found that the latent trait measured by the three discrimination tests had a correlation of 0.46 with intelligence and a correlation of 0.66 with non-verbal intelligence. The covariance between each of the three stimulus discrimination tasks and measures of intelligence was completely overlapping. The three discrimination tasks appear to have methodologically distinct requirements. The tasks involving the presentation of an initial array of 49 rectangles require an individual to maintain diffuse attention in order to notice a change in a relatively complex array. By contrast, the classic inspection time task involves focused attention on a relatively simple stimulus. All of the tasks share the common feature of requiring the ability to rapidly process information involving stimulus discriminations.

Deary (1999) reported the results of a similar analysis of auditory discrimination tasks. He administered three tests of auditory discrimination ability and three tests of intelligence — the Cattell Culture Fair, the Raven and the Mill Hill Vocabulary — to a group of adolescents. The auditory discrimination tests included the Seashore pitch discrimination test, a pitch discrimination task for stimuli presented for 20 ms, and an auditory inspection time task involving a threshold for the minimal exposure required to accurately discriminate between tones clearly varying in pitch. Deary (1999) was able to fit a model to these data that indicated that the three auditory measures defined a single latent trait and the three intelligence measures defined a single latent trait. The correlation between the latent traits was 0.64. Model fits were degraded for a model that assumed there was only a single latent trait suggesting that g and auditory discrimination ability are related but should not be construed as being defined by a single latent trait.

Deary's studies indicate that there is a core ability to process information rapidly permitting an individual to discriminate between stimuli that is substantially related to measures of intelligence — particularly to measures of non-verbal intelligence. Deary's studies do not examine the panoply of potential discrimination measures that are related to intelligence. Auditory and visual spection time tasks and pitch discrimination tasks are not included in a common nalysis. Whether a latent trait analysis would indicate a common discrimination oility that is substantially related to *g* for this expanded array cannot be ascertained om the available literature. It is also the case that the two studies conducted by eary and his colleagues, as well as the infant studies, are compatible with a theory nat assumes that a singular *g* construct derives from a singular ability to rapidly ncode features of stimuli leading to an ability to discriminate differences between imuli.

ehavioural genetic analyses

ehavioural genetic analyses provide support for a theory that assumes that the nitary structure of *g* derives from the influence of genotypes on phenotypic nanifestations of *g*. Four different kinds of analyses are relevant.

1) Heritability of g vectors. From a psychometric perspective *g* may be defined by ctor loadings. Pedersen et al (1992) administered a battery of tests to a sample f older monozygotic and dizygotic twins reared together and apart. They found nat the vector defining the *g*-loadings of the tests was correlated 0.77 with the ndependently ascertained vector defining the heritabilities of the tests. These esults imply that there is an isomorphic relationship between the psychometric tructure of *g* and the influence of genes on tests that define that structure.

2) Relationships among tests. The *g* construct derives from the finding that tests of ntellectual ability form a positive manifold. Petrill et al (1998) analysed ovariances among tests of ability for three different twin samples. Their genetic ovariance analyses indicated that covariances among tests of ability were primarily ttributable to common genetic influences rather than to environmental nfluences. These results provide additional support for the isomorphic elationship between the psychometric phenotypic manifestations of the *g* onstruct and the influence of genes on the phenotypic manifestation of the tructure of relationships among tests.

3) Covariances between psychometric and elementary information processing measures. Neubauer t al (2000) analysed relationships between two elementary information rocessing measures (a Sternberg memory scanning test and a Posner letter natching task) and intelligence for a relatively large sample of twins. They found hat approximately two-thirds of the phenotypic relationship between elementary nformation processing measures and psychometric measures was attributable to ommon genetic influences. These results indicate that psychometric indices of *g* and elementary information processing correlates of g derive from commo genetic influences.

(4) Social outcomes. It is well known that g is related to important socially relevar outcomes such as educational attainments, intergenerational occupation mobility and income. Rowe et al (1999) analysed relationships between g an educational attainments and income for a large sample of siblings. They foun that common genetic influences accounted for approximately two-thirds of th covariance between g and income and educational attainments.

The behavioural genetic analyses indicate that the nomological network of law and relationships that triangulate the meaning of the g construct in its logical spac is related to genetic influences. g-loadings, covariances among diverse tests c ability, relationships between g and elementary information processing abilitie and relationships between g and socially relevant outcomes are all related t common genetic influences.

Conclusion

Psychometric, experimental, behavioural genetic and sociologically oriente research may be construed as supporting a hegemonic position for g. g is th essential construct in the domain of intellect.

References

Carroll JB 1993 Human cognitive abilities. Cambridge University Press, Cambridge

Carroll JB 1997 Theoretical and technical issues in identifying a factor of general intelligence. Ir Devlin B, Fienberg SE, Resnick DP, Roeder K (eds) Intelligence, genes and success. Springe Verlag, New York, p 125–156

Colombo J 1993 Infant cognition. Sage, Newbury Park, CA

Deary IJ 1999 Intelligence and visual and auditory information processing. In: Ackerman PI Kyllonen PC, Roberts RD (eds) Learning and individual differences: process, trait, an content determinants. American Psychological Association, Washington, DC, p 111–134

Deary IJ, Stough C 1996 Intelligence and inspection time: achievements, prospects, an problems. Amer Psychol 51:599–608

Deary IJ, McCrimmon RJ, Bradshaw J 1997 Visual information processing and intelligenc Intelligence 24:461–479

Detterman DK 1994 A system theory of intelligence. In: Detterman DK (ed) Current topics i human intelligence, vol 4: Theories of intelligence. Ablex, Norwood, p 85–115

Detterman DK 1999 The psychology of mental retardation. Int Rev Psychiatry 11:26–33

Gustafsson J-E 1999 Measuring and understanding g: experimental and correlation approaches. In: Ackerman PL, Kyllonen PC, Roberts RD (eds) Learning and individu differences: process, trait, and content determinants. American Psychological Associatior Washington, DC, p 275–292

orn JL 2000 A basis for research on age differences in cognitive abilities. In: McCardle JJ, Woodcock RW (eds) Human cognitive abilities in theory and practice. Riverside, Chicago, IL, in press

ubauer AC, Spinath FM, Riemann R, Borkenau P, Angleitner AA 2000 Genetic and environmental influences on two measures of speed of information processing and their relation to psychometric intelligence: evidence from the German Observational Study of Adult Twins. Intelligence, in press

dersen NL, Plomin R, Nesselroade JR, McClearn GE 1992 A quantitative genetic analysis of cognitive abilities during the second half of the life-span. Psychol Sci 3:346–352

trill SA, Plomin R, Berg S et al 1998 The genetic and environmental relationship between general and specific cognitive abilities in twins 80 years and older. Psychol Sci 9:183–189

ose S, Feldman J 1995 Prediction of IQ and specific cognitive abilities at age 11 from infancy measures. Develop Psychol 31:685–696

owe DC, Vesterdal WJ, Rodgers JL 1999 Herrnstein's syllogism: genetic and shared environmental influences on IQ, education, and income. Intelligence 26:1–19

kolov YN 1969 Perception and the conditioned reflex. Macmillan, New York

ernberg RJ 1988 The triarchic mind: a new theory of intelligence. Viking, New York

ernberg RJ, Ferrari M, Clinkenbeard P, Grigorenko EL 1996 Identification, instruction, and assessment of gifted children: a construct validation of a triarchic model. Gift Child Quart 40:129–137

ISCUSSION

Hinde: I have an extremely naïve question, just to set my mind at rest — I am sure will just be brushed aside. We have heard a lot about how the different sorts of telligence all latch onto *g*. Yet I know so many mathematicians who are almost literate, and so many literary people who are just about innumerate. Do you ever ook at the distributions of these things? Do you ever do categorical analysis? All e hear about is correlation coefficients — Pearson's and Spearman's — and orrelation coefficients are so misleading unless you categorize and eyeball your ata.

Brody: For variables that are continuously distributed, we're much better off ooking at correlations. I would certainly not dismiss the notion that there are any special abilities: those of us who believe in *g* would never deny that. David ubinski has done wonderful work dealing with people who have very special ighly developed skills in spatial and mechanical abilities, indicating that these eople are often overlooked within formal education. Some of these people do ery well in things like lab work. When you are talking about your initial xample of mathematicians who are considered illiterate, I think that may be isleading. They may be illiterate relative to somebody who is a poet, but they re not illiterate relative to the general population. For example, they may be our standard deviations above the mean in mathematical ability, but only one andard deviation above the mean in verbal ability. We all have specialized bilities: I can't walk around the corner without getting lost — I think I must be e one exception to the rule that there is such a thing as *g*!

Hinde: I accept all that, and to be honest I've heard it before. But you haven answered my question: do you ever eyeball the data? It is shown clearly in studies temperament, for example, that if you categorize the data and look at the extrem separately you get quite different relations (Hinde 1997, Kagan 1994).

Brody: David Lubinski could answer that.

Lubinski: I have an article under review now (Lubinski et al 2000), looking subjects that were genotyped last year in the first genetic marker study of gene intelligence (Chorney et al 1998). These profiles are based on kids who were the t one in 10 000 in either mathematical reasoning or verbal ability. We had 3. subjects who we arbitrarily categorized in three groups. One was called the hig flat group, and they had verbal and quantitative reasoning abilities within o standard deviation of each other. Then we had two tilted profiles: a high verb group whose verbal ability was one standard deviation beyond their math matical reasoning ability, and a high mathematical group whose quantitative scor were one standard deviation beyond their verbal scores. The proportion doctorates among this group was 50 times base rate expectations: half of the people either had law degrees, MDs or PhDs. But if you look at the specific area the high verbal group were in law and philosophy, the high maths were in th physical sciences and mathematics, and the high flat group were intermediate distributed. We therefore got very different outcomes as a function of nich picking. When we add educational and vocational preferences, we can make eve better predictions (Achter et al 1999).

Mackintosh: The infant habituation studies are clearly important in that the correlate highly with much later IQ. However, you suggested that what infa habituation measures were quantifying was speed of encoding and thus speed discrimination, which was the same process underlying later performance o inspection time tasks. As I have argued elsewhere (Mackintosh 1998) that seem plausible. But if it is true, then you haven't got anything that greatly illuminates th nature of *g*, because inspection time doesn't correlate well with *g*.

Brody: I know the study you are referring to, and I don't think it is a definiti analysis (Crawford et al 1998). They used the Wechsler test. The *g* factor that yo get out of the Wechsler tends to be crystallized. All the research on inspection tim shows it's more predictive of non-verbal intelligence. I think if you had broader *g*, or a *g* that reflected more *gf*, you would get a very different resul The other problem with that study is that it used only a single inspection tim measure. In order to answer this question definitively, if a battery of inspectio time tasks were to be combined with a diverse battery of psychometr measures, this would permit the extraction of a core discrimination trait tha would have a very high correlation with a *g* factor derived over a broad rang of tests. While I think Ian's study that you're citing goes against the analysis, don't think it's definitive.

Mackintosh: I'm aware that it is unfair to cite unpublishable data, but we have one a study ourselves in which we give various marker IQ tests for verbal ability, uid intelligence and perceptual speed, and inspection time correlates with erceptual speed but not with the other two characteristics. When you do the artial correlations, the correlation of inspection time with Raven's is entirely ttributable to its correlation with measures of perceptual speed and nothing else. 1uch the same conclusion is also suggested by the recent study of Burns et al 1999).

Brody: You may be right. I think we need a large-scale study, where you have a ange of cognitive tasks.

Deary: It is a brave or naïve man who will throw an epithet like perceptual speed t a psychometric test, and thereby think that he is measuring it. Nathan Brody, ith regard to the interpretation you put on our work on the latent trait analysis of number of different information processing tasks (Deary et al 1997), I don't want ny sort of disagreement between us to be exaggerated. I see the main job of that tudy as expelling some doubts about why the correlation between inspection time nd psychometric intelligence exists. The main force against a reductionistic nterpretation has been that the correlation occurs because of idiosyncrasies in the ask. Once one puts together a number of diverse tasks, and boils down a latent rait, that to some extent rests one's mind and gives us a licence to then go on and ook at some lower level things, like doing more psychophysiology on the nspection time task and exploring it further. It is not that I'm unhopeful about t, I just don't think you can stop there and say we now know what our underlying construct is. It simply gives you a licence for more work and a wee bit f optimism. I would halt you if you said that you then knew that it was processing peed: I think that's been the problem in this area — that we have stopped too early nd rested on some knowledge that we don't have.

Brody: I think the problem is largely that people try to take a task like inspection ime and begin to decompose it, pointing out its complexity and the variety of potential influences and confounds which go into performance. My point is that he strategy of cutting across the tasks to extract the latent trait forces you to think nuch more broadly about the meaning of that latent trait. What impressed me in our study was that the covariance between each of your independent measures of nformation processing in *g* was completely overlapping, despite the fact that they ad some degree of difference in their methodological requirements. If you look at single measure, you may always be getting correlations for all sorts of things that re idiosyncratic to that measure. As you measure more broadly and try to extract he common core, you then have to face what is it that is in common across the core hat might in fact be accounting for some more general construct.

Deary: That was the rationale for our study. Can I mention the Bielefeld study of wins that you talked about (Neubauer et al 2000)? I know it has not been published yet, but I have seen it too. I agree that if one takes the elements of the Sternberg an Posner tasks, their correlations with psychometric abilities are mediated by geneti effects. How much does that tell you? Well, it tells you as much as we know abou how valid the decomposition of the Sternberg and Posner tasks are. Yo mentioned a couple of times the phrase 'elementary information processing'. would dispute that. It is well known that the theoretically interesting aspects o both of these tasks — the slope in the case of the Sternberg task, and the NI-P difference in the case of the Posner task — do not have a special correlation with psychometric ability (Neubauer 1997, Lohman 1994, 1999). This leaves one with the intercept parameters, which are these sort of globules of mess: we don't know what they are, and they weren't the reasons the tasks were picked up by differentia psychologists in the first place. To what extent do you think you can defend th claim that we've learned anything about the elementary processing bases o psychometric intelligence?

Brody: In the literature there are only three studies in which anybody has looke at an elementary information processing task and its correlation with genera intelligence, and have then done a genetic covariance analysis (Ho et al 1988 Vernon 1983, F. M. Spinath, A. C. Neubauer, R. Riemann, P. Borkenau & A Angleitner, unpublished paper, 9th Bienn Meet Int Soc Stud Individ Differ 1999). All of them show substantial genetic mediation of that relationship. Bu the problem with all three of the studies is that in no case have the elementar information processing tasks used been those I would take to be most importan in trying to understand the relationship between *g* and some parameters o information processing. We do need a much better study. The right way to do the study is to get a core ability that extends across a variety of elementar information processing tasks, and then look at the genetic covariance analysis. agree that we don't have a good behaviour genetics study using the best of th information processing tasks. This needs to be done.

Rutter: Following through on Robert Hinde's earlier query, let me put this slightly different way. It seems indisputable that in the population as a whole abilities of one kind tend to intercorrelate with abilities of other kinds. I have n problem with calling that *g*: it functions in a way that you and others have describec during this meeting. What I'm not quite so sure about is what that tells us about th nature of intelligence. Here, the exceptions seem to me to be the area of interest. It i true that if you look at people who have unusual talents in the general population you get the sort of cohesive picture that you describe. But there are idiot savant who are quite different, and they are not that rare. In our own study of autisti individuals, when unusual skills were defined psychometrically, requiring tha the special skill should be at least one standard deviation above the genera population mean and at least two standard deviations above the person's own mean across cognitive tests, about 10% of autistic individuals showed a specia

kill: that's a non-trivial number. Similarly, in studies of cognitive processes, one of the ways in which leverage has been exerted to pull apart different cognitive functions has been to investigate individuals with brain injuries or medical conditions that have a differential impact on cognitive skills, with some affected and others not. It is easy using these strategies to find special skills and to show that they can function in ways that are independent of g. The question is, what does this tell us about the overall understanding of the nature of intelligence?

Brody: From a pragmatic point of view, I think they are different questions. There is an example I often use with my students. They all take the SAT, so they now they have an SAT quantitative score and an SAT verbal score. I say to them, 'Look, we can do two things: we can get an average score. We could also say that a person is better in one of these two categories, and that tells us something about the kinds of courses he or she is likely to take.' I don't see where the study of one means that you shouldn't study the other, or that one is more legitimate than the other: it's different focal point. In the field of intelligence, we have the problem of understanding why there are these covariances, and trying to understand what implications they have for our understanding of individual differences. At the same time, that doesn't exhaust our understanding of individual differences in intellectual abilities, or as David Lubinski pointed out (correctly), it does not help us to understand the ways in which people use their abilities in everyday life. Many of us who are interested in general intelligence are great fans of the work of Phil Ackerman, who has large-scale studies that include interests, personality and cognitive abilities.

Maynard Smith: I wanted to raise the same question that Michael Rutter has just raised. I'm speaking completely as an outsider, but something that has always puzzled me about 'intelligence' is the range in ability. Compare the individual differences in intelligence with individual differences in the ability to run 100 metres. If the fastest people in the world can run 100 metres in about 10 seconds, I guess that almost all of us when we were young and healthy could do it in 20 seconds, and nobody could do it in 5 seconds. The range of variability is sensible. Yet, there are people out there who can factorize six figure numbers in their head quickly — I'm not stupid mathematically, but I can't. I have a job with four figure numbers. And there are other people with different skills. The reason this is puzzling to me is that it says that you can have a brain which will do the equivalent of running a hundred metres in 5 seconds, without as far as I can see necessarily paying a great price in some other trait. In other words, the brain can do particular tasks enormously better than it does without paying a big price. So why doesn't it?

Jensen: One thing we must realize about g is that it acts as a threshold variable for creativity or super-performance in many other fields. You don't find any outstanding musicians with low g. You may find idiot savants who can play the piano by ear, and numerical savants who can calculate the cube root of a 200 digit number in their heads, but they don't become outstanding musicians or mathematicians. There are two Nobel prize winners who didn't make the Terman gifted class (i.e. IQ above 140), but their IQs were in the high 130s, and as children they were mathematical prodigies.

Pomiankowski: A comment on John Maynard Smith's point. In my own work, am studying flies with big eyespans, and I'm interested in how this character affect their choice by females. I'm worried about size. Bigger flies are more active, but I'm interested in eyespan, so I have to create a set of flies in my experiments which are all standardized for size. Size is a general property and everything else scales with it just as *g* is a general property that scales all the different specific attributes. John' question is really asking about these specific attributes.

Lubinski: With respect to size, 50% of the common variance in cognitive tests is *g*, and that's where the size comes from (Lubinski 2000). There are other domains of individual differences, such as personality, and educational and vocational interests, that don't structure hierarchically (Lubinski 2000). There are no general factors, but there are a number of clusterings: vocational interest has 6, some people say personality has 5 or 7, but there's not a hierarchy. The reason *g* gets most of the attention is because it has the biggest, broadest and deepest social correlates: these include educational credentials, income and rate of learning These other group factors that are under it do account for additional variance and are very helpful in terms of niche picking in the kind of environmental ecology people seek out and strive to stay into. But they don't account for as much variance as *g*.

References

Achter JA, Lubinski D, Benbow CP, Sanjani H 1999 Assessing vocational preferences among gifted adolescents adds incremental validity to abilities: a discriminant analysis of educational outcomes over a 10-year interval. J Educ Psychol 91:777–786

Burns NR, Nettlbeck T, Cooper CJ 1999 Inspection time correlates with general speed of processing but not with fluid ability. Intelligence 27:37–44

Chorney MJ, Chorney K, Seese N et al 1998 A quantitative trait locus (QTL) associated with cognitive ability in children. Psychol Sci 9:159–166

Crawford JR, Deary IJ, Allan KM, Gustaffson J-E 1998 Evaluating competing models of the relationship between inspection time and psychometric intelligence. Intelligence 26:27–42

Deary IJ, McCrimmon RJ, Bradshaw J 1997 Visual information processing and intelligence Intelligence 24:461–479

Hinde RA 1997 Through caegories towards individuals: attempting to tease apart the data. In Cairns RB, Bergman LR, Kagan J (eds) Methods and models for studying the individual Sage, Thousand Oaks, CA, p 11–32

Ho HZ, Baker L, Decker SN 1988 Covariation between intelligence and speed of information processing: genetic and environmental influences. Behav Genet 18:247–261

Kagan J 1994 Galen's prophesy: temperament in human nature. Basic Books, New York

Lohman DF 1994 Component scores as residual variation (or why the intercept correlates best). Intelligence 19:1–11

Lohman DF 1999 Minding our p's and q's: on finding relationships between learning and intelligence. In: Ackerman PL, Kyllonen PC, Roberts RD (eds) Learning and individual differences: process, trait, and content determinants. American Psychological Association, Washington, DC, p 55–76

Lubinski D 2000 Assessing individual differences in human behavior: 'Sinking shafts at a few critical points'. Annu Rev Psychol 51:405–444

Lubinski D, Webb RM, Morelock M J, Benbow CP 2000 Top 1 in 10,000: A 10-year follow up of the profoundly gifted. submitted

Mackintosh N J 1998 IQ and human intelligence. Oxford University Press, Oxford

Neubauer AC 1997 The mental speed approach to the assessment of intelligence. In: Kingma J, Tomic W (eds) Advances in cognition and education: reflections on the concept of intelligence. JAI Press, Greenwich, CT, p 149–174

Neubauer AC, Spinath FM, Riemann R, Borkenau P, Angleitner A 2000 Genetic and environmental influences on two measures of speed of information processing and their relation to psychometric intelligence: evidence from the German Observational Study of Adult Twins. Intelligence, in press

Vernon PE 1983 Speed of information processing and general intelligence. Intelligence 7:53–70

General intelligence and the definition of phenotypes

Douglas K. Detterman

Department of Psychology, Case Western Reserve University, Cleveland, OH 44106, USA

Abstract. From Spearman's famous 1904 paper to Carroll's recent book on factor analytic results from a multitude of studies, there has been one consistent conclusion: '*g*', or general intelligence, is the factor that defines the phenotype for intellectual functioning. It is no overstatement to say that *g* is undoubtedly the most important psychological construct discovered in this century. It predicts more and is implicated in a wider range of behaviour than any other psychological construct. The empirical support for *g* is extensive and overwhelming. It would seem that *g* is the perfect phenotypic definition of intelligence. I argue that it is not the perfect phenotype. If we are to understand intelligence, we need to define a new, more elaborate definition of intelligence taking *g* as the starting place. It must be remembered that *g* is a statistical abstraction. Current formulations of *g* are largely silent about the composition of *g*. I argue that *g* is actually made of further separable basic cognitive processes and does not represent a single underlying entity. These basic cognitive processes are integrated into a complex system in the brain that makes them difficult to identify. None the less, until these basic processes are identified and related to brain function there are a number of findings that cannot be explained and this will inhibit scientific progress.

2000 The nature of intelligence. Wiley, Chichester (Novartis Foundation Symposium 233, p 136–148

General intelligence and the definition of phenotypes

There is no doubt about general intelligence or *g*. For nearly 100 years, no matter how the data are analysed, a general factor emerges from any battery of mental tests. This general factor is highly predictive of academic achievement as well as many other outcomes including education, occupational status, income and other important social variables. As scientific stories go, the history of *g* is almost boring in its regularity. Despite torturous methods of factor analysis, attacks from outraged critics and even long periods of being ignored, *g* just keeps reappearing like the insistent relative that won't go away.

It has taken us 95 years to fully realize *g*'s importance — this is now thoroughly detailed in books like Jensen's (1998) *The g factor*. Looking back from our present perspective of enlightenment, *g* is certainly the most robust phenomenon in the social sciences and it is a wonder that it has taken us so long to see it clearly, especially when people as smart as Galton, Spearman, Thorndike, Turstone and Jensen have been steadily working on the problem. Of course, things always seem complicated until we understand them and then they are simple. Now that we know the overriding importance of *g*, what should we do?

I believe we are on the verge of a very productive period in our understanding of human intelligence. Not only do we know a great deal about *g*, we also have the tools to understand the origins of *g*. Plomin and his associates (Hill et al 1999) have developed methods of DNA pooling and dense marker maps that will allow, in a reasonably short time, the identification of genes associated with intelligence. One gene, *IGF2R* on chromosome 6, has already been identified (Chorney et al 1998) and others will certainly be found in the next few years.

We also have methods for studying the activity of living, working brains. These methods include positron emission tomography (PET) (Haier et al 1988, 1992), functional magnetic resonance imaging (fMRI) (Hacke et al 1994) and averaged evoked potentials (AEP) (Ertl & Schafer 1969) to name a few. We have already seen provocative results from these techniques but there is little doubt there will be much more progress in the future. These methods have the potential for identifying the brain processes associated with particular cognitive behaviours. More importantly for intelligence research, they offer a method of studying individual differences in living organisms differing in ability.

Intelligence researchers are in a position to trace *g* from genes, to brain, to behaviour. Twenty, or even ten, years ago this possibility was little more than science fiction. Today there is little doubt that it can and will be done. It is likely that general intelligence will be the first behavioural trait that will be described at the level of genes, brain and behaviour. If I am right, what we learn will have immense implications for social policy in diverse ways. Many of the issues currently decided by personal prejudices will be settled once and for all and will restrict or curtail the options that can be legitimately debated.

What we know least about now are the environmental influences on general intelligence. It is ironic that such a large portion of intelligence research, certainly more than half, has been devoted to the study of environmental effects yet there has been so little actual progress. It may be that we will have to come to a more complete understanding of the biological bases of *g* before we can have a full appreciation of how environment contributes to *g*'s development. Environment may be the most difficult aspect of intelligence to understand because individual effects are small and idiosyncratic.

Given this optimistic future, what is the most important thing that needs to be done? I will argue that the first and most important goal of research should be to develop an accurate phenotypic behavioural definition of general intelligence. This may seem odd since there are so many potential opportunities waiting in genetic and brain research. Don't we know just about all there is to know about g at the behavioural level? In truth, we don't know what g is.

In my view (Detterman 1982, 1987, 1994), g is only the surface manifestation of a complex system and it is our task to understand the underlying complexities of this system. After all, g is a statistical concept. g simply indicates that mental tests are all positively correlated. It does not explain why this positive correlation occurs. We must have a reasonable explanation for this pervasive positive correlation if we are to ever relate genes and brain function to those behaviours that make up general intelligence. I will argue that g is really composed of a small set of basic cognitive abilities knit into a cohesive system and that it is these basic abilities that we must identify before we can fully understand the phenotypic character of g. Following are the reasons that argue for this position.

(1) If g was the manifestation of a single underlying variable, we should have identified that variable by now. That variable should manifest itself as a large correlation with g. Given the reliability of g and the lower reliability of cognitive measures, we should conservatively expect that if a single variable caused g, we should consistently and reliably obtain correlations over 0.70 between that variable and g. There have been many suggestions about the kinds of variables that might account for g. These include speed of information processing, accuracy of information processing, complexity of neural processing, and speed of neural conduction. Some studies have even produced large correlations between g and the measure being examined. However, these studies are seldom fully replicable and when they are the correlations are not as large as in the original study.

(2) Basic cognitive tasks have low correlations with each other. Summarizing over all the studies that have been done that attempt to relate cognitive ability to g, the general finding is not large correlations but small to moderate correlations. Some have been so distressed by this finding they have talked about the 0.30 barrier meaning that it is very difficult to obtain correlations between cognitive tasks and g over 0.30. What do these small correlations mean?

Small correlations are just what would be expected if g was a set of independent processes. If there were 10 equally important processes, each process would account for 10% of the variance. Taking the square root the 0.1 yields the expected correlation of 0.32. Because neither tests of g nor cognitive tests are completely reliable, we should expect uncorrected correlations to be well below 0.30 (assuming there are 10 independent and equally weighted abilities composing g).

The small-to-moderate correlations one obtains from correlations of cognitive tasks with g are very strong evidence that g is not a single thing but is composed of a system of separate cognitive abilities. On the other hand, there is little or no compelling evidence that any cognitive variable shows large and consistent correlations with *g*. *g* must be composed of separate cognitive abilities. There is no other reasonable explanation for these empirical facts.

3) Basic cognitive tasks predict g. If there is a set of cognitive abilities that form *g*, then measures from those cognitive tasks should be able, when combined, to predict *g*. I have been investigating this possibility for over 15 years. My students and I have developed a battery of basic cognitive tasks that measure things like memory, learning and perceptual processes. The 10 tasks included in the battery were selected based on a theoretical model and because they represented the range of cognitive tasks known to correlate with intelligence. They are all very simple cognitive tasks much more like what you would find in the typical experimental psychologist's laboratory than on an intelligence test. These tasks have been fully described elsewhere (Detterman 1990).

All of the tasks are similar in format and use the same stimuli. Tasks are presented by computer and responses are made on a touch screen. The tasks were thoroughly piloted before being administered as a battery. The average reliability of the measures obtained from the tasks is around 0.80. This battery, in my opinion, is both psychometrically and cognitively fairly crude. I believe it could be substantially improved upon and so the results I present here are conservative.

This battery, which we call CAT (Cognitive Abilities Tests), has been administered to a number of samples varying in size from 40–860. These samples are summarized in Table 1. In each case, a separate measure of intelligence was obtained. These measures differ across the samples. One of our main interests in testing these groups was to determine if the measures from this battery would predict general intelligence.

Table 2 shows the results. In each case, multiple regression was used to combine variables from the CAT tasks to predict IQ. The multiple correlations obtained ranged from 0.63 to 0.93 with a mean of 0.79 and a standard deviation of 0.11. There are many ways to compute multiple regression with the wealth of data provided by CAT. Table 2 shows that several different methods were used including cross validation. Even when we use variables that have correlations of 0.25 or less with intelligence, we obtain a multiple correlation with IQ of 0.63. Cross validation yields a multiple correlation almost as high as that obtained in the original sample.

Several things are worth pointing out about the original data sets. One of the data sets has an extended range because subjects were selected at the extremes of ability. Another has a restricted range because Air Force recruits were used. In the USA at that time, Air Force recruits were highly selected. None of the correlations in Table 2 have been corrected for range restriction (or extension) or for

TABLE 1   Characteristics of four samples on standardized measures of intelligence

Sample	n	Subjects	Test	Mean	SD	Range
1	40	Combined group	WAIS-R	91.5	25.5	49–132
	20	College students		115.6	7.8	94–132
	20	Mentally retarded		67.5	7.6	49–80
2	141	Randomly selected high school students	WAIS-R	108.0	18.3	53–150
3	860	Air force enlistees (80% M, 20% F)	AFQT(%) (S) Gen. (T)	61.7 5.7 53.7	17.6 1.1 5.3	28–99 4–9 45–67
4	575	Twins (6–13 years old)	PPVT	104.2	15.9	52–147

%, percentile; AFQT, Armed Forces Qualification Test; PPVT, Peabody Picture Vocabulary Test; S, Stanine ($M = 5$, $SD = 1.96$); T, T-score; WAIS, Wechsler Adult Intelligence Scale.

TABLE 2   Multiple R's and size of first principal component for four samples

Sample description of regression analyses	No. Var	R	%Var 1st PC
	Sample 1		
Major variables	22	0.93	17.8
Lowest r's	8	0.81	
	Sample 2		
All major variables	Step	0.87	26.6
Low to moderate r's	23	0.81	
Same var. as Sample 1	19	0.83	
$r < 0.25$	Step	0.63	
	Sample 3		
30 major variables	Step	0.67	14.2
	Sample 4		
Major variables	Step	0.76	27.5

PC, principal component.

unreliability. Not surprisingly, when such corrections are made the mean multiple correlation increases substantially.

Though one can argue about methods, there is little doubt about the general conclusion. No matter how the data are analysed, no matter if the methods are conservative or liberal, no matter what test of intelligence is used, a set of cognitive measures can predict IQ as well as IQ tests predict each other. This is very strong support for the hypothesis that *g* is composed of a set of cognitive abilities.

(4) Basic cognitive tasks do not show a large general factor. When batteries composed of tests of general intelligence are factor analysed, the finding for nearly 100 years now has been that a large first general factor emerges. This is the statistical evidence that makes *g* an inescapable conclusion. This first principal factor usually accounts for between 40% and 80% of the total variance. However, this is not the case when basic cognitive tasks are factor analysed. As shown in the last column of Table 2, when the major variables from CAT are factor analysed, the first principal component accounts for only 18–28% of the total variance. That is, no large general factor emerges.

It could not be otherwise. The magnitude of the first principal component or factor is dependent on the average correlation among the variables in the matrix. Since the correlation among basic cognitive tasks is small, the proportion of variance accounted for has to be small. This is not a chance relationship. Proportion of variance accounted for by the first factor is computed from the eigenvalue for that factor. The eigenvalue is directly related to the average correlation among variables in the matrix. In fact, the average correlation among variables can be computed directly from the eigenvalue for that factor.

Even though basic cognitive tasks can be combined to predict *g*, they themselves do not show a large general factor. Therefore, basic cognitive tasks do not serve as proxies for *g*. Instead, each appears to provide its own independent contribution to *g*. This finding supports my original contention that *g* is composed of a complex system of separate cognitive abilities.

(5) Data from rats show that systems that contribute to g are independent. The findings from human data are supported by studies with rats. Thompson et al (1990) lesioned rats in various brain areas and then tested them on a number of tasks. When they factor analysed the resulting data, they found brain areas that they thought corresponded to psychometric *g*. While some of these areas were in the cortex, others were in lower centres of the brain. Most interestingly, though, each portion of the brain implicated in psychometric *g* involved a different brain system.

These data provide strong support for the notion that *g* is composed of independent processes united into a single system. The problem with these data is, of course, that they are from rats. However, in at least one sense, this is also the strength of the data. Laboratory rats are bred for minimum variability. Most scientists find individual differences to be a nuisance and would prefer not to deal with them. That Thompson et al (1990) were able to find the results they did even in rats with individual differences bred out is a tribute to the robustness of the effect.

(6) Many genes contribute to intelligence.   It is becoming increasingly clear that g depends on many genes. These genes probably each have separate and largely independent effects on g. I think that this makes it unlikely that we will ever find a single variable underlying g. What is more likely is that these genes contribute independently to brain processes that in turn result in independent cognitive abilities combined into an integrated system.

(7) g does not explain the diversity of intellectual behaviour.   Galton first described intelligence as a general disposition. While this is what g suggests, there appears to be great variety in what people do well. Cattell explained this in terms of investment while Gardner has suggested multiple intelligences. Despite the lack of evidence for Gardner's position and others like it, there is a persistent and unshakeable belief that general intelligence is multifaceted. While this seems to be a contradiction in terms, it is only a contradiction if g is viewed as being caused by a single variable. If g consists of several cognitive processes, then intelligence could easily be multifaceted. The correlation that yields g would result from the interrelationship of the parts of the system.

(8) Idiot savants and other forms of exceptionality suggest a complex system underlying g.   Idiot savants have long puzzled those interested in intelligence. While there is no generally accepted explanation of savants, the most frequently forwarded explanation is that portions of the system are preserved. Such an explanation is only consistent with an account of g that proposes multiple cognitive abilities.

(9) Cognitive tasks and even more complex tasks correlate differently at different levels of cognitive ability.   Detterman & Daniel (1989) found that if the IQ distribution was divided into parts and correlations computed separately for each part of the distribution, those in the lowest IQ ranges had the highest correlations among subtests included in the matrix. This finding also held for cognitive tests. What this means is that g is actually larger for low IQ subjects than high IQ subjects. Conversely, it means that high IQ persons have greater variability in their patterns of performance than low IQ subjects.

(10) g is good at general prediction but not good at differential diagnosis.   One hope of the original inventors of tests was that they would be prescriptive and tell us exactly what to do about somebody with a low IQ. Though we are able to differentially diagnose individuals with low IQ into diagnostic categories such as Down's syndrome, Williams syndrome, autism, learning disability and attention deficit hyperactivity disorder, I know of no evidence that these groups can be differentiated cognitively even though it is the cognitive aspects of the disorder that are frequently most salient. Why is this?

One explanation would be that g is g and if two people have the same IQ we should expect no difference in their cognitive behaviours. But then the question is why do clinical reports persist in describing these individuals as cognitively different? I think the reason is that they are cognitively different but that we have not developed cognitive tests sensitive enough to detect these differences. If that is so, then only an explanation of g that included independent cognitive abilities knit into a general cognitive system would explain these differences.

We now know beyond a shadow of a doubt that g, or general intelligence, is what carries the explanatory weight in individual differences in ability. It is g that predicts important social variables and will be of vast importance in resolving many current social controversies. We know g is important. Unfortunately, we do not know what g is.

I believe g is a set of independent cognitive abilities tied together into a well-integrated system. I have presented evidence here that I think provides strong support for that position. There is no more important task facing intelligence researchers than understanding exactly what these cognitive abilities are and how we can measure them. What we learn about genetics and the brain from the new methodologies will certainly be important for a comprehensive understanding of g. But if we are to completely understand g, we must have a more precise definition of its phenotypic characteristics.

Acknowledgement

Parts of this work were supported by Grants No. HD07176 from the National Institute of Child Health and Human Development, Office of Mental Retardation.

References

Chorney MJ, Chorney K, Seese N et al 1998 A quantitative trait locus (QTL) associated with cognitive ability in children. Psychol Sci 9:159–166

Detterman DK 1982 Does 'g' exist? Intelligence 6:99–108

Detterman DK 1987 Theoretical notions of intelligence and mental retardation. Am J Ment Defic 92:2–11

Detterman DK 1990 Computerized cognitive abilities tests for research and teaching. Micro Psychol 4:51–62

Detterman DK 1994 A system theory of intelligence. In: Detterman DK (ed) Current topics in human intelligence, vol 4: Theories of intelligence. Ablex Publishing, Norwood, NJ, p 85–115

Detterman DK, Daniel MH 1989 Correlations of mental tests with each other and with cognitive variables are highest for low IQ groups. Intelligence 13:349–359

Ertl JP, Schafer EWP 1969 Brain response correlates of psychometric intelligence. Nature 223:421–422

Hacke EM, Hopkins A, Lai S 1994 2D and 3D high resolution gradient echo functional imaging of the brain: venous contribution to signal in motor cortex studies. NMR Biomed 7:54–62 (erratum: 1994 NMR Biomed 7:374)

Haier R J, Siegel BV, Nuechterlein KH et al 1988 Cortical glucose metabolic rate correlates of abstract reasoning and attention studied with positron emission tomography. Intelligence 12:199–217

Haier R J, Siegel B, Tang C, Abel L, Buchsbaum MS 1992 Intelligence and changes in regional cerebral glucose metabolic rates following learning. Intelligence 16:415–426

Hill L, Craig IW, Asherson P et al 1999 DNA pooling and dense marker maps: a systematic search for genes for cognitive ability. NeuroReport 10:843–848

Jensen AR 1998 The g factor: the science of mental ability. Praeger, Westport, CT

Thompson R, Crinella FM, Yu J 1990 Brain mechanisms in problem solving and intelligence: a lesion survey of the rat brain. Plenum Press, New York

DISCUSSION

Miller: The finding that intercorrelations between tasks are higher for lower *g* subjects is very interesting from the genetic point of view. It seems to suggest that in so far as those phenotypic correlations reflect genetic covariances, *g* is being caused mostly by harmful mutations that have pleiotropic effects on multiple systems and that *g* does not necessarily reflect a spread of different strategies. That is, *g* reflects damage caused by particular mutations with multiple effects. This could account for why correlations between tasks are higher at lower *g*. Is that a coherent idea?

Detterman: Are you saying just that there's a sort of accumulation of these mutations at the lowest levels? Why does it consistently come up across generations?

Miller: If the optimal phenotype — that is the 'unmutated' genome, the species-typical genome — represents high *g*, then as you accumulate more and more deleterious mutations that each have pleiotropic effects in multiple systems, they're going to introduce the correlations between deficits in multiple systems. This will in turn introduce higher intercorrelations at lower *g* levels.

Detterman: That could be the case. I know that at the lower end, for instance, a number of facial anomalies are correlated with mental retardation.

Rutter: I'm not quite sure how you're using the term 'mutations'. All genetic variations are in an ultimate sense 'mutations'. Presumably, you are talking about new mutations that are deleterious. You are then postulating that these are functioning right across the range. It is not that you're getting a jump up when you're hitting the retarded range: you're getting it within the normal range. I find it a surprising notion that the variations in *g* within the normal range are due to accumulation of abnormal mutations.

Maynard Smith: I've thought all along that this is an obvious explanation of what I've been listening to. This would explain it very nicely.

Jensen: In other words, you are saying that without these deleterious mutations we would all be highly intelligent and there would be no *g* factor, because each of these various component abilities wouldn't be correlated at all. The thing that makes them correlate is that different people have different amounts of these mutations.

Maynard Smith: I am suggesting that most of the genetic variance is due to deleterious mutation. This is probably true: why wouldn't it be like that?

Detterman: The other side of that coin is that smart people get all the good genes.

Gangestad: Most mutations have very small effects. Most deleterious mutations are also not fresh. We each carry on average up to 200 deleterious mutations that will eventually be taken out. These have occurred over generations, and each one has only a certain probability that it will be removed in any particular generation. Across individuals, the number of mutations should be close to normally distributed, with substantial variance. What is being talked about here is not just the rare mutation that creates mental retardation.

Rutter: John Maynard Smith, can you follow through on your argument because I am not sure that I understand it. I'm aware from my reading of your work that if I'm puzzled by what you say, you're much more likely to be right than I am, so I'm wary of taking issue with you. But I don't understand why you think the evidence is suggesting that new pathological mutations are playing a role here. If one is looking at pathological conditions in general medicine, most of the genetic effects that we know anything about—and this is still quite a small number—are normal allelic variations.

Maynard Smith: What do you mean by normal allelic variations?

Rutter: By 'normal' I mean that they occur commonly in the general population without being associated with the disease. In a sense all allelic variations are mutations, but in medical genetics one would tend to make a distinction between a gene for phenylketonuria which is obviously causing pathology, as opposed to ApoE4 which is a normal variation but nevertheless carries with it an increased statistical risk for Alzheimer's.

Maynard Smith: I'm persuaded that measures of g have a high heritability. This means that there is genetic variance in the population from some source or another. One can have all sorts of ideas about the nature of that genetic variability. I agree with you that we're not talking here about things like phenylketonuria which, if you are homozygous for it, you are way off this scale. But there's every reason to believe that the human genome probably undergoes about two deleterious mutations per individual per generation. Most of these will have a very small effect. In the human species in particular, because of our medical services mean that people like me can survive who wouldn't in a hunter–gatherer society, much of the genetic variance is likely to be maintained by recurrent deleterious mutations. These will likely be mildly deleterious mutations balanced by selective removal of mutations. When one talks about these mutations being recent, it is just that deleterious mutations don't hang around forever. The individual mutation will sooner or later get eliminated, but lots more will have occurred in the meanwhile. I would want to go away for a week with a computer, pencil and paper to develop a model of this kind before I was sure that it would explain the kinds of correlation structures that have been discovered, but I'm pretty sure that it would. I think I am agreeing very much with the kind of multifactorial image that Douglas Detterman was giving of what g is about.

Jensen: It seems to me, the next question to ask would be whether there is a general factor of overall fitness in some sense. There may be a general factor of biological fitness that is highly related to the psychometric g factor.

Anderson: In Duchenne's muscular dystrophy, the boys that get Duchenne's have lower IQs on average than boys who don't carry the gene. Although many of them are in the normal intelligence range their mean is shifted about one standard deviation down. This would be a deleterious mutation for intelligence but not as dramatic as phenylketonuria. With your mechanism, is the collapsing of the variance dependent upon the loss of IQ? Or if you took Duchenne's boys with this deleterious mutation and matched them for ability with boys who didn't have the mutation, would they still show less variance in IQ scores, or higher intercorrelations among ability tests? Could we look for increased correlations as a result of a deleterious mutation if we matched on ability, or do the two necessarily go together?

Houle: I'm a fan of the idea that deleterious mutations may be involved in such general traits as g. But I'm very sceptical of this idea that that would explain this change in the correlation with IQ level, if in fact the average number of mutations carried would be in the order of 100. You are still looking at well functioning people carrying lots of deleterious mutations. I don't think there is any reason to believe that the variance in mutation number within those correlates would be different.

Maynard Smith: But the point is that this is not a hard question to answer.

Detterman: One complication I wondered about, is exactly what is a deleterious mutation? Many of these genes that in the homozygous state produce mental retardation, in the recessive state actually confer some reproductive advantage, even though they may lower IQ. There is evidence for phenylketonuria, for instance, and Tay Sach's disease.

Houle: There may be plausible theories, but I don't think there's solid evidence of that. Genetically, the better explanation is that these are more common than average because of drift and founder effects.

Brody: How many principal components do you need to predict intelligence in your battery?

Detterman: To completely reproduce it you need all the principal components. The correlations are very low, so you need a lot of principal components. The thing that I find most telling is that if you look through Carroll's book arefully, he has a lot of trouble with cognitive measures. They do not fit moothly into his scheme.

Karmiloff-Smith: I would like to come back to the issue about whether it is ossible to differentiate different phenotypes on the basis of psychometric tests. n my field we have to use psychometric tests because there is no other acceptable vay of matching different phenotypes. Take the Wechsler adult intelligence scale WAIS): if you look at the pattern of scores on individual subtasks, we find ifferent patterns for Down's syndrome, Williams syndrome and autism, for xample, despite the same overall score. But non-standardized tests differentiate hese phenotypes far better.

Detterman: Generally, in the literature, subtest scatter has not been a useful liagnostic tool. There is a huge history of attempts to use scatter to diagnose ead injury and all sorts of things. They have been largely unsuccessful.

Karmiloff-Smith: Perhaps head injury is different to the genetic syndromes.

The point I'm trying to make is that the overall scores alone don't tell us very nuch. If we take one of the syndromes that I have looked at, Williams syndrome, ndividuals with this syndrome are particularly good at face processing. They score n the normal range on tasks like the Benton Face Processing test. But if you ctually probe this, people with Williams syndrome go about solving the task in different way to the normal controls. The former use featural strategies, the latter onfigural strategies. So similar behavioural scores again are based on different ognitive processes. I would like to probe in more depth the behavioural scores n which you're basing your correlations, and ask what the cognitive process is hat underpins that score. It can be very different across different subtests and cross different populations or age groups.

Detterman: I think you're exactly right. In fact, that's the point I was trying to nake. If we understood the cognitive processes that relate to that performance, we :ould diagnose differentially. But we don't understand those cognitive processes)ecause we haven't taken the care to do what psychometricians and everybody rom Spearman on has been telling us to do.

Karmiloff-Smith: Then the leap from trying to map between brain processes and he scores you get on psychometric tasks is huge. Should you not be doing the :ognitive analysis first? Overt behaviour and cognitive process are not the same hing.

Detterman: I think one has to define the behaviour — the cognitive aspects of the)henotype — before we can understand which brain processes are important. The)rocess of understanding the cognitive aspects is going to point to certain brain)rocesses. Just to give you an idea, the fMRI work that we did was basically uninterpretable. We did get areas that showed heightened activity but I can't igure out what the results mean. These tasks are all much more complex than we magine, and they do involve strategies and all sorts of other processes that we don't well understand. Don't misunderstand me: I think discovering g was a important step forward, but now I think we have to do the harder task of tryin to understand what it is. If you look at an autistic child and compare them with Down's syndrome child, you know that there are cognitive differences betwee them. Why are we so dumb that we can't find a test that will distinguish the tw conditions?

s there a *g* factor for fitness?

)avid Houle

)epartment of Biological Science, Florida State University, Tallahassee, FL 32306-1100, 'SA

Abstract. Biological fitness is a directly observable quantity with well-known causal components, in contrast to the latent '*g*' factor of psychometrics. The study of the causes of variation in fitness should therefore be simpler than the study of variation in mental abilities, but a paucity of data has kept the nature of genetic variation in fitness obscure. We can define an '*f*' factor as variation creating positive correlations among components of fitness. There is little doubt that such *f* factors exist. Perturbations of populations such as mutation or environmental change create such patterns of positive correlation. However, natural selection will tend to minimize variation in any *f* factor, so it is much less clear whether *f* causes quantitatively substantial genetic variation within populations. Experimental data are consistent with variation in an *f* factor within some natural populations. As predicted, *f* is less important in populations where natural selection has had more opportunity to reshape the correlation matrix. Although one can incorporate variation in *g* into a study of variation in human fitness, the pace of change in our environment suggests that the results would neither reflect the conditions under which *g* evolved nor predict future evolutionary changes in *g*.

2000 The nature of intelligence. Wiley, Chichester (Novartis Foundation Symposium 233) p 149–170

This paper is motivated by speculations that human mental abilities and volutionary fitness should have some simple relationship. For example, there are)ersistent fears that IQ may be evolving to a lower level in modern society Herrnstein & Murray 1994), and we will hear an argument from Geoffrey Miller ater in this book that the '*g*' factor evolved to reflect the fitness of an individual Miller 2000, this volume). In evolutionary genetics, the relevant questions are vhether one expects much variation in fitness within a typical population of)rganisms and how that variation might be correlated with other traits. I have aken the view that a large proportion of the variation in the components of itness may be caused by overall quality of individuals. An implication of this dea is that one ought to be able to find a pattern of positive correlations among hese components. From such a pattern one could of course estimate a factor that xpresses this relationship, and it would have a structure and possible nterpretations much like the *g* factor of psychometrics. I will call this typothetical factor '*f*'.

149

Fitness and its components

Fitness is the number of descendants that an individual is expected to have Inherited variation in fitness is the necessary and sufficient condition for evolution by natural selection. Because much of the variation in fitness is no inherited, and is therefore irrelevant to evolution, the partitioning of variation i fitness between genetic and non-genetic causes is central to evolutionary biology

Although fitness is readily defined, measuring the fitness of genotypes is a exceedingly difficult task. Following an individual and its offspring through lif is difficult for many organisms; replicating a particular genotype and followin the fates of many such sets of individuals would often require a host of miracles Experimental systems exist where the fitness of genotypes of fitness can be studie (Stratton 1995, Travisano et al 1995, Fowler et al 1997), but the speci circumstances necessary to obtain these relatively comprehensive measures mak the estimates of dubious generality. A somewhat different difficulty arises with th fitness of humans; the same advances in medicine, technology and organizatio that potentially allow studies over the lifetime of individuals are correlated wit drastic changes in our environment that make the estimates of fitness obsolete b the time the data are collected.

Faced with the formidable difficulties of estimating fitness, evolutionar biologists have turned to estimates of the life-history parameters that collectivel determine fitness. Fortunately, these are easier to measure than fitness. Fo example, in the simple case of a stable population without parental care, fitness i the product of survival to age x (l_x) times the rate of reproduction at age x (m_x integrated over the whole lifespan. A convenient approximation is the sum o survival and reproduction over a discrete series of ages. Then fitness of genotyp i follows from the expected number of offspring, W, an individual has during it lifetime as:

$$W_i = \sum_{x=1}^{\infty} l_{xi} m_{xi}.$$

I will define any phenotype that is monotonically related to fitness as a fitnes component. The l's and m's are thus components of fitnesses.

Natural selection will tend to maximize W by increasing the frequency o genotypes with the highest W_i values. R. A. Fisher showed that fitness increase at a rate determined by the variance in fitness among genotypes when fitness i standardized to a mean of 1

$$\Delta \bar{w} = V_w.$$

This is known as Fisher's Fundamental Theorem of Natural Selection. In the absence of perturbations to the population or environment, fitness increases until the best genotypes are fixed and no variance in fitness remains.

Causes of variation in fitness components

Fisher's Fundamental Theorem and the assumption of no perturbations suggest that there should be no variance in fitness. This assertion is difficult to test directly. Burt (1995) reviewed 13 estimates of the variance in fitness in six different species, and only two were significant. Because one cannot prove absence, the meaning of this result is unclear. Of course many examples of directional changes in populations suggest that variance in fitness is often present (Endler 1986). Experimenters have usually had to content themselves with measuring fitness components, and these very often display substantial genetic variance (Houle 1992, Mousseau & Roff 1987, Roff & Mousseau 1987). Two interpretations of this result are possible, and are most easily introduced with a simple model (Houle 1991).

Figure 1 represents genes that underlie the life history of a hypothetical simple organism. This beast has a larval period during which it feeds and grows, then it metamorphoses into an adult, which then must find a mate and rear its offspring but does not feed. Thus all the resources at its disposal are acquired during the larval period and spent during adulthood. The functional genetic architecture that underlies the expression of the two fitness components is represented by the arrows. These processes fall into three classes. Many processes influence the amount of resources that an individual acquires prior to metamorphosis. Another set of loci, which might be a small number, influence the allocation of

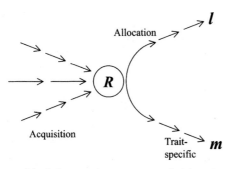

FIG. 1. A simple model of the genetic processes underlying the expression of fitness in a hypothetical organism. Arrows represent the genetic loci or pathways involved, R the limiting resources the organism acquires, *l* the phenotypes that determine survival and *m* the phenotypes that determine fecundity.

resources to one trait or another. Finally, loci must exist that influence only one trait or the other but not both. The genetic variance in each trait will consist of the sum of variances due to acquisition, allocation and trait-specific loci.

Traditionally, biologists have focused on allocation of resources. The metamorph has the choice of allocating its resources to structures that promote survival, perhaps spines and armour, or of saving its resources for the eggs it may lay, should it survive. Many choices may be optimal, because the increase in survival from allocating more resources to l could compensate for the fecundity costs of that lost allocation to m. Variation in fitness components could therefore be maintained without genetic variance in fitness. I will call this the 'optimal world' case. Using phenotypic observation or manipulation, or comparisons among populations, biologists have found evidence for trade-offs among many life history traits (Stearns 1992, Sinervo & Basolo 1996, Rose et al 1996). However, the optimal-world scenario requires not just the existence of trade-offs but that the genetic variation in life history in natural populations be primarily due to them.

Most tests of this more stringent requirement have involved picking one potential trade-off and studying it carefully. Traits that trade-off should be negatively correlated, but a failure to find a particular negative correlation is not very meaningful, as the variation in each trait might actually be involved in a trade-off with some unstudied trait. For example, Charlesworth (1990) considered a model of a life history consisting of three stages, characterized by five fitness components, with trade-offs between survival and reproduction and between reproduction at different ages. He generated a correlation matrix of these traits assuming that all of the variation was due to differences in these trade-offs, shown in Table 1. Not all of the correlations were negative, even though this case conforms perfectly to the optimal-world scenario. A recent review of the literature found that 40% of the relevant correlation estimates were negative (Roff 1996) and that the median estimate was 0.4. The median standard error of the estimates is 0.26, so estimation variance accounts for some but probably not all of the negative estimates. Overall, Roff's review provides some evidence for the importance of trade-offs.

The alternative to the 'optimal world' is that perturbations continually prevent the population from attaining one of the optimum states. This is the 'cruel world' case. There may be a few life-history strategies that are optimal for a given set of environmental circumstances, but there are certainly many that are sub-optimal. The world is cruel when it converts high-fitness genotypes to lower-fitness ones through changes in the environment or mutation. In the cruel world, genotypes poor at acquiring resources and with low values of all fitness components may be common.

There is good evidence that movement of genotypes (Burt 1995, Stratton 1995, Blondel et al 1999) and changes in environments (Kalisz 1986, Schemske &

TABLE 1 Factor analysis of a correlation matrix among life history traits from Charlesworth (1990), generated on the assumption that all variation is due to trade-offs among traits

Trait	Correlation matrix				Factor correlations[a]	
	m_1	m_2	m_3	l_2	F1	F2
m_1					0.966	−0.486
m_2	−0.892				−0.978	0.038
m_3	−0.453	0.0			−0.207	0.999
l_2	−1.000	0.892	0.453		−0.966	0.486
l_3	0.892	−1.0	0.0	−0.892	0.978	−0.038

By convention, survival to age 1 is collapsed into the parameter for reproduction at age 1.
[a]Factors extracted in a principal-factor analysis and rotated to a Harris–Kaiser case II orthoblique solution by the HK routine in SAS 7.0. The correlation between the resulting factors is 0.24.

Horvitz 1989, Hairston & Dillon 1990) are important sources of genetic variation. This sort of variation would be expected to increase genetic correlations, in contrast to the optimal-world case. Some believe that laboratory studies of field-evolved populations are therefore biased toward rejecting the optimal-world scenario and are not relevant to the question (Service & Rose 1985).

Mutation continually creates new genotypes that are less fit. This process may seem to be a trivial nuisance because any particular mutation is unlikely to arise. However, every locus in the genome must be capable of influencing fitness, so for complex metazoans in the order of 10^5 loci are capable of expressing deleterious mutations. Current evidence suggests that each metazoan embryo carries at least one new deleterious mutation, in addition to the load of mutations inherited from its parents (Eyre-Walker & Keightley 1999, Lynch et al 1999). A substantial amount of the genetic variance in fitness components may be the signature of new deleterious mutations that natural selection has not yet eliminated (Houle et al 1996).

There is good direct evidence that mutation creates positively correlated variation among life-history traits. Table 2 gives the correlation matrix from an experiment of mine (Houle et al 1994) in which a genetically homogeneous population was allowed to accumulate mutations in the absence of natural selection. All of the correlations are positive, and none is significantly different from 1. This result suggests that the number of acquisition loci, those that perform basic functions on which all phenotypes depend, is much greater than that of loci that allocate resources or affect traits independently. Overall, data from *Drosophila melanogaster* support the idea that the genetic complexity that

TABLE 2   Correlations of fitness components due to the second chromosome i
D. melanogaster after 44 generations of mutation accumulation

Trait	m_{5-6}	m_{27-28}	Male longevity	Female longevity	Productivity[b]
Fitness in Sved test[a]	0.69[†]	0.69**	0.66[†]	0.88*	0.61*
m_{5-6}		0.67**	0.68[†]	0.64	0.76[†]
m_{27-28}			0.56[†]	0.82**	0.45[†]
Male longevity				0.78*	0.61[†]
Female longevity					0.61*

[†]$P < 0.10$; *$P < 0.05$; **$P < 0.01$.
[a]The fitness index is the equilibrium frequency of the test chromosome in competition with a balance
chromosome (Houle et al 1992).
[b]Productivity is the product of fecundity of parents times the viability of their offspring.
Data from Houle et al (1994).

underlies a trait is a good predictor of how much it is affected by mutation and tha
the amount of mutation for a trait is correlated with the amount of genetic variatio
found in that trait in an outbred population (the standing variation) (Houle 1998)

The essence of the cruel-world scenario is that natural selection is continuall
pursuing an elusive optimum that the population is being pushed away from
The result is genetic variance in fitness and positive correlations among fitnes
components, that is, the existence of an '*f*' factor.

Factor analysis and the causes of variation

My simple model brings to mind some of the arguments in psychometrics abou
the nature of variation in mental abilities. Psychometricians have tended t
emphasize either 'general' variation in mental abilities, analogous to th
acquisition component in my model, or trait-group specific abilities. I do no
know of any champions of the view that mental abilities should be subject t
trade-offs. With this exception, the model I have shown corresponds fairly wel
with the widely accepted hierarchical partitioning of mental abilities into grou
factors and *g*. By analogy, it is clear that multivariate analyses of fitnes
components could be used to help determine the relative importance of thes
different sources of variation. If variation from acquisition predominates, the
we should see a pattern of positive correlations among fitness components, tha
is, an *f* factor. If trait-specific causes predominate, we should see weak correlation
among traits. If allocation variance predominates, the primary factors would sho
both negative and positive loadings like those seen after factor analysis on th
theoretical 'optimal world' example shown in Table 1. In this case, the pattern o
loadings corresponds to the constraints assumed in the model.

TABLE 3 Loadings of life-history traits on the first eigenvector in the data of Tatar et al (1996). m_x is adult fecundity on day x, and l_x is the probability of survival from day x-7 to x.

Trait	Component
m_3	−0.16
m_7	0.25
m_{10}	0.23
m_{14}	0.42
m_{17}	0.25
m_{21}	0.28
m_{24}	0.28
m_{28}	0.25
l_7	0.18
l_{14}	−0.02
l_{21}	0.19
l_{28}	0.25
l_{35}	0.30
l_{42}	0.30
l_{49}	0.28

All we need then is a representative sample of well-estimated genetic correlation matrices (**G**) to test the cruel and optimal scenarios. Here, this promising research program runs into trouble: we simply do not have any examples of correlation matrices that cover a complete sample of fitness components.

An examination of the best available **G** matrix is very revealing of the difficulties in this kind of study. Tatar et al (Promislow et al 1996, Tatar et al 1996) studied adult fecundity and longevity in *D. melanogaster*. This study is exemplary in that the sample sizes are enormous (65 000 flies), and it was conducted under the same laboratory conditions the base population had evolved in, so the flies were presumably well adapted. For all these advantages, the correlation matrix still does not cover the entire life history, omitting larval survival and male mating success. Therefore some of the variation observed may be due to trade-offs with these unmeasured components. Despite the huge sample size, the estimates still have high variances; 9 of the 112 correlations are outside their bounds. This problem leads to difficulties in factor analyses, so I have limited myself to a

principal components analysis. Table 3 shows the loadings of traits on the fir
eigenvector.

Overall, there are many positive elements in this vector, and those with negativ
loadings have relatively small scores. This eigenvector might therefore represe
an f factor, depending on the interpretation of the variables with negative score
Because very few flies died in the first two weeks of adult life, neither l_7 nor l_{14} ha
significant additive genetic variance or covariance, so these correlations at
probably not meaningful. The negative loading of m_3 is more convincing, as
has significant genetic variance and is significantly negatively correlated with l_{4}
Day 3 is near the peak of adult fecundity in this population, and there is probabl
substantial mortality in the crowded continuous culture the stock has evolved ir
so fecundity early in life could be one of the most important determinants of fitnes
The trade-off of early fecundity with late-life fitness is also consistent with a grea
deal of evidence showing costs to reproduction and the evolutionary lability of lif
span in this species (Partridge & Barton 1993, Rose et al 1996). Although th
principal components analysis by itself is certainly not convincing, it has
plausible interpretation under the optimal-world scenario. On the other hand
the abrupt change of loadings between days 3 and 7 seems biologicall
implausible. Although this analysis suggests a direction for further work, th
implications of the result are unclear.

Direct comparisons between mutational covariances and the standin
covariances within populations are possible for some trait pairs i
D. *melanogaster*. For example, the mutational correlation between egg-to-adul
survival and the rate of developmentl is strongly positive and not significantl
different from 1, whereas the correlation within a natural population is near 0 an
not significant (Yoshimaru & Mukai 1985). This pattern is consistent with
substantial positive contribution to the covariance from mutation and with
winnowing of much of this variation by natural selection, so that the standin
correlation has a proportionally larger contribution from allocation or trait
specific variances.

In summary, there is good evidence that both optimal-world and cruel-worl
scenarios supply variation in fitness components, but the quantitative balanc
between the two is unclear.

What about g?

The argument so far has all been about fitness components, whose partia
correlation with fitness is positive by definition. For any other trait, such as size
bristle number, or the g factor of psychometrics, fitness will not automaticall
increase if an individual has more of it. In a cruel world, the probability of such
positive relationships with arbitrary characters is higher, as maladapted individual

:an plausibly fail at whatever they attempt, and half maladapted individuals do half well at everything. This will not be the case in the optimal world, however, where :he careful balance suggests that nothing will be positively correlated with fitness, not even fitness components. Our current inability to determine how cruel the world is leaves the possibility of simple correlations of arbitrary traits with fitness possible but not assured.

To see the difficulties of inferring the relationship of fitness and arbitrary traits, let us consider body size and growth rates. In many organisms, fecundity scales with size, so size may be a good predictor of fitness. For example, in the planktonic crustaceans of the genus *Daphnia*, size at birth, growth rates and fecundities are positively genetically correlated with projected fitnesses (Lynch & Spitze 1994). The weakness of these studies is that they were all carried out in the lab in the absence of predators, so these conclusions about the relationship of growth rate and size with *Daphnia* fitness may not be robust. For example, if the risk of predation increases with size, then high growth rates and large size would carry a substantial fitness cost not reflected in measures of lab fitness.

I am afraid that a similar indeterminacy must accompany any attempt to determine the relationship between *g* and fitness in humans. Certainly, further study of the relationship between demography and *g* might have considerable descriptive interest, but our current population is much like that of *Daphnia* in glass jars — we are insulated from most sources of mortality early in life to a much greater degree than in our evolutionary past. In *Daphnia* we can hope to do an experiment including the missing components of fitness in a more natural environment. In humans, we would have great difficulty inferring the range of environments that we evolved in, and we cannot even hope to recreate those environments or populate them with experimental subjects. Furthermore, changes in human demography seem to have accelerated over the last 500 or so years, and there is little sign that these changes are ceasing. In addition, the increase in performance on IQ tests over the past 50 years suggests that the impact of environmental change on *g* is also considerable (Jensen 1998). It therefore seems likely that current estimates of these relationships are neither likely to illuminate our evolutionary history, nor enable us to predict our evolutionary future.

Acknowledgements

Thanks to Geoffrey Miller for sharing unpublished manuscripts, to Marc Tatar for providing unpublished data, and to Ann Thistle for editing the manuscript.

References

Blondel J, Dias PC, Perret P, Maistre M, Lambrechts MM 1999 Selection-based biodiversity at a small spatial scale in a low-dispersing insular bird. Science 285:1399–1402

Burt A 1995 The evolution of fitness. Evolution 49:1–8

Charlesworth B 1990 Optimization models, quantitative genetics, and mutation. Evolution 44:520–538

Endler J A 1986 Natural selection in the wild. Princeton University Press, Princeton, NJ

Eyre-Walker A, Keightley PD 1999 High genomic deleterious mutation rates in hominids. Nature 397:344–347

Fowler K, Semple C, Barton NH, Partridge L 1997 Genetic variation for total fitness in *Drosophila melanogaster*. Proc R Soc Lond Ser B Biol Sci 264:191–199

Hairston NG Jr, Dillon TA 1990 Fluctuating selection and response in a population of freshwater copepods. Evolution 44:1796–1805

Herrnstein R J, Murray C 1994 The bell curve. Free Press, New York

Houle D 1991 Genetic covariance of fitness correlates: what genetic correlations are made of and why it matters. Evolution 45:630–648

Houle D 1992 Comparing evolvability and variability of quantitative traits. Genetics 130:195–204

Houle D 1998 How should we explain variation in the genetic variance of traits? Genetica 102, 103:241–253

Houle D, Hoffmaster DK, Assimacopoulos S, Charlesworth B 1992 The genomic mutation rate for fitness in *Drosophila*. Nature 359:58–60 (erratum: 1994 Nature 371:358)

Houle D, Hughes KA, Hoffmaster DK et al 1994 The effects of spontaneous mutation on quantitative traits. I. Variance and covariance of life history traits. Genetics 138:773–785

Houle D, Morikawa B, Lynch M 1996 Comparing mutational variabilities. Genetics 143:1467–1483

Jensen AR 1998 The *g* factor: the science of mental ability. Praeger, Westport, CT

Kalisz S 1986 Variable selection on the timing of germination in *Collinsia verna* (Scrophulariaceae). Evolution 40:479–491

Lynch M, Spitze K 1994 Evolutionary genetics of *Daphnia*. In: Real LA (ed) Ecological genetics. Princeton University Press, Princeton, NJ, p 109–128

Lynch M, Blanchard J, Houle D et al 1999 Spontaneous deleterious mutation. Evolution 53:645–663

Miller G 2000 Sexual selection for indicators of intelligence. In: The nature of intelligence. Wiley, Chichester (Novartis Found Symp 233) p 260–275

Mousseau TA, Roff DA 1987 Natural selection and the heritability of fitness components. Heredity (Edinburgh) 59:181–197

Partridge L, Barton NH 1993 Optimality, mutation and the evolution of ageing. Nature 362:304–311

Promislow DEL, Tatar M, Khazaeli AA, Curtsinger JW 1996 Age-specific patterns of genetic variance in *Drosophila melanogaster*. I. Mortality. Genetics 143:839–848

Roff DA 1996 The evolution of genetic correlations: an analysis of patterns. Evolution 50:1392–1403

Roff DA, Mousseau TA 1987 Quantitative genetics and fitness: lessons from *Drosophila*. Heredity (Edinburgh) 58:103–118

Rose MR, Nusbaum TJ, Chippindale AK 1996 Laboratory evolution: the experimental wonderland and the Cheshire cat syndrome. In: Rose MR, Lauder GV (eds) Adaptation. Academic Press, San Diego, CA, p 221–241

Schemske DW, Horvitz CC 1989 Temporal variation in selection on a floral character. Evolution 43:461–465

Service PM, Rose MR 1985 Genetic covariation among life-history components: the effect of novel environments. Evolution 39:943–945

Sinervo B, Basolo AL 1996 Testing adaptations using phenotypic manipulations. In: Rose MR, Lauder GV (eds) Adaptation. Academic Press, San Diego, CA, p 149–185

tearns SC 1992 The evolution of life histories. Oxford University Press, Oxford

tratton DA 1995 Spatial scale of variation in fitness of *Erigeron annuus*. Am Nat 146:608–624

atar M, Promislow DEL, Khazaeli AA, Curtsinger JW 1996 Age-specific patterns of genetic variance in *Drosophila melanogaster*. II. Fecundity and its genetic covariance with age-specific mortality. Genetics 143:849–858

ravisano M, Mongold JA, Bennett AF, Lenski RF 1995 Experimental tests of the role of adaptation, chance, and history in evolution. Science 267:87–90

oshimaru H, Mukai T 1985 Relationships between the polygenes affecting the rate of development and viability in *Drosophila melanogaster*. Jpn J Genet 60:307–334

DISCUSSION

Brody: I think I can come up with one example where there is evidence for additive covariance. There are studies of the genetic covariance between intelligence and academic achievement. Both twin studies and adoption studies tend to show that the covariance between intelligence and academic achievement is primarily genetic. They give somewhat comparable estimates of the degree to which genetic covariances are involved. I assume that if an adoption design and a twin design give you somewhat comparable data, we're looking therefore at additive covariance between those two things. Does this have any relevance?

Houle: The problem with this argument is that it may be that g is responsible for academic achievement, so you're not really measuring two different things, as you might potentially be with verbal or mathematical or spatial abilities.

Jensen: What you need is a design based on correlations and cross-correlations between parents and children, because parents and children have just the additive variance in common.

Houle: You still have the environmental effects to deal with.

Jensen: That is true. We know that there is a lot of dominance variance in intelligence, or you wouldn't get a high degree of inbreeding depression of IQ or g. It is higher than for many other polygenic traits.

Gangestad: You don't need a lot of dominance variance to get inbreeding depression on a trait, if most of the trait's genetic variance is due to mutations. With rare mutations there are very few double recessive mutations, and therefore, almost all of the variance caused by each mutation is merely additive, even if the effect of double recessives is nonadditive. So rare mutations can produce low dominance variance yet substantial inbreeding depression.

Brody: I disagree with Arthur Jensen: the heritability of g itself is additive. In adoption studies involving children who have been adopted for long periods, such as in the Colorado study, by the time the adoptees get to age 15 or 16, the biological parent–child correlations run close to 0.3. There is some restriction of range in that study. At age 16 peak heritability probably hasn't been reached, so if you double that you're beginning to get estimates that are very close to what happens in twin studies. I think a lot of genetic variance in intelligence over the lifespan tends to be additive.

Jensen: A lot of what counts as additive variance is due to dominant genes. If you had 100% dominant genes, you would still have a big component of additive variance. That is, if every gene for intelligence was either dominant or recessive at every locus, the minimum of additive variance would be 25%.

Houle: You are correct that additive variance may be caused by recessive genes but I don't follow your 25% remark. For one locus, additive variance is a function of the allele frequency of the less dominant allele (q), the difference in phenotype between the two homozygous genotypes ($2a$), and the deviation of the heterozygote phenotype from the average phenotype of the two homozygotes (d). The actual function is

$$V_A = 2q(1-q)[a + d(2q-1)]^2.$$

When inheritance is additive and $d=0$, then V_A reaches a maximum when the allele frequencies are 0.5. When there is dominance, then the maximum is shifted towards higher values of q, so that when the recessive allele is rare, additive variance is low. A figure showing this relationship can be found in Falconer & Mackay (1996, Fig. 8.1). A great deal of data shows that most genetic disorders are caused by at least partially recessive alleles. Since these will be maintained at low frequency by selection, they do not cause a great deal of additive genetic variance. The *Drosophila* data suggests that the lower the effect (a) of an allele, the more additive the allele will be, so that alleles of small effect can explain more of the additive genetic variance than you might think.

Gangestad: My understanding of the genetic correlations between different mental abilities tests is that they tend to mirror the phenotypic correlations. We might expect there to be a lot of additive genetic covariance there. But the genetic correlations that might be most interesting from a standpoint of looking at *g* as some sort of a fitness indicator would be genetic correlations between it and other markers of fitness: health indicators, growth parameters, etc.

Jensen: There is a correlation between *g* and longevity recently reported (Smits et al 1999).

Gangestad: That's interesting, though you would want to know the genetic correlation; this could be a nutritional effect. David Houle, I was a little surprised by your final conclusion, in which you stated that you don't think that we are going to be able to understand much about the forces that account for existing genetic variation. Don't you think that genetic correlations between fitness traits could be informative?

Houle: I am pessimistic, because I see modern humans as in a similar position to *Daphnia* in the lab: we're basically outside our historically relevant viability regime. Now, natural selection is mainly acting on fertility differences, at least in the first

orld. This is a perfectly legitimate environment to ask about evolution in, but it's
ot going to be informative about the past. We're still probably looking at genes
hat have hung around from the past. Nor is our environment likely to remain the
ime, because medical care will probably continue to change. In that sense, I'm not
ire a correlation now would be anymore meaningful than looking at *Daphnia*
utside of their pond.

Gangestad: How fast would the genetic correlations change between traits that
lay have been valuable in the past? Genetic correlations involving longevity and
cundity may change immediately, but genetic correlations with health and
rowth and so on may change more slowly.

I have a question for you. There's a lot of talk in evolutionary biology about the
nportance of coevolutionary processes in maintaining genetic variance, with the
rimary one being host–parasite/pathogen coevolution. How important do you
tink coevolutionary processes are, as opposed to mutation?

Houle: My best estimate of how much genetic variation mutation must account
or, in terms of variance within *Drosophila*, is probably in the order of 20% (Houle
: al 1996), and that's a conservative estimate. The remaining 80% could well be
counted for by polymorphisms maintained by the sorts of things you're talking
bout, such as disease interactions. However, an alternative is that mutation–
election balance maintains far more than 20%. There is lots of room for
ncertainty about the quantitative importance of mutation.

Rutter: In my introductory remarks I expressed scepticism about whether the
orrelations for social success and so on were relevant to this issue. What value is
here in thinking about *g* in relation to evolutionary fitness?

Houle: In theory a great deal. In humans, I am sceptical about what data we could
ather now that would be very informative. The study of non-human systems
ould provide a good deal more. In humans there has almost certainly been very
rong positive selection in favour of some kind of brain function. In mice this
robably hasn't occurred. One of the things I think would be informative would
e that if we found that *g* existed in mouse and rat, and then went and found it
xisted in the squid which has a completely different brain system and history of
volution. This would suggest that whatever leads to the general factor is a
onsequence of something much more general than just the specifics of our
volutionary history. Perhaps a comparative approach would be more
iformative than looking within current populations.

Harnad: You touched on the fact that some of the questions we like to ask about
hether *g* is in fact a fitness measure are short-circuited by something analogous to
ie *Daphnia* situation: we are currently out of our ancestral environment of
volutionary adaptation (EEA). I have a conceptual question about the
cological validity of IQ tests. We're asking in a sense about the ecological
alidity of IQ tests; whether they indeed measure fitness and they're ecologically

valid. What is the likelihood that the tests that are being constructed now — measure the kinds of things that we're interested in today in this non-EEA — a ecologically valid? Are you hoping that the ones that load highly on g will loa highly on those portions of the test that actually measure things that we adaptive in the EEA?

Humphrey: On the news last year I heard a report about someone who wanted join the police force in New London, Connecticut, and had been turned down the grounds that he had too high an IQ. They said they had done research which had showed that the optimal range for IQ for the police in Connecticut w between 95–115, and this man had an IQ of 125. I'm not suggesting that th police force corresponds all that closely to the EEA, but doesn't this give some reason to question whether high IQ would in fact have been adaptive in th EEA? One answer perhaps to John Maynard Smith's question about why natur selection hasn't given all members of the human population the most brilliant minds is because in the past this wouldn't have been optimal. There are bits ar pieces of evidence around suggesting that having too good a memory, for exampl actually might not be a good strategy: if you have too good a memory — of th kind which turns up occasionally in the cases of pathology in human beings — actually steers you away from another strategy for solving problems in the worl which is the use of high-level concepts, rules and abstract thinking. There's th famous case of Mr S, the mnemonist studied by Alexander Luria, who was brilliant natural calculator and had perfect photographic recall, but in other wa turned out to be amazingly stupid.

Harnad: Borges had a short story, *Funes the memorious*, that did an even better jc of limning all the handicaps of Mr S in Luria's *Mind of a mnemonist*.

Humphrey: Coupled with that, there is evidence that our ancestors not long ag may generally have had considerably better memories, and perhaps would hav scored higher on some of the factors that load on g than we do today. In th 1960s Donald Farrer did some experiments with chimpanzees which seemed show that chimpanzees have a capacity for 'picture memory', far beyond wh normal humans are capable of today (Farrer 1967). If we have subsequently lo this kind of capacity, perhaps the reason may have been that human beings wit worse memories actually tended to do better in the long run precisely because the had an incentive to develop improved ways of categorizing and storin information — through high level concepts, language and so on. Taking wh might have looked at the time like a step backwards could actually have led taking two steps forward.

Detterman: Just a point of information: memory is not very heavily loade on g.

Harnad: Could I suggest a dichotomy that might describe the dividing lin between the ancestral EEA tasks/skills and contemporary ones? This idea can com a conference on heuristic strategies in Berlin. It is the difference between 'on-ine' and 'off-line' skills. On-line skills are the kind that you would need in order to perform the task in the real world in real time. Off-line skills are the (language and naths-conferred) ones that allow you to calculate off-line on your own time, to be pplied later. Much in our current world is loaded on off-line skills. To what extent re our psychometrics biased in that direction?

Lubinski: As culture evolves, especially as you look at how we develop from ndustrialized to an information-based society, one of the things that goes along vith that is that we have more niches to operate in (Lubinski 1996). There is good vidence that a general factor has utility in multiple niches. There are also distinct niches for the group factors to manifest themselves. The best example I can think of s C. P. Snow's 'Two cultures', the humanist and the scientist. There is good psychometric evidence that if you look at profiles of abilities, the humanists peak on verbal skills and vocational interest in the art and social realms, and the scientists peak on quantitative and spatial visualization. Although they have comparable *g* factors, they have different profiles: scientists are more interested in sophisticated gadgets and things (Achter et al 1999, Humphreys et al 1993). We carve out these niches for ourselves. One of the reasons that there are these occasional intellectual pattles between humanists and scientists is because they have different criteria in erms of what constitutes a intellectually satisfying explanation of a phenomenon Lubinski 2000). In psychology, we have this huge debate in clinical versus actuarial prediction. The data are in that if you want to make predictions about people, you're better off using psychologists to point to variables, but after that point you're better off using a regression formula or discriminative function analysis (Dawes et al 1989, Grove & Meehl 1996). But a lot of clinical psychologists who haven't been trained in quantitative traditions would rather lo armchair forecasts. The evidence is in, but there is still this conflict. I think what a more complex and multifacteted society affords is the opportunity to hrive in different niches. There is not only more diversity now in our gene requencies, but there is also more diversity in our culture: there are more niches and we have a more complex society.

Whiten: One way in which we can still find out more about the cognitive challenges of something like our EEA is to study contemporary hunter–gatherers. I have looked at this literature for various reasons. One of the things I was struck by, comparing human hunting with the hunting strategy that's used by large predators or by non-human primates, is the extent to which it involves more off-line processing (Whiten 1999). For example, when !Kung hunters are hunting, instead of getting within direct vision of the prey, they do an enormous amount of cracking, which is an abstract kind of process. They look at tracks on the ground and try to make inferences about where the animals are and what would be the best place to hunt them from. But even when they hit the prey animal with an arrow they will then often let the prey get away and inspect the debris around, from which they make inferences about where that prey is going to go and how long it will last. The next day they come out with a party of helpers to gather the prey having worked out roughly where it's going to be. So the key activity of hunting is actually quite abstract for human hunter–gatherers. It has always struck me as tragic that these peoples, now disappearing quite fast, have been studied by anthropologists, but hardly at all by cognitive psychologists. We have almost missed that chance. Even less seems to be known of the cognitive structure of the gathering that is done mostly by women.

Harnad: Arthur Jensen has done a terrific job refuting the claim that IQ tests are biased in some way, because people love to criticize them as being designed just for our own culture. Would an IQ test that would be predicting the skills that are needed in order to get by in palaeolithic society be higher or lower in *g*-loading? Would they be higher because that is closer to the EEA?

Brody: There is a design to answer your question. If you took someone who was high in skills in one culture and did a cross-cultural adoption study, would the adopted child of that person be advantaged in acquiring the kind of cultural contents that we value? My guess is that the answer would be yes. It's very hard to think of contexts in which *g* is not useful: the Connecticut policeman example given earlier is instructive. It is not that the data show that people with higher IQ don't do well as policemen. The reason for that prediction, which is actually based on some empirical results, is that policeman who have a higher IQ don't stay in the job.

Harnad: Why an adoption study? It is not the !Kung's genetics that is of interest here; it is their environment.

Brody: The genes that are relevant to the acquisition of intellectual skills may be the same in different cultures.

Gangestad: It is an empirical question that we can't really answer from the armchair, but I have more anecdotal evidence that fits with what Andy Whiten suggested. I've talked a lot with the folks who studied the Ache, a hunter–gatherer group from South America. They claim that many of the second-order representation skills that involve a lot of scenario building are important in Ache hunting. It turns out that a guy doesn't reach his peak as a hunter until he's about 30–35, even though his physical skills are well developed by the time he is 18. It is mostly a matter of acquiring knowledge and being able use that knowledge on the spot. I don't know whether this means that *g* is what counts, but that is a plausible possibility.

Flynn: With regard to the cross-cultural validity of IQ tests, the IQ gains over time data show that the Dutch gained 20 IQ points on Raven's over a 30-year period, and the Israeli's 9 points in 15 years. So the cultural distance a society travels over time seems to make IQ tests invalid as measures of ntelligence. None the less, you would still find IQ tests valid within each group. That is, within the Dutch of 1982, the IQ tests would still predict all he individual differences in academic success they normally do and within he Dutch of 1952, they would also make all of the usual predictions accurately. However, the advantage of the Dutch of 1982 over the Dutch of 1952, a 20 IQ point advantage, didn't bring the expected differences between the two societies. The Dutch data are particularly impressive. They compared the recruits with their own fathers, and they had an 18 point IQ advantage on Raven's, i.e. well over one standard deviation. In other words, there is a difference between working on the level of explaining individual differences, and on the level of comparing groups. On the latter level the IQ tests often have great difficulties when there's some cultural distance involved.

Harnad: The Flynn effect occurs on modern IQ tests in modern societies: it is interesting, but I don't see its bearing on the kind of question that Andy Whiten was raising.

Flynn: I'm merely commenting on the chance remark that IQ tests have been shown to be free from cultural bias: that depends on whether you are using them within a culture or between cultures.

Harnad: We need people to construct valid tests in the !Kung environment for whatever it takes to get ahead in that environment, and to see empirically whether those tests end up being higher or lower on *g*-loading.

Deary: Michael Rutter, you asked earlier whether psychometric *g* was relevant to evolutionary success. We've heard from psychometricians and evolutionary biologists that it might be that some cognitive abilities are predictive of some ability to do things that are valued within a society. Is anybody actually applying these things to your question, about the relevance of *g* to evolutionary/reproductive success? Are these societal 'success' variables proximal to evolutionary reproductive success, or are they just other reinstantiations of what David Lubinski talked about on the first day of this meeting?

Miller: There are good data that in the Ache hunters of Amazonia, studied by Kim Hill, there is a strong correlation between hunting ability in males and reproductive success, particularly their rates of extra-pair copulations. The number of kids they produce within their primary relationship is not that much higher than those produced by poor hunters, but they have a lot more illegitimate kids. A number of other anthropologists have traced good correlations between a lot of these indicators of 'social success' among hunter–gatherers and actual reproductive success. If we could just find the *g*-loadings of the activities that they do, then we would have a more complete story to tell.

Whiten: The hunters vary enormously in hunting *success*, too. This is interesting in respect of the evidence I mentioned earlier, about human hunting methods being highly cognitive, in conjunction with the findings you've just outlined.

Humphrey: Parallel data were produced by Napoleon Chagnon on the Yanomamo. He showed a fitness correlation with the number of people that an individual had killed in battle. Men who had killed became sexually attractive.

Nesse: The additional aspect here is that participating in raids allowed the men to capture women and bring them back.

Detterman: I want to ask opinions about the data that I know about on fitness and IQ, showing that from Cattell to Vining, family size is declining among higher IQ individuals and increasing among lower IQ individuals.

Harnad: The resolution of the Vining (1986) 'problem' thing came from Perusse (1993) in Quebec, who showed that although family size is declining among those with higher IQs and incomes, it is still true that the richer you are the more sperm you will 'exchange'. Contraception has got in the way, but the old correlation is still there.

Suddendorf: This has only occurred during the last 100 years or so.

Nesse: It is an environmental novelty. People get more sex, have more partners, are more attractive and stay married longer if they are higher up in the hierarchy. The fact that they have fewer children is merely a result of the novel factor of birth control.

Detterman: What are the implications of that?

Nesse: That our minds are not designed to maximize fitness in the presence of birth control! There is one implication I think is quite profound, which is that to the extent that there's heritability of a wish for having children (there's some evidence that there is heritability on that trait), this should be very strongly selected for.

Harnad: I didn't know that there was a genetic connection between knowledge of consequences of reproduction, and yearning for children.

Nesse: There is no knowledge component to this. Linda Mealey did this study with Nancy Segal (Mealey & Segal 1993). They have shown that if you ask women in their 20s, 'Do you want children?' and calculated the heritability on that, it comes out at 0.3–0.35. It is a simple finding and I don't want to stand on it, but if someone asks you how natural selection is shaping humans in our current environment, I think that's the answer.

Pomiankowski: I would like to comment on David Houle's pessimistic view. I don't think we need to be so pessimistic, for two reasons. If you are interested in the genetic structure of *g* in the current human population, you want some internal comparison. It may be that *g* has a very high additive genetic variance today and this can be ascertained by comparison with other traits, for instance other psychological traits. Perhaps they have different additive effects. This may tell us something interesting. Second, is it very interesting to know this genetic structure, anyway? What will knowledge of the additive genetic variance and covariance really tell us? They're not really going to tell us an awful lot about evolutionary history. They aren't necessarily the questions we want to ask when we are addressing the nature of intelligence, which is the title of this symposium. I don't know that we have to be so pessimistic.

Houle: I am pessimistic about solving problems by looking at current patterns of genetic variance and covariance. The idea of mutation load being expressed through complex phenotypes is an idea that stems from this. It offers a very simple explanation for why *g* exists despite the fact that, as Douglas Detterman was saying, we have got separate abilities which are organized into one complex system. It is saying that there exist features which may not be involved with mental function at all, but which affect the health of that system. If you have a university in a city that doesn't function well, it's not going to be an attractive university. I don't think I can test that idea through looking at genetic variances now in the human population, but it is an interesting idea that is worth pursuing in other contexts.

Detterman: I think the environment has changed dramatically. If you look at the proportion of people completing education in the USA, for instance, it's very high: nearly 90% complete high school now, whereas the number of people who completed high school in 1895 was about 5%. Certainly, *g* is becoming more important as an academic predictor in some sense.

Houle: If in fact, you could go to primitive populations and find that *g* was just as useful there as it is in modern societies, then that would be wrong. A plausible set of things to believe here would be that *g* is an old property of brains. Brains would be expected to function better or less well within species, as Britt Anderson's data suggest in a completely different context, and that that function is reflecting the same kinds of factors causing variation among humans: mutation load, changes in the environment, perhaps disease. All such factors would have an impact on anything complex or costly that an organism does, like running a big brain that mediates complex behaviours. I don't claim that this scenario has been demonstrated, but I think it's an interesting idea that needs to be investigated.

Hinde: A more naïve question: what's the relation between this discussion as to why we have *g* and whether it is adaptive, and the suggestion that it is due to the effects of deleterious genes?

Miller: I hope there's a tight relationship. Most of David Houle's talk was music to my ears, except for his pessimism.

Rutter: So what is the connection between the two?

Miller: If *g* is principally a reflection of mutation load, and it's not a component of fitness but rather it is a subfactor of fitness, this might explain its heritability, the intercorrelations among mental traits that might be quite distinct at an architectural level, and it might explain the increase in correlations between them at low *g*.

Houle: An interesting example of how that might work was provided by the work on hypoglycaemia and test-taking ability. If for some reason you had genetic variation in your ability to maintain blood sugar level, averaged over time, individuals would show variance in *g* not through anything that is happening in their brain. The brain is energetically expensive and depends on everything that we do with the rest of our bodies to function properly. One way this might be testable is that when we start mapping genes for intelligence, I would predict that some of the genes will turn out to be involved in processes, like regulating blood sugar, that are not directly involved in brain function.

Maynard Smith: Depending upon whether one thinks that the genetic variance in a trait arises primarily by recurrent deleterious mutations and a balance between that and selection, or one thinks that it's a property of the fact that being good at this makes you bad at that, so you have a trade-off, you would get quite different correlation structures in your data. And the one thing that we seem to know a lot about is the correlation structure of the data. We ought to be able to argue back from the correlation structure to the kind of genetic variance which is likely to be present and how it arose.

Nesse: I have another naïve question. You were talking about deleterious mutations, and it gives the impression that there are good genes and bad, abnormal genes, as if someone designed something and then these abnormal things came in. Is that right?

Houle: Let's suppose that the mutation–selection balance maintains all variation, which is probably not true, but may be true to a large extent. Then you would expect that any particular mutation would be very rare, but bad. It would still be legitimate in that situation to say that there are good genotypes at all these different loci, so that the normal PKU allele is common, because it is good, and then there are deleterious genotypes that are kept rare by natural selection. This is an extreme example with a discrete choice between normality and a disastrous disease. There are intermediate cases where you have alleles which are a little bit deleterious. Studies from *Drosophila* suggest that the average deleterious mutation is decreasing fitness by around 1%. Natural selection will be pretty bad at eliminating such a gene: it will stick around on average about the inverse of that selection coefficient, about 100 generations, before it would die out. So it could become slightly common within a local population, but you wouldn't expect any of these mutations to explain a great deal of the variation across a whole species. If you find a widespread polymorphism, that would suggest some other process maintaining genetic variation. And in that case, you would get into much more complicated questions of saying what's normal and what's abnormal.

Nesse: You say that on average we each carry 30 deleterious mutations. This means that some people are going to carry 28, and some people are going to carry 32: the question then becomes how much variance there is, and whether that's sufficient to allow natural selection to discriminate effectively between those people carrying more or fewer mutations.

Houle: That's a good question, and raises the sexual selection issues. But one fairly solid way of looking at this is that in *Drosophila* there are good data that if you maintain flies in such a way that natural selection can't act for or against phenotypes, fitness declines around 1% per generation in the lab (Shabalina et al 1997). By Fisher's fundamental theorem, to get equilibrium natural selection has to improve fitness 1% per generation to counteract that. This leads to the prediction that the coefficient of variation of fitness should be around 10%. This is fairly substantial. It is more variable than your average morphological trait, which has coefficients of variation around 5% (Houle 1992).

Maynard Smith: The other variation that is likely to exist in any population, including the human one, is the degree of inbreeding of particular individuals. This is going to lead to substantial differences between different individuals in the number of slightly deleterious recessive genes that are being expressed.

Detterman: There is a peculiar finding in the literature that when someone has Down's syndrome, their IQ correlates as highly with their parents' IQ as does a normal sibling's. I wonder if this is consistent with what we are discussing.

Rutter: The data are contradictory: this effect comes up in some studies but not in others.

Detterman: I have a student who has done a dissertation on this. She has found this in a large sample.

Maynard Smith: I don't think that need contradict what has been said here. The difference between someone with Down's syndrome and their parents is that the child has an extra chromosome. The child will still resemble the parents at other gene loci. There would still be genetic similarity between parent and offspring.

Detterman: Wouldn't you expect it to be reduced?

Houle: Perhaps not on some scales of mental functioning, but it could well be reduced on the scale measured by the test. You could imagine that performance falls at such a level where the test is no longer detecting the underlying variance among individuals who are just answering at random.

Detterman: One other question. The Plomin mapping study has decided to look at normal and high IQ subjects only, I think for this reason. Is that a good choice?

Houle: Actually, I would take the maximum variance, and look at low IQ and high IQ subjects. The trouble is what you will detect with those screens with moderate sample sizes of a few hundred. You would be very unlikely to pick up one of these deleterious recessive alleles, and your statistical power would be very small. What I expect will be the progression of this is that mapping studies will pick out a few genes that have large effects and are probably not maintained by this process of mutation–selection balance. The real question is how much unexplained variance is going to remain after we've picked off the easy genes: is it going to be 80% or is it going to be 10%?

Nesse: Would you anticipate that genes for high IQ would be the same as genes for low IQ?

Houle: Yes. If it's multifactorial, it's all relative, so that a good allele could well occur in a low IQ person. One of the results that some claim on the basis of quantitative trait loci studies is that if you look at their effects, they're extremely context dependent. That is, if you put the same marker in a different background, you get an extremely different expression of that gene. Unfortunately, there are statistical issues here which I don't think have been worked out.

References

Achter JA, Lubinski D, Benbow CP, Sanjani H 1999 Assessing vocational preferences among gifted adolescents adds incremental validity to abilities: a discriminant analysis of educational outcomes over a 10-year interval. J Educ Psychol 91:777–786

Dawes RM, Faust D, Meehl PE 1989 Clinical versus actuarial judgment. Science 243:1669–1674

Falconer DS, Mackay TFC 1996 Introduction to quantitative genetics, 4th edn. Addison Wesley Longman, Harlow

Farrer DN 1967 Picture memory in the chimpanzee. Percept Mot Skills 25:305–315

Grove WM, Meehl PE 1996 Comparative efficiency of formal (mechanical, algorithmic) and informal (subjective, impressionistic) prediction procedures: the clinical/statistical controversy. Psychol Public Policy Law 2:293–323

Houle D 1992 Comparing evolvability and variability of quantitative traits. Genetics 130:195–204

Houle D, Morikawa B, Lynch M 1996 Comparing mutational variabilities. Genetics 143:1467–1483

Humphreys LG, Lubinski D, Yao G 1993 Utility of predicting group membership: exemplified by the role of spatial visualization for becoming an engineer, physical scientist, or artist. J Appl Psychol 78:250–261

Lubinski D 1996 Applied individual differences research and its quantitative methods. Psychol Public Policy Law 2:187–203

Lubinski D 2000 Assessing individual differences in human behavior: 'sinking shafts at a few critical points'. Annu Rev Psychol 51:405–444

Mealey L, Segal NL 1993 Heritable and environmental variables affect reproduction-related behaviors, but not ultimate reproductive success. Pers Individ Differ 14:783–794

Perusse D 1993 Cultural and reproductive success in industrial societies: testing the relationship at the proximate and ultimate levels. Behav Brain Sci 16:267–283

Shabalina SA, Yampolsky LY, Kondrashov AS 1997 Rapid decline of fitness in panmictic populations of *Drosophila melanogaster*. Proc Natl Acad Sci USA 94:13034–13039

Smits CH, Deeg DJ, Kriegsman DM, Schmand B 1999 Cognitive functioning and health as determinants of mortality in an older population. Am J Epidemiol 150:978–986

Vining DR 1986 Social versus reproductive success: the central problem of humane sociobiology. Behav Brain Sci 9:167–187

Whiten A 1999 The evolution of deep social mind in humans. In: Corbalis MC, Lea SEG (eds) The descent of mind. Oxford University Press, Oxford, p 173–193

How can psychological adaptations be heritable?

J. Michael Bailey

Department of Psychology, Northwestern University, 209 Sheridan Road, Evanston, IL 60208-2710, USA

Abstract. By Fisher's fundamental theorem, selection depletes additive genetic variation. However, moderate heritabilities are invariably obtained for psychological traits, even those that have been under intense selection. Examples include sociosexuality (interest in emotionally uncommitted sex), schizophrenia and sexual orientation, which have all been subject to strong sexual selection. A number of factors can help maintain (or at least slow depletion of) genetic variation. These include antagonistic pleiotropy; geographic or temporal variability in optimal phenotypes (and hence genotypes); mutational pressure (especially in the context of parasite resistance dynamics); and existence of heritable strategic variation or morphs. I discuss the likelihood that these factors maintain heritable variation for intelligence. I then review some evolutionary hypotheses regarding variation in some specific psychological traits.

2000 The nature of intelligence. Wiley, Chichester (Novartis Foundation Symposium 233) p 171–184

High intelligence is universally admired, and it seems intuitively obvious that more intelligent people have advantages over less intelligent people. Members of *Homo sapiens* have much larger brains than their ancestors did, and this almost certainly reflects directional selection for higher intelligence (Dunbar 1992). Although there are no clear criteria for determining whether a particular characteristic is an adaptation, the complexity and distinctiveness of human intelligence make it a highly plausible candidate. If high intelligence has been so advantageous to our ancestors, why are there such noticeable differences among us in intelligence? Furthermore, why are those differences moderately heritable? If genes for low intelligence have been disadvantageous, why are they still with us?

The paradox of heritable variation for adaptive (and their logically necessary complement, maladaptive) traits applies more generally than merely to intelligence. Indeed, in the human behaviour genetics literature most traits are moderately heritable. (Elsewhere I have recommended the generalization that $h^2 = 0.40 \pm 0.20$ as 'Bailey's Law' [Bailey 1997].) This appears to be true even of traits associated with reproductive success, such as schizophrenia versus normality (Gottesman 1991) and homosexuality versus heterosexuality (e.g. Bailey & Pillard 1991, Bailey et al 2000a).

Fisher's fundamental theorem (1958) states that selection removes additive genetic variance, and thus should diminish narrow sense heritability. Because of Fisher's argument (which is mathematically correct), scientists have argued until recently that additive heritability was *prima facie* evidence that the trait was evolutionarily neutral (e.g. Tooby & Cosmides 1990). However, the ubiquity of additive genetic variation, even for traits subject to strong selective forces, has forced evolutionary biologists to try to account for the routine violations of Fisher's fundamental theorem.

In my chapter, I first summarize some of the most plausible explanations for why, even if a trait is associated with increased reproductive success, we would expect it to remain at least somewhat heritable. When possible, I will address the potential relevance of each general explanation to an account of variation in intelligence. Next, I consider hypotheses of adaptive, or strategic, genetic variation. Finally, I consider several other psychological traits whose genetic variation has intrigued scientists. For each, I briefly review the status of hypotheses regarding the persistence of trait variation.

Factors that maintain genetic variation

Mutation

The raw material of evolution is provided by genetic mutation. Because even the highest mutation rates are low, it has often been assumed that mutation cannot help much in explaining how genetic variation persists despite selection. Favourable mutations should quickly (in evolutionary scale) become fixed in the population, and unfavourable mutations should quickly be eliminated. However, it has recently become evident that we have underestimated the mutation rate. One current estimate is that on average, each human carries one or two fresh mutations (Kondrashov 1988). Because mutations introduce noise into a highly selected, finely tuned system, their effect will most often be negative with respect to fitness. Although some mutations have horrendous phenotypic effects that are incompatible with life, most have much smaller effects, which allow but impede reproduction.

Mildly deleterious mutations are eventually eliminated from the gene pool, albeit much more slowly compared with lethal mutations. Because mildly deleterious mutations are common, there is probably important variation in the number of such mutations that we carry. That is, humans vary in genetic quality. Thus, we have an incentive to distinguish between potential mates. Because females make a larger investment than males in reproduction, they have an especially strong incentive to be picky about a potential mate's genes. Mutation is an important component of theories of sexual selection (Rice 1988).

Variation is most likely to be maintained by mutation when a trait is affected by genes at many different loci. Miller (2000, this volume) points out that because the human brain is so complex, any mutation is likely to affect intelligence. He also offers the hypothesis that some aspects of human intelligence are sexually selected.

Environmental variation

If the optimal phenotype varies regionally, genetic variation will tend to be maintained. The controversial idea that differences between human races and ethnic groups in intelligence may be partly genetic depends on the validity of the scenario that there has been geographic variation in optimal intelligence level (e.g. Rushton 1995).

Pathogens help insure genetic diversity across time (Tooby & Cosmides 1990) and place (Gangestad & Buss 1993). Genes that confer resistance to common parasites at one time are unlikely to remain the most resistant at a much later time, because as successful genes become more common, pathogens will rapidly evolve to hone in on them. On average, rare genotypes will be the most parasite resistant. Parasite resistance is another respect (along with mutational load) in which individuals of a species may vary in genetic quality. Because brain development is probably sensitive to developmental perturbations, intelligence may be a good marker of individual differences in parasite infestation. One test of this hypothesis would be to correlate geographic variation in parasite prevalence with importance of potential mates' intelligence.

Antagonistic pleiotropy

Most genes have many phenotypic effects. An allele that is evolutionarily advantageous with respect to one trait may be disadvantageous with respect to another. For example, in some species genotypes that reproduce the earliest may be relatively short-lived (Rose & Charlesworth 1980). The antagonistic pleiotropy hypothesis of ageing, that genes that confer early benefits are responsible for many of ageing's detrimental effects (Williams 1957), is another example.

Are there genetic costs to higher intelligence? Jensen (1998) has reviewed evidence that myopia is genetically correlated with higher intelligence, and it is plausible that difficulty in seeing sights at a distance would be evolutionarily disadvantageous. Intelligence is positively correlated with brain size (Willerman et al 1991), and larger brains may be metabolically costly.

Frequency dependent and density dependent selection

Perhaps the most interesting potential explanation of the persistence of genetic variation, at least from the perspective of evolutionary behavioural science, is that part of the variation represents different genetically based life history strategies. This possibility raises a number of complex issues, some of which I address in the next section. Assuming this possibility is plausible, why doesn't the best strategy win? One solution to this problem is that how good a strategy is may depend on its frequency (frequency dependent selection). One strategy may be best until it becomes too frequent, at which point another strategy works better. Alternatively, the success of a strategy may depend on population size (density dependent selection). At low population density, a strategy (attempting to fill a certain niche) may be superior to alternatives, but as population size increases, it may become less so. Frequency and density dependent selection can lead to one form of adaptive genetic variation, in which different genetic morphs pursue different life history strategies. The general issue of strategic variation, or variation in life history strategies, including heritable life history variation, has provoked a great deal of interest among evolutionary psychologists, and thus I devote the next section to clarifying some relevant issues.

Strategic variation

The general issue of adaptive genetic variation among humans has been intensely debated (Tooby & Cosmides 1990, Wilson 1994). Following Wilson (1994) I use 'adaptive' (alternatively, 'coordinated') genetic variation to refer to genetic variation that is the product of natural selection. Such variation is not only allowed by evolutionary processes but is created by them.

Tooby & Cosmides (1990) have provided the most formidable argument against the possibility of adaptive genetic variation. The argument concerns the genetics of polygenic systems. Most human behavioural variation is polygenic. Two genetically determined alternative strategies will differ at many genetic loci, across several chromosomes. The problem with the coevolution of two alternative strategies is that fortuitous combinations of genes will be broken apart during recombination. For example, assume that 'Dads' (dependable mates, high investment) and 'Cads' (undependable mates, low investment) represent two possible genetically determined life history strategies. These strategies are behaviourally complex and surely would differ, on average, at many loci. Whenever someone with a 'Dad' genotype mated with someone with a 'Cad' genotype (or anyone with a genotype different from 'Dad'), the adapted genotypes would both be destroyed.

Wilson (1994) has argued that it is premature to dismiss the possibility of adaptive genetic variation. Both simulations (e.g. Wilson & Turelli 1986) and empirical data (Wilson 1998) suggest that complex polymorphisms (involving at least two loci) can be maintained in a population if their fitnesses are sufficiently high, even if intermediate forms have relatively low fitness. In one model (Wilson

& Turelli 1986), the prevalent phenotype is well adapted to niche 1, but poorly adapted to niche 2. A mutant phenotype is better adapted than the prevalent phenotype to niche 2, although less well adapted to niche 2 than the prevalent phenotype is to niche 1. The mutant phenotype is said to be 'crudely adapted' to niche 2 (Wilson & Turelli 1986). This assumption is biologically plausible, because it would be surprising if a mutant were as well adapted for any niche as the prevalent phenotype, which has evolved to fill the primary niche. The mutant phenotype can spread if niche 1 is overexploited and niche 2 is underexploited. Hence, the model requires density dependence.

One important implication of the model (and frequency dependent analogues) is that they require a small number of genes (perhaps one or two) that have important (hence presumably detectable) effects. Thus, traits hypothesized to vary due to density or frequency dependence may be especially good candidates for genetic linkage studies.

Contingent variation

Adaptive genetic variation is not the only possible cause of adaptive phenotypic variation. People sometimes assume that behavioural adaptations are fixed and inflexible, but there is no reason why this must be true. A gene can code for phenotypic flexibility, given environmental input. For example, people may possess the ability to assess their own mate value (Landolt et al 1995) and to pursue different mating strategies on the basis of what they infer. Moreover, these 'decisions' (for they are surely mostly unconscious) may be made using a species-typical adapted mental algorithm. That is, human nature may be contingent, programmed such that fundamentally different circumstances lead to fundamentally different outcomes. By this model, we all possess the basic architecture to pursue different strategies.

The evolution of a contingent human nature simply requires that across generations, humans are regularly exposed to different environments in which different strategies would work best. Genes that have different, optimal, effects in different environments (i.e., which show gene–environment interaction) are selected. Genes that affect sexual differentiation have been selected this way. Such genes have different effects in the presence of testosterone than they do in its absence. It is also possible that genes have been selected to yield different phenotypes contingent on information about one's own genetic endowment. In their discussion of this possibility, to which they refer as 'reactive heritability', Tooby & Cosmides (1990) offered the example of an evolved programme to be more aggressive when one has a stronger body, but to be less aggressive when one has a weaker body. One's strength is likely to be a highly genetic trait. If so, and given the evolved programme, trait aggression would also be highly heritable.

This would be so even if the evolved programme were species-typical and hence not at all heritable.

Human psychological variation

In this section, I briefly review evolutionary hypotheses of variation for several psychological traits that have captured the interest of evolutionary scientists: sociosexuality, schizophrenia, sexual orientation and psychopathy.

Sociosexuality

Sociosexuality is the tendency to engage in casual, uncommitted sex. Those who seek casual sexual encounters have an unrestricted sociosexual orientation, and those who avoid them have a restricted orientation (Simpson & Gangestad 1991). Although evolutionary psychologists have focused a great deal of attention on the sex difference in sociosexuality, for which there is a compelling evolutionary explanation (e.g. Symons 1979, Buss 1994), they have until recently ignored its within sex variation. The variation within sexes is both substantially larger than the between sex variation and moderately heritable (Bailey et al 2000b). The sex lives of restricted and unrestricted individuals differ markedly in ways that would seem to have important evolutionary implications. How is the genetic variation in sociosexuality maintained?

Gangestad and Simpson have provided a detailed theory of male sociosexuality variation (Gangestad & Simpson 2000). Men vary in their genetic quality, largely due to mutational pressure in the context of parasite resistance dynamics, which impedes allelic fixation. Men with good genes have low levels of developmental instability, and some indicators of developmental instability are detectable. Women prefer men with low levels of developmental instability, and hence such men have more mating opportunities and can invest less in particular women. Thus, variation in male sociosexuality tracks variation in male genetic quality. The most direct evidence for this hypothesis consists of replicated correlations between fluctuating asymmetry and sociosexuality in men. Fluctuating asymmetry is a putative marker of developmental instability. On average, more symmetric men have more sex partners and invest less in each, compared with more asymmetric men (Gangestad & Simpson 2000). This work represents the most successful evolutionary account to date of human psychological trait variation.

Schizophrenia

Schizophrenia is moderately to highly heritable (Gottesman 1991). It also has a marked negative impact on reproductive success, particularly for men, who have less than half the number of offspring compared with other men (Gottesman 1991, 196–207). The prevalence of schizophrenia (approximately 1%) is much higher than would be expected given its impact on reproductive success. Crow (1995) has proposed that schizophrenia is an unfortunate by-product of the development of language during the speciation of *H. sapiens*. His argument primarily consists of marshalling evidence that schizophrenia is related to anomalies of cerebral asymmetry. He theorizes that genetic variation for schizophrenia reflects genetic variation in the rate of development of the two cerebral hemispheres (which also affects handedness), and posits that a single gene is responsible. Allelic variation at the putative locus is maintained by heterozygote advantage in cognitive ability. Crow's theory is quite elaborate considering its limited empirical support. In particular, there is little support for a simple genetic contribution to handedness (Gangestad et al 1996) or of heterozygote superiority with respect to reproductive success of the putative gene. Yeo et al (1999) have suggested that schizophrenia is a consequence of developmental instability, which is a consequence of mutational pressure and pathogens. This model is the same one that Gangestad & Simpson (2000) have successfully applied to male sociosexuality variation. It is somewhat less successful regarding schizophrenia, however. In the case of sociosexuality, there is a well-explicated connection between developmental instability and low interest in casual sex among men. Women prefer men with low developmental instability, and men with high instability get fewer mating opportunities. There is thus no benefit to the latter having high motivation for sexual variety, because they will not have the opportunity to act on it. It is much less clear why developmental noise should lead to auditory hallucinations, flat affect and social withdrawal.

Sexual orientation

Homosexuality is even more common than schizophrenia, with a prevalence exceeding 2% for adult men and 1% for adult women (Laumann et al 1994). Homosexuality appears to reduce reproductive success even more than schizophrenia, with one study finding about an 80% reduction (Bell & Weinberg 1978). Sexual orientation appears to be modestly heritable (Bailey & Pillard 1991, Bailey et al 2000a). Because of its high prevalence and negative impact on reproductive success, homosexuality is an evolutionary anomaly. (To say that homosexuality is an evolutionary anomaly is to say nothing about its social or moral acceptability.) It is such an evolutionary anomaly that it has inspired a great deal of speculation. A review of relevant hypotheses is beyond the scope of this chapter (but see McKnight 1997). No hypothesis has generated compelling data or has gained scientific consensus. Indeed, no one has showed that any existing hypothesis is even mathematically plausible. Thus, homosexu orientation remains a fascinating challenge to evolutionary psychology.

Psychopathy

Because psychopaths cause great harm to others, predominant aetiologic hypotheses have stressed failures of normal development. However, recent several researchers have suggested that psychopathy represents an alternative li history strategy (Colman & Wilson 1997, Lalumiere et al 1996, Mealey 1995 Specifically, they have hypothesized that psychopaths succeed by exploitir others for resources and sexual opportunities. Both frequency depende (Colman & Wilson 1997, Mealey 1995) and environmental contingency (Meale 1995) models have been proposed.

Conclusions

Scientists have only recently begun to pay serious attention to the evolution psychological trait variation. Because we are at an early stage in this science, an because evolutionary hypotheses are intrinsically difficult to test, there is current an excessive ratio of speculation to data. However, there have also been importan theoretical and empirical advances, particularly in the domain of sexual selectio (e.g. sociosexuality). Interdisciplinary effort, including both experts on relevan phenotypes and evolutionary biologists — just the kind of group who comprise this meeting — will be needed to progress far.

Acknowledgements

I am indebted to Gregory Cochran and Steve Gangestad for invaluable discussions, and to Jo Linsenmeier for her comments on a draft of the manuscript.

References

Bailey JM 1997 Are genetically based individual differences compatible with species-wic adaptations? In: Weisfeld GE, Weisfeld CC, Segal NL (eds) Uniting psychology ar biology: Integrative perspectives on human development. American Psychologic Association, Washington, DC, p 81–90

Bailey JM, Pillard RC 1991 A genetic study of male sexual orientation. Arch Gen Psychiatr 48:1089–1096

Bailey JM, Dunne MP, Martin NG 2000a Genetic and environmental influences on sexu orientation and its correlates in an Australian twin sample. J Pers Soc Psychol 78:524–536

Bailey JM, Kirk KM, Zhu G, Dunne MP, Martin MP 2000b Do individual differences i sociosexuality represent genetic or environmentally-contingent strategies? Evidence fro the Australian Twin Registry. J Pers Soc Psychol 78:537–545

Bell AP, Weinberg MS 1978 Homosexualities: a study of diversity among men and women. Simon and Schuster, New York

Buss DM 1994 The evolution of desire: strategies of human mating. HarperCollins, New York

Colman AM, Wilson JC 1997 Antisocial personality disorder: an evolutionary game theory analysis. Legal Criminol Psychol 2:23–34

Crow TJ 1995 Aetiology of schizophrenia: an evolutionary theory. Int Clin Psychopharmacol (suppl 3) 10:49–56

Dunbar RIM 1992 Neocortex size as a constraint on group size in primates. J Hum Evol 22:469–493

Fisher RA 1958 The genetical theory of natural selection. Dover, New York

Gangestad SW, Buss DM 1993 Pathogen prevalence and human mate preferences. Ethol Sociobiol 14:89–96

Gangestad SW, Simpson JA 2000 The evolution of mating: trade-offs and strategic pluralism. Behav Brain Sci 23, in press

Gangestad SW, Yeo RA, Shaw P, Thoma R, Daniel WF, Korthank A 1996 Human leukocyte antigens and hand preference: preliminary observations. Neuropsychology 10:432–428

Gottesman II 1991 Schizophrenia genesis. Freeman, San Francisco

Jensen AR 1998 The *g* factor: the science of mental ability. Praeger, Westport, CT

Kondrashov AS 1988 Deleterious mutations and the evolution of sexual recombination. Nature 336:435–440

Lalumiere ML, Chalmers LJ, Quinsey VL, Seto MC 1996 A test of the mate deprivation hypothesis of sexual coercion. Ethol Sociobiol 17:299–318

Landolt JA, Lalumiere ML, Quinsey VL 1995 Sex differences in intra-sex variations in human mating tactics: an evolutionary approach. Ethol Sociobiol 16:3–23

Laumann EO, Gagnon JH, Michael RT, Michaels S 1994 The social organization of sexuality: sexual practices in the United States. University of Chicago Press, Chicago, IL, p 283–320

McKnight J 1997 Straight science? Homosexuality, evolution, and adaptation. Routledge, London

Mealey L 1995 The sociobiology of sociopathy: an integrated evolutionary model. Behav Brain Sci 18:523–541

Miller G 2000 Sexual selection for indicators of intelligence. In: The nature of intelligence. Wiley, Chichester (Novartis Found Symp 223) p 260–275

Rice WR 1988 Heritable variation in fitness as a prerequisite for adaptive female choice: the effect of mutation–selection balance. Evolution 42:817–820

Rose M, Charlesworth B 1980 A test of evolutionary theories of senescence. Nature 287:141–142

Rushton JP 1995 Race, evolution, and behavior: a life history perspective. Transaction, New Brunswick, NJ

Simpson JA, Gangestad SW 1991 Individual differences in sociosexuality: evidence for convergent and discriminant validity. J Pers Soc Psychol 60:870–883

Symons DT 1979 The evolution of human sexuality. Oxford University Press, New York

Tooby J, Cosmides L 1990 On the universality of human nature and the uniqueness of the individual: the role of genetics and adaptation. J Pers 58:17–67

Willerman L, Schultz R, Rutledge JN, Bigler ED 1991 *In vivo* brain size and intelligence. Intelligence 15:223–228

Williams GC 1957 Pleiogropy, natural selection, and the evolution of senescence. Evolution 11:398–411

Wilson DS 1994 Adaptive genetic variation and human evolutionary psychology. Ethol Sociobiol 15:219–236

Wilson DS 1998 Adaptive individual differences within single populations. Philos Trans R Soc Lond B Biol Sci 353:199–205

Wilson DS, Turelli M 1986 Stable underdominance and the evolutionary invasion of empty
    niches. Am Nat 127:835–850
Yeo RA, Gangestad SW, Edgar C, Thoma R 1999 The evolutionary genetic underpinnings of
    schizophrenia: the developmental instability model. Schizophr Res 39:197–206

DISCUSSION

Dunbar: Perhaps one oughtn't get too worried about the apparent infertility of
smarter people. The situation is more complex because of the costs of rearing
children. Ruth Mace and one or two others have developed models recently that
show rather nicely that when the costs of rearing start to bite — the cost required to
place your offspring in advantageous positions in society, which is the problem we
have now in a highly educational-based society — it really pays you to have fewer
children, given that there's likely to be a correlation then between IQ and social
economic achievement. This apparent negative correlation may be something
similar to David Lack's findings on optimum clutch size in birds. Offspring
number is contingent upon circumstances, and restricting the number of children
may be an optimal strategy in terms of lineage survival.

Bailey: I didn't mean to suggest that this was part of any theory of the evolution
of intelligence, except that I do think it suggests that intelligence is related
somehow to reproductive patterns.

Humphrey: If it is right that intelligent people are investing more in their fewer
children, we would expect also to find a sex bias in their children. We would expect
higher IQ to be correlated with a bias towards having boys.

Dunbar: I don't know about IQ, but a number of studies have shown that the
richer sector of the population invests more heavily in their sons than daughters,
and the poorer sector invests more heavily in their daughters. Various studies (e.g.
Bereczkei & Dunbar 1997) have shown that this applies, even down to the level of
how long mothers breast-feed their children for.

Nesse: We have just completed a study at Michigan using the Panel Study for
Income Dynamics, which I think is the only population representative sample to
address this question. Matt Keller is the leader of this project. We went in expecting
Trivers–Willard effects to be found, and after doing 65 different comparisons with
seven or eight different outcome variables, including breast-feeding, amount of
hugs per day, money spent on the care of the child were compared by different
class. We found no effect whatsoever and as a result have reconsidered the
fundamental thinking of the Trivers–Willard logic. It is entirely possible that it
occurs in other societies, but we think we have definitive evidence that it does
not occur in the USA.

Humphrey: One of the clearest examples of this Trivers–Willard effect in humans
comes from new work by Peter Sykora (unpublished results), in which he has

ɔoked at the sex ratio in relation to infanticide in Czechoslovakia over the period ɔanning the end of communism. He predicted that after the fall of communism ⱱhen people felt insecure and worried about the future, mothers show a new bias ɡainst sons and in favour of daughters. He got the police record and showed ɦat in the five years before 1990, there were 1.4 times as many boys killed as ʓirls, but in the five years following, there were 3.5 times as many boys killed s girls.

Maynard Smith: I'm curious about the prediction from evolutionary game ɦeory, that a genetic polymorphism can be maintained, with different ndividuals adopting different strategies. Can you offer any plausible examples of ɔlaces where a genetic polymorphism or a strategic one exists in the human ɔopulation maintained by that kind of frequency-dependent selection?

Nesse: How about different morphs in fish?

Maynard Smith: There are plenty of non-human examples. I was really thinking ɔf these rather puzzling human behavioural syndromes, as to whether any of them ɖo make sense from a game theory point of view.

Bailey: You can make up stories of all kinds, but there is no real evidence. Ⱶowever, people haven't really looked. It strikes me that by the Wilson ɹrgument, that's where you should be able to find major gene effects in human ɔehaviour. They are not looking there, however, they are looking in chizophrenia, which seems to me to be a terrible evolutionary candidate.

Maynard Smith: Is that because it is not a major gene?

Bailey: It is because it would be so easily weeded out if it were.

Nesse: What are the fitness decreases for schizophrenia?

Bailey: Men reproduce at about half the rate when they have schizophrenia.

Nesse: Is this a significant enough fitness decrease that we have to look for some ⱪind of pleiotropic benefit? How do we explain this kind of thing from a genetic ⱱiewpoint?

Gangestad: The evidence for schizophrenia as well as lots of other neural ɖevelopmental disorders, is that it is caused by developmental disruption fairly ɵarly on. It may well be caused by mutations.

Maynard Smith: It's horribly frequent.

Gangestad: It is 1% over the lifetime, but perhaps 10% of individuals have some ɹspects of the syndrome: although this 10% reproduce at a rate greater than half the ɔopulation average, it is almost certainly less than the population average.

Nesse: I have a speculation. If in fact we believe that, for whatever reasons, ntelligence has been quite rapidly selected over the last few thousand ʒenerations, is it possible that such rapid selection for one particular trait would ɵither drag along with it deleterious genes, or more likely, cause trade-offs in other raits that would make one vulnerable to other kinds of problems? The model here s the upright posture of humans. It has advantages, but unfortunately we pay a high price for it that will take another million years to fix. Could the same thing have happened if there had been rapid selection for high intelligence?

Suddendorf: Is there a connection between schizophrenia and high IQ?

Deary: Higher IQ is protective against at least being diagnosed as having schizophrenia (David et al 1997).

Rutter: The predictive power comes from both IQ and developmental delays way before the onset of schizophrenia. It seems likely to be involved in the predisposition in some sort of way, but whether that is genetic or due to environmental hazards is still a matter of debate. There is also debate as to whether this is diagnosis-specific or not. For quite a long time people saw this as an early marker of a genetic liability to schizophrenia. But the fact that similar although weaker associations have been found for bipolar disorder throws that in question.

Gangestad: I would expect that intelligence would coevolve with a number of things, one of which would be investment in maintaining the soma. The way life history theorists talk about body size is that increased body size is associated with increased net energy gain, but it comes at the cost of building the bigger body. What is optimal body size depends somewhat on mortality rate. Some people such as Hillard Kaplan consider intelligence to be a capital investment in the self that only pays off over time. Kaplan and colleagues have recently claimed that investment in intelligence should coevolve with an increased effort to maintain the soma, thereby increasing the period during which the investment can pay off (Kaplan et al 2000). The major cost is delayed reproduction, not necessarily some deleterious trait.

Rutter: Is the delayed reproduction general? This is certainly pervasive now, but was that true, for example, at the turn of the century?

Gangestad: I'm speaking here of the non-reproductive developmental period. The comparative primate data are of interest here. Across species, body size of course predicts brain size. Group size also predicts brain size. But if you co-vary out these variables another predictor of brain size is delay of first reproduction. It seems as though there is a cost paid for growing a larger brain, independent of growing a larger body.

Karmiloff-Smith: Isn't the period of postnatal brain growth relevant here?

Gangestad: I'm not aware of good comparative data relevant to that issue.

Dunbar: It seems that the really key correlation is the one between non-visual neocortex size and the period of juvenility between weaning and first reproduction, in other words the period of socialization. In humans, neocortex is the bit that's increased out of all proportion. It suggests that there is a very strong emphasis on socialization—the software programming, as it were, is becoming crucial at this point, it's not just the hardware that's the issue.

Miller: I'm wondering whether we should be a little bit cautious about aggregating data about reproductive success with respect to IQ over very different socioeconomic groups and different subcultures. We live in a very curious modern society where there are many different mating pools, and somebody within a particular mating pool is rather unlikely to meet a long-term partner from a different mating pool. Have there been serious attempts to compare the reproductive success of bright lawyers to dumb lawyers, or bright taxi drivers to dumb taxi drivers? This would help tease out these subculture-specific effects within each mating pool.

Bailey: I doubt that that's been done. I'm not sure I agree that's the thing to do, because IQ might be strategic in getting people into the different pools in the first place.

Rutter: The question you pose must be answerable within a many available data sets. Any of the large-scale longitudinal studies should be able to provide data on this.

Humphrey: I want to come back to the question of whether stupidity is strategic, and rephrase it slightly. Is it possible that ordinariness is strategic? Earlier I raised the matter of the Connecticut police force not wanting recruits with high IQ. But these days at any rate, if extra clever people aren't wanted in the police force they'll certainly be wanted somewhere else — at least in a society like the modern USA, where there are so many possible different niches to be filled. So everyone can find employment to match their talents, and we get the kind of monotonic relationship between IQ and worldly success that David Lubinski described in his paper (Lubinski 2000, this volume). However, in the environment in which we evolved, the range of opportunities for an individual were certainly not as large. If you were too bright or too dull to make a good member of the stone age task force you couldn't just go off and find some more appropriate occupation. If you didn't fit in, you would potentially be in considerable trouble. Under those conditions, to have been at an extreme in IQ, as in any other trait, might in fact have been maladaptive. And there surely wouldn't have been the same monotonic relationship between IQ and success, because there wouldn't have been a specialized niche for the high IQ people to succeed in.

Maynard Smith: I wouldn't follow that argument too far, because something has differentiated us from chimpanzees in evolutionary terms in rather a short period. The fact that we talk and do sums and they don't has to be genetic rather than environmental, so there has to have been powerful selection in favour of IQ. If selection had been for the guy in the middle this wouldn't have happened.

I don't think there's anything theoretically implausible about that the notion that if a population is being selected rather strongly to acquire some new trait such as the ability to talk, occasionally a genotype might arise which would be disastrous. I'm thinking of these conditions like schizophrenia which are far too frequent to be easily explained, and which do appear to have at least some kind of genetic component. I have this image of this population of intelligent birds, which have been selected very powerfully for the ability to fly, sitting around in the Novartis Foundation asking, 'Why is the frequency of chaps who break their necks falling out of trees so high?' There could be a risk in being too bloody clever that could account for the schizophrenics and depressives, and so on. The high frequency of conditions such as schizophrenia really is a puzzle.

References

Bereczkei T, Dunbar RIM 1997 Female-biased reproductive strategies in a Hungarian gypsy population. Proc R Soc Lond B Biol Sci 264:17–22

David AS, Malmberg A, Brandt L, Allebeck P, Lewis G 1997 IQ and risk for schizophrenia: a population-based cohort study. Psychol Med 27:1311–1323

Kaplan H, Hill K, Lancaster J, Hutardo AM 2000 A theory of human life history evolution Evol Anthropol, in press

Lubinski D 2000 Intelligence: success and fitness. In: The nature of intelligence. Wiley Chichester (Novartis Found Symp 233) p 6–27

Social complexity and social intelligence

School of Psychology, University of St Andrews, St Andrews, Fife KY16 9JU, UK

Abstract. When we talk of the 'nature of intelligence', or any other attribute, we may be referring to its essential structure, or to its place in nature, particularly the function it has evolved to serve. Here I examine both, from the perspective of the evolution of intelligence in primates. Over the last 20 years, the Social (or 'Machiavellian') Intelligence Hypothesis has gained empirical support. Its core claim is that the intelligence of primates is primarily an adaptation to the special complexities of primate social life. In addition to this hypothesis about the function of intellect, a secondary claim is that the very structure of intelligence has been moulded to be 'social' in character, an idea that presents a challenge to orthodox views of intelligence as a general-purpose capacity. I shall outline the principal components of social intelligence and the environment of social complexity it engages with. This raises the question of whether domain specificity is an appropriate characterization of social intelligence and its subcomponents, like theory of mind. As a counter-argument to such specificity I consider the hypothesis that great apes exhibit a cluster of advanced cognitive abilities that rest on a shared capacity for second-order mental representation.

2000 The nature of intelligence. Wiley, Chichester (Novartis Foundation Symposium 233) p 185–201

Introduction

'Social intelligence' — a challenge to tradition

When we talk of the 'nature' of a human attribute like intelligence, we may mean several things. I shall highlight two. First, we may have in mind the 'essential nature' of intelligence. What exactly does intelligence amount to, when we subject it to scientific scrutiny? What is its structure and how does it operate?

The second, alternative sense of 'nature' can be thought of as shorthand for 'natural history'. Where and how does intelligence fit into the rest of the natural world? Why have certain forms of intelligence evolved? What are their functions?

These two sides of the 'nature' of intelligence are likely to be intimately related, as we should expect of the structure and function of any evolved phenomenon.

Intelligence is expected to have the structure it has because of the particular role evolutionary forces have shaped it to play in the natural world. Conversely, the 'nature' (structure) of intelligence at any one point in evolution will have shaped the role its descendant modifications play.

Thinking about these two sides of the 'nature of intelligence' is essential to make sense of the implications of the subject matter of this paper: social intelligence. The idea of 'social intelligence' arose as studies of primate social life became more numerous and sophisticated in the 1960s and 1970s. The basic proposition formulated perhaps most influentially in Humphrey's (1976) paper, 'The social function of intellect', is that primate intelligence is primarily an adaptation to the special complexities of primates' social lives. This, of course, connects immediately with one of the two senses of 'the nature of intelligence': if the hypothesis is correct, the evolutionary *raison d'être* of intelligence can be traced to one crucial segment of primates' environments — their societies. To understand intelligence in nature, this is where we would have to focus our studies. This was (and still is) a radical proposition, because academic analysis of intelligence has focused almost exclusively on non-social or technical realms. IQ has traditionally been assessed with scant regard to the social world. This means that if the 'social intellect hypothesis' is correct, the study of intelligence has neglected the principal factor that can explain its existence.

The implications might be no less radical for the other sense of the 'nature of intelligence'. If intelligence has been shaped by social forces, its very architecture may be explicable by the demands of social life — intelligence might not only have been created by social factors, but might contain design features specifically structured for dealing with this social world.

That primate intelligence was selected for primarily by the social world, and that it is adapted particularly to deal with that world, are hypotheses open to empirical test. One might be true and not the other. Thus, it could be true that primate intelligence exists because of the demands of social life; yet the nature of that intelligence might be sufficiently flexible that it finds equal application across social and non-social domains of primates' lives. General-purpose flexibility is, after all, one of the traditionally defining features of intelligence. The question of whether primate intelligence is indeed general-purpose, or whether its structure is biased to deal with social problems, is one we shall revisit.

Whatever the answer to this latter question, there is one aspect of the social intellect hypothesis that seems to offer undeniable explanatory power. If a complex social environment favours the offspring of the most socially intelligent individuals, those offspring will likely generate yet greater levels of social complexity as they mature. Social intelligence would thus have the inherent potential to spiral to new heights with each new generation.

Machiavellian intelligence': the hypothesis supported

Following Humphrey (1976), some have talked of 'the social intelligence hypothesis' (e.g. Kummer et al 1997), but 'social' is not really an adequate label. Many species are social, often living in larger groupings than do primates, without evidencing great intelligence. What is argued to be special about primates is their social complexity, as exemplified in the cultivation of alliances and coalitions (Harcourt & de Waal 1992). In a society that includes coalitions, computing the optimal social strategy will often require account to be taken not only of one's dyadic relationship with others, but additional polyadic relationships too. Primate social tactics have frequently been described as manipulative or political (de Waal 1982) and a variety of deceptive ploys have been recorded (Whiten & Byrne 1988a). Social manouevres often fit the cunning advice that Nicolò Machiavelli (1513) offered to Italian princes in the service of outwitting and subjugating their competitors and underlings. Accordingly, in collating the first volume dedicated to the topic, Byrne & Whiten (1988) talked not of the 'social' but rather the 'Machiavellian' intelligence hypothesis (MI hypothesis). The term has now passed into conventional usage in the cognitive sciences (Whiten 1999a).

Two potential confusions about the hypothesis should be dispelled at this point. First, although primatology spawned the hypothesis, it is important to acknowledge there is nothing about it that should constrain it to non-human primates. To be sure, the hypothesis arose because of the need to explain forms of intelligence and encephalization that exceed those of most mammals. But the proposition that social complexity will be coupled with high intelligence applies to any taxon that exhibits social complexity, primate or otherwise. Moreover, focusing *within* the primates, one form of the hypothesis may help to explain the rapid elaboration of intelligence and encephalization in humans during the last two million years of evolution (Whiten 1999b, cf. Miller 2000, this volume).

A second potential source of confusion about the MI hypothesis is that in everyday talk, 'Machiavellian' often connotes a self-centred attitude and this has naturally extended into some academic usages (Wilson et al 1996). However, although the behaviour of an animal is expected to favour its own ultimate reproductive interests, cooperation can be one way to promote this and it is widespread in primates (Harcourt & de Waal 1992); it is an important component of the Machiavellian complications of interest. In addition, primates can exploit the knowledge of others socially, either directly by scavenging or indirectly by observational learning (Russon 1997). The latter thus brings even cultural learning within the remit of the MI hypothesis.

So, is the MI hypothesis right? The diverse papers that made up *Machiavellian intelligence* (Byrne & Whiten 1988) were not really concerned to test the hypothesis as such. Rather, when assembled together they suggested that the hypothesis held much promise. In the following years, however, the predictions of the hypothesis — or more specifically, the component of the hypothesis that proposes intelligence to be critically generated by social complexity — began to be tested (e.g. Dunbar 1995). The approach has rested on examining correlations between proxies for intelligence on the one hand, and for social complexity on the other, because direct measures that would do real justice to either of these target variables have yet to be attained.

The proxy for intelligence has been encephalization: brain size, appropriately corrected for body size, or the relative size of components of the brain associated with intelligence or 'higher cognitive functions', notably the neocortex. Social complexity has been estimated by measuring the size of social groups or, more recently, the typical size of cliques that groom together intensively (Dunbar 1998). The question has been whether such indicators of social complexity explain variance amongst primate taxa better than do indicators for rival explanatory pressures concerning the physical environment. Examples of the latter include the size of the animals' range and the proportion of fruit in the diet, which would be expected to correlate with encephalization if intelligence is an adaptation for dealing with such demands as foraging.

These analyses require care and ingenuity, for there are many alternative measures (many ways of correcting for the effects of body size, for example), many alternative statistics and sources of bias to be avoided, such as the effects of phylogenetic relationships between the species used. Analyses have gradually become more sophisticated in all these respects, details of which are far beyond the scope of this short paper. The principal outcome of this work is easy to summarize, however; the results of the more recent studies favour the MI hypothesis over the principal competing hypotheses corresponding to physical or technical factors (Barton & Dunbar 1997, Dunbar 1998) (see Fig. 1).

Components of social complexity
and social intelligence

These correlational analyses provide encouraging support for the MI hypothesis. However, the variables on which they rest are still relatively crude. Our accumulating picture of social complexity is much richer than indicated by group size or even clique size; similarly, the cognitive processes we call 'intelligent' are more diverse and complex than indices like neocortex ratio. In this section, encouraged by the outcome of the correlational work to date, I outline a dissection of what social complexity may entail, given our present understanding. I then do the same for social cognition, thus addressing both senses of the 'nature of intelligence' alluded to at the outset of this paper.

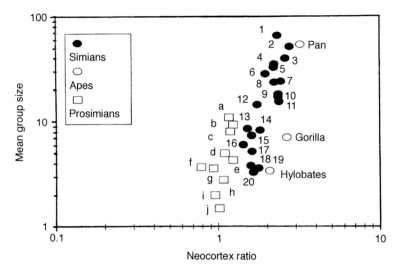

FIG. 1.   Mean group size plotted against neocortex ratio (neocortex relative to rest of brain) for individual genera, shown separately for prosimians, simians (monkeys) and apes (after Dunbar 1998). Simians: 1, *Miopithecus*; 2, *Papio*; 3, *Macaca*; 4, *Procolobus*; 5, *Saimiri*; 6, *Erythrocebus*; 7, *Cercopithecus*; 8, *Lagothrix*; 9, *Cebus*; 10, *Ateles*; 11, *Cercocebus*; 12, *Nasalis*; 13, *Callicebus*; 14, *Alouatta*; 15, *Callimico*; 16, *Cebuela*; 17, *Saguinus*; 18, *Aotus*; 19, *Pithecia*; 20, *Callicebus*. Prosimians: a, *Lemur*; b, *Varecia*; c, *Eulemur*; d, *Propithecus*; e, *Indri*; f, *Microcebus*; g, *Galago*; h, *Hapalemur*; i, *Avahi*; j, *Perodictus*.

Dimensions of social complexity

As our understanding of primate societies has deepened, the expression 'social complexity' occurs more and more frequently. However, it has not been subjected to systematic analysis. Tom Sambrook and I have begun an assault on this task, attempting as far as possible to identify components of social complexity that in principle could be independently measured, even where this is currently difficult in practice (e.g. A. Whiten & T. Sambrook, unpublished paper, Am Soc Primatol, July 1994, Sambrook 1995).

Table 1 lists a number of proposed dimensions of social complexity in primates. Our approach to complexity has been that at the most abstract level, one system is 'more complex' than another if it contains more elements and, even more importantly, more combinations or links between the elements. This conception underlies our approach to both social complexity and cognitive complexity. The social complexity we want to define is that which is predicted to require a more intelligent brain to engage with it, if biological fitness is to be maintained or enhanced (Sambrook & Whiten 1997). One society might thus count as more complex than another if to succeed in it, a member had, for example, to process

TABLE 1   Some dimensions of social complexity in primates

Dimension	*Scope*
Levels of social structure	Extent to which social environment is structured: a) by interactions constituting relationships; b) by relationships constituting political networks, or differentiated into consistent roles (see text).
Dyadic complexity	Greater complexity where an individual's interactions with others are more common (e.g. higher rate of interaction, or more interactants); similarly, where more relationships are the rule (as in analyses based on clique size: see Dunbar 1998). Further dyadic-level complexities include reciprocity (in grooming, for example) and exchange (where one type of benefit is traded for another). There is evidence for both these types of complexity in primates (Cords 1997).
Polyadic complexity	Complexities of interaction involving three or more parties, as recognized by Kummer (1967) and now well documented amongst primates (Harcourt & de Waal 1992, Cords 1997). Triadic complexity can also exist at the relationship level (de Waal 1982).
Variability of response	A social initiative may receive very variable responses, even from the same individual on different occasions, in part because of dependence on allies' availability.
Instability	Relationships vary in stability, creating a pressure to track their status.
Complexity of prediction	The above factors make prediction of the social behaviour of others complex to predict. One measure of this might be the number of factors needed to predict to a certain level of probability. For example, where such factors as rank and availability of allies needs to be considered in addition to rank of protagonist, there is greater social complexity.
Demographic complexity	Although group size in itself may not imply great complexity, it may do so in concert with components like those sketched above. Such factors as turnover (e.g. rate of immigration and emigrations, and possibly group fission) may also be considered background demographic components of the social complexity that the Ego may be faced with.

more items of social information, recognize more combinations of such items, store more information, make more decisions, anticipate more varied outcomes and/or predict new outcomes.

This may sound dangerously circular: if social complexity is defined by reference to cognitive processing requirements, surely the more refined MI hypotheses we are trying to generate are going to get confirmed automatically! But this would be to misunderstand the enterprise. The aim is instead to define components of social complexity that are predicted to afford more complex processing, to define components of intelligence that are predicted to handle social complexity and then, having independently measured samples of each, test for the relationships expected between them.

Space permits little explication here of the measures described in Table 1, beyond the outlines in the table itself. One that begs comment concerns levels of social structure. The earliest substantial analysis of the complexity of primate social structure by Hinde (1976) distinguished three levels: (1) social structure, constituted by the totality of (2) relationships in the group, which are in turn constituted by regularities in (3) interactions between specific individuals. Hinde's scheme is an important foundation to any analysis of social complexity, but a shift in perspective appears to be needed for our purposes. Hinde's analysis dissected structure from the bird's eye perspective of the ethologist; here we are instead concerned with complexity from the perspective of a group member ('Ego'). Ego does appear to face greater social complexity where more levels are present, as in the case where interactions are structured into the relationships typical of anthropoid society. However, Hinde's social structure level appears to amount simply to the sum of Ego's relationships within the group, so we must question if there is really a third 'social structure' level of complexity from Ego's perspective. Nevertheless, a level beyond direct relationships can perhaps be envisaged in the form of such phenomena as politics (where relationships between X and Y may affect those between Ego and X, and Ego and Y) and the existence of societal roles (like 'kingmaker'), which differentiate alternative pathways relationships might take. Other dimensions of social complexity are briefly outlined in Table 1.

Components of social intelligence

Whiten & Byrne (1988b), in attempting to describe the scope of Machiavellian intelligence, were struck by a paper by Sternberg et al (1981) that aimed to establish what the public at large takes intelligence to be. This is surely an important enterprise, because although science can establish the extent to which natural phenomena conform to any given criteria for intelligence, scientists cannot do the same for the definition of intelligence itself. Intelligence is whatever people generally mean by the term, and any scientist who attempts to legislate otherwise courts confusion. Interestingly, when interviewed by Sternberg et al, people described intelligence in terms of a considerable diversity of facets, which Byrne and I found we could map rather well to aspects of social intelligence emerging in the new scientific literature (Table 2). The scope of these is further described in Table 3. This does not claim to be an exhaustive analysis but illustrates the idea of component abilities within the concept of social intelligence.

Machiavellian intelligence and modularity

There is a long-standing debate about whether intelligence is a general-purpose capacity or instead encompasses subcomponents. Such subcomponents might be

TABLE 2   People's everyday notions of intelligence, and components of primate social intelligence

People's everyday conceptions of intelligence[a]	Components of primate social intelligence[b]
'knowledgeable about a particular field of knowledge'	social knowledge
'able to apply knowledge to problems' 'shows creativity' 'is a good source of ideas' 'identifies connections between ideas'	solving social problems
'appreciates knowledge for its own sake' 'displays interest in the world around'	curiosity about social world
'sensitive to other people's needs and desires'[c] 'converses well'	social expertise
'interest in learning and culture'	social learning

[a]Aspects of the public's definitions of intelligence (after Sternberg et al 1981).
[b]Related aspects of primate social intelligence.
[c]Factor analysis in the Sternberg et al study identified a reliable factor of 'social competence', second only to 'problem-solving skills' in defining people's conceptions of everyday intelligence.

differentiated in terms of their dedication to particular functions, like spatial memory versus reasoning, and they may be thought of as mental modules (writers vary in their insistence on additional criteria for the module concept: compare Fodor [1983] and Baron-Cohen [1994]). By their nature, such components might find expression to varying degrees in different individuals or species.

Where Machiavellian intelligence stands with respect to such distinctions depends on which version of the MI hypothesis is at stake. In one version, intelligence is defined as a general-purpose ability (typically, general-purpose problem-solving, consistent with the findings of the Sternberg study cited in Table 2), and the MI hypothesis is that intelligence in this sense has been most forcefully shaped by social selection factors, in a taxon such as anthropoid primates.

Another form of the MI hypothesis goes one step further and proposes that the very architecture of intelligence will be intrinsically 'social'; it will be structured in ways adapted to dealing particularly with the unique characteristics of the social environment.

The case for social modules

Dissection of components of social intelligence like those listed in Table 3 seems to imply a modular structure. It suggests there is cognitive specialization for dealing with the social world (rather than the physical world of food items, tools, etc.), and

TABLE 3 Some components of Machiavellian intelligence in primates

ocial knowledge	Primates carry a store of social information about their companions' characteristics, relationships and past behaviour, which they can apply to novel social situations. The extent of knowledge about who is affiliated with whom, and who did what to whom in the past, was strikingly demonstrated by vervet monkeys' enhanced tendency to fight with the relatives of a monkey who attacked their own kin sometime in the last two hours (Cheney & Seyfarth 1990).
ocial curiosity	Note that Cheney and Seyfarth's finding means that the two fighting animals need not have directly interacted in this period; they were instead just intent observers of the social scene around them. Clearly, they actively monitor their social worlds and pick up information that may not be vital at the time, but which may be utilized adaptively later on.
ocial problem solving	Primates may harbour large stores of knowledge about their social worlds, yet as Whiten & Byrne (1988b) noted, 'extensive social knowledge only makes an individual really clever if the individual does something clever with the knowledge'. The solution of problems that are relatively novel has the greatest claim to be intelligent. The scientific difficulty is that novel social problems, even if they can be identified, by their nature tend to lack replication. It is thus relatively rich narrative accounts that tend to carry the most relevant observations, with an accumulating corpus of apparently novel social problem-solving (e.g. de Waal 1982, Goodall 1986). Several of the episodes of tactical deception collated by Whiten & Byrne (1988a) appeared to fall into this category.
Social sensitivity	The Machiavellian monkey is competing in a world of other Machiavellian monkeys, and success may depend upon an astute and sensitive reading of others' behaviour. For example, our corpus of tactical deception indicated that primates are often sensitive to the attentional focus of others, which they both monitor and manipulate, sometimes to the extent of temporarily inhibiting attention to a critical locus so that others will not become aware of this interest (Whiten & Byrne 1988a). This capacity has recently been experimentally confirmed (Tomasello et al 1998).
Social learning	An individual can exploit the knowledge of others by learning from them. Like other items in this table, social learning itself is manifested in many different forms (Russon 1997, Whiten 2000).

moreover, that different capacities exist for dealing with different aspects of that world; different species might thus be socially intelligent to varying degrees, with respect to such possibilities as are shown in the table.

However, there have been few attempts to tackle the case for social modules empirically in research on non-human primates. The most concerted treatment is due to Cheney & Seyfarth (1990), who presented data in support of the contention that vervet monkeys are more sophisticated in their social cognition (e.g. their social knowledge—see Table 3) than in the cognitive achievement evident in their dealings with aspects of their physical environment, like predators

There has been much more theoretical and empirical treatment of the question of socio-cognitive modules in research with human subjects. Cosmides (1989) Gigerenzer (1997) and Cummins (1998), for example, have presented evidence that reasoning in such social domains as detecting cheating operates far more efficiently than when applied to equivalent non-social issues. Within the massive research literature that has developed over the last decade on the child's developing 'theory of mind', the existence of specialized modules subserving this capacity has been based on a different kind of contrast: deficits and delays in mindreading abilities in autism, relative to other, non-social cognitive functions that are spared (Baron-Cohen 1995).

Hierarchies of social modules?

In the face of all the empirical and theoretical analyses cited above, it seems difficult to entertain the idea that all the components of Machiavellian intelligence can be reduced to the operation of some kind of 'generalized intelligence' that just 'happens' to be applied to various aspects of the social world. However intermediates between the hypothesis of a single 'general intelligence' and that positing multitudinous modules are also conceivable. One candidate is the capacity for what Perner (1991) has called 'secondary representation', the ability to entertain multiple mental models, which emerges in children's second year Whiten (1996) and Suddendorf (1998) have independently proposed that just such an ability may underwrite a cluster of capacities, such as simple 'mindreading' and complex imitation, that appear to emerge together in great apes, as they do in children. Here, we have the idea of an ability that is to some degree 'general purpose', forming the cognitive foundation for a cluster of processes with more specific functions and structures, yet 'modular' to the extent that its primary functional context might be the social sphere.

Concluding remarks

The idea of social or Machiavellian intelligence is still quite new, and although already influential, the essential complexity of its subject matter means that we are probably just scratching the surface in our attempts to understand it. However, the first proper tests of the MI hypothesis have supported it, giving encouragement to deeper attempts to dissect both the cognitive capacities involved and the dimensions of social complexity to which they are adapted. It

ould be over-simple to say that 'the nature of intelligence is social', but the study
f Machiavellian intelligence may have profound, and still insufficiently
ecognized, implications for the central subject matter of this volume.

References

aron-Cohen S 1994 How to build a baby that can read minds: cognitive mechanisms in
   mindreading. Cah Psych Cog 13:513–552
aron-Cohen S 1995 Mindblindness: an essay on autism and theory of mind. MIT Press,
   Cambridge, MA
arton RA, Dunbar RIM 1997 Evolution of the social brain. In: Whiten A, Byrne RW (eds)
   Machiavellian intelligence II: evaluations and extensions. Cambridge University Press,
   Cambridge, p 240–263
yrne RW, Whiten A 1988 Machiavellian intelligence: social expertise and the evolution of
   intellect in monkeys, apes and humans. Oxford University Press, Oxford
heney DL, Seyfarth RM 1990 How monkeys see the world: inside the mind of another species.
   University of Chicago Press, Chicago, IL
ords M 1997 Friendships, alliances, reciprocity and repair. In: Whiten A, Byrne RW (eds)
   Machiavellian intelligence II: evaluations and extensions. Cambridge University Press,
   Cambridge, p 24–49
osmides L 1989 The logic of social exchange: has natural selection shaped how humans reason?
   Studies with the Wason selection task. Cognition 31:187–276
ummins DD 1998 Social norms and other minds: the evolutionary roots of higher cognition.
   In: Cummins DD, Allen C (eds) The evolution of mind. Oxford University Press, Oxford,
   p 30–50
e Waal FBM 1982 Chimpanzee politics. Jonathan Cape, London
unbar RIM 1995 Neocortex size and group size in primates: a test of the hypothesis. J Hum
   Evol 28:287–296
unbar RIM 1998 The social brain hypothesis. Evol Anthropol 6:178–190
odor JA 1983 The modularity of mind. MIT Press, Cambridge, MA
igerenzer G 1997 The modularity of social intelligence. In: Whiten A, Byrne RW (eds)
   Machiavellian intelligence II: evaluations and extensions. Cambridge University Press,
   Cambridge, p 264–288
oodall J 1986 The chimpanzees of Gombe: patterns of behavior. Harvard University Press,
   Cambridge MA
Harcourt AH, de Waal FBM 1992 Coalitions and alliances in humans and other animals. Oxford
   University Press, Oxford
Hinde RA 1976 Interactions, relationships and social structure. Man 11:1–17
Humphrey NK 1976 The social function of intellect. In: Bateson PPG, Hinde RA (eds) Growing
   points in ethology. Cambridge University Press, Cambridge, p 303–321
Kummer H 1967 Tripartite relations in hamadryas baboons. In Altmann SA (ed) Social
   communication among primates. University of Chicago Press, Chicago, IL, p 63–71
Kummer H, Daston L, Gigerenzer G, Silk, J 1997 The social intelligence hypothesis. In:
   Weingart P, Richerson P, Mitchell SD, Maasen S (eds) Human by nature: between biology
   and the social sciences. Lawrence Erlbaum Associates, Hillsdale, NJ, p 157–179
Machiavelli N 1513 The prince. (Engl transl: 1961 Penguin Books, Harmondsworth)
Miller G 2000 Sexual selection for indicators of intelligence. In: The nature of intelligence.
   Wiley, Chichester (Novartis Found Symp 233) p 260–275
Perner J 1991 Understanding the representational mind. MIT Press, Cambridge, MA

Russon AE 1997 Exploiting the expertise of others. In: Whiten A, Byrne RW (ed
    Machiavellian intelligence II: evaluations and extensions. Cambridge University Pres
    Cambridge, p 174–206
Sambrook TD 1995 Social complexity in a large and small group of olive baboons. PhD thesi
    University of St Andrews, Scotland
Sambrook TD, Whiten A 1997 On the nature of complexity in cognitive and behaviour
    science. Theory Psych 7:191–213
Sternberg R J, Conway BE, Ketron JL, Bernstein M 1981 People's conceptions of intelligence.
    Pers Soc Psychol 41:37–55
Suddendorf T 1999 The rise of the metamind. In: Corballis MC, Lea SEG (eds) The descent (
    mind: psychological perspectives on hominid evolution. Oxford University Press, Oxfor(
    p 218–260
Tomasello M, Call J, Hare BJ 1998 Five species of nonhuman primates follow the visual gaze (
    conspecifics. Anim Behav 55:1063–1069
Whiten A 1996 Imitation, pretence and mindreading: secondary representation in comparativ
    primatology and developmental psychology. In: Russon A, Bard KA, Parker ST (ed(
    Reaching into thought: the minds of the great apes. Cambridge University Pres
    Cambridge, p 300–324
Whiten A 1999a The Machiavellian intelligence hypothesis. In: Wilson RA, Keil F (eds) MI'
    encyclopedia of the cognitive sciences. MIT Press, Cambridge, MA, p 495–497
Whiten 1999b The evolution of deep social mind in humans. In: Corballis MC, Lea SEG (ed(
    The descent of mind: psychological perspectives on hominid evolution. Oxford Universit
    Press, Oxford, p 173–193
Whiten A 2000 Primate culture and social learning. Cognit Sci 24, in press
Whiten A, Byrne RW 1988a Tactical deception in primates. Behav Brain Sci 11:233–273
Whiten A, Byrne RW 1988b Taking (Machiavellian) intelligence apart. In Byrne RW, Whiten (
    (eds) Machiavellian intelligence. Oxford University Press, Oxford, p 50–65
Wilson DS, Near D, Miller RR 1996 Machiavellianism: a synthesis of the evolutionary an
    psychological literatures. Psych Bull 119:285–99

DISCUSSION

Harnad: One of the things you're probably familiar with in cognitiv
psychology is the implicit/explicit distinction in learning. Do you think of thes
social capacities as being implicit or explicit? Do they need to be explicit? This i
related a little to the on-line/off-line dichotomy that I was trying to float earlier. Th
capacity to make these implicit things explicit is very close to the heart of the kin(
of thing that makes humans different.

Whiten: That is not an easy question to answer. You talk about the implicit
explicit distinction, but that is cast in different ways by different authors
Typically, 'explicit' seems to boil down to 'verbalized', which does not apply t(
non-human primates.

Harnad: I'll give an example. We are not surprised if an alligator mother lunges a
anybody approaching her young, and we don't feel we have to confer specia
cognitive capacities upon her: the behaviour is just part of whatever it is tha
makes her protect her young in the first place. That sense of rage whe(

nething threatens your property could be diffused and doesn't have to be made ›licit in any way. It is just something you act on, and that could be diffused across ›cial group; and it could be stretched out in time and remain completely implicit :hat way. Do you think that the kinds of skills that you have been studying have v need to be explicit?

Whiten: This depends on which taxa one is talking about.

Mackintosh: How would you set about distinguishing between explicit and plicit learning in problem-solving in chimpanzees?

Whiten: Again, I'm not clear about what the distinction is really meant to be, in ‹ non-verbal case.

Mackintosh: For inarticulate animals, all you can do is pose an inarticulate 1avioural question, and they either do or do not produce the correct 1aviour. That is usually regarded as implicit knowledge. They cannot answer ‹ explicit question: what information do you recollect from this learning :sode?

Suddendorf: One way one might be able to operationalize explicit knowledge is the basis of the distinction between procedural (implicit) and declarative :plicit) representation, where declarative representations allow an individual to egrate information about separate associations (Dickinson 1980). Halford et al ›98) point to relational match-to-sample tasks as a measure of the ability to ›licate representations because participants have to map binary relations. In velopmental psychology it is usually the Piagetian stage six of sensorimotor velopment (reached at about 18 months) that is regarded as the first sign of ›licit representation (e.g. Russell 1996). In the middle of the second year ants begin to pretend, to understand hidden displacement, to recognize :mselves in mirrors and to attribute intentions and emotions to others. All :se skills may be based on (explicit) secondary representations (Perner 1991). In :tence, for example, the child has to hold a primary representation of reality and a coupled secondary representation of the pretend situation. While various species ιy have developed explicit knowledge, current comparison with the data from man development shows empirical support for all of these skills only in the great e species (Suddendorf 1998, 1999).[1]

Lubinski: The better example is the great apes that have been trained to use sign ιguage, and then have spontaneously trained their offspring.

Humphrey: 'Training' here is an exaggeration.

›r related arguments see Whiten (1996, 2000). The symposium bursary to Thomas ddendorf facilitated collaboration by Suddendorf and Whiten to pursue this issue. The nuscript 'Mental evolution and development: evidence for secondary representation in dren, great apes and other animals' is available from either of the authors.

Karmiloff-Smith: It is not sign language they learn; it's merely a sort lexical stringing, words listed one after another, not the grammar of hum language.

Humphrey: I would like to come back to the point raised at the beginning of yc paper about whether social intelligence is a separate, encapsulated faculty. Whe wrote 'The social function of intellect' (Humphrey 1976) I thought I was talki about the evolution of intelligence across the board. Though I did indeed sugg that the primary advantage to human beings of high level intelligence lay in th ability to cope with the complexities of social life, I've never been persuaded th this social intelligence was somehow shut off from the rest of the mind and r available for solving non-social problems. Given all the other evidence we' been hearing about for the correlation of different aspects of intelligence, would in fact be very odd if social intelligence were out on a limb. Do you rea want to hold out against this and insist on a modular view?

Whiten: I was wanting to be non-committal about that. I was saying that soc modularity of intelligence is one alternative. But as I also noted, explicit testing that has been minimal in primatology. It is mainly people working with huma who have been advocating special social modules.

Humphrey: I'd agree that there may be a special module for mind-reading human beings. But mind-reading and social problem-solving capacities aren't t same thing. You need two things to be a fully capable social human being: to very clever *and* to have the capacity for developing a theory of mind. When th are put together, you get the astonishing abilities that we have. But the intelligen arm of the package may in fact not be an encapsulated module.

Whiten: Indeed. However, this depends on how you define intelligence. There surely some sense in which having a theory of mind makes you more socia intelligent. Notwithstanding Premack & Woodruff's (1978) quip that t chimpanzee may not be intelligent enough to be a behaviourist, the current sta of evidence means one can question whether a chimpanzee is intelligent enough have a theory of mind (Whiten 1996, 1998). This is so even though chimpanzees a probably the most socially intelligent and socially complex primates.

Suddendorf: You would have to come up with some causal chain: just having sa that social complexity might be related to social intelligence doesn't expla anything, because the causality can go both ways. In order to explain why have stayed in this mental arms race in social intelligence, you would have either resort to a runaway selection mechanism, or argue for some spin-off bene outside the social domain which allows you to support the investment in a larg brain.

Humphrey: Incidentally, the arms race needn't relate to social complexity as suc what's more important is psychological complexity — and this doesn't necessar imply a large and complex social group. You only need one other person

evelop a highly complicated relationship, and to get into third, fourth and fifth
vels of intentionality — as can happen, say, in a chess game.

Houle: I was struck by your list of characteristics of what might be social
ntelligence, in terms of going to primate societies, and how easy that would be
o apply to humans. One could ask people about their social relations and
mpirically determine the relationship between *g* and the aspects of social
nowledge or social prediction. Has anyone done that?

Brody: From time to time people in the psychometric tradition have looked at
neasures of social intelligence. There is relatively little evidence indicating that
ognitive intelligence is related to social intelligence.

Whiten: Well, that would appear to be consistent with social modularity. But
vhat kind of tests have been used? I worry whether paper and pencil tests will get
t the real social intelligence at stake.

Brody: Guilford (1967) studied social intelligence. He would give subjects a
catement and ask them what kind of person might say that.

Detterman: Sternberg has come up with a much more interesting test. He takes
pictures of people who have various relationships: it could be a guy holding his arm
round someone else's girlfriend, or his own girlfriend, for example. People are
hown these pictures and then they have to decide the nature of these people's
elationships. He finds that social intelligence is much higher in women.

Brody: He doesn't find that social intelligence is related to *g*, does he?

Detterman: I can't remember. I don't think that there is any evidence that it is
ndependent of *g*.

Suddendorf: I showed you data yesterday indicating that, at least in childhood,
ocial intelligence (as measured by theory of mind tasks) is moderately correlated
vith measures of general intelligence.

Karmiloff-Smith: I want to add a caution about autism and the kind of
onclusions we've drawn from that about the so-called social module. Generally,
n abnormal psychology, if you get an uneven pattern, research has focused on
mpaired domains, and the tests of other domains are quite superficial. Take
dyslexia: there has been lots of work on reading and then some quick
psychometric measures of the rest that is ostensibly normal. But almost every
ime you actually probe the rest in any depth, you find subtle deficits. I don't
hink enough work has been done on the non-social aspects of autism, on what
ne might call 'theory of physics', where a similar kind of reasoning might be
nvolved in drawing inferences about physical phenomena rather than social
phenomena. We just don't know yet. In the case of Williams syndrome, in 1995 I
laimed theory of mind was relatively unimpaired. This was naïve, because now
hat we have probed it in more depth, we have found that people with Williams
yndrome are quite good at some low-level aspects which might be called socio-
ffect, as opposed to social cognition. They are good at empathy and can read

expressions on faces like 'sad' or 'happy'. But if tests are slightly more comple:
including expressions like 'guilty' for instance, they can no longer succeed. An
they tend to perform poorly on tests really measuring social cognition. W
shouldn't jump to the conclusion that because people with autism hav
difficulties in the social world, that there exists a social module.

Whiten: In the discussion after Randy Nesse's talk when we discussed module
versus social specializations, you seemed more comfortable with a relativel
blurred view of specializations, rather than encapsulated modules?

Karmiloff-Smith: The infant brain may start out with a number of differer
learning mechanisms slightly more suited to certain kinds of input than othe:
(Elman et al 1996). But I think that the notion that evolution has create
independently functioning, ready-made modules with representational content i
naïve — but it's a popular notion. The evolutionary psychologists have jumped o
data from adult abnormal psychology to make such claims.

Suddendorf: Many other acknowledged deficits that characterize autism, such a
obsession with routine, stereotyped behaviour, preoccupation with parts of a:
object, echopraxia and echolalia, can hardly be explained as secondary deficit
caused by a defect in a presumed social cognition module. Autistic children als
have a deficit on creativity tasks. The clinical picture is far more complex than
malfunctioning discrete module for social cognition.

Mackintosh: One of the conclusions from the work on social intelligence, on m
reading, is that this is a wholly misleading term. There are a lot of separate socia
skills which tend not to correlate very highly with one another, other tha:
correlating a bit with *g*.

References

Dickinson A 1980 Contemporary animal learning theory. Cambridge University Pres
Cambridge
Elman JL, Bates E, Johnson MH, Karmiloff-Smith A, Parisi D, Plunkett K 1996 Rethinkin,
innateness: a connectionist perspective on development. MIT Press, Cambridge, MA
Guilford JP 1967 The nature of human intelligence. McGraw-Hill, New York
Halford GS, Wilson WH, Phillips S 1998 Processing capacity defined by relational complexity
Behav Brain Sci 21:803–864
Humphrey NK 1976 The social function of intellect. In: Bateson PPG, Hinde RA (eds) Growin
points in ethology. Cambridge University Press, Cambridge, p 303–321
Perner J 1991 Understanding the representational mind. MIT Press, Cambridge, MA
Premack D, Woodruff G 1978 Does the chimpanzee have a 'theory of mind'? Behav Brain Sc
1:515–526
Russell J 1996 Development and evolution of the symbolic function: the role of workin,
memory. In: Mellars P, Gibson K (eds) Modelling the early human mind. McDonal:
Institute, Cambridge, p 159–170
Suddendorf T 1998 Simpler for evolution: secondary representation in apes, children, an:
ancestors. Behav Brain Sci 21:131

Suddendorf T 1999 The rise of the metamind. In: Corballis MC, Lea S (eds) The descent of mind: psychological perspectives on hominid evolution. Oxford University Press, Oxford, p 218– 260

Whiten A 1996 When does smart behaviour reading become mindreading? In: Carruthers P, Smith P (eds) Theories of theories of mind. Cambridge University Press, Cambridge, p 277– 292

Whiten A 1998 Evolutionary and developmental origins of the mindreading system. In: Langer J, Killen M (eds) Piaget, evolution and development. Lawrence Erlbaum, Hove, p 73–99

Whiten A 2000 Primate culture and social learning. Cognit Sci, in press

IQ gains, WISC subtests and fluid *g*: *g* theory and the relevance of Spearman's hypothesis to race

James R. Flynn

Department of Political Studies, University of Otago, PO Box 56, Dunedin, New Zealand

Abstract. IQ gains over time were calculated for each WISC (Wechsler Intelligence Scale for Children) subtest and the subtests ranked by size of gain. Verbal similarities led at 20 points per generation — larger than gains on Raven's Progressive Matrices. Similarities measures on-the-spot problem-solving (something akin to fluid *g*); verbal subtests that do not measure this show low rates of gain. WISC subtests were also ranked by their correlations with Raven's, the latter being used as a marker for fluid *g*. The *r* between the two hierarchies was calculated to approximate a correlation between IQ gains and fluid *g*. The result of 0.50 contrasts with the negative correlation between IQ gains and the *g* generated by factor analysing the WISC battery itself, which is generally viewed as predominately a crystallized *g*. In sum, it appears that human groups can make massive fluid *g* gains in a period too short to accommodate radical change in the speed and efficiency of neural processes. Moreover, once gains in intelligent behaviour over historical time are seen to be independent of brain physiology, does *g* really provide a criterion for assessing their significance? Finally, not only a measure of fluid *g* (which is highly heritable) but also inbreeding depression are shown to be correlated with IQ gains — gains overwhelmingly environmental in origin. Therefore, correlations between such genetically influenced factors and the size of the black/white IQ gap do not show that the gap has a genetic component.

2000 The nature of intelligence. Wiley, Chichester (Novartis Foundation Symposium 233) p 202–227

This paper falls into three parts. The first ranks WISC (Wechsler Intelligence Scale for Children) subtests by the magnitude of the post-1948 score gains over time on each subtest. The second ranks WISC subtests by the magnitude of the correlation between Raven's and each subtest. Raven's gives each subtest a weighting for fluid *g*. The correlation between the subtest gain hierarchy and the subtest Raven's hierarchy is calculated and found to be positive, a result consistent with the hypothesis that recent IQ gains are largely fluid *g* gains. The third part uses the fact that IQ gains correlate with variables genetically influenced (fluid *g* and inbreeding depression) to clarify the race and IQ debate.

Score gains and WISC subtests

The existent WISC data cover five periods and four nations. The label WISC is used to refer to the subtests and scales that all three editions of the WISC have in common. When referring to the various editions, the first will simply be called the WISC, the revised edition the WISC-R, and the third the WISC-III. The American editions were normed in 1947–1948, 1972 and 1989 respectively. So when the standardization samples are used to measure IQ gains over time, the periods are 24.5 and 17 years. The West German WISC was normed in 1954, the WISC-R in 1981, giving a period of 27 years. The Austrians used the West German WISC (1954) and their gains are measured not by comparing the performance of a later standardization sample, but rather by using 2318 subjects tested at a Viennese clinic (but deemed normal) between 1962 and 1979. Since the mid-point of those years is 1970–1971, their period is put at 1954 to 1970–1971 or at 16.5 years. The Scottish WISC was normed in 1961–1962, the WISC-R in 1983–1984, giving a period of 22 years. Scottish gains were measured only on WISC items that were left unaltered and therefore, estimates exist only for six of the 10 subtests usually administered (Flynn 1984, 1987, 1990, 1999a, Table 1, Schubert & Berlach 1982).

Table 1 first focuses on the 10 WISC subtests and gives the gains for each subtest for every period and nation. The gains are then converted into rates over a common period of 30 years, so that comparisons between nations can be made. These rates are summed and averaged. The averages are not weighted by the number of subjects used to estimate IQ gains, because the various numbers are not comparable. The two US estimates and the West German one are based on subjects who took both an earlier and a later edition of the WISC ($n=245$, 206 and 124); these subjects are, of course, merely a vehicle for comparing the norms set by an earlier and a later standardization sample. The Austrians scored 2318 subjects against an edition normed at an earlier date. The Scots consist of 297 subjects from the WISC-R standardization sample who were scored against WISC norms. Setting aside non-comparability, weighting by numbers would advantage the Austrian data which are clearly the weakest of the five. Another alternative, weighting by length of the period IQ gains cover, was also rejected. This would advantage the West German data which are perhaps the next weakest.

Finally, Table 1 translates the average subtest rates of gain from scaled score points (SD$=3$) into IQ points (SD$=15$), so that subtest gains can be compared to gains (also projected over 30 years) for WISC Verbal, Performance and Full Scale IQ. As far as possible, the same studies were used for all estimates, so as to maximize comparability. As Table 1 note 'd' indicates, the fact that the Scottish performance data are incomplete poses a problem (Flynn 1990, Tables 2 and 4). The right-hand column of Table 1 makes the relevant comparisons: the 10 subtests are ranked by magnitude of the average IQ rate of gain; and the rates on

TABLE 1 IQ gains and WISC[a] subtests: subtest, verbal and performance gains compared

	US: WISC to WISC-R		US: WISC-R to WISC-III		West Germany		Austria		Scotland		Sum of rates	Ave SS rate	Ave IQ rate
	Gain 24.5 years	Rate 30 years	Gain 17 years	Rate 30 years	Gain 27 years	Rate 30 years	Gain 16.5 years	Rate 30 years	Gain 22 years	Rate 30 years			
	SD=3[c]										SD=3[c]		SD=15
A[b]	0.36	0.44	0.3	0.53	−0.5	−0.56	−0.4	−0.73	−0.88	−1.20	−1.52(÷5)=−0.304		(×5)=−1.52
I	0.43	0.53	−0.3	−0.53	1.0	1.11	0.2	0.36	0.70	0.95	2.42(÷5)=0.484		(×5)= 2.42
V	0.38	0.47	0.4	0.71	2.6	2.89	1.0	1.82	0.00	0.00	5.89(÷5)=1.178		(×5)= 5.89
Com	1.20	1.47	0.6	1.06	2.4	2.67	0.1	0.18	3.20	4.36	9.74(÷5)=1.948		(×5)= 9.74
PC	0.74	0.91	0.9	1.59	4.8	5.33	0.6	1.09	0.61	0.83	9.75(÷5)=1.950		(×5)= 9.75
OA	1.34	1.64	1.2	2.12	2.4	2.67	1.0	1.82	–	–	8.25(÷4)=2.063		(×5)=10.32
Cod	2.20	2.69	0.7	1.24	2.8	3.11	1.1	2.00	–	–	9.04(÷4)=2.260		(×5)=11.30
PA	0.93	1.14	1.9	3.35	4.8	5.33	0.9	1.64	–	–	11.46(÷4)=2.865		(×5)=14.33
BD	1.28	1.57	0.9	1.59	4.8	5.33	1.8	3.27	–	–	11.76(÷4)=2.940		(×5)=14.70
S	2.77	3.39	1.3	2.29	4.7	5.22	2.1	3.82	3.69	5.03	19.75(÷5)=3.950		(×5)=19.75
	SD=15												SD=15
Verbal	6.56	8.03	2.4	4.24	11.4	12.67	2.96	5.38	9.72	13.25	43.57(÷5)=		8.71
Perfor	8.37	10.25	7.4	13.06	27.3	30.33	7.65	13.91	–	–	67.55(÷4)=		16.89
F. Scale	7.91	9.69	5.3	9.35	21.5	23.89	5.91	10.75	–	–	53.68(÷4)=		13.42

(Continued)

TABLE 1 (*Continued*) Average IQ rates (of gain over 30 years) compared: English-speaking vs. German-speaking (SD = 15)

	Arithmetic	Information	Vocabulary	Verbal	Performance	Similarities
United States & Scotland	−0.38	1.58	1.97	8.51	14.81[d]	17.85
West Germany & Austria	−3.23	3.68	11.78	9.03	22.12	22.60

Data and sources: discussed in text.

[a]WISC is used generically to refer to subtests common to the WISC, WISC-R and WISC-III.

[b]Full names of subtests: A, arithmetic; BD, block design; Cod, coding; Com, comprehension; I, information; OA, object assembly; PA, picture arrangement; PC, picture completion; S, similarities; V, vocabulary.

[c]Values within the 'box' are subtest scaled scores (SS scores) based on SD = 3; values outside are IQ scores based on SD = 15.

[d]The estimate for the combined United States and Scotland performance gains includes a rough estimate of Scottish performance gains. The latter were put at a rate of 21.11 IQ points per 30 years based on a comparison of Scottish and white American standardization samples (Flynn 1990).

the three scales immediately follow. Some of the results match expectations (Flynn 1994). Gains are lowest on Arithmetic, Information and Vocabulary, the crystallized subtests that measure the accomplishments intelligent people acquire. The more fluid subtests, that is, the remaining two verbal subtests and all of the performance subtests, show large gains ranging from about 10–20 points. The preponderance of performance subtests among those showing large gains is reflected in the fact that Performance IQ gains are almost double Verbal IQ gains: 16.89 points as compared to 8.71 points, with Full Scale in between at 13.42.

However, two results merit comment. First, Table 1 (continued) compares IQ rates of gain in the English-speaking nations (USA and Scotland) with those in the German-speaking nations (West Germany and Austria). The latter are somewhat higher for Performance IQ and therefore for Full Scale IQ. But the dramatic difference is on the Vocabulary subtest, where gains are virtually nil for English-speaking children while large, at almost 12 points, for German-speaking children. Independent data from Northern Ireland (Lynn 1990) and England (Raven et al 1994, Table MHV 3) confirm low gains for English-speakers.

Second — and this came as a surprise — Similarities shows huge gains. All of the other verbal subtests trail behind the performance subtests, but Similarities tops the list at almost 20 points. It is hard to imagine any explanation for this other than the fact that one must think or perform on the spot. It consists of questions such as, 'What do water and salt have in common?'; and the subject must formulate alternatives like, 'Both chemical elements', or 'both in the ocean', or 'both at the dinner table', and choose from among them. Similarities gains probably exceed Raven's gains: excellent data put the latter at no more than 18 points per 30 years (Flynn 1998a, p 56). Therefore, it appears that the matrices format is not an important factor in massive IQ gains. If it were, gains should diminish on a test like Similarities where it is absent. Therefore, causal hypotheses related to a visual format, such as that the advent of video games and computers are dominant causes (Greenfield 1998), must at least be supplemented (U. Neisser, unpublished paper, International Society for the Study of Individual Differences and the Behavior Genetics Association, July 4 1999).

Raven's correlations and WISC subtests

Rushton (1999) questioned whether IQ gains represent g gains. He ranked the WISC subtests in terms of the magnitude of their g-loadings, took IQ gain hierarchies from each of the five data sets, and got negative correlations averaging just above −0.3. The g used was, of course, derived from factor analysis of the WISC subtest battery itself: as Jensen (1987, p 96) points out, such a g would tend toward the crystallized pole of the spectrum. Flynn (1999b) noted that post-

1948 IQ gains are by far largest on tests of fluid g and hypothesized that ranking the WISC subtests in terms of fluid g would change the correlations from negative to positive. The obvious test of this hypothesis was to rank the WISC subtests by their correlations with Raven's. Jensen (1998, p 38) asserts that when the g-loadings of tests within a battery are unknown, the correlation of Raven's with each test is often used; and Raven's is the universally recognized measure of fluid g.

John Raven made his archives available and an effort was made to locate all studies giving the relevant correlations. Studies were rejected if the mean IQ of subjects fell below the normal range and on methodological grounds. For example, Mehrotra (1968) administered the US WISC to children in India for whom English was a second language and who had difficulties coping with four of the 10 subtests. Semler & Iscoe (1966) administered only eight of the subtests: including their data would have affected the subtest Raven's correlation hierarchy; and inflated the correlation between that hierarchy and the subtest IQ gains hierarchy. This left five studies with a total of 483 subjects, aged 6–11 years, 423 taking the Coloured Progressive Matrices and 60 the Standard Progressive Matrices.

Table 2 cites the studies retained and uses a weighted average to merge the correlations they gave between Raven's and WISC subtests. As a preliminary, the resulting fluid g hierarchy was compared to those that resulted when Rushton ranked WISC subtests by crystallized g, that is, the g-loadings derived from factor analysis of the WISC-R and WISC-III respectively. The hierarchies were uncorrelated: the values for r_s and r ranged from negative 0.10 to positive 0.18. Turning to correlations between the subtest Raven's hierarchy and the subtest IQ gains hierarchy, Table 2 gives four results. The values are lower than those earlier reported by Flynn (1999c) but all four show a robust positive correlation (reliabilities partialled out). When Scottish IQ gains are included, the rank-order correlation (r_s) is 0.41, the Pearson correlation (r) 0.40. When Scottish gains are excluded, the values are 0.44 and 0.50. The Scottish data make a difference because they give IQ gains for only six subtests; and, as Table 2 shows, they therefore affect the subtest IQ gains hierarchy. They will be excluded from analysis hereafter.

However, the Scottish data did deserve to be included in Table 1 because they are informative on points having to do with IQ gains taken in isolation. They confirm the other data by showing losses over time on Arithmetic and huge gains on Similarities; they confirm the tendency for English-speaking nations to gain far less on Vocabulary than German-speaking nations.

Table 2 combines subjects taking the WISC-III ($n=28$), the WISC-R ($n=91$), and the WISC ($n=364$). Brosier (G. Brosier, personal communication 1998) used the WISC-R, not the WISC as the published summary of his results erroneously states. John Raven (J. Raven, personal communication 1998) supplied detail about

TABLE 2 Raven's[a] correlations and WISC[b] subtests — correlations between subtest Raven's correlation and subtest IQ gain

	Martin & Wiechers (1954)		Barratt (1956)		Kostamska (1982)		Brosier (1986)		Kleuwer et al (1995)		Total Products	Total Nos.		Raven's correlation (average)	Raven's rank	IQ gain rank[c]	Reliabilities[d]
	Raven's correlation	× No. (=100)	Raven's correlation	× No. (=60)	Raven's correlation	× No. (=204)	Raven's correlation	× No. (=91)	Raven's correlation	× No. (=28)							
A[e]	0.66	66.0	0.540	32.40	0.320	65.280	0.43	39.13	0.40	11.20	214.01	÷ 483	=	0.443	4	1/1	0.77
I	0.47	47.0	0.585	35.10	0.267	54.468	0.44	40.04	0.41	11.48	188.09	÷ 483	=	0.389	1	2/2	0.85
V	0.73	73.0	0.561	33.66	0.497	101.388	0.49	44.59	0.49	13.72	266.36	÷ 483	=	0.551	9	3/4	0.86
Com	0.70	70.0	0.075	4.50	0.387	78.948	0.43	39.13	0.33	9.24	201.82	÷ 483	=	0.418	3	4/3	0.77
PC	0.62	62.0	0.415	24.90	0.490	99.960	0.46	41.86	0.44	12.32	241.04	÷ 483	=	0.499	6	5/6	0.77
OA	0.73	73.0	0.388	23.28	0.490	99.960	0.56	50.96	0.30	8.40	255.60	÷ 483	=	0.529	8	6/5	0.70
Cod	0.60	60.0	0.332	19.92	0.357	72.828	0.38	34.58	0.04	1.12	188.45	÷ 483	=	0.390	2	7/7	0.72
PA	0.58	58.0	0.300	18.00	0.553	112.812	0.49	44.59	0.54	15.12	248.52	÷ 483	=	0.515	7	8/8	0.73
BD	0.74	74.0	0.601	36.06	0.643	131.172	0.58	52.78	0.62	17.36	311.37	÷ 483	=	0.645	10	9/9	0.85
S	0.62	62.0	0.589	35.34	0.360	73.440	0.45	40.93	0.47	13.16	224.89	÷ 483	=	0.466	5	10/10	0.81

Correlations between subtest Raven's correlation and subtest IQ gain — reliabilities partialled out

r_s (including Scottish gains)	0.41	r_s (without Scottish gains)	0.44
r (including Scottish gains)	0.40	r (without Scottish gains)	0.50

[a] Coloured Progressive Matrices or Standard Progressive Matrices depending on age of subjects.
[b] WISC is used generically to refer to subtests common to the WISC, WISC-R and WISC-III.
[c] Subtest 'IQ gain rank' and size of gain (needed for r) from Table 1. First rank is including Scottish gains, second is without — see text.
[d] WISC-R subtest reliabilities—see text.
[e] Full names of subtests: A, arithmetic; BD, block design; Cod, coding; Com, comprehension; I, information; OA, object assembly; PA, picture arrangement; PC, picture completion; S, similarities; V, vocabulary.

he number and age of Brosier's subjects. The three versions of the WISC were nalysed separately. Predictably, the reduction in the number of subjects did not ffect r_s, the values differing from those in Table 2 by only minus 0.02 to plus 0.03. 'redictably, it did increase the measurement error for r: the value was 0.24 for the VISC-III (with only 28 subjects) rising to 0.55 for the WISC (with 364 subjects). Fable 2 uses the subtest reliabilities from the WISC-R. First, it is the connecting ink for IQ gains, which run either from the WISC to the WISC-R or from the VISC-R to the WISC-III. Second, in terms of test content, the WISC and WISC-II are closer to the WISC-R than they are to one another. However, using eliabilities from the WISC and WISC-III makes no difference: the values for ioth r and r_s differ from those in Table 2 by only minus 0.03 to plus 0.03.

Table 2 refers to post-1948 IQ gains and shows that there is a positive correlation if 0.50 between the magnitude of those gains and a measure of fluid g. This is onsistent with other evidence. Colom et al (2000) have analysed Spanish IQ gains between 1979 and 1995 on the subtests of the Differential Aptitude Test, elected as a battery for which factor analysis would give a g predominately fluid n character. They found a positive correlation of 0.78 between magnitude of score gains and factor loadings. Flynn (1998a, 1999b) has emphasized the contrast ietween IQ gains prior to World War II and post-war gains. The latter are argest by far on tests of fluid g like Raven's. I will provide a brief sketch of a heory that is at least consistent with the pattern of IQ gains. It is yet to be videnced, although a research design has been proposed (J. R. Flynn, inpublished paper, International Society for the Study of Individual Difference ind the Behavior Genetics Association, 4 July 1999).

Let us borrow the notion of 'mental energy' from Spearman. Human beings nvest their mental energy to meet the cognitive demands posed by their social nvironment. In America, between World War I and World War II, the major challenge posed for the mass of people was exposure to the cognitive demands of econdary education. Millions of people were now expected to go beyond say a iixth grade education to complete the 12th grade. In response, they developed ietter arithmetical skills, larger vocabularies and larger stores of general nformation. They also developed enhanced abstract problem-solving skills, iecause formal schooling always encourages the latter to some degree. Since the 'ormer would register on tests skewed towards crystallized g and the latter on tests kewed towards fluid g, the pattern of IQ gains would not favour one over the ither. About 1948, I suspect that the cognitive demands of secondary school 'eached a 'saturation point', that is, they attained a complexity beyond which children (at least white American children) could not be motivated to respond 'or perhaps did not have the capacity to respond). In addition, beginning about 1948, there was an attitude shift. Perhaps because of certain 'triggers', such as the lecline of the depression psychology with its pragmatic flavour, the growth of

leisure, the growth of leisure pursuits that exercise the mind, smaller families s
that parents took their children's 'whys' more seriously, people began to b
willing to invest their mental energy into solving non-practical problems to a
unprecedented degree. People suddenly found that other people were demanding
that they take intellectual interaction 'for its own sake' more seriously. Therefore
score gains on school-relevant mental tests tailed off and gains on abstract problem
solving tests escalated. This would produce score gains on tests with a fluid bias a
the expense of tests with a crystallized bias. There are signs that the end of the 20th
century may see an end even to the escalation of abstract problem-solving skills
certainly, people cannot be willing to invest infinite time and energy into this kind
of thinking.

These facts and this theory have implications that may not be evident. First
history can produce robust correlations between IQ gains and measures of fluid
in a period far too short for biological evolution to affect the neural processe
relevant to intelligent behaviour. It may be said that other factors, like hybrid
vigour or better nutrition, could upgrade those processes without any evolution
of the brain's structure. The Dutch gained 8 IQ points on Matrices in 10 years
measured by cohorts born in 1954 and 1964 respectively (Flynn 1987). The
Israelis gained 5 points in 8 years, measured by cohorts born in 1959 and 196
(Flynn 1998b). I do not think anyone can make a case for hybrid vigour or
alleviation of large nutritional deficiencies in either of those cases. Returning to
the United States, there is an exaggerated notion of the extent to which mobility
(and therefore hybrid vigour) are peculiar to recent times. In 1870, 23 per cent of
Americans were living in a state other than the one of their birth; in 1970, the figure
was 32 per cent (Mosler & Catley 1998). Second, what relevance does g have to
testing the significance of IQ gains over historical time? The fact that g correlate
with physiological factors may mean that it is a pointer to brain structures that
evolve over the aeons of evolutionary time. There is no doubt that g predict
outcomes for individuals competing with one another within a particular
generation, that is, at a particular place and time. But neither of these establishe
its credentials as a criterion to assess cognitive developments that affect a whole
society over historical time.

IQ gains over time reveal the shifting cognitive demands American society made
on its members during the 20th century. The history of how Americans responded
in terms of developing new areas of intelligent behaviour can be told without any
reference to g. Whether the pattern of investment of mental energy in different
areas, reflected in the magnitude of score gains on different cognitive tests
happened to correlate with the g-loading of those tests has no real relevance. Let
us imagine that the correlation was nil or negative. Would this mean that the
cognitive gains were second-class citizens or somehow less significant? Here a
sports analogy may help. The ten events of the decathlon contain more events

hat cater to speed and spring in one's legs than to strength. The 100 metres, 400 metres, hurdles, high jump and long jump clearly cater to the former. Even the 500 metres will be easier for a runner than a weight man. Only the shot put, discus and javelin clearly cater to strength, with the pole vault requiring both speed and strength. Therefore, a g derived from factor analysis of the whole battery will be skewed towards speed and spring. Now imagine that over 30 years, American society develops a romance with strength but no enhanced love of speed. The pattern of performance gains on the ten events will have a negative correlation with decathelon g. But the gains in athletic performance, the greater distances the shot, discus and javelin are put or hurled will be no less real for that; and what they tell us about shifting social demands no less significant.

In sum, correlations with g should be kept to their proper sphere, that is, used as pointers to brain physiology and predictors of competitive advantage. It may be said that if there is no necessary connection between g and the evolution of human intelligence over historical time, then g theory claims no applicability. After all, Jensen (1998) now denies that g makes any reference to intelligence as a psychological phenomenon. Fair enough, then it is agreed that we must look elsewhere for illumination of the fascinating history of American intelligent behaviour in the 20th century. However, setting aside the question of whether or not there is a necessary connection between g and intelligence, it is fortuitous that recent IQ gains do show a positive correlation with measures of fluid g. As we shall see, this correlation allows us to demonstrate the irrelevance of the Spearman hypothesis to the race and IQ debate.

Genetically influenced variables and race

The Spearman hypothesis states that black/white IQ differences will tend to be largest on tests with the greatest g-loading. Rushton (1997) believes this suggests a method for diagnosing whether the black/white IQ gap has a potent genetic component. You rank WISC subtests by the size of the racial IQ gap; you then rank them for variables known to be genetically influenced, not just the size of their g-loadings but also things like inbreeding depression; and if the hierarchies correlate, you conclude that a significant portion of the racial IQ gap is caused by genetic differences. Stephen J. Gould is taken to task for ignoring this 'critically important finding'.

Flynn (1999a) noted that the WISC subtest IQ gain hierarchy correlated with inbreeding depression; yet, post-1948 IQ gains are overwhelmingly environmental in origin; so Rushton's method reached a demonstrably false conclusion (that IQ gains must have a large genetic component). Rushton (1999) replied that if you took both inbreeding depression and g-loading into account, and did a factor analysis on variables inclusive of them plus both the WISC subtest black/white hierarchy and the WISC subtest IQ gains hierarchy, you got two clusters: IQ gains isolated; all other factors together. He concluded that IQ gains stood aside because of their environmental causality; while the other three were revealed to share genetic causality.

Rushton's factor analysis has been revised in three ways. First, Rushton entered five data sets for IQ gains over time, that is, data for each period and each nation. As Jensen (1998, p 30) points out, this is a mistake: multiple data sets for a single variable are likely to have more in common with one another than they do with anything else; therefore, the factor analysis will be biased towards isolating them as a separate cluster. We enter a single data set for IQ gains, namely, the averaged data from Table 1. Second, although virtually all of Rushton's data is from the WISC-R, he enters black/whites IQ differences from both the WISC-R and the WISC-III. We discard the latter. Third, we use the WISC subtest fluid g hierarchy from Table 2 rather than Rushton's crystallized g hierarchies. This should make no difference in terms of the logic of the method: fluid g is at least as highly genetically influenced as crystallized g (Jensen 1998, p 124).

Table 3 provides both the correlation matrix for our four variables and the factor analysis of that matrix. Note that the correlation between inbreeding depression and IQ gains (0.28) is almost identical to the correlation between inbreeding depression and black/white differences (0.29). The correlation between fluid g and IQ gains is identical to the correlation between fluid g and black/white differences (0.50). So if these correlations show that black/white IQ differences are genetically influenced, post-1948 IQ gains must be genetically influenced to the same degree. Jensen and Rushton argue that about two-thirds of the black/white IQ gap is genetic in origin: few would care to argue a similar thesis concerning IQ gains. As for the factor analysis, Table 3 uses Pearson correlations (r) and shows inbreeding depression isolated on the second component, and all other variables clustered on the first component. Factor analysis using rank-order correlations (r_s) shows IQ gains and fluid g together on the first component, inbreeding depression and black/white differences together on the second component. Both analyses put inbreeding depression and fluid g into separate boxes; yet, these two variables have genetic influence in common. Therefore, neither analysis can be taken to distinguish genetic from environmental causality without absurdity.

Conclusion

The data contained herein are not robust. The data on WISC IQ gains come from four nations and at this late date, the number of subjects is unlikely to be augmented. On the other hand, as Rushton (1999) points out, the fact the data sets intercorrelate so strongly suggests that they represent a reliable

TABLE 3 Correlation matrix and factor analysis of four variables — Pearson (*r*) with reliabilities partialled out

	IQ gains	Fluid g-loadings	Inbreeding depression	Black/white differences
IQ gains	1.00	0.50	0.28	0.21
Fluid g—loadings	0.50	1.00	0.03	0.50
Inbreeding depression	0.28	0.03	1.00	0.29
Black/white differences	0.21	0.50	0.29	1.00

Data: From Table 1, IQ gains (ave. IQ rates — delete Scots). From Table 2, Fluid *g*—loadings (Raven's cor. ave.) and reliabilities. Inbreeding depression and black/white differences from Rushton (1999) as follows:

	A	I	V	Com	PC	OA	Cod	PA	BD	S
Inbredding depression	5.05	8.30	11.45	6.05	5.90	6.05	4.45	9.40	5.35	9.95
Black/white differences	0.61	0.86	0.84	0.79	0.70	0.79	0.45	0.75	0.90	0.77

A, arithmetic; BD, block design; Cod, coding; Com, comprehension; I, information; OA, object assembly; PA, picture arrangement; PC, picture completion; S, similarities; V, vocabulary.

	Principal components			
	Unrotated loadings		Varimax rotated loadings	
	I	II	1	2
IQ gains	0.74	−0.03	0.69	0.25
Fluid g—loadings	0.80	−0.48	0.92	−0.15
Inbreeding depression	0.47	0.86	0.12	0.97
Black/white differences	0.73	0.00	0.68	0.28
Percentage of total variance explained	48.59	24.31	45.18	27.72

phenomenon. The data on correlations between Raven's and WISC subtests are sparse: four American studies and one Polish. We suspect our results will hold up for this reason: IQ gains over time on Raven's are huge; and no one has thought of a hypothesis to explain them other than that people really have got better at what Raven's measures (fluid *g*). It is encouraging that Colom et al (2000) have found a higher correlation between IQ gains and a measure of fluid *g* (0.78 to our 0.50) in data that pose fewer problems.

Let us assume that evidence eventually confirms a strong correlation betwee
IQ gains and fluid g. We could then state a strong conclusion: the method of taki~
x in conjunction with y and z, y and z known to be genetically influenced, and th~
showing they all have something in common, is simply bankrupt — as a method
diagnosing whether x is genetically influenced. It makes no difference whether y~
use correlations or factor analysis: all they show is that the variables ha~
something in common. Neither method tells you what they have in commo~
certainly not that they share genetic causality. Counter examples have be~
provided to dramatize this. It is not just a matter of our analysis (using fluid
providing a counterweight to Rushton's analysis (using crystallized g). O~
analysis challenges the whole endeavour: if a method produces an absu~
conclusion in one case, its conclusions cannot be trusted. Pile up as ma~
correlations between genetically influenced factors and the black/white IQ gap
you want. Do they signify anything?

No theory is needed to discredit a method that generates false assertions, but
would be good to have an explanation as to why it fails. As for inbreedi~
depression, two groups can differ for height purely due to environmental facto~
The better the test for height, the larger the difference will be and also the more th~
test will be affected by inbreeding depression. Does that show that the height g~
between the two groups is really genetic in origin? As for g, two groups can be fac~
with different cognitive demands or respond differently to the same cogniti~
demands, thanks to purely social or environmental factors. Their differenti~
response can produce different cognitive skills that involve school-releva~
problem-solving or abstract problem-solving or both, and these will simulate
group difference in either crystallized g or fluid g or both. Therefore, the fact th~
there is a positive correlation between the magnitude of their performan~
differences and the magnitude of g-loadings does not necessarily signal
physiological difference, much less a genetic difference. Whether this theory h~
applicability to g differences between black and white is problematic. But o~
thing is certain: verification of the Spearman hypothesis concerning black ar~
white cannot settle the race and IQ debate.

Acknowledgements

William T. Dickens supplied the statistical analysis, with assistance from Jennifer Eichberg~
and Megan Monroe.

References

Barratt ES 1956 The relationship of the progressive matrices (1938) and the Columbia men~
    maturity scale to the WISC. J Consult Psychol 20:294–296

Brosier G 1986 Coloured progressive matrices: intercorrelations between CPM and sub-tests of WISC. In Raven J (ed) Manual for Raven's progressive matrices and vocabulary scales, research supplement no 3: a compendium of North American normative and validity studies. Lewis, London, p 67

Colom R, Juan-Espinosa M, Garcia LF 2000 The secular increase in test scores is a 'Jensen effect'. submitted

Flynn JR 1984 The mean IQ of Americans: massive gains 1932 to 1978. Psychol Bull 95:29–51

Flynn JR 1987 Massive IQ gains in 14 nations: what IQ tests really measure. Psychol Bull 101:171–191

Flynn JR 1990 Massive IQ gains on the Scottish WISC: evidence against Brand et al's hypothesis. Irish J Psychol 11:41–51

Flynn JR 1994 IQ gains over time. In: Sternberg RJ (ed) The encyclopedia of human intelligence. Macmillan, New York, p 617–623

Flynn JR 1998a IQ gains over time: toward finding the causes. In: Neisser U (ed) The rising curve: long-term gains in IQ and related measures. The American Psychological Association, Washington, DC, p 25–66

Flynn JR 1998b Israeli military IQ tests: gender differences small, IQ gains large. J Biosoc Sci 30:541–553

Flynn JR 1999a Evidence against Rushton: the genetic loading of WISC-R subtests and the causes of between-group IQ differences. Pers Individ Differ 26:373–379

Flynn JR 1999b Reply to Rushton: a gang of gs overpowers factor analysis. Pers Individ Differ 26:391–393

Flynn JR 1999c Searching for justice: the discovery of IQ gains over time. Am Psychol 54:5–20

Greenfield P 1998 The cultural evolution of IQ. In: Neisser U (ed) The rising curve: long-term gains in IQ and related measures. The American Psychological Association, Washington, DC, p 88–123

Jensen AR 1987 The g beyond factor analysis. In: Ronning RR, Glover JA, Conoley JC, Witt JC (eds) The influence of cognitive psychology on testing. Lawrence Erlbaum Associates, Hillsdale, NJ, p 87–142

Jensen AR 1998 The g factor: the science of mental ability. Praeger, Westport, CT

Kleuver RC, Smith DK, Green KE, Holm CB, Dimson C 1995 The WISC-III and Raven coloured progressive matrices test: a pilot study of relationships. Paper presented at the Annual Meeting of the American Educational Research Association, April 1995, San Francisco, CA

Kostanska L 1982 Wspolzaleznosc Kolorowych Matryc J. C. Ravena, Krotkiej Skali Inteligencji, i Skali Inteligencji D. Wechslera Dla Dzieci (Interdependency of the Raven's coloured matrices, a short intelligence scale, and Wechsler's Intelligence Scale for Children) Zagadnienia Wychowawcze a Zdrowie Psychiczne 5:29–39

Lynn R 1990 Differential rates of secular increase of five major primary abilities. Soc Biol 38:137–141

Martin AW, Wiechers JE 1954 Raven's colored progressive matrices and the Wechsler intelligence scale for children. J Consult Psychol 18:143–144

Mehrotra KK 1968 The relationship of the WISC to the progressive matrices. J Psychol Res 12:114–118

Mosler D, Catley B 1998 America and Americans in Australia. Praeger, Westport, CT

Raven JC, Court JH, Raven J 1994 Manual for Raven's progressive matrices and vocabulary scales (section 5A). Oxford Psychologists Press, Oxford

Rushton JP 1997 Race, intelligence and the brain: the errors and omissions of the 'revised' edition of S. J. Gould's *The mismeasure of man* (1996). Pers Individ Differ 23:169–180

Rushton JP 1999 Secular gains in IQ not related to the g factor and inbreeding depression — unlike black–white differences: a reply to Flynn. Pers Individ Differ 26:381–389

Schubert MT, Berlach G 1982 Neue Richtlinien zur Interpretation des Hamburg Wechsler
    Intelligenztests für Kinder (HAWIK). (New guidelines for the interpretation of th
    Hamburg Wechsler Intelligence Tests for Children (HAWIK).) Z Klin Psychol 11:252–279
Semler IJ, Iscoe I 1966 Structure of intelligence in negro and white children. J Edu Psycho
    6:326–336

DISCUSSION

Bailey: To what extent you would argue that these IQ gains are more than gain
in ability to do well on IQ tests?

Flynn: I've often been misinterpreted on that point. Initially, I was confronted
with the naïve reaction that these IQ gains had brought about a golden era: tha
there had been enormous escalations of intelligence in a simple sense. I thought
'That can't be so; my kid isn't much brighter than I am; there hasn't been a
renaissance equivalent to classical Greece!' Think what a rise of 20 IQ points in a
generation means: classrooms should be filled with gifted kids. I would like today
to put it a little differently. I think we should talk about how people invest their
mental energy. People are challenged by their environments and they adapt. Let me
describe three phases. First, throughout human history, people have invested their
undifferentiated mental capacity, call it what you will — intelligence — into
everyday life. They didn't need much motivation to develop the skills to cope
with their kinship groups and ordinary social interchange. Second, between
World Wars I and II, for the first time people had to adapt to mass education
beyond the primary level. I suspect that the IQ gains, which Tuddenham
measured between the two wars, reflect a massive investment of capacity into
dealing with a school environment. This would mean a gain in crystallized g and
since schools to some degree teach you to think abstractly, there would be fluid g
gains as well. Third, since World War II, I think there's been an attitude shift: for a
whole range of reasons there's been a massive investment of mental energy into
abstract problem-solving. Thus we see the pattern of post-1948 gains. I am
talking about school children. The fact that people today may be intellectually
challenged by university after 16 doesn't affect these data. I think that by about
1945 the investment of human intelligence in school made school about as
complicated and cognitively demanding as teachers and kids were willing to put
up with: it reached a saturation point and crystallized g gains stopped. Then after
World War II, there is this massive investment into abstract problem-solving and
fluid g gains escalated. What real world effects would I expect because of IQ gains
since 1945? I'd expect the age of chess grandmasters would be dropping: that
appears to be true. That you would probably have more promising theoretica
physicists and pure mathematicians, but of course they might not actually realize
this potential, because government funding is so barbarous these days that we
strangle them all in the cradle. It would be very hard to detect unfulfilled talent

'm not saying there would be no real world effects, but I think they would be
pretty limited. I think all of this counts against the unitary nature of intelligence.
As several people have remarked, human beings are challenged to adapt to new
environmental situations. There was the unitary model that we had from Cattell:
fluid *g* is invested in vocabulary and general information, and that's the origin of
crystallized *g*. But it seems that the two *g*'s can be functionally much more
independent than that. Since World War II, I think there's been a massive
investment of intellectual energy into abstract problem-solving, boosting fluid *g*,
but we reached a saturation point about 1948 on school, resulting in little gain in
crystallized *g*. I suspect we're reaching a saturation point now on abstract problem-
solving. You can't escalate skills forever, and I suspect that even fluid *g* IQ gains are
failing off. Some of the Scandinavian data indicate this. I have never thought that
IQ gains were totally empty, I just think the post-1948 ones do not have the wide
range of real world consequences that you would normally expect.

Miller: I think these data are interesting, particularly in Table 3 this correlation
between IQ gains and inbreeding depression. Even in relatively sophisticated
behaviour genetics, it's often portrayed that there's a zero-sum game between
genetic and environmental influences in explaining behaviour. But what we
heard this morning from David Houle and what we'll hear tomorrow from
Andrew Pomiankowski suggests that often the traits that are most highly
condition-dependent — that are the most susceptible to the environmental
quality — often tend to be traits that also show the largest genetic variance. They
might end up showing the same heritability, for example, as those that are relatively
condition-independent and low in genetic variance. But what seems to be
happening here, is that some of these IQ gains are happening in mental traits that
are both highly condition-dependent and genetically influenced: it is not a trade-
off.

Flynn: The purpose behind that table was solely to show that Rushton can't use
his method as he does. The only function of this table is to say that merely because
you find correlations between genetically influenced factors and the black/white IQ
gap, it does not settle whether the black/white IQ gap is genetically caused. Phil
just says it: if you read *Race, evolution and behavior*, he says 'we now have the clinching
evidence' (Rushton 1995).

Humphrey: Your positive feedback model of what is happening is very
convincing. The question becomes, why did it take off when it did? You
suggested the coming of television, but there may be a simpler answer. If one
thinks of Robin Dunbar's estimates of what the typical group size would have
been in past human history, it is about 150. And the number of peers with whom
anyone would in the past have had to compete would have been relatively less than
that. But then around the beginning of the 20th century, the world began to open
up and the pool of potential competitors and idealized models vastly increased. So

the conditions were suddenly in place for the feedback process of IQ chasing IQ t take off as never before.

Flynn: I agree that television is of marginal importance. The 'feedback model' i not described in my paper here but in Dickens & Flynn (2000).

Humphrey: This idea that the IQ gains were spurred by competition an awareness of the larger world of people to be emulated might also explain th relative poor performance of blacks—who sociologists claim are generally nc so competitive over these issues.

Flynn: People have often attributed to me the idea that the causes of generationa differences in IQ must be similar to the causes of black/white IQ differences. I hav never at any time said that. I have never said that IQ gains over time shows th black/white IQ gap to be environmental. Although, even if the causes ar different, they do make an environmental hypothesis more plausible, for reason that would take us far afield. Note in Table 3, that the correlation between IQ gain and the black/white IQ differences is relatively low: it is 0.21. I have never though there is a commonality of causality there. I don't think that Chinese/white IC differences are caused by the same thing as Filipino/Chinese IQ differences. I would seem to me quite bizarre if all these group IQ differences had a common cause

Jensen: There is another Flynn effect, in the physical realm, and that's for heighi There have been comparable increases in height over the same period. For example J. M. Tanner (University of London) mentions that 10-year-old children today i London schools are four inches taller than they were 100 years ago. Since Worl War I there have been the same kinds of increases to about the same extent i standard deviation units. There are other parallels as well. For example, th correlations between different body measurements have remained the same ove this time, despite the increase in height. And the differences between variou national and ethnic groups that differ in height has continued to exist.

Flynn: The Japanese have gained a lot on Americans.

Jensen: This is especially interesting because the heritability of height is 0.95. Thi shows the independence of the heritability and the mean value. Now an interestin question is, why have psychologists got so worked up over the Flynn effect for IQ while there's been no great excitement about this 'Flynn effect' for height?

Flynn: I'm glad you said that. In your work in 1973, you did you use the high heritability of IQ to cast doubt on the fact that there could be environmenta explanations of the black/white IQ gap. If I understand what you're saying, you now think that was a mistake in reasoning.

Jensen: Yes, if that is, in fact, what I actually said. I would refer readers to chapte 7 of my 1973 book (Jensen 1973).

Flynn: With regard to the height gains, I am baffled too, but I started talking with the biologists in Otago. They convinced me that I was getting into deep water: the said biologists are puzzled by it but know a lot about increases in species size fo

imals. I know you've often thought that perhaps improved nutrition was
sponsible for these gains in height.

Jensen: Nutrition and a number of other health factors.

Flynn: Richard Lynn said that nutrition was probably responsible for the IQ
ins. I don't deny that it was probably responsible for the gains early in this
ntury, but the Dutch gained eight points between those born 1954 and 1964,
d there is no indication that there was an enormous upgrading in the Dutch
et over this period. If you look at the Dutch that were gestated during the great
utch famine, they don't even show up as a blip.

Jensen: That's a more complicated issue, because there was differential fetal loss
ring the famine period.

Flynn: But you did bring it into your 1973 book, as an example to why nutrition
obably didn't affect IQ very much.

Jensen: Well I hope I've changed in some of my views over the years!

Brody: I'm delighted that you have raised the whole notion of the social context
which heritability in genetic influences takes place. One of the things Herrnstein
d Murray demonstrated in their book is that social class is less predictive than IQ
r many outcomes. But if you look at the R^2 values of the extent to which those
o variables are predictive, once you get out of the domain of academic
hievement, you're accounting for a small portion of variance. This is a point
ey don't make. It is also worth noting that even with respect to the connection
tween IQ and academic performance, which is well established, this is not a
atement about the limits of what kids can learn. Compare American kids in the
ird or fourth grade with kids in Japan: as far as I can tell, looking at well-designed
oss-national educational surveys, there is something close to a one and a half
andard deviation difference in learning mathematical concepts. There is little or
 evidence that there are large differences in IQ between these groups. I believe
at intelligence is highly heritable — I think this is what the data show. But this
s few implications for malleability or saying that the social context is not
ediating anything, or saying that we can't do better in terms of providing much
tter educational opportunities for all children in our society.

Flynn: In my book on Asian Americans, I did a study of Japanese and Chinese
ildren born in America between 1945 and 1949, plus those who came to America
 that time and were educated in America. If they had higher IQs than white
mericans it was only marginal. Yet data suggest that a Chinese American kid
uld spot a white American kid 7 IQ points, and match them for the credentials
at got them into university. If you look at the occupational profiles in the cohorts
 the 1980 census, you would have sworn that the Chinese kids had a mean IQ of
0 rather than 100. Of course one-third of that was due to the seven points. It
eant that the relevant IQ threshold for entry into high-status jobs was 93 for
hinese, as compared to a white threshold of 100. The other 13 points came from

their capitalization rate. That is, 80% of Chinese kids above 93 were professional managers or technical, whereas only 60% of white kids above 100 were. characterize this by saying if a Chinese kid has a fiancée and he or she says, 'Don go to Stanford, stay with me,' the Chinese kid gets another fiancée. An Iris American kid may actually stay. There are important factors that influence grou achievement other than IQ.

Maynard Smith: You said that you thought that the reason for the post-Wor War II gain was an increased interest in abstract thinking. Why do you thir this?

Flynn: After World War II, a number of things occurred. In America at least, tl depression psychology began to wear off and people were less pragmaticall oriented. There was also more leisure and people started doing leisure activitie that were fun in terms of using ideas for their own sake. There were few children and I think parents began interacting with kids by satisfying the curiosity more. I suspect there were a whole range of subtle triggers that mac people invest their intellectual energy into problem-solving for its own sak even if it had no obvious pay-off in terms of school learning or everyday lif However, this is just a suspicion. I've tried to formulate a research design th will allow me to collect data on the subject; it's not easy.

Jensen: Why do you so minimize the physical side of the possible cause of this I gain? It is not just nutrition that has improved, but also prenatal care, obstetr techniques and so on: these don't all hit the whole population at once. If the were responsible there would be a gradual change until some asymptote reached. Apparently, the height increase is already saturated and is dropping off.

Flynn: What do the biologists say about that? I would be interested to know.

Maynard Smith: The increase in the height in kids in Britain over the last 50 year and I gather this is true in the USA also, has nothing whatever to do with tl general observation that mammalian species get larger with time. The latter is statement about genetic change.

Flynn: To answer Arthur's question, I don't take the physical causes light before World War II. But look at the data after World War II. In the Netherland 18-year olds made an IQ gain of eight points between 1972 and 1982. I asked peop there whether there was any conceivable increase in care of kids or diet and the said, 'No'. Actually, most of them were amazed: they thought their kids we poisoning themselves with fast foods! I talked to the Israelis too, because 1 year olds there gained nine IQ points between 1970 and 1985, and I dre another blank.

Jensen: There are experimental studies showing that nutritional supplements ca increase IQ. But this depends on the subjects having had deficiencies to begin wit although they are subtle deficiencies in the sense that other children in the sam family don't show those deficiencies.

Hinde: I was surprised that you don't lay more emphasis on changes in rearing practice during the periods you discuss: the change from Truby King to Spock and Bowlby; the change from bringing up children in kibbutzim to the increased emphasis on parent–child relationships in Israel; and the change in hospital regimes in allowing parents to visit. All these changes in the children's early development have happened during this period and are likely to have affected development.

Flynn: I hinted at this in the sense that post-World War II parents are probably more conceptually interactive with their kids and take them more seriously. I know when I was raised, if I came to my father with a question, he was not enormously receptive. But with my own child, when he came to me with a little number theorem he invented, I used to show him simple proofs. This is not a negative statement about my father: he went into factory work at age 12 and he was a busy man, and he wasn't used to kids asking questions. Dr Spock, I can see as a cause: he signalled a more flexible and conceptually rich child–parent interaction. But I am a bit sceptical about the hospital visits.

Hinde: I was brought up as a Truby King baby, and fed regularly on a schedule every six hours. I have always been told that was the root of all that was the matter with me!

Gangestad: It would be interesting to see in which subpopulations the largest gains are made. My understanding is that it is the lower end of the IQ distribution.

Flynn: Only in some of the data. In other data, the gains go right up through the scale. For example, I have the Dutch Raven's curve. There's a problem right at the top end because of a ceiling effect, but throughout most of the curve, there are gains at all levels. I published in the *American Journal of Mental Deficiency* the data from WISC to WISC-R. Admittedly, there weren't many samples above 120, but the gains were pretty uniform from 70 up to 115. They may be a little greater at the bottom. You don't find truncated variance in most of the IQ gains data. You would think that if the gains are at the bottom and not above the mean, you would find over time that raw score variance would decline. However, it doesn't in some of the data sets.

Houle: I was going to ask about changes in variance which could be very informative here. I'm wondering whether you are adequately taking into account the changing nature of the test.

Flynn: I'm talking about tests that haven't been altered. In the Israeli data, the same derivative from Raven's was used over the entire period. The Dutch was the same, so was the Norwegian and the French. For the Raven's data at least the test was invariant. Interestingly, you don't find a wildly different pattern between unaltered and altered tests. You do find some differences between nations. I'm convinced that US gains on Wechsler IQ tests since World War II have been less

than those in Scotland, Austria and Germany, though the data is so bad in som
cases it's hard to tell.

I have a lot of trouble with cross-national comparisons, because often the onl
really good data are the Raven's military data. This is often the only set of data tha
gives a saturation sample on an unaltered test. You can get into a lot of problem
with the others. I'm not saying the Raven's data never differ: gains tailed off i
Norway beginning in about 1972–1973, while they seem to go on quite robustl
in Israel at least through 1985 and in the Netherlands until 1982. They are reachin
what I call 'saturation point' at different places at different times, but it would b
wonderful to know whether they started at different times in those places. By th
way, male and female aren't different in Israel: Israel tests women, and while yo
only get an 80% sample of women I developed techniques for estimating the tai
There, the male/female gains were similar. They also had a verbal test they hadn'
changed, and as usual the gains on that verbal test were far lower than the Raven'
gains.

Gangestad: Why do you think the gains in West Germany are twice what they ar
in the USA?

Flynn: I don't know. They are also very high in Scotland.

Gangestad: Would it be informative to look at the height gains in West German
and Scotland, and compare them with those in the USA, to see if there is an
comparability?

Flynn: I thought of that, but I just got exhausted. I got the Dutch height gain
and I thought, 'What am I getting into?' It took me six years to collect the IQ data
and someone else is going to have to do the height data. I wrote a book on mora
philosophy instead.

Next year I am going to look at the Scottish data, because it allows one to chec
whether, despite IQ gains, item hierarchy has remained relatively similar. Arthu
Jensen has pointed out that one of the interesting things about the black/white IC
gap is what small differences there are in item hierarchy mimic age differences. H
pointed out that black 13-year olds have something like the item hierarchy of whit
10-year olds. We've got the 13-year olds' and 10-year olds' item hierarchy data fron
Scotland. It will be interesting to find whether the 10-year olds of the later grou
mimic the 13-year olds of the earlier group.

Rutter: Arthur Jensen, you were saying psychologists haven't paid attention t
height changes, but they have. In 1975, Jack Tizzard used height specifically t
refute your argument that the within-group heritabilities in IQ meant that it wa
likely that the between-group explanation for black/white differences in IQ wa
genetically determined. He made the point that the heritability of IQ has alway
been high, but in spite of that, there was a 12 cm rise in average height in Londo
schoolboys between 1900 and 1950. Interestingly, as far as one can tell, th
heritability hasn't altered one iota over that period.

Two points need to be made with respect to the possible role of obstetric factors in the secular rise in IQ. First, the evidence for a causal effect of obstetric complications on variations within the normal range of IQ is very weak. Major complications that are associated with brain abnormalities as revealed by scanning findings do, of course, predispose to cognitive impairment but they affect a tiny proportion of children. Minor complications not associated with demonstrable brain abnormalities seem to have a negligible effect on intelligence. Thus, for example, in a systematic comparison of twins and singletons, we found that although obstetric complications were much commoner in twins, they did not relate at all to differences in cognitive functioning within twins, within singletons, or between the two groups. Rather, the lag in language development found in twins relative to singletons seemed to be a function of the patterns of mother–child communicative interaction that differed between twins and singletons (Rutter et al 2000). Second, although it certainly is the case that over the last half century there have been massive improvements in both obstetric and neonatal care, it is likely that this has not affected the overall rate of serious obstetric complications. That is because, although babies who would have experienced such complications in the past no longer do so, it is also the case that babies who would have died in the past now survive and that a substantial proportion of them are left with sequelae. The net effect may well be no overall change over time in the rate of surviving children who experienced serious obstetric complications.

There are two other issues that we need to remember with regard to the Flynn effect. First, it is by no means confined to IQ. The evidence of secular trends in other variables is very strong (Rutter & Smith 1995). At the same time that the mean IQ has gone up, so too there has been a rise in crime rates, suicide rates in young people, and drug and alcohol use. As James Flynn noted, the secular rise has been found for many traits, some advantageous and some disadvantageous. Second, a rise in the level of a trait, such as IQ, need not necessarily affect individual differences. For example, the Duyme et al (1999) study published a few months ago looked at the effects of late adoption in French children who were removed from parents because of abuse or neglect and who were adopted between the ages of four and six with an IQ measure prior to adoption. The rise in IQ as measured at the follow-up in adolescence was substantial and was significantly related to the qualities of the adoptive home. Those in low socioeconomic status (SES) homes showed a mean rise of eight IQ points, whereas those in higher SES homes showed a mean rise of 20 points. However, the correlations over time between the pre-adoption IQ and the adolescence IQ were the same in those showing large and those showing small rises in IQ. Although it would be a mistake to view the domains of causal influences on level and on individual differences as necessarily different (see Turkheimer 1991), equally they are not necessarily the same (see Rutter & Smith 1995).

Miller: I believe these IQ gains are real. The question of why there has not been renaissance is interesting, and might be instructive in thinking about human evolution. In certain domains there has been a renaissance: the total number of books published, music CDs released and the number of scientific publications has skyrocketed in this period. But to some extent because social competition is often a zero-sum game, we don't see any socially beneficial effects of increased IQ. I was at Stanford, for example, when federal funding for a particle collider was cut, and the 300 physics PhDs who were working on it, suddenly couldn't work in physics anymore. So they went to Wall Street and became quantitative analysts, where their job is to try to out-predict the other physicists working in the other investment banks and try to figure out what the stock markets might do tomorrow. They are not necessarily producing any net social benefits. Do you think that's the sort of explanation for why there hasn't been the renaissance you might expect?

Flynn: Well you see when I first saw the data, I had to analyse them from two perspectives. Some people were saying that these IQ gains are real, therefore all of our grandparents must have been mentally retarded. My father could keep score at a baseball game, and the average Dutchman of 20 years ago knew what offside was in soccer: they weren't mentally retarded, even though on current norms the average IQ was 75. As for the social effects, I think you're right. In the research design I've set up, I will simulate the IQ gap between two generations (I'm going to try to get two groups that are matched for arithmetic, vocabulary and general information, but the second group beats the first for Matrices, Block design and Similarities). I would be very surprised if the test score difference does not signal a real world effect, at least in the sense that the second group does more of the advanced maths and physics courses and does better at them. But that does not mean we will find more pure mathematicians. It breaks your heart to see the talent in physics and mathematics that's going down the drain. When I was at Cornell, I was rooming with someone at his wits end, who had 200 or 300 citations and 30 articles on meson physics and was just about to go to Wall Street. It might be the real world effects would be more visible if it weren't for countervailing social trends.

Houle: What about at the low end? The IQ scale was in part derived to help detect children with real learning disabilities. The prediction is that the low end of the IQ scale really can't function. If what you are saying is true IQ tests should no longer predict disability at the same level it did 50 years ago.

Flynn: Let me give you another illustration. Take someone in 1918, who hadn't had to cope with a beyond primary school environment, hadn't invested their intellectual energy into things that would give them good IQ scores or vocabulary and arithmetic. But they may well have been quite capable of coping with everyday life. There is a difference between not having invested your intelligence in what gives you a good IQ score, and being unable to do it. The current person with an IQ of 75 has every opportunity to invest their intelligence in the sort of domains that would give them a better IQ score. So their IQ of 75 or below has a very different significance than the person who hasn't had the same chance.

Houle: Basically we are saying that the heritability of IQ is remaining the same, and it seems to mean the same thing relative at least at the high end of the scale. But I just don't see how that argument can apply at the lower end.

Flynn: People say that everyday life has got more complicated, and that maybe our parents were as unintelligent as these IQ scores indicate and they got by because they had a simpler world to deal with in 1918 than we do today. I'm not entirely convinced of this. When I was a kid, my cousins up north had to know how to put their own motor cars together. In some ways, everyday life was a lot tougher: being a farm wife was a considerable organizational feat. So, I'm not entirely convinced there's been this great upgrading of the complexity of everyday life. This is why I selected sport as an example. In 1918, 1948 and 1980, people attended baseball games that were the same in complexity. And at all times they tended to keep score. If you have someone with a WAIS IQ of below 75 today, even if they are a keen sports fan, they often don't know what a sacrificed fly is and they may not even know the number of players on a team. If you go back to 1918, the average person has an IQ of 75 on today's norms, but they could all keep score at baseball games and they knew what a sacrificed fly was.

Rutter: You may be right that life was as demanding in the past, but what certainly has changed is the job market. Over the same period that IQ has gone up, the proportion of unskilled and semi-skilled jobs in the USA and UK has halved (Rutter & Smith 1995). The scholastic prerequisites for jobs have risen greatly. Of course, that does not necessarily mean that the IQ demands are greater today than in the past, but IQ and scholastic achievement are associated. There are fewer job opportunities now for individuals with limited cognitive skills because there are fewer unskilled jobs.

Houle: It seems to me in some respects the cognitive demands must be the same. Learning to read is the same now as it was in 1900.

Harnad: Am I just being curmudgeonly if I say that the situation seems a little bit worse now? What has been expressed so far is surprise that there are not comparable academic performance gains to show for these IQ test performance gains. In contrast, I thought the idea was that it was actually the reverse: achievement is actually going down, grade inflation is rife, and the maximum digestible unit that can be taught in schools has actually been shrinking while IQ has been rising?

Flynn: When I published my 1984 article on US IQ gains in *Psychological Bulletin*, it was the time of the great scholastic aptitude decline. Since then, they have got better data, and they argue that if you look at the junior SAT, which was given to a more universal sample, there was little or no decline. Even so, it is still surprising that there were these massive gains on IQ tests and scholastic achievement on the junior SAT did no more than remain stable. They have dumbed down the textbooks of course.

Harnad: From personal experience I would say that the essays have dumbed down.

Jensen: Not only that, there is an increasing percentage of the high school population that takes the SAT. You have to control for that.

Flynn: That's why I have mentioned the junior SAT data, which does control for that. When I wrote that article, I did try to allow for cohort size, and my calculation at the time still showed that there was a drop, but not as big a drop as appeared. I was also impressed by the fact that there were absolutely fewer top scores. During that period, the number of people getting 700 or above fell off numerically, which was much more difficult to explain in terms of the wider group taking it.

Jensen: One explanation is that there are changes in the occupational structure and the birth rates in different segments of the distribution over different generations. This can have effects in these small parts up at the top of the scale.

Mackintosh: I wanted to go back to David Houle's point which I don't think has been answered. 50 years ago if you scored below 70 on an IQ test you were mentally retarded and unable to lead an independent life. X per cent of the population fell into that category. Very few people would score below 70 on a 50-year-old IQ test today. So far fewer people should be incapable of leading an independent life today than 50 years ago.

Flynn: I thought that Spitz was convinced that though they may have dropped off, they hadn't disappeared to the degree that you are talking about.

Houle: I would guess that we have the same proportion of retarded people in the sense that they don't function in society now even after these IQ gains. This seems to pose a real paradox.

Flynn: It does indeed, and I've given you the best answer I have. Nick Mackintosh may be right. I read Spitz's book: he said in the USA there has been a drop in people unable to cope, but not a dramatic drop. You would think that if the IQ gains are real at the level of coping with everyday life, then that group would have very radically diminished. I have given the only reason I can give as to why I think that didn't happen. I think the gains reflect no greater capacity to cope with everyday life: instead, they reflect a tendency towards abstract problem-solving of a sort that doesn't affect everyday life much in terms of coping with the fundamentals of social interaction. This may be a totally inadequate explanation.

Rutter: I don't understand why there is a paradox. The finding on mildly retarded children is that post-school, the great majority of them function in the general population: they have jobs, they marry and they have children. They do less well compared to other people, though. The reason why I don't think this is a paradox is that this was the case before and it is still the case now. The issue comes in terms of competition. Competition is essentially comparative, and wherever you are, it's a question of whether or not you are at the bottom of the pile relative to other people. If everybody goes up but you're still at the bottom of the pile you can't compete.

Humphrey: There are some hurdles that have an absolute height to them, like learning to read. The paradox is that while IQ has gone up, there doesn't seem to have been any change in this respect.

Flynn: Take a basketball example. There's been this great escalation of basketball skills. What does it mean? It means that people can shoot with both right and left hands and can make fade-away jump shots. An escalation of skills of that sort isn't going to reflect too much who can't walk properly, that is, who is disabled at the other end of the spectrum. I think the IQ gains are more like that.

Houle: Then you should get a change in the variance.

Flynn: Real-world performance variance perhaps, but not reflected in IQ scores.

Maynard Smith: Is it irreligious to assert that perhaps IQ tests aren't a very good measure of performance?

Detterman: You have said, and Wendy Williams has documented, that there are a lot of changes going on in schools that make them worse — spending less time on academic subjects, books are dumbed down — would you predict that there is going to be a decline?

Flynn: I haven't studied it like Wendy has. I said that a more free interaction between parent and child which encourages curiosity and thinking abstractly on one level, might at the same time undermine children's attitude towards teachers as mentors and makes them retreat into their peer group at an earlier age. The latter could mean a more limited fund of general information and vocabulary. But in this I'm just a total amateur, speculating as to what common causes could both bring this rise in abstract problem solving ability and could also make kids more resistant to the fundamentals of education.

References

Dickens WT, Flynn JR 2000 Heritability vs. environmental effects. Psychol Rev, in press

Duyme M, Dumaret A-C, Tomkiewicz S 1999 How can we boost IQs of 'dull children'? A late adoption study. Proc Natl Acad Sci USA 96:8790–8794

Jensen AR 1973 Educability and group differences. Methuen, London

Rushton JP 1995 Race, evolution and behavior. Transaction, New Brunswick, NJ

Rutter M, Smith DJ (eds) 1995 Psychosocial disorders in young people: time trends and their causes. Wiley, Chichester

Rutter M, Thorpe K, Golding J 2000 Twins as a natural experiment to study the causes of language delay. Mental Health Foundation, London

Tizard J 1975 Race and IQ: the limits of probability. New Behav 1:6–9

Turkheimer E 1991 Individual and group differences in adoption studies of IQ. Psychol Bull 110:392–405

Mutation, selection and the heritability of complex traits

Andrew Pomiankowski

The Galton Laboratory, Department of Biology, University College London, London NW1 2HE, UK

Abstract. It has been suggested that complex traits, like intelligence, have low heritabilities. This hypothesis stems from the idea that strong selection for higher intelligence has led to the fixation of genetic variation for this trait. The same hypothesis has been framed for complex sexual ornaments used in courtship display. These traits are also subject to directional selection, in this case caused by sexual selection. However, contrary to the hypothesis, comparative data shows that sexual ornaments have higher additive genetic variation than similar non-sexual traits. It appears that the number of variable genes and the effect per genetic locus have increased for sexual ornaments. Theory suggests this is due to selection for extreme phenotypes resulting in condition-dependent expression of sexual traits. Experimental work on the stalk-eyed fly, *Cyrtodiopsis dalmanni,* confirms that the male sexual trait (exaggerated eyespan) is more sensitive to environmental conditions than other non-sexual traits (wing dimensions and female eyespan). This environmental sensitivity has a genetic basis and environmental stress enhances genetic differences. It is likely that genetic variation in intelligence is maintained in a similar fashion.

2000 The nature of intelligence. Wiley, Chichester (Novartis Foundation Symposium 233) p 228–242

Introduction

The aim of this chapter is to review genetic variation underlying exaggerated sexual traits. At first sight this has nothing to do with the nature of intelligence. However, there is one question in intelligence research that data and theory on sexual traits can usefully shed light.

It has been suggested that complex traits, like intelligence, have low heritabilities. The reason given is that intelligence has been subject to persistent strong selection for higher values, and this has depleted additive genetic variation underlying the trait. If this view is correct, most variation in intelligence will be due to environmental (or non-additive genetic) variation.

228

A similar proposition has been put forward for secondary sexual traits. Male sexual traits differ from ordinary morphological traits in a number of ways. They are often highly complex and exaggerated (e.g., the peacock's tail), and show high rates of evolutionary divergence between species (e.g., in the birds of paradise). Measurements of variation in reproductive success in species with exaggerated sexual traits, show that these traits are under strong directional selection, in this case caused by female mate preferences and male–male sexual competition, both of which favour larger trait values (Andersson 1994). Again, it has been argued that this leads to the fixation of much of the additive genetic variation in sexual traits (Taylor & Williams 1982).

Genetic variance in sexual traits

Before addressing these arguments about how selection alters the level of additive genetic variation, it is instructive to examine the data. A recent literature search was carried out of studies that measured the heritability of sexual traits (Pomiankowski & Møller 1995). A comparison was made of the additive genetic variation in sexual and similar non-sexual traits from the same species. Ideally the same trait from the female (or the non-sexually selected sex) was used for comparison. When this was not available, another non-sexually dimorphic trait was used.

The coefficient of additive genetic variance CV_A was used to compare the additive genetic variance in sexual and non-sexual traits. This standardizes the additive genetic variance with respect to the mean value of the trait, $CV_A = \sqrt{V_A}/\bar{X}$ (Houle 1992). An adjustment of this kind was needed as sexual traits are often exaggerated and hence larger than the non-sexual trait they were compared with, and we expect the variance to scale with trait size. Heritability is another potential measure which scales additive genetic variance to the total phenotypic variance, $h^2 = V_A/V_P$. This is also an informative index for comparing traits but can be misleading as a low heritability may reflect a lack of additive genetic variance or an excess of environmental or non-additive effects (e.g., dominance). The main result of the comparative review was the complete lack of evidence for depleted additive genetic variance in sexual traits (Fig. 1). The additive genetic variance in the sexual traits was clearly not low, contributing over 60% to the total phenotypic variance. Contrary to expectation, the additive genetic variance was significantly higher in sexual traits, whereas the residual variance (environmental and non-additive) did not differ between sexual and non-sexual traits. The higher additive genetic variation in sexual traits contributed to a higher phenotypic variance as well.

These results should not be taken as cast in stone. Many of the estimates of additive genetic variation were made from small samples and few controlled for common environmental effects (e.g., maternal effects) and so may be

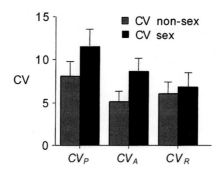

FIG. 1. Means and standard errors of the coefficient of phenotypic variance (CV_P), the coefficient of additive genetic variation (CV_A) and the coefficient of residual variation (CV_R). Comparison is made between paired data for sexual and non-sexual characters from the same species (Data from Pomiankowski & Møller 1995, $n = 16$).

overestimates. But these deficiencies are likely to affect variance estimates both in sexual and non-sexual traits. Another problem has been uncovered by Alatalo et al (1997), who showed a publishing bias. Post-1988 studies showed higher heritabilities for sexual traits than pre-1988 studies, but this change was not reported for non-sexual traits. Alatalo et al (1997) suggest that 1988 marks the turning point in acceptance of handicap models of sexual selection which assume that females choose mates for genetic benefits (Pomiankowski 1988). In this new climate, additive genetic variation in sexual traits was expected, and led to more publications with this result. Whether this sociological explanation is true or not, the evidence for a publication bias suggests caution.

What maintains genetic variance?

These results suggest that the logic, strong selection causes low genetic variance, is too simple. What it leaves out is that different traits have different genetic architectures. In particular, the number of genes that contribute to variation differ between traits and are subject to evolutionary change. Equilibrium genetic variance not only reflects selective loss but also mutational input. Higher genetic variance is therefore expected in traits affected by more loci. This point is well known and underlies the observation that traits closely related to fitness, like life history traits, have higher standardized genetic variance (Houle 1992).

A similar logic can be applied to sexual traits. Pomiankowski & Møller (1995) suggested that persistent directional selection caused by female mate preferences disproportionately favours individuals with higher trait values. Such selection favours increased phenotypic variance and so selects for an increase in the number of loci and the effect per locus on sexual traits. The net effect will be to increase the genetic variance of sexual traits. This view echoes an idea originally put forward by Haldane (1932) that directional selection often as a side consequence selects for changes in the variance.

A similar idea was put forward by Rowe & Houle (1996) who argued that many sexual traits have evolved strong condition-dependent expression. If the marginal cost of further exaggeration of a sexual trait is lower for individuals in higher condition than for individuals in poor condition, we expect that the size of the sexual trait will evolve to be an increasing function of condition. This formulation is well known to biologists interested in the evolution of sexual traits as the handicap principle (Pomiankowski 1988, Iwasa & Pomiankowski 1994, Rowe & Houle 1996).

Condition in this case may be taken as a general measure of some of the major fitness components of an organism, for example, its ability to accumulate resources, the absence of deleterious mutations, or even a simple trait like size. As a large proportion of the genome contributes to condition, which is a complex summary of many processes (Price & Schluter 1991), genetic variation in condition is predicted to be large. To the degree that sexual trait development reflects condition, it too will have high genetic variance.

We can follow the logic of this argument with a quantitative genetic model of the size of a sexual trait (Iwasa & Pomiankowski 1994),

$$s = t + t'v. \tag{1}$$

The genetic contribution to size of the sexual trait (s) has two parts, one that is condition independent (t) and the other that is condition dependent ($t'v$), where condition is denoted by v. The genetic variance of s can be estimated as (Rowe & Houle 1996),

$$G_s \approx G_t + \bar{t}'^2 G_v + \bar{v}^2 G_{t'}. \tag{2a}$$

Given that $G_{t'}$, the genetic variation in the rule for converting condition into sexual trait size, is likely to be small,

$$G_s \approx G_t + \bar{t}'^2 G_v. \tag{2b}$$

So if condition-dependence is strong (i.e., $t' > 0$), genetic variation in the sexual trait will largely depend on genetic variation in condition, as for most traits $G_v \gg G_t$.

To some extent all traits show condition-dependent expression. For example, most traits scale with body size. The important question is whether we expect condition-dependence to be greater in sexual traits? We can study this by following the evolution of a trait subject to sexual selection. Say females prefer to mate with males with larger traits. This will lead to increases in s. This enlargement is opposed by natural selection which acts against increases in trait size beyond the optimum for survival (e.g., the peacock's tail is good for attracting females but impedes male flight and predator avoidance). The key assumption concerns how this natural selection cost depends on condition. Following the assumption of the handicap principle given above,

$$\text{costs} \propto \frac{1}{1 + kv} s^2. \tag{3}$$

Here we arbitrarily scale the natural selection optimum to zero, and any deviation from this increases costs. As trait size increases (larger s) or deviates from the natural selection optimum, costs increase. These costs vary with condition (coefficient k). If $k > 0$, an individual in good condition (high v) suffers relatively smaller fitness loss compared to an individual in poor condition (low v) for the same trait size (s).

If we allow trait size to evolve given these assumptions about selection, it is straightforward to show that at equilibrium the relative condition-dependence is (Iwasa & Pomiankowski 1994),

$$\frac{t'}{t} = k. \tag{4}$$

Where costs of sexual trait exaggeration strongly depend on condition (large k), we expect condition-dependence (t') to be large as well.

To summarize, we have shown that traits with strong condition-dependent expression have high genetic variation. This is expected because many genes contribute to condition, so the mutational input and standing genetic variation in condition will be large. Condition-dependence evolves when the cost of trait exaggeration depends on condition. Sexual traits are thought to have evolved strong condition-dependent expression because of the pressure generated by female mate preference for exaggerated trait values. So we expect sexual traits to show high genetic variation.

Evidence for condition-dependence

These ideas can now be backed up by experimental work. I will illustrate this by my own work using the stalk-eyed fly *Cyrtodiopsis dalmanni*. Males of this species have greatly exaggerated eyespan and females prefer to mate with males with wider eyespan (Wilkinson & Reillo 1994). Fortunately the flies are easy to rear in large numbers under controlled laboratory conditions. We tested whether the size of the exaggerated male sexual ornament (eyespan) was more sensitive to condition than the size of the homologous eyespan trait in females or to other non-sexual traits (wing dimensions).

In the first experiment (David et al 1998), condition was experimentally manipulated by allowing larvae to develop at different food densities (a 20-fold spread, from low density to very high density). As predicted, male eyespan showed a marked decrease in size as larval density increased (Fig. 2). But so did the non-sexual traits (Fig. 2). This revealed that condition-dependence was a general feature of sexual and non-sexual traits in insects.

However, several strands of evidence showed that male eyespan was more sensitive to environmental conditions (David et al 1998). There was a strong sex × density interaction, with male eyespan declining much more conspicuously than female eyespan over the same range of stresses (Fig. 2). The sex difference persisted when we examined relative eyespan size (dividing by body size). Finally, a linear model with body size and larval density as effects showed that male eyespan declined with larval density even when body size scaling had been accounted for, but that female eyespan did not.

This experiment established that male eyespan (sexual trait) is more sensitive to environmental stress than non-sexual traits. However, this greater condition-dependence is paradoxical, as sensitivity to environmental variation can potentially mask genetic effects. To address this concern, we designed a second experiment to investigate how genetic variation affected the development of sexual and non-sexual traits (David et al 2000). Experimental males were mated to virgin females to generate full and half-sib families. Larvae from each family were exposed to three food environments (corn, spinach, cotton wool) of decreasing nutritional value.

Again sexual and non-sexual traits were compared, whilst controlling for general body size effects (David et al 2000). All traits measured were genetically variable. But only the sexual trait (male eyespan) showed a genetic basis to environmental condition-dependence that was independent of body size scaling (Fig. 3). Genetic variation in male eyespan increased under food stress but despite this, rankings of genotypes were maintained across environments. So rather than masking genetic variation, stressful environments magnified the differences between genotypes in male eyespan. Similar patterns were non-existent or considerably weaker in the non-sexual traits (female eyespan and wing dimensions in both sexes).

Discussion

These experiments show that the sexual trait (male eyespan) in stalk-eyed flies is a unique character. Both sexual and non-sexual traits decreased in size under

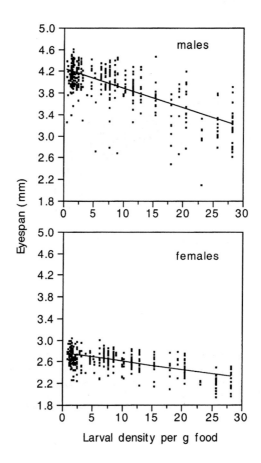

FIG. 2   Decreases in male and female eyespan in stalk-eyed flies subject to increasing larval density (David et al 1998). Male eyespan (sexual trait) is more sensitive to larval density than female eyespan (non-sexual trait).

environmental stress. However, this condition-dependence was largely a scaling response to changes in body size for the non-sexual traits. In contrast, the sexual trait showed condition-dependence after body size effects had been accounted for, and this condition-dependence had a genetic basis.

These results are consistent with handicap models of sexual selection (Pomiankowski 1988, Iwasa & Pomiankowski 1994, Rowe & Houle 1996). The models predict that complex and exaggerated sexual traits which signal male genetic quality (e.g., elongated eyespan in stalk-eyed flies, long tails in peacocks) evolve strong condition-dependent expression. The central assumption is that the

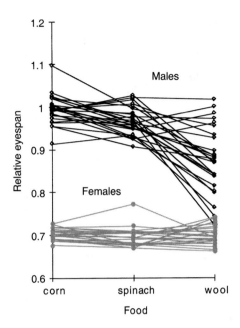

FIG. 3. Genotypic responses for relative male and female eyespan across the three environments of decreasing nutritional value (corn, spinach, cotton wool). Relative values are eyespan divided by thorax length for each individual. Each line represents the mean eyespan of a group of full sibs (five offspring in each environment). Genetic variation in relative male eyespan increases from good to poor environments (reprinted from David et al 2000).

marginal cost of producing a larger trait must be smaller for individuals with higher condition. This assumption about fitness remains to be fully evaluated.

Returning to the original theme of this paper, how do these results help explain the significantly higher measures of genetic variation found in sexual traits? If the expression of sexual traits is strongly condition-dependent, then we expect that many genes that affect the general condition of an individual will also affect sexual trait size. So a consequence of the evolution of exaggeration and complexity will be an increase in the mutational input and hence higher genetic variation in sexual traits.

How do these results relate to the nature of intelligence? They firstly demonstrate that strong selection and rapid evolution do not necessarily result in a denudation of genetic variation. In fact, directional selection can result in an increase of genetic variation. If selection causes an increase in the number of genes that contribute to a trait or the effect of each variable locus, then we can expect that genetic variation will increase. If general condition makes a significant contribution to intelligence, as seems likely, then we can expect that genetic variation in intelligence will be maintained despite persistent selection on intelligence.

Another possibility is that intelligence has evolved as a sexual trait (Miller 2000, this volume). Although there is some evidence in favour of this hypothesis, it remains to be established whether sexual selection had a major role in the evolution of intelligence. However, the rapid increase in brain size (and presumably intelligence) in human history, whatever the cause, may have involved a similar expansion in the number of genes affecting brain development, and hence a knock-on effect increasing genetic variation.

Summary

Traits like intelligence that have been subject to strong directional selection are predicted to have low additive genetic variation. Similar arguments have been made about sexual traits. However, sexual traits have higher additive genetic variation than similar non-sexual traits. Theoretical developments show that directional selection on sexual traits can cause an increase in additive genetic variation when condition-dependent expression is favoured. Similar selection may have acted on intelligence and so have maintained genetic variation in this trait.

Acknowledgements

My research is supported by a Royal Society University Research Fellowship and Research Grants from the Natural Environment Research Council. I am greatly indebted to my co-workers on the stalk-eyed fly experiments, Tracey Bjorksten, Patrice David, Kevin Fowler and Andy Hingle, and to collaborations with Yoh Iwasa and Anders Paper Møller.

References

Alatalo RV, Mappes J, Elgar MA 1997 Heritabilities and paradigm shifts. Nature 385:402–403
Andersson M 1994 Sexual selection. Princeton University Press, Princeton, NJ
David P, Hingle A, Greig D, Rutherford A, Pomiankowski A, Fowler K 1998 Male sexual ornament size but not asymmetry reflects condition in stalk-eyed flies. Proc R Soc Lond B Biol Sci 265:2211–2216
David P, Bjorksten T, Fowler K, Pomiankowski A 2000 Condition-dependent signalling of genetic variation in stalk-eyed flies. Nature 406:186–188
Haldane JBS 1932 The causes of evolution. Longman, London
Houle D 1992 Comparing evolvability and variability of quantitative traits. Genetics 130:195–204
Iwasa Y, Pomiankowski A 1994 The evolution of mate preferences for multiple handicaps. Evolution 48:853–867

Miller G 2000 Sexual selection for indicators of intelligence. In: The nature of intelligence. Wiley, Chichester (Novartis Found Symp 233) p 260–275

Pomiankowski A 1988 The evolution of female mate preferences for male genetic quality. In: Harvey P, Partridge L (eds) Oxford surveys in evolutionary biology, vol 5. Oxford University Press, Oxford, p 136–184

Pomiankowski A, Møller AP 1995 A resolution of the lek paradox. Proc R Soc Lond B Biol Sci 260:21–29

Price T, Schluter D 1991 On the low heritability of life history traits. Evolution 45:853–861

Rowe L, Houle D 1996 The lek paradox and the capture of genetic variance by condition dependent traits. Proc R Soc Lond B Biol Sci 263:1415–1421

Taylor PD, Williams GC 1982 The lek paradox is not resolved. Theor Pop Biol 22:392–409

Wilkinson GS, Reillo 1994 Female choice response to artificial selection on an exaggerated male trait in a stalk-eyed fly. Proc R Soc Lond B Biol Sci 255:1–6

DISCUSSION

Harnad: Concerning the notion that these male traits validly signal fitness to females: females have both sons and daughters. I assume that it is to a male's advantage to fake these traits, if this is possible, but it is also to the advantage of the female that they not be faked. How do the prospects of her sons affect the fakeability of these traits?

Pomiankowski: The central answer to that lies in the concept of handicap: a signal provides good information about a male's fitness if it is costly. If we want to know whether a man has a lot of money, for instance, and we can see that he owns a Ferrari we know this is the case. I could fake being wealthy by hiring a Ferrari for a couple of days, but I could do no more than this. There are costs associated with producing and maintaining these big signals, which are differential on the quality of the individuals bearing them. The peacock with its huge tail is expending a lot of energy on it, because he can afford to do this. The female is therefore getting good information about his genotype which is contributing to his quality. It is an uncheatable signal of his worth.

Harnad: I have no idea where you would expect intelligence researchers to pick up on this work. Eye stalk width is not functional. As to the extent to which signs of *g* are detectable, *g* itself is so eminently functional, how could it fit into this paradigm?

Pomiankowski: We have had this debate before. Is having a high *g* functional in terms of fitness? We don't know. There are some signs that it is in terms of success, but we also have indications that it is not. Having intelligence is a good thing. Having a tail is a good thing: it enables you to fly. Having eyes on stalks is good: it enables you to see. These features are intrinsically good, but what is the optimal trait size? In the eye stalk, it is probably much shorter than males currently have. There are related species in which females don't care which males they mate with, and in these the males don't have long eye stalks.

Harnad: I know the costs of having widely spaced eyes, but is there even a tin advantage to this? In intelligence, every time you crank up *g* it is better in *some* way for the individual, even though it may be disadvantageous in other ways. I don' see how cranking up wider and wider eye spacing is going to be any benefit to an individual in the same way that enhanced *g* will be.

Pomiankowski: One idea about eyespan is that you want your eyes on stalks to facilitate binocular vision.

Harnad: What about peacock tails?

Pomiankowski: I don't think there is any value in having a huge tail Aerodynamically it is a nightmare. It is a physical encumbrance and costs a lot to produce.

Harnad: To my layman's view, that seems like a big disanalogy between the two cases.

Pomiankowski: If one was going to follow the logic that the brain is a sexually selected organ, one would have to argue hypertrophy beyond what is optimal for everyday life.

Maynard Smith: I would probably want to argue with you about that. There really is a quite sharp distinction between two processes which may be going on in sexual selection. They both happen, but in different cases. In the case of the stalk eyed fly or the peacock, having these exaggerated features is intrinsically a cost. As far as individual survival is concerned, the male is better off without these features But if (and only if) it is true that an organism with high fitness can afford to produce this structure without killing itself whereas an organism with low fitness cannot afford this, it does pay a female to choose the male with such a handicapping feature, because she knows she is getting value in other respects. The alternative is that in a sensible fly, such as *Drosophila subobscura,* the female chooses a male who can dance athletically. Anything you do to a male to make it move less well means that the male cannot keep up with the female when she dances. This is a genuinely different mechanism from the one that Andrew Pomiankowski is talking about. In the one case there is a signal which is honest because of its cost; in the other you have what I call an 'index': something which for causal reasons reflects what the female actually wants. One ought to keep these two mechanisms rather separate in one's mind. I'm open minded as to whether being clever is like having a long tail, no good to anyone and something that only very fit people like me can afford, or whether it is actually intrinsically useful.

Harnad: Is there doubt in your mind about this?

Maynard Smith: In relation to music, yes. Music has to be a peacock's tail.

Rutter: Are you suggesting that the mechanisms will be different in these two examples you give? I agree that they are functionally very different, but will the genetic mechanisms necessarily be different?

Maynard Smith: They needn't be.

Pomiankowski: If a female could detect a fit male directly, this would be preferable.

Maynard Smith: A female *Drosophila* can tell every time the difference between an inbred male and an outbred one. She will not mate with an inbred male for hour after hour, but give her an outbred one and she will mate in a couple of minutes. She does this by dancing, and she is getting a direct measure of fitness. This is very sensible of her.

Pomiankowski: The cases I have been describing are brief encounters. Perhaps his dancing is a direct display of fitness, but it seems to me that dancing itself is a waste of a male's energy, just as producing long eye stalks is.

Maynard Smith: It takes only a couple of seconds, whereas the inbred male dances for hour after hour.

Pomiankowski: He must be dancing badly.

Maynard Smith: He dances slowly: he can't see very well or coordinate very well.

Pomiankowski: So dancing quickly is a tricky thing for the male to do.

Maynard Smith: General athletic and sensory ability is an important component of fitness in a fly, quite independent of courtship.

Houle: I wanted to pick out another strand of sexual selection theory. The general problem that this falls under is why should a female or a choosy mate care who their mate is? These cases like the stalk-eyed fly are one extreme where there is no parental care and very little likelihood of males passing material benefits to their mates. These are special cases which are very interesting because of the theoretical questions that they raise, but in many other organisms — notably those with parental care — the direct benefit model is a plausible alternative. In this scenario, you display your quality to a mate, and your quality has a much more direct impact on the offspring that you might care for together. If you choose a lousy mate, they may not take good care of the kids. This can lead to exaggerated displays that have these sorts of properties.

Humphrey: I would suggest that John Maynard Smith's distinction isn't anything like so clear-cut as he is making out. Even a peacock's tail has direct markers of fitness, such as the symmetry of the eyes on the tail and its glossiness. It is no more costly to produce a tail which has beautifully symmetrical eyes than one which is not so symmetrical: it is just that only the more fit males are able to accomplish this.

Maynard Smith: It is hard to make really clear distinctions. There are two kinds of processes going on; they mix in different proportions in different places.

Gangestad: In many species, females will see males compete with one another, and in these encounters their physical abilities are tested. The traits themselves are quite functional: greater size and physical fitness. They look more functional than stalks for eyes.

Maynard Smith: They get exaggerated though, beyond the optimal level.

Gangestad: There is a viability cost paid for with increased fecundity.

Pomiankowski: In the weaver bird, the male weaves a nest. He also has bright yellow coloration. If you force a male to make his nest out of useless materials, he will still make a nest, and if he has bright yellow coloration, females want to mate with him whatever his nest is like. The female thus chooses the male primarily on what he looks like. Then she enters the nest, and if it is made out of rubbish, she will abandon him. She looks at the resource he is giving her, and she doesn't look at him. There are other birds in which the male brings food to the female, thus demonstrating his foraging ability. It seems to me to be likely that those things are going to be directly assessed. We are thinking that females also want to be bothered about deleterious mutations, and we discussed yesterday that variation in brain function is rife and may be caused by deleterious mutations. Perhaps the female is getting at that through something to do with g.

Gangestad: When considering attractive features in birds in relation to male parental care across species, sometimes the males are doing more feeding, in other cases they are doing less. Interestingly, what predicts very well what attractive males will be doing is the extra-pair paternity rate within the species. Where there is a lot of extra-pair paternity, the attractive males seek and get extra-pair copulations and they accordingly spend less time feeding. In species in which the extra-pair paternity rate is low, the attractive males provide more feedings. In some cases, it may be possible to distinguish what attractiveness advertises by measuring whether attractive males are doing more or less.

Miller: Andrew Pomiankowski, when you talked about accelerating selection and this idea that selection favours increased phenotypic variance, you argued that this would increase the number of loci and the strength of loci effects on the sexual character. Could you explain more about how this would happen? To some non-biologists this might sound a little 'magical'. Are you a fan of David Houle's genic capture model, or do you have a different view about how this works?

Pomiankowski: I don't have a particular axe to grind on this one. Traits are probably all to some degree under stabilizing selection. When we bring in the idea that they vary with condition or with fitness in other respects, we know that fitness is under directional selection. So, it seems that if these traits are condition dependent, they will be under persistent directional selection. What I argued depends on the type of directional selection. If the directional selection equally favours big things as it disfavours small things, then there will be no selection on the variance. But if it highly favours extreme features, it is essentially selecting for high variance. How would you get high variance? It seems to me that you could get it in a number of ways, which is why I don't have any particular view. You can get it by recruiting extra genes, or by boosting the existing genes in some way, making their allelic variance more potent.

Miller: It might be worth connecting the dots a little and saying that you get these accelerating fitness functions under polygyny when mating competition is a 'winner take all' contest, and the top male gets a highly disproportionate number of mates.

Maynard Smith: There is a difficulty here as to who 'you' is referring to: the individual doesn't have a high variance, it is the population that does. Are you sneaking in a bit of group selection here? I'd like to see it spelt out in a model to show that it would work without group selection.

Pomiankowski: There is no group selection, the arguments are set out in Pomiankowski & Møller (1995).

Anderson: You are saying that it is a logical possibility that g is essentially directly unrelated to fitness, but it is identifiable by the females in mate selection, and it indexes other things that are useful for fitness. Is this correct?

Pomiankowski: Yes, the argument is that females want to know how many deleterious mutations a male has and uses intelligence as a means of getting at that information.

Suddendorf: The problem then is why don't we observe a sexual dimorphism in intelligence?

Pomiankowski: I agree that is a problem, but we can sneak out of this by saying that there many cases where there is no sexual dimorphism of a sexually selected feature. One example is in grebes: both male and females have elaborate courtship displays. In the species we have been talking about the females are doing the choosing, the males are displaying (e.g., the peacock). This is because there is a big asymmetry in investment as males are not contributing to parental care.

Suddendorf: And in these short-term mating strategies we find that males do not have the strong selection criteria that the females do.

Miller: If g is basically an index of fitness and if it is indeed the case that fitness is determined by the deleterious mutation load, there is not going to be sexual dimorphism in mutation load. After all, the two sexes basically share the same genes except those on the Y chromosome.

Rutter: Let me come back to the question of the extrapolation of Andrew Pomiankowski's work to intelligence. The extrapolations that we have been talking about are, to my mind, too complicated. It seems that you have provided an answer to the question on empirical findings that I posed in the introduction. Although evolutionary theory suggests that when equilibrium is reached, additive genetic variance should be zero, I queried whether that is actually borne out with empirical data. You have such data and have shown that in fact this does not happen. You put forward two possible explanations as to why that might be so, in terms of selection for variance and condition dependence. Yesterday we also had other explanations in terms of how one knows when equilibrium has been reached, and what sort of assumptions one is making about the way it operates in the world.

But it does seem that the paradox that Geoffrey Miller posed in putting forward the basis for this symposium is not a paradox any longer. Is this sort of extrapolation wrong?

Pomiankowski: I think it was naïve to believe the lek paradox as formulated — that there will be no genetic variance. This has been shown to be wrong. What explains the existence of variance and if it happens to be higher in sexual traits is a matter for experimental investigation. The fact that both sexual traits and g may share high additive variance may have no significance, since these may have completely different explanations.

Reference

Pomiankowski A, Møller AP 1995 A resolution of the lek paradox. Proc R Soc Lond B Biol Sci 260:21–29

The quantitative and molecular genetics of human intelligence

Peter McGuffin

Social, Genetic and Developmental Psychiatry Research Centre, Institute of Psychiatry, King's College London, De Crespigny Park, Denmark Hill, London SE5 8AF, UK

Abstract. General cognitive ability or *g* as measured by IQ tests has been the most intensively studied trait in human behaviour genetics. Although there has been much debate about how best to describe and measure intelligence, this is addressed elsewhere in this volume and here I will assume that there is utility in the concept of general intelligence and review the data showing that, whatever it is, *g* is familial and influenced by genes. Next, I will briefly describe some of the main quantitative genetics models that have been used in trying to tease out the genetic and environmental sources of variation. Finally, I will outline current molecular genetic research aiming to locate and identify genes influencing human intelligence and try to predict the directions in which such research will lead.

2000 The nature of intelligence. Wiley, Chichester (Novartis Foundation Symposium 233) p 243–259

Familial correlations in IQ

Francis Galton is usually credited as being the founder of behavioural genetics with his famous treatise on the familial transmission of various kinds of mental and physical talent, *Hereditary genius* (Galton 1869). Galton had his own theory of 'blending' inheritance and wrote in ignorance of the findings of his contemporary Gregor Mendel and his particulate theory of inheritance. Galton might also now be criticized for a too-ready acceptance of the idea of familial transmission, which can be equated with what we would now call genetic transmission (*genetic* being a term that was not coined until some years later by Bateson in 1901). Nevertheless Galton, even if he did not work out the full details, suggested both twin and adoption studies as ways of disentangling the effects of shared environment and shared genes. Galton was also the first to put forward the method of correlation. In the time since Galton produced these important insights, a vast body of data has accumulated on IQ, presented in the form of correlations between pairs of relatives, including those from intact families, from twins and from relatives separated by fostering and adoption.

Some of the key data are summarized in Table 1, which is taken from a classic review by Bouchard & McGue (1981), and updated by Plomin (1993) and Bouchard (1998). The table also shows the genetic correlation or average proportion of genes held in common for the various classes of relative. For most categories, there is a fairly obvious and striking relationship between the genetic relationship and the average correlation in general intelligence. However, the role of environment is also apparent. For example monozygotic (MZ) or identical twins who have all their genes in common and share a common environment are highly correlated but not perfectly correlated for IQ, suggesting that environment not shared by twin pairs has an influence. They are however more highly correlated than dizygotic (DZ) twins who have, on average, half their genes in common and, like MZ twins, share a common environment. MZ and DZ twins reared apart are less similar than twins reared together and unrelated individuals show an average weighted correlation in general intelligence of 0.28 in childhood. Both observations suggest that shared environment plays a role.

Another aspect worth noting is that mating with respect to this phenotype is not random. Spouses, who in western industrialized societies usually share zero genes in common, show a high average correlation of 0.33, not much below that of DZ twins reared apart. The exact mechanisms underlying such assortative mating can be debated, but there are at least two possible explanations. The first is that people tend to be directly influenced by similarity in general intelligence in selecting their mates — so called 'phenotypic homogamy'. However, there may be also an element of social homogamy. That is, people tend to meet their partners in the same class at school, university or at work. Since there is a fairly strong relationship between educational and career attainment and IQ, this will in turn induce a positive correlation in general intelligence.

Having made the basic observation that the pattern of correlation of pairs of relatives suggests a role both for genes and environment in variation in general intelligence, the next question is how strong these roles are. To answer this we need to briefly consider what are the appropriate quantitative genetic models.

Quantitative genetics

By their design, intelligence tests tend to provide measures that are normally distributed in the population. In common with other continuously distributed complex traits, it seems likely that intelligence is contributed to by multiple factors and that the genetic component is polygenic (Plomin et al 1994). That is there are multiple genes, each of which on its own has comparatively small effect. It is also usually assumed in most basic quantitative models that polygenes tend to

TABLE 1   Correlations for general cognitive ability

	Number of pairs	Weighted average Correlation	Genetic Correlation
Monozygotic twins reared together	4672	0.86	1.0
Monozygotic twins reared apart	162	0.75	1.0
Dizygotic twins reared together	5546	0.60	0.5
Dizygotic twins reared apart	73	0.38	0.5
Siblings	26473	0.47	0.5
Half siblings	200	0.31	0.25
Cousins	1176	0.15	0.125
Unrelated reared together, childhood	689	0.28	0
Unrelated reared together, adulthood	398	0.04	0
Spouses	3817	0.33	0

Data from Bouchard & McGue (1981) and Bouchard (1998).

behave in an additive fashion. However, it is possible to have non-additive effects within loci (dominance) as well as interactions between loci (epistasis).

At the simplest level therefore, we can partition the variation in a phenotype such as general intelligence (V_p) into components explained by genes (V_g) and environment. We can further divide the environment into a shared environment that tends to make relatives similar (V_c) and the non-shared environment that makes relatives different from each other (V_e). (Because non-shared environment cannot be distinguished in such models from variation resulting from measurement error, this component is also sometimes referred to as residual environment.) Thus:

$$V_p = V_g + V_c + V_e.$$

Commonly, we wish to know the heritability of a trait (h^2) or the proportion of variation attributable to genetic effects. Strictly speaking heritability is defined as the proportion of variation explained by *additive* genetic effects (V_a). Hence

$$h^2 = V_a/V_p.$$

If there are also non-additive effects, $h^2 = V_g/V_p$ defines 'broad' heritability or degree of genetic determination.

Similarly, we might wish to know the proportion of variance explained by shared environment (c^2):

$$c^2 = V_c/V_p.$$

Figure 1 shows a simple path diagram where P_1 and P_2 are the phenotypes of a pair of relatives, in this case siblings or twins. The expected value of the correlation between P_1 and P_2 is, in the calculus of path analysis, the sum of the connecting paths between the two. Thus there is a connecting path via genotypes (G_1 and G_2) and though the common environment (CE). This provides us with an expression

$$r = Bh^2 + c^2.$$

In the case of MZ twins, the correlation, B, between phenotypes G_1 and G_2 is 1 while for DZ twins the correlation if 0.5. Therefore, data on twins provides us with a pair of simultaneous equations, which by substitution and rearrangement, gives a straightforward formula for h^2 (Falconer & McKay 1996)

$$h^2 = 2(r_{M2} - r_{D2}).$$

We can also solve for c^2

$$c^2 = 2r_{D2} - r_{M2}.$$

If we take the average correlations for twin reared together in Table 1 and use these formulae, we obtain an estimate of heritability of 0.52 and of c^2 of 0.34. An even

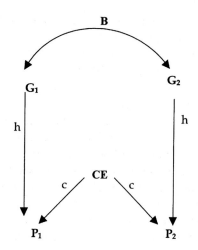

FIG. 1.   A simple path model of the sources of resemblance between twins or pairs of siblings. G_1 and G_2 are genotypes with correlation B, CE is common environment, P_1 and P_2 are phenotypes and h and c are path coefficients.

simpler way of obtaining an estimate of c^2 is directly from the correlation between unrelated individuals reared together. As we see from Table 1, during childhood this correlation at 0.28 is close to that calculated from MZ and DZ twin data (most of which again were based upon childhood measurement). By the same token the correlation for MZ twins reared apart can be considered as a direct estimate of broad heritability. In fact we see in Table 1 that the correlation between twins reared apart is rather higher than our estimate obtained from the twin data on subjects reared together. With the widespread availability of high speed computers, structural equation modelling approaches can carry the techniques derived from path analysis much further, incorporating data from multiple classes of relatives (such as those in Table 1) and use maximum likelihood approaches to compare the fit of alternative models (Neale & Cardon 1992, McGuffin et al 1994). It is also possible, rather than treating environment purely as an unobserved or latent variable, to attempt to incorporate environmental measures. For example Rice et al (1980) used socioeconomic status (SES) as an environmental index in their path model and estimated that the heritability of IQ was reduced to a fairly modest level of a little over 0.3. However these authors assumed that SES is a 'pure' environmental measure, whereas in fact we know that it is fairly highly correlated with general intelligence and it could be argued that general intelligence as much a 'cause' of SES as the other way around.

Intra-uterine shared environment

Most of the debate concerning shared environment and intelligence has been to do with the common environment in which children are raised. However, some studies have attempted to examine the effects of intra-uterine effects. The majority of MZ twins are dichorionic (DCMZ), usually sharing a placenta but not a chorionic sac. However, approximately one-third of pairs are monochorionic (MCMZ). Unfortunately, it is usually difficult to obtain information on placenta types but Rose et al (1980) were able to carry out a study on a small sample of adult twins who could be assigned to the MCMZ, DCMZ and dizygotic categories. They found that both types of MZ twins were significantly more similar than DZ twins on verbal sub-tests of the Wechsler adult intelligence scale (WAIS) but for another subtest, block design, only the MCMZ and not the DCMZ twins were more highly correlated than the DZ pairs. This provides some suggestion that the degree to which intra-uterine environment is shared may have a lasting influence on resemblance for some specific cognitive abilities in twins.

A more recent study carried this argument further: Devlin et al (1997) criticized the conventional lumping together in quantitative genetic analyses of 'maternal effects' (which should include intra-uterine effects) and, what they described as shared 'external' environment. They proposed a variant on the classic type of model described above, by introducing additional sources of variance resulting from maternal effects that are different for twins and other categories of siblings. The full model also allowed for dominance effects and was fitted using the data, already referred to, of Bouchard & McGue (1981). Devlin et al found that maternal effects accounted for about 20% of the covariance between twins compared with 5% between siblings. The narrow sense heritability (variance explained purely by additive genetic effects) was 34% while the broad sense heritability was 48%.

Although the obvious implication of the analysis by Devlin et al (1997) is to support the contention of Rose et al (1980) that the very early environment may have a long lasting effect, this has been criticized on the grounds that the data analysed by Devlin et al omitted correlations on individuals reared apart, particularly those where the measurements have been made in adult life (Bouchard 1998). Such data together with recent twin data on older cohorts suggest that the relative contribution of genes and environment to general cognitive ability is not static but rather changes over time.

Temporal changes in genetic and environmental contributions

Bouchard (1998) has recently pointed out that in their classic review, he and McGue (Bouchard & McGue 1981), by combining data on all unrelated individuals reared together, entirely overlooked the striking effect of age on c^2. When the data are separated according to age, quite different patterns emerge in childhood and adult life. As shown in Table 1, there is a fairly substantial correlation in childhood but a near zero correlation in adults. That this might occur was actually suggested by one of the earliest adoption studies. Unlike most such studies, which have involved one-off measures of IQ, Skodak & Skeels (1949) managed to follow up 100 individuals raised in foster homes and test them on four separate occasions over the course of about 15 years. Because of tracing difficulties, the sample size became steadily reduced on each occasion of testing, but the final sample was considered to be fairly representative of the starting population. The fostered children's IQ showed an increasing correlation over time with the IQ and educational attainment of their biological mothers. After an initial increase in similarity with foster mother's IQ up to the age of about 7, the foster mother–child resemblance for IQ began to decrease. A more recent longitudinal study, the Colorado Adoption Project (DeFries et al 1994) found that between infancy and 15 years of age, the correlation for g between adopted-away offspring and their biological mothers increased in a way that mirrored control (non-adoptive) parent–offspring pairs to reach a level of about 0.3. By contrast the correlations between adopting parents and their non-biological offspring remained around zero.

Twin correlations for IQ for different age groups are summarized in Table 2. As we see, there is a modest increase in the MZ correlation over time with a gradual decrease in the DZ correlation. This together with the near zero correlation for unrelated individuals reared together, but tested as adults, suggest that the effect of c^2 diminishes over time whereas heritability increases. This would also be compatible with a rather higher estimate of heritability that we mentioned earlier coming from adult MZ twins reared apart compared with that based on the combined correlations of monozygotic and dizygotic twins.

Recent results based on a sample of Swedish twins reared together also provide general support for a reduction in common environment effects with age (McClearn et al 1997). Twins aged 80 years or more were studied and only those without cognitive or memory impairment were included. The estimated heritability was 0.62 and the shared environmental effect could be dropped without deterioration in fit of the model.

In summary, quantitative genetic studies have recently converged on a consensus that general intelligence is at least moderately and perhaps highly heritable. As McGue (1997) has remarked 'that the IQ debate now centres on whether IQ is 50% or 70% heritable is a remarkable indication of how the nature–nurture debate has shifted over the past two decades'. That said, much interest has now begun to shift towards the goal of actually being able to locate and identify genes involved in cognitive ability.

Gene mapping approaches

Molecular genetics has revolutionized our understanding of rare Mendelian disorders and traits and is beginning to have a substantial impact on the study of complex phenotypes. The elegantly simple logic of positional cloning is that genetic linkage analysis allows the position of a gene locus to be identified within a region of the genome (i.e. the 23 pairs of human chromosomes). Further fine

TABLE 2   Changes in twin correlations (r) over time

Age group	r MZ	r DZ
4–6	0.58	0.78
6–12	0.58	0.82
12–16	0.6	0.83
16–20	0.57	0.82
Adult	0.4	0.83

Data from McGue et al (1993).

mapping can then be carried out first by genetic methods including further linkage studies and studies of linkage disequilibrium followed by physical mapping to pinpoint the position of the gene more exactly. Genes within that region are then identified and scrutinized to see which is involved in the trait. Once the gene itself is cloned, sequence and structure and can be studied, the protein for which it encodes is identified and the molecular variation resulting in phenotypic differences can finally be understood. The whole process has been spectacularly successful in single gene disorders. Although of course what has been set out here in a few sentences, in reality may be time consuming. In the case of the Huntingdon' disease gene it has taken more than a decade to go from linkage to detailed protein chemistry studies.

The first added complication when we turn to complex traits is that mapping using linkage analysis is much more difficult. Nevertheless, the mapping of so called quantitative trait loci (QTLs) has progressed rapidly in the past decade in laboratory plants and animals in which experimental crosses are possible. This has lead to successes in mapping QTLs contributing to characteristics of tomato fruits (Paterson et al 1988), traits such as blood pressure in rodents (Hilbert et al 1991) and, more recently, emotionality in mice (Flint & Corley 1996).

In humans we have to rely on the types of crosses that individuals choose for themselves. One approach is to attempt to find families in which multiple individuals are affected or are at the extreme on some continuous measure and assume that there is a prospect of detecting a gene of large effect. This has been successful in mapping rare genes causing early onset forms of Alzheimer's disease, but has been less successful in detecting genes involved in other psychiatric disorders (McGuffin et al 1994, Owen & Cardno 1999). The approach also worked in mapping a quantitative locus influencing serum leptin and fat mass (Comuzzie et al 1997). However, for such methods to work, the effect size must be fairly large so for example in the case of leptin levels, about 47% of variance was accounted for by a single gene. It is highly likely that in the case of cognitive ability, multiple genes of small effect are involved and therefore other methods need to be considered.

Rather than studying extended pedigrees, one general alternative approach is to search for allele marker sharing in pairs of relatives. Using this approach Cardon et al (1994) localized a gene contributing to reading disability on the short arm of chromosomes 6. This has subsequently been supported by Grigorenko et al (1997), who also reported evidence of a contributed locus on chromosome 15 in a region of interest previously identified by Smith et al (1983). Despite these positive and replicated findings, power calculations suggest that sibling pair methods can only detect genes that account for a fairly large proportion of total phenotypic variation. QTLs contributing less than 10% of phenotypic variance are unlikely to be detectable, unless the sample size is enormous, consisting of several ousand sibling pairs (Fulker & Cardon 1994). In our own work on cognitive ility we have therefore focused on association studies which have an advantage being able to detect QTLs of much smaller effect.

ssociation studies

he standard approach to allelic association is simply to compare allele frequencies a sample of cases with a disorder and a sample of ethnically matched controls. he case–control design is easily extended to quantitative traits by selecting 'cases' ho have an extreme score on the quantitative measure and comparing them with ntrols who have near average scores. The attraction of case control allelic sociation studies, in addition to the simplicity of their design, is that they have ng be known to be capable of detecting genes of small effect. For example dwards (1965) pointed out that the well-replicated association between uodenal ulcer and blood group O accounts for only about 1% of the variance in ability to develop the disorder. Similarly, McGuffin & Buckland (1991) showed at the proportion of variance counted for by HLA associations with various seases was in the order of 3% and even the strongest known association etween HLA B27 and ankylosing spondylitis was only around 20%. The rawback of allelic association studies is that association only occurs either if the arker *itself* contributes to the trait or if the marker is so close to the trait locus that e relationship is undisturbed over many generations of recombination, i.e. there *linkage disequilibrium* (LD). Association studies are therefore potentially much ore powerful than linkage approaches, but whereas linkage can be detected ver fairly large distances, association studies are 'short-sighted' (Plomin et al 994). The genome can be measured in recombination units called centimorgans M) and is about 3500 cM long. Linkage can be detected at distances of 10 or more M but LD is only likely to occur in most populations at distances of less than 1 cM.

andidate genes

he most direct approach to detecting allelic association is to focus on olymorphisms in or very close to genes that encode for proteins thought to be elevant to the biochemical basis of the trait. When it comes to cognitive ability the ange of possible candidates is wide. Therefore in a first attempt to search for ssociation, Plomin et al (1995) examined a total of 100 polymorphisms onsisting of 18 multi-allelic and 72 bi-allelic markers. These were selected on the road basis that they were at or near genes that are expressed in the brain. A omparison of allele distributions was made in three groups of subjects having igh, middle and low scores on IQ test and positive results followed up on a eplication sample. There were some promising preliminary findings including

loci on chromosome 6p and mitochondrial polymorphisms. However, the latt
failed to replicate on an independent sample (Petrill et al 1998). The next stage
this project has therefore been to move on to a systematic whole genome search

Genome search for LD

At the beginning of the 1990s we suggested (McGuffin et al 1992) that once a den
human genetic linkage map had been developed with very closely spaced marker
a whole genome search for LD with complex traits would become feasible even
outbred populations. Although the standard textbook view has been that such a
approach is not feasible (Strachan & Read 1996), the climate of opinion is changin
(Risch & Merikanges 1996). A major problem, as we have noted is that LD is onl
likely to be detectable over very short distances of less than a centimorga
Assuming a sex-averaged genome length of 3500 cM, this means that at lea
2000 markers would be required for a genome search and most would regar
even this as an optimistically small estimate.

We recently carried out a pilot search on chromosome 6q. This was selecte
because it is likely to be among the first large chromosomes whose DN
sequence would be completely determined as part of the Human Genom
Project. So as to increase power with a manageable number of subjects, w
studied 52 children with extremely high *g* (IQ greater than 160) and compare
with 50 controls with average *g* (mean IQ 101) (Chorney et al 1998). A total of 3
markers were studied of which one, insulin-like growth factor 2 receptor (*IGF2R*
reached significance when the most common allele was compared with all othe
alleles in the two groups. This was replicated in a second high *g* and averag
control comparison. There were findings in the same direction in further grou
selected for high maths ability and high verbal ability. Combining all the data usin
Cochran's method, gave a *P* value of less than 0.00003 which withstands correctio
for multiply testing. Although these results are clearly worth pursuing, we hav
estimated that the *IGF2R* association accounts for less than 2% of the variance in
we cannot claim to have discovered the 'gene for' IQ! Furthermore, the grid o
markers used in this study on chromosomes 6q, although it involved a larg
amount of genotyping, was comparatively widely spaced and far from ideal for
systematic search

Attention is therefore turning to approaches that enable very high throughpu
genotyping. Currently, there is particular interest in developing maps of singl
nucleotide polymorphisms (SNPs) that can be rapidly detected on glass boun
microarrays (Asherson et al 1998). However we have been pursuing a
alternative approach which is to carry out the initial genome screen using DN
pooling. We have already noted that the very minimum number of evenly space
markers to perform a genome wide search is 2000. Thus in our current stud

arching for QTLs involved in IQ and in which we have 200 unrelated subjects with high IQ and 100 with average IQ, we would need to perform at least 600 000 individual genotypings (Daniels et al 1998a). However, using DNA pooling we can simply combine the DNA from all the subjects in the high group and those in the middle IQ group reducing the number of genotypings in the initial phase to a more manageable 4000.

In brief, the approach is an extension of the now routine high throughput semi-automated genotyping using a DNA sequencer where simple sequence repeat polymorphisms (SSRPs) are fluorescently labelled and the resultant data analysed by computer. There are a number of difficulties using SSRPs resulting from 'tutter' bands and differential amplification. However, these are in part overcome using a simple statistic which compares the allele image patterns (AIPs) in the two groups by calculating a difference in areas by overlaying the traces derived from the two samples (Daniels et al 1998b).

We have applied this approach using 147 roughly evenly spaced markers on chromosome 4. The strategy is to carry out the initial screen with a fairly liberal criterion for statistical significance and then to attempt to replicate the positive results on an independent sample carrying out conventional individual genotyping. On chromosome 4, we have interesting preliminary results with three significant QTLs associations that withstand replication on the independent sample (Fisher et al 1999). This requires follow up on yet further samples with an even finer marker grid. In the meantime an entire genome scan using over 3000 microsatellite markers is nearing completion in our labs and those of our collaborators in the University of Wales College of Medicine.

Conclusions and future directions

There can be little doubt that there is an important heritable contribution to g and it appears that this increases from childhood through to adult life and persists even in the non-demented elderly. The existence of a fine grain map of the human genome based on microsatellite markers and the development of high throughput screening using DNA pooling has enabled the first genome scan for linkage disequilibrium to be carried out. This has produced some interesting preliminary results which need further investigation. Newer techniques including detection of SNPs on microarrays will further facilitate mapping of QTLs that influence g. Speed of progress in the next stage, positional cloning proper, will depend on how closely regions of interest can be initially defined by LD mapping but the production of a publicly available SNP map of 100 000 evenly spaced markers corresponding to a spacing of one SNP roughly every 0.03 cM) will aid this. This together with the completion of a draft version of the human genome

sequence which has recently been announced means that genes contributing to
may be identified (as opposed to just located) within a matter of years.

References

Asherson P, Curran S, McGuffin P 1998 Molecular genetics — approaches to gene mapping
CNS 1:18–22

Bouchard TJ Jr 1998 Genetic and environmental influences on adult intelligence and speci
mental abilities. Hum Biol 70:257–279

Bouchard TJ Jr, McGue M 1981 Familial studies of intelligence: a review. Science
212:1055–1059

Cardon LR, Smith SD, Fulker DW et al 1994 Quantitative trait locus for reading disability o
chromosome 6. Science 266:276–279

Chorney MJ, Chorney K, Seese N et al 1998 A quantitative trait locus (QTL) associated wit
cognitive ability in children. Psychol Sci 9:159–166

Comuzzie AG, Hixson JE, Almasy L et al 1997 A major quantitative trait locus determinin
serum leptin levels and fat mass is located on human chromosome 2. Nat Gene
15:273–276

Daniels J, McGuffin P, Owen MJ, Plomin R 1998a Molecular genetic studies of cognitiv
ability. Hum Biol 70:281–296

Daniels J, Holmans P, Williams N et al 1998b A simple method for analyzing microsatellite alle
image patterns generated from DNA pools and its application to allelic association studie
Am J Hum Genet 62:1189–1197

DeFries JC, Plomin R, Fulker DW 1994 Nature and nurture during middle childhood
Blackwell, Cambridge, MA

Devlin B, Daniels M, Roeder K 1997 The heritability of IQ. Nature 388:468–471

Edwards JH 1965 The meaning of the associations between blood groups and disease. Ann Hur
Gen 29:77–83

Falconer DS, Mackay TFC 1996 Introduction to quantitative genetics, 4th edn. Addison Wesle
Longman, Harlow

Fisher PJ, Turic D, McGuffin P et al 1999 DNA pooling identifies QTLs for general cognitiv
ability in children on chromosome 4. Hum Mol Genet 8:915–922

Flint J, Corley R 1996 Do animal models have a place in the genetic analysis of quantitativ
human behavioral traits? J Mol Med 74:515–521

Fulkner DW, Cardon LR 1994 A sib-pair approach to interval mapping of quantitative trait loc
Am J Hum Genet 54:1092–1103

Galton F 1869 Hereditary genius: an inquiry into its laws and consequences. Macmillan, Londo
(1962 World, Cleveland, OH)

Grigorenko EL, Wood FB, Meyer MS et al 1997 Susceptibility loci for distinct components o
developmental dyslexia on chromosomes 6 and 15. Am J Hum Genet 60:27–39

Hilbert P, Lindpaintner K, Beckmann JS et al 1991 Chromosomal mapping of two geneti
loci associated with blood-pressure regulation in hereditary hypertensive rats. Natur
353:521–529

McClearn GE, Johansson B, Berg S et al 1997 Substantial genetic influence on cognitive abilitie
in twins 80 or more years old. Science 276:1560–1563

McGue M 1997 The democracy of the genes. Nature 388:417–418

McGue M, Bouchard TJ Jr, Iacono WG, Lykken DT 1993 Behavioral genetics of cognitiv
ability: a life-span perspective. In: Plomin R, McLearn GE (eds) Nature, nurture and
psychology. American Psychological Association, Washington, DC, p 59–76

cGuffin P, Buckland P 1991 Major genes, minor genes and molecular neurobiology of mental illness. A comment on 'quantitative trait loci and psychopharmacology' by Plomin, McLearn and Gora-Maslak. J Psychopharmacol 5:18–22

cGuffin P, Owen M, Gill M 1992 Molecular genetics of schizophrenia. In: Mendlewiecz J, Hippius H (eds) Genetic research in psychiatry, vol 1. Springer-Verlag, Berlin, p 25–48

cGuffin P, Owen MJ, O'Donovan MC, Thapar A, Gottesman I 1994 Seminars in psychiatric genetics. Gaskell, London

eale MC, Cardon LR (eds) 1992 Methodology for genetic studies of twins and families. Kluwer Academic, Dordrecht, The Netherlands

wen MJ, Cardno AG 1999 Psychiatric genetics: progress, problems and potential. Lancet (suppl) 354:SI11–SI1

aterson AH, Lander ES, Hewitt JD, Peterson S, Lincoln SE, Tanksley SD 1988 Resolution of quantitative traits into Mendelian factors by using a complete linkage map of restriction fragment length polymorphisms. Nature 335:721–726

etrill SA, Ball D, Hill L et al 1998 Failure to replicate a QTL association between a DNA marker (EST00083) and IQ. Intelligence 25:179–184

omin R, Owen MJ, McGuffin P 1994 The genetic basis of complex human behaviors. Science 264:1733–1739

lomin R, McClearn GE, Smith DL et al 1995 Allelic associations between 100 DNA markers and high versus low IQ. Intelligence 21:31–48

lomin R 1993 Nature and nurture: perspective and prospective. In: Plomin R, McClearn GE (eds) Nature, nurture and psychology. American Psychological Association, Washington, DC, p 459–485

ice J, Cloninger CR, Reich T 1980 Analysis of behavioural traits in the presence of cultural transmission and assortative mating: appplications to IQ and SES. Behav Genet 10:73–92

isch N, Merikangas K 1996 The future of genetic studies of complex human diseases. Science 273:1516–1517

ose RJ, Boughman JA, Corey LA, Nance WE, Christian JC, Kang KW 1980 Data from kinships of monozygotic twins indicate maternal effects on intelligence. Nature 283:375–377

kodak M, Skeels HM 1949 A final follow-up study of one hundred adopted children. J Genet Psychol 75:85–12

mith SD, Kimberling WJ, Pennington BF, Lubs HA 1983 Specific reading disability: identification of an inherited form through linkage analysis. Science 219:1345–1347

trachan T, Read AP 1996 Human molecular genetics. BIOS Scientific, Oxford

DISCUSSION

Miller: One of the themes of the discussion yesterday was the question of whether genetic variation in intelligence is due to a kind of strategic polymorphism where there might be balanced selection for low *g* and high *g*, or whether it is due to a mutation–selection balance. If genetic variation is due mostly to mutation, one would not necessarily expect there to be a small set of genes that are consistently mutated across the entire species. One might expect that in the tens of thousands of genes that contribute to brain growth there would be a large number of mutations that are quite idiosyncratic. These might be localized in particular families or particular subpopulations, but not necessarily replicated across different human groups. In contrast, the strategic

polymorphism theory would predict that there will be a few genes accounting f(
the variation that are consistent across different groups. It seems that the allel
association research method shouldn't work very well if the mutation theory
right, or am I misunderstanding the situation?

McGuffin: You are quite right. What gives me cause for optimism, however,
the fact that where people have looked for QTLs and found them, it isn't a classic
Fisher-type polygenic pattern, which is that there is a huge number of genes of tir
effect. What we tend to find is that there are a few genes of comparatively big effec
and there is a kind of scree of genes which have much smaller effects tailing awa'
This is true for any sort of quantitative trait, such as how big a tomato plant grow

Houle: I have a question related to that. The cases where QTL mapping has bee
very successful have usually involved wide crosses among things that have bee
selected to be different. An example would be comparing wild tomatoes wit
commercially bred strains, where there are enormous differences in phenotyp(
I'm not aware whether any of the human projects that have not just been lookin
at single genes have progressed to the point where one can say whether that patter
which holds for domesticated plants and animals is also true for an outbre
population of which humans would be a good example. Do you have any insigl
on this?

McGuffin: It is more complicated in humans because we can't design breedin
programmes, so we have to make do with people's own breeding programme:
There is no doubt that it is preferable to map genes of large effect: it is easier t
deal with a trait where there are extreme examples, such as attempts to map th
genes involved in obesity in families where there are clear cases of obesit
segregating. When we look at complex diseases such as schizophrenia c
diabetes, the picture is mixed. In diabetes there has been a lot of success i
mapping the genes that have a relatively large effect, such as HLA, but there i
huge debate about whether any of the other loci actually matter. Schizophreni
has been a total mess, with very few replications coming up. In mapping comple
traits in humans, one either sits back and assumes we are never going to be able t
do it, or one gets on and has a go. This comes back to the debate I mentioned abou
how many markers it will take to span the genome for a linkage disequilibriun
map. The difference of opinion is somewhere between a couple of thousand, lik
I mentioned, and several hundred thousand. If you take the latter figure and all th
genes have a tiny effect, this will be an impossible task.

Whiten: You showed a chart early on of correlations in IQ in various sibs, and
was interested in the one involving adopted sibs, with the correlation falling t(
about zero by adulthood. You later showed one looking at twins of differen
ages, but these *weren't* adopted. Do we know what the story is for twins who *ar'*
adopted? Does the correlation fall to zero also for DZ twins by adulthood? Wha
about MZ twins?

McGuffin: The most recent data come from Tom Bouchard's Minnesota twin studies. The adult correlation in twins reared apart is just under 0.8.

Suddendorf: Could this work be supportive of the hypothesis regarding sexual selection? Earlier on we heard that sexual selection leads to condition-dependent expression of sexual traits. If there is a poor environment there is a far greater variance in the phenotype. If *g* is the phenotype we are interested in and it is indeed a sexually selected trait, we would expect to see greater variance in *g* in poor environments than in good environments. Is there any evidence for this? Could the twin studies lend support to this idea by allowing us to investigate the differential effects of environmental differences? If we had a population of MZ twins reared apart with one twin living in a poor and the other in a rich environment, then the group reared in the poor environment should show greater variance than their twins in the rich environment.

McGuffin: I don't know whether this argument can provide any support either way. The problem about heritability is that it is just the proportion of variance explained. Of course, if you increase the variance, and all this increase is coming from increased environmental variance, heritability must be less. Heritability only applies to the population in which you measure it: it is a population measure and has no meaning at an individual level.

Miller: But isn't there already evidence that the heritability of IQ is lower for children in very poor environments.

McGuffin: I don't know, but the prediction would be that if you simply increase the environmental variance, heritability must go down.

Rutter: That has to be the case, of course, if genetic and environmental effects are separate, but the situation is more complicated in the common circumstance in which there are gene–environment correlations and interactions. If susceptibility to disadvantageous environments is strongly genetically influenced, an increased environmental effect will be associated with an increased heritability; that is because, rather misleadingly, the gene–environment interaction is included in the genetic term (see Rutter 2000).

Deary: The title of this symposium is 'The nature of intelligence', and I would like to explore how much these studies will take us towards the nature of intelligence. You said that you didn't like the idea of genes giving a 'blueprint', and you suggested that they were more like a 'recipe'. A recipe has two components: ingredients and a method. It is the method that explains how to put the ingredients together to provide the phenotype. Can I suggest that the genes will give us only a partial recipe list, because we know there are things other than genes that contribute to mental ability. If we take just the one example of the *IGF2R* gene as an ingredient, how does this fit into the method? Is there a mechanistic trail from differences in that gene to differences in ability phenotype that is tractable?

McGuffin: That is a fascinating question, but I don't have an answer.

Nesse: IGF2R is a peculiar gene in that it is sexually imprinted, and it has been proposed to be related to male–female competition over the size of the offspring. Have you any thoughts about this?

McGuffin: In these studies we have been using that gene as a marker of an association. It could be that gene or something close to it.

Deary: You actually didn't say very much about the phenotype that you are measuring in the IQ QTL project. How are you defining this?

Detterman: A portion of the data are from a twin study that we did earlier, and we defined them in terms of IQ and selected within an IQ range. We used the Wechsler scales.

Lubinski: For the IQ 160 group we used a combination of tests to get to that extreme level safely. Robert Plomin wanted to make sure that everyone had IQs of 160 or above, so this value was the lower cut (Lubinski et al 2000). The longitudinal study that I am involved in is based on a talent search, where we give children in the seventh grade who score in the top three percentage points on any number of routine tests at school an opportunity to take a college entrance exam, which is the SAT. The subjects selected for this study had either scored 700 on the SATM or 630 on the SATV before age 13 (Lubinski et al 2000). We didn't want tilted profiles, so we made sure that they were within one standard deviation. Over half scored 630V and 700M before age 13. I am very confident that the mean IQ of these subjects is beyond the high 170s.

Detterman: Interestingly enough, the hardest subjects to get are the average ones.

Karmiloff-Smith: You said that you are not concentrating on the lower end of the normal curve. Lower still, you had different syndromes, many of which give rise to mental retardation. Why can't what we already know about the genetics of these syndromes contribute to the exploration of the link with *g*?

McGuffin: That is a good question. The trouble is that most of those syndromes can be seen as 'spanners in the works' rather than as examples of how the works function normally. They often lead to disastrous changes.

Karmiloff-Smith: In many cases these individuals have IQs in the upper 60s and lower 70s. It isn't that disastrous.

McGuffin: I take your point. We have looked at some of the genes. One of the common disorders is fragile X, which is a common sex-linked form of mental retardation where there is a trinucleotide repeat stuck on one end of the gene. It is an unstable mutation, and once it gets to a certain length the whole thing is methylated and the gene is effectively switched off. We looked at minor forms of this unstable mutation to see whether it had any relation at all to IQs in the normal range. It doesn't. We think it is probably safer to concentrate on the middle of the range.

Flynn: If your project is successful, will it solve controversies over group differences? The children of the top third and bottom third occupationally in the

USA have a very stable 10 point IQ gap. There are good reasons for thinking that there is a genetic component in that. There is also the 15 point IQ gap between US whites and blacks over which there is much more controversy. If you were successful, would you be able to say that there is a relevant genetic difference between these two groups, and that this kind of difference is to the disadvantage of group B and to the advantage of group A? If you can reach such conclusions, you will have an interesting future ahead of you!

McGuffin: It might well do. I don't know how definitive any answer will be, but we may come up with a complicated solution involving quite a lot of different genes. It is interesting to see some of the reactions that this type of work produces. I worked in a department in Cardiff in close association with the medical genetics department, where my close colleague and friend Peter Harper thought it was perfectly OK to look for genes involved in depression or schizophrenia, but he thought it was unacceptable to look for genes related to cognitive ability.

Rutter: When one has got to that point, would you not anticipate that there may well be the problem that these genes may work differently in different populations. If one takes the example of ApoE4 and Alzheimer's disease, we know from several studies that there are major differences in rates of Alzheimer's disease between people in Africa and whites in the USA. But there are not any differences in the distribution of the ApoE4 gene, and ApoE4 does not predict Alzheimer's in Africa although it does in the USA (Hendrie et al 1995a,b, Osuntokun et al 1995). What this means is unclear, but it reinforces the fact that we need to take into account the context when looking at genetic effects. It could of course come out all very tidily that black–white or social class differences simply come down to allelic frequencies, and that this is a satisfactory explanation. I expect that in reality the situation will turn out to be more complex.

References

Hendrie HC, Hall KS, Hui SL et al 1995a Apolipoprotein E genotypes and Alzheimer disease in a community study of elderly African-Americans. Ann Neurol 37:118–120

Hendrie HC, Osuntokun BO, Hall KS et al 1995b Prevalence of Alzheimer's disease and dementia in two communities; Nigerian Africans and African Americans. Am J Psychiatry 152:1485–1492

Lubinski D, Webb RM, Morelock MJ, Benbow CP 2000 Top 1 in 10,000: A 10-year follow up of the profoundly gifted. submitted

Osuntokun, BO, Sahota A, Ogummiyi AO et al 1995 Lack of an association between Apolipoprotein E ε4 and Alzheimer's disease in elderly Nigerians. Ann Neurol 38:463–465

Rutter M 2000 Negative life events and family negativity: accomplishments and challenges. In: Harris T (ed) Where inner and outer worlds meet. Essays in honour of George W Brown. Taylor & Francis, London, in press

Sexual selection for indicators of intelligence

Geoffrey Miller

Centre for Economic Learning and Social Evolution, University College London, Gower Street, London WC1E 6BT, UK

Abstract. Many traits in many species have evolved through sexual selection specifically to function as 'fitness indicators' that reveal good genes and good health. Sexually selected fitness indicators typically show (1) higher coefficients of phenotypic and genetic variation than survival traits, (2) at least moderate genetic heritabilities and (3) positive correlations with many aspects of an animal's general condition, including body size, body symmetry, parasite resistance, longevity and freedom from deleterious mutations. These diagnostic criteria also appear to describe human intelligence (the *g* factor). This paper argues that during human evolution, mate choice by both sexes focused increasingly on intelligence as a major heritable component of biological fitness. Many human-specific behaviours (such as conversation, music production, artistic ability and humour) may have evolved principally to advertise intelligence during courtship. Though these mental adaptations may be modular at the level of psychological functioning, their efficiencies may be tightly intercorrelated because they still tap into common genetic and neurophysiological variables associated with fitness itself. Although the *g* factor (like the superordinate factor of fitness itself) probably exists in all animal species, humans evolved an unusually high degree of interest in assessing each other's intelligence during courtship and other social interactions — and, consequently, a unique suite of highly *g*-loaded mental adaptations for advertising their intelligence to one another through linguistic and cultural interaction. This paper includes nine novel, testable predictions about human intelligence derived from sexual selection theory.

2000 The nature of intelligence. Wiley, Chichester (Novartis Foundation Symposium 233) p 260–275

Introduction: sexual selection for fitness indicators

During sexual courtship, animals often advertise the quality of their genes, bodies and minds, in order to attract the best possible mate (Cronin 1991, Miller 1997, 1998). The peacock's tail, the elk's antlers and the nightingale's voice all evolved through sexual selection as 'fitness indicators': traits specifically evolved to advertise good genes, good health and/or good psychological functioning (Andersson 1994). This paper argues that many human mental traits also evolved through sexual selection as fitness indicators, to advertise a particular component of fitness called 'intelligence', also known as the g factor.

When choosing sexual partners, animals have particularly high incentives to favour partners with above-average 'fitness' (heritable genetic quality). This is because, under Mendelian inheritance, the genetic quality of one's mate determines half the genetic quality of one's offspring. In genetic terms, low fitness corresponds not so much to 'genetic load' (the number of fully recessive mutations on single-gene Mendelian traits—which tends to be phenotypically invisible), but to the number of mildly harmful, partially recessive mutations on the many genes ('quantitative trait loci') underlying complex polygenic traits—which tend to be manifest in phenotypic functioning.

The whole point of fitness indicators is to advertise differences in heritable fitness between individuals. This gives them some unusual features as biological adaptations, compared to ordinary survival adaptations (Miller 2000, Miller & Todd 1998). Survival adaptations usually evolve to be genetically and developmentally canalized to create the optimal phenotype, leading to low apparent heritability and minimal differences between conspecifics. By contrast, fitness indicators evolve to be costly, complex displays that are so difficult to grow, maintain and produce that only the highest-fitness individuals can afford to produce them in the optimal, most sexually attractive form. Whereas survival adaptations tend to minimize between-individual differences, fitness indicators tend to amplify them dramatically (Hasson 1990, Pomiankowski & Møller 1995, Rowe & Houle 1996).

The evolution of most survival adaptations can be modelled using standard optimization theory, but the evolution of fitness indicators can only be modelled using a form of evolutionary game theory called signalling theory (Bradbury & Verhencamp 1998). A central lesson from modern signalling theory is that fitness indicators must have high marginal costs in order to be reliable, or else low-fitness pretenders would be able to afford an impressive display as easily as a high-fitness signaller (Grafen 1990, Johnstone 1995). This is called 'the handicap principle' (Zahavi & Zahavi 1997): fitness indicators typically impair survival (they are 'handicaps'), but increase sexual attractiveness and hence reproductive success. They are analogous to conspicuous consumption (Veblen 1899): a wasteful display of luxury that reliably reveals an individual's wealth because the poor cannot afford the waste.

Fitness and intelligence

'Fitness' is a statistical abstraction across the efficiency levels of many different adaptations serving different survival and reproductive functions. The 'g factor' is a statistical abstraction across the efficiency levels of many different mental adaptations. How are these two constructs related?

So far, biologists have not used factor analysis to analyse fitness in the same way that psychometricians have used it to analyse human intelligence. Fitness cannot be measured directly, but biologists have developed a number of moderately reliable measures that probably correlate positively with general biological fitness, including body size, body mass, body symmetry and low parasite load (Møller & Swaddle 1997). I conjecture that, given a large representative sample of mature individuals from a particular species, and a number of different fitness measures of proven reliability, the correlation matrix between all such fitness measures will usually contain all positive entries — the same sort of positive manifold discovered by Spearman in 1904, in relation to the g factor. Given this positive manifold of fitness measures, it would be possible to use standard factor analysis methods to recover a general fitness factor, which could be called the f factor (for a similar idea, see Houle 2000, this volume).

Prediction 1.   Factor analysis of reliable fitness measures obtained from a large representative sample of individuals from any wild species will reveal a general fitness factor, an 'f' factor, analogous to the 'g' factor in psychometrics. This f factor will account for a substantial proportion of between-individual variance in the fitness measures, and will prove moderately heritable under normal ranges of environmental conditions.

This prediction is implicit in most modern biological research on sexual selection (e.g. Møller & Swaddle 1997, Furlow et al 1997), but is worth making more explicit. The f factor prediction is quite different from the standard assumption in behavioural ecology that trade-offs between traits should give rise to negative correlations between many fitness measures.

The f factor ('fitness') would probably be superordinate to the g factor ('intelligence'), just as the g factor is superordinate to the spatial intelligence factor and the verbal intelligence factor. (Obviously, such hierarchies of factors can only be recovered through hierarchical factor analysis, which does not force lower-order factors to be orthogonal to one another.) If f is superordinate to g, then we might more parsimoniously explain why human intelligence is positively correlated with so many biological traits such as height, health, longevity and bodily symmetry (see Jensen 1998, Furlow et al 1997): all of these traits, including intelligence, are tapping into a general fitness factor.

Prediction 2.   The g factor will prove subordinate to the f factor. That is, individual differences in 'intelligence' partly reflect individual differences in biological fitness that are not specific to psychological or neurophysiological functioning.

If g is subordinate to f, we should be careful about interpreting correlations between g and measures of social, economic or reproductive success (e.g. Lubinski 2000, this volume): such correlations should be attributed to the effect of 'intelligence' only if the subordinate g factor accounts for significant variance in those measures beyond that which is accounted for by the f factor itself. Likewise, any behaviour-genetic study claiming to find a quantitative trait locus associated with human 'intelligence' (e.g. Chorney et al 1997, McGuffin 2000, this volume) should demonstrate that the locus has g-specific effects, and not just a generally positive effect on fitness.

Now, consider the implications of predictions 1 and 2 from the viewpoint of sexual selection theory. An animal choosing a sexual partner is trying to select the individual with the highest possible heritable fitness, corresponding to the f factor. the g factor is a major component of f (i.e. if the g factor itself has a high f-loading in this particular species), then g makes a convenient fitness indicator. This implies that any behavioural capacity with a high g-loading may also have a reasonably high f-loading. That is, any behaviour that requires high 'intelligence' can function as a fitness indicator in sexual selection. If g has a high f-loading, then the mechanisms of mate choice should evolve to favour courtship displays and behaviours with high g-loadings. Behaviours that are particularly indicative of high 'intelligence' should prove particularly attractive.

Prediction 3. Mate choice mechanisms should favour courtship behaviours with high g-loadings, as cues of heritable fitness (insofar as g has a high f-loading). Generally, a mental trait's sexual attractiveness should correlate positively with its g loading.

Evolutionary psychology research suggests that intelligence is a major criterion in human mate choice. Buss (1989) found that, across all 37 cultures he investigated, intelligence was the second most-desired trait in a sexual partner (kindness was the most desired). Although males are not very choosy about the intelligence of short-term sexual partners, both sexes become equally, and extremely, choosy about the intelligence of long-term sexual partners (Kenrick et al 1990), which are much more likely to produce offspring. The method of correlated vectors (Jensen 1998) also shows that assortative mating is very focused on g-loaded mental traits. For example, spouses correlate more highly for their vocabulary sizes (a highly g-loaded trait) than they do for digit span (a modestly g-loaded trait).

Sexual selection for g-loaded intelligence indicators

Courtship behaviours evolve in response to the pressures of mate choice. If mate choice mechanisms in a particular species are favouring highly g-loaded behaviours as fitness indicators, then sexual selection would shape those behaviours accordir to the standard predictions of fitness indicator theory. The behaviours shou evolve to have higher marginal costs, higher coefficients of genetic ar phenotypic variation, higher complexity and higher f-loadings (by virtue of eve higher g-loadings).

Elsewhere, I have argued that many of our uniquely human mental trai evolved mainly through sexual selection, due to the mate choices made l ancestral males and females (Miller 1998, 1999, 2000, Miller & Todd 1998 These traits may include our capacities for language, art, music, generosit creativity and humour. Here, I am emphasizing that these capacities may hav evolved to advertise biological fitness principally through their ability advertise intelligence: their f-loadings may be carried almost entirely by their loadings. In other words, our most distinctive mental traits may have evolve not so much because they yielded some survival advantage during tl Pleistocene, but because they were sexually attractive intelligence indicators th yielded reproductive advantages.

Prediction 4. Most of our uniquely human mental abilities should sho particularly high g-loadings and f-loadings, compared to more ancient ment capacities common to other great apes, primates or mammals. Like oth sexually selected fitness indicators, they should also show higher coefficients genetic variation and phenotypic variation, and at least moderate heritabilities.

Though we often attribute high intelligence to someone capable of impressi verbal, visual or musical behaviour, it is not so clear whether the link betwee intelligence and fitness is consciously understood. However, very little abo mate choice is consciously mediated, nor need it be. Presumably peahens do n consciously appreciate that a large, symmetrical peacock tail indicates a lower th average number of mildly deleterious, partially recessive mutations on genetic lc associated with fitness — they only need to feel attracted to such tails, ar evolution keeps track of the correlations.

If sexual selection favoured intelligence indicators, why is there no sexual dimorphism in the g factor?

Because males and females of any mammalian species share almost all of the sar genes (except those on the tiny Y chromosome), we would not expect any sexu dimorphism in the f factor itself, which is basically just average genetic quali across a whole genotype. Fathers selected through mate choice for high fitne would produce high-fitness daughters, not just high-fitness sons. Insofar as the factor is highly f-loaded, this may help explain why there appears to be no sexu dimorphism in the g factor (Jensen 1998). Even if sexual selection were driv

itirely by female choice favouring highly intelligent males, as long as the g factor
:pended on genetic variation at mostly autosomal loci, average g would increase
. both sexes at the same rate. Darwin's 'Law of Equal Inheritance' expressed the
.me idea (see Lande 1987).

However, sexual selection theory would still predict sexual dimorphism in the
ublic behavioural manifestations of intelligence, because the reproductive
:nefits of such displays would usually be higher for males than for females given
>me degree of polygyny (see Buss 1994, Ridley 1993). (Also, the marginal costs of
ich displays would be higher for females, given the competing demands of
regnancy and maternal care.) Demographic data on the production of costly,
ifficult, public displays of intelligence, such as painting pictures, writing novels,
roducing jazz albums and publishing philosophical speculations, reveals a very
rong dimorphism, with males producing about 10 times more displays than
males, and male display rates peaking in early sexual maturity, corresponding
> the peak of courtship effort (Miller 1999).

rediction 5.   Despite the sexual equality in the g factor itself, the human display
:haviours that show the highest sexual dimorphism should show the highest g-
>adings, functioning as the most effective displays of intelligence. Likewise, the
isplay behaviours that show the sharpest peak in young adulthood (at the peak of
>urtship effort) should show the highest g-loadings.

Iow can the g factor be reconciled with
volutionary psychology's massive modularity hypothesis?

volutionary psychologists have argued that evolution would have produced
uman minds composed of hundreds of distinct psychological adaptations, each
:dicated to solving a particular problem of survival or reproduction under
icestral conditions (Cosmides & Tooby 1994, Tooby & Cosmides 1990, Pinker
)97). This 'massive modularity' argument goes well beyond Howard Gardner's
. 983) 'multiple intelligences' theory, which posited only seven distinct faculties.
ut like Gardner's theory, the massive modularity view seems difficult to reconcile
·ith the existence of the g factor. If the mind has so many parts, why should the
ficiencies of those parts be positively inter-correlated, such that they yield such a
>bust g factor?

Ian Deary (2000, this volume) and Arthur Jensen (2000, this volume) have
ghtly argued that we must distinguish between the species-typical human
)gnitive architecture (which may be massively modular), and the factor-analytic
ructure of individual differences in cognitive functioning (which yields a unitary
factor). This distinction is obvious in the case of fitness itself: to claim that there is
i f factor in a particular species (which can capture individual differences in

general health and condition) is not to claim that a typical individual of that species is composed of just one bodily organ. The f factor is not a single gene or a single physical organ, and the g factor ('intelligence') is not a psychological organ. Rather, the g factor arises because each mental organ taps into the same basic set of genetic and neurophysiological variables (Jensen 1998). The existence of the g factor leaves completely open the question of how many psychological adaptations comprise human nature; it is not inconsistent with a highly modular mind.

A more interesting question is why we attach the honorific label of 'intelligence' to some of our modular psychological adaptations, and not to others. For example, why did Gardner (1993) choose the seven 'intelligences' (linguistic, logical-mathematical, spatial, musical, body-kinaesthetic, interpersonal, intrapersonal) that he did? His explicit criteria for distinguishing an intelligence from a non-intelligence are almost identical to the criteria that modern evolutionary psychologists (e.g. Pinker 1997) use to distinguish any modular, psychological adaptation from anything else. According to Gardner's explicit criteria (e.g. potential isolation by brain damage, a distinctive developmental history, evolutionary plausibility), dozens of psychological adaptations (including species-typical capacities for face recognition and social inference) should qualify as 'intelligences'.

However, Gardner alludes to an implicit criterion that actually does all the work: 'intelligences' are skills highly valued by a particular society. For example, Gardner rejects face recognition as an 'intelligence' because 'this ability does not seem highly valued by cultures' (Gardner 1993, p 61). In my terms, Gardner has picked out some of the highly g-loaded intelligence indicators, and what he calls 'culturally valued', I would call 'sexually attractive'. (Whenever social scientists talk about 'social status', evolutionary psychologists see the footprints of sexual selection.) Likewise, the evidence that Robert Sternberg (1988) cites for his 'triarchic theory' of intelligence — the fact that 'intelligence' to ordinary people connotes practical, social and academic forms of intelligence — suggests that there are practical, social and academic types of intelligence indicators.

However, the notion of intelligence indicators raises some problems for a strong version of the massive modularity view. If each psychological adaptation was totally modular at all levels of description (genes, developmental pathways, brain circuits, cognitive operations), then there would be no such thing as the g factor and no module could function as a very good fitness indicator either. Indicators are most reliable when they have some intrinsic correlation with the variable they are indicating, by virtue of sharing some lower-level biological processes. Total mental modularity would make intelligence indicators totally unreliable: efficiency in one behavioural domain would have no correlation with efficiency in other domains.

In fact, if sexual selection favoured certain psychological adaptations specifically as intelligence indicators, then those adaptations should be specifically designed to have a high degree of functional overlap with many other psychological adaptations — at least at the genetic, developmental and neurophysiological levels, if not at the cognitive and behavioural levels. The main way for an intelligence indicator to evolve a high g-loading would be to recruit a large number of genes, developmental pathways and brain circuits into its operation. Typically, this might be accomplished by evolving a very high degree of psychological complexity that draws upon a wide range of cognitive operations and mental representations. Conversation, art, music and humour do precisely that. According to this theory of intelligence indicators, the psychological complexity of such behaviours evolved not because complex survival problems demanded complex solutions, but because complex courtship displays are more easily disrupted by low fitness and low intelligence, and therefore make better indicators of both high g and high f.

Why is intelligence still heritable after all these years?

If the g factor is subordinate to the f factor, then the surprisingly high heritability of human intelligence may reflect the heritability of fitness itself across many species.

According to traditional population genetics, fitness should not remain heritable in any species at evolutionary equilibrium, because selection should remove any alleles that result in below-optimal fitness. However, molecular genetic research since the 1960s has shown surprisingly high amounts of fitness-related genetic variation in wild populations. Also, sexual selection theory since the 1980s has emphasized that optimal fitness is a moving target (Hamilton et al 1990), due to co-evolution between each species and its pathogens, parasites, predators and competitors. Moreover, the constant hail of mutations often keeps species from converging to optimal fitness, even when the fitness optimum is stable (see Eyre-Walker & Keightley 1999, Kondrashov 1995). Apparently, fitness remains at least moderately heritable in most species most of the time, and this is why mate choice mechanisms still bother to pay attention to fitness indicators (see Charlesworth 1987, Pomiankowski & Møller 1995, Møller & Swaddle 1997, Rowe & Houle 1996).

From this perspective, the continuing heritability of human intelligence may be a special case of the heritability of fitness itself, which is the evolutionary norm. But there is another effect called 'genic capture' (Rowe & Houle 1996) that may account for the especially high heritability of sexually selected fitness indicators, including intelligence indicators. In so far as intelligence indicators are favoured because they advertise general fitness, intelligence indicators should evolve to recruit an ever larger number of genes and developmental pathways into their operation, so they reveal more information about the quality of an individual's genome. In particular they should increase their 'mutational target size': their vulnerability to harmfu mutations, wherever they occur (Rowe & Houle 1996). (This follows th handicap principle: the easier a trait is to mess up through mutations, inbreeding injury, or disease, the better a fitness indicator it makes, and the more it will b favoured by sexual selection). The human brain apparently depends upon a ver large proportion of the human genome, which gives it a wonderfully larg mutational target size, from sexual selection's viewpoint. (Of course, if ever human gene were expressed in the human brain, the g factor would be identical t the f factor.) This leads to some final predictions that molecular genetics method should be able to test within a few years:

Prediction 6. A mental trait's g-loading should correlate positively with the numbe of quantitative trait loci upon which it depends.

Prediction 7. The g score indicated by a mental trait should correlate negatively witl the number of mutations affecting those loci.

Prediction 8. A mental trait's g-loading should correlate positively with its f loading.

Prediction 9. A mental trait's g-loading and f-loading should both correlat positively with its heritability.

The theory of sexual selection for intelligence indicators might not turn out t have the virtue of truth, but at least it has the virtues of falsifiability and consilience

References

Andersson M 1994 Sexual selection. Princeton University Press, Princeton, NJ
Bradbury JW, Vehrencamp SL 1998 Principles of animal communication. Sinauer, Sunderland MA
Buss DM 1989 Sex differences in human mate selection: evolutionary hypotheses tested in 3 cultures. Behav Brain Sci 12:1–49
Buss DM 1994 The evolution of desire: human mating strategies. Basic Books, New York
Charlesworth B 1987 The heritability of fitness. In: Bradbury JW, Andersson MB (eds) Sexua selection: testing the alternatives. Wiley, Chichester, p 21–40
Chorney MJ, Chorney K, Seese N et al 1998 A quantitative trait locus associated with cognitiv ability in children. Psychol Sci 9:159–166
Cosmides L, Tooby J 1994 Origins of domain specificity: the evolution of functiona organization. In: Hirschfeld LA, Gelman SA (eds) Mapping the mind: domain specificity i cognition and culture. Cambridge University Press, New York, p 85–116
Cronin H 1991 The ant and the peacock: altruism and sexual selection from Darwin to today Cambridge University Press, Cambridge
Deary I 2000 Psychometric intelligence differences and brain function. In: The nature o intelligence. Wiley, Chichester (Novartis Found Symp 233) p 58–78

yre-Walker A, Keightley PD 1999 High genomic deleterious mutation rates in hominids. Nature 397:344–347

arlow FB, Armijo-Prewitt T, Gangestad SW, Thornhill R 1997 Fluctuating asymmetry and psychometric intelligence. Proc R Soc Lond B Biol Sci 264:823–829

ardner H 1993 Frames of mind, 2nd edn. Basic Books, New York

rafen A 1990 Biological signals as handicaps. J Theor Biol 144:517–546

amilton WD, Axelrod R, Tanese R 1990 Sexual reproduction as an adaptation to resist parasites (a review). Proc Natl Acad Sci USA 87:3566–3573

asson O 1990 The role of amplifiers in sexual selection: an integration of the amplifying and Fisherian mechanisms. Evol Ecol 4:277–289

oule D 2000 Is there a *g* factor for fitness? In: The nature of intelligence. Wiley, Chichester (Novartis Found Symp 233) p 149–170

ensen AR 1998 The *g* factor: the science of mental ability. Praeger, Westport, CT

ensen AR 2000 The *g* factor: psychometrics and biology. In: The nature of intelligence. Wiley, Chichester (Novartis Found Symp 233) p 37–57

ohnstone RA 1995 Sexual selection, honest advertisement, and the handicap principle: reviewing the evidence. Biol Rev Camb Philos Soc 70:1–65

enrick DT, Sadalla EK, Groth G, Trost MR 1990 Evolution, traits, and the stages of human courtship: qualifying the parental investment model. J Personal 58:97–116

ondrashov AS 1995 Contamination of the genomes by very slightly deleterious mutations: why have we not died 100 times over? J Theor Biol 175:583–594

ande R 1987 Genetic correlation between the sexes in the evolution of sexual dimorphism and mating preferences. In: Bradbury JW, Andersson MB (eds) Sexual selection: testing the alternatives. Wiley, Chichester, p 83–95

ubinski D 2000 Intelligence: success and fitness. In: The nature of intelligence. Wiley, Chichester (Novartis Found Symp 233) p 6–36

IcGuffin P 2000 The quantitative and molecular genetics of human intelligence. In: The nature of intelligence. Wiley, Chichester (Novartis Found Symp 233) p 243–259

Iiller GF 1997 Mate choice: from sexual cues to cognitive adaptations. In: Characterizing human psychological adaptations. Wiley, Chichester (Ciba Found Symp 208) p 71–87

Iiller GF 1998 How mate choice shaped human nature: a review of sexual selection and human evolution. In: Crawford C, Krebs D (eds) Handbook of evolutionary psychology: ideas, issues, and applications. Lawrence Erlbaum, Mahwah, NJ, p 87–129

Iiller GF 1999 Sexual selection for cultural displays. In Dunbar R, Knight C, Power C (eds) The evolution of culture. Edinburgh University Press, Edinburgh, p 71–91

Iiller GF 2000 Mental traits as fitness indicators. Expanding evolutionary psychology's adaptationism. Ann NY Acad Sci 907:62–74

Iiller GF, Todd PM 1998 Mate choice turns cognitive. Trends Cognit Sci 2:190–198

Iøller AP, Swaddle JP 1997 Asymmetry, developmental stability and evolution. Oxford University Press, New York

inker S 1997 How the mind works. Norton, New York

omiankowski A, Møller A 1995 A resolution of the lek paradox. Proc R Soc Lond B Biol Sci 260:21–29

idley M 1993 The red queen: sex and the evolution of human nature. Viking, New York

owe L, Houle D 1996 The lek paradox and the capture of genetic variance by condition dependent traits. Proc R Soc Lond B Biol Sci 263:1415–1421

ternberg R 1988 The triarchic mind: a new theory of intelligence. Viking, New York

ooby J, Cosmides L 1990 The past explains the present: emotional adaptations and the structure of ancestral environments. Ethol Sociobiol 114:375–424

eblen T 1899 The theory of the leisure class. Macmillan, New York

Zahavi A, Zahavi A 1997 The handicap principle: a missing piece of Darwin's puzzle. Oxfo
University Press, New York

DISCUSSION

Bailey: Have you given up the sexual dimorphism in *g* too easily? The indire
evidence is that the single, best established sex difference in the brain is brain siz
even after controlling for body size. Do you know Jackson's data? He argues th
part of the reason why IQ tests don't show sex difference is because the items th
show sex difference are discarded. He presented data showing a difference of a fe
points when this is corrected for (D. N. Jackson, unpublished paper, 1st Int Beha
Dev Symp, 25–27 May 1995). Finally, it is well established that variation in IQ
higher for men than for women.

Miller: I'm not sure whether variation in *g* itself is higher in men. At least wit
respect to the behavioural advertisements of intelligence, it is true that from th
risk-seeking model that Andrew Pomiankowski advocated one would expe
higher variation in males than in females. The more relevant question
whether *g* is an index of fitness: if so, one would not expect sexual dimorphis
in *g*, because there should be no sexual dimorphism in overall average fitnes
This is less true if *g* is more like a costly indicator (rather than an index) c
fitness. The fact that there is a sex difference in brain size even after controllin
for body size suggests that brains are costly and they might be functioning mo
as indicators. I am still not sure what the relation is between the *g* factor and brai
size in that regard.

Hinde: Kittiwakes who don't breed successfully in one year find new mates th
next year. Is there any place in your system where you can account for matching, a
opposed to absolute value? Not everybody prefers the same mate, fortunatel
Attitude similarity is one of the critical factors in mate selection.

Miller: I have done some work with Peter Todd on mate search strategies. In th
work we predict that if there is general variation in fitness, then because of th
mating market you are probably going to end up with someone of similar fitnes
since you cannot afford to attract someone of higher fitness (they want someone a
least equal to themselves). If this is true, then one would expect psychologic
adaptations to evolve that prefer similarity itself. This keeps you from wastin
effort going after mates who won't have you anyway.

Hinde: All attempts to confirm that hypothesis for attractiveness have failed.

Miller: There is certainly a learning process: adolescents tend to aim too high
and then they learn what their limitations are and their criteria regress to what the
can afford.

Flynn: With regard to the sex differences for *g*, I have studied the Israeli militar
data, which is virtually a saturation sample of males. Although on average onl

% of females are sampled, there is enough variation from year to year to get a
ood estimate of the total population. These tests were not rigged for sexual
uality: one was a derivative from Raven's, which certainly has not been rigged.
he verbal test is derived from the old army alpha, which was not selected for sex.
hese show women about one point higher on the verbal, which consists of
uestions like, 'What is the last letter of the word that is the opposite of white?'
n the matrices the women are about 1.5 points below, but it is a heavily speeded
st, so visual memory might be the decisive factor there. I must admit that I'm
eptical that the brain size difference is significant between the sexes.

Jensen: The brain size difference itself is certainly significant, but it is not highly
rrelated with IQ — the correlation is about 0.4. There are any number of tests
here selection is not based on sex. The British Intelligence Scale is one of these,
d shows no sex differences whatsoever. The most interesting thing to me is that if
u put sex into a factor analytic battery, and put it into the correlation matrix as a
chotomous variable, it doesn't show any loading on g, even though it has
adings on just about every other factor. This is true for a fairly large battery of
fferent tests. I doubt that brain size itself is either a necessary or sufficient
ndition for high intelligence. A former student of mine has been studying true
idgets, who are about the size of three-year-old children, with correspondingly
nall heads, and they have a normal distribution of intelligence, and they are just as
telligent as their non-midget siblings (Kranzler et al 1998). I can't get excited
out the idea of sex differences in g.

Detterman: Related to that, has anyone ever looked at head size as being a factor
attractiveness?

Miller: Not that I know of.

Gangestad: It seems that smaller heads on males might be more attractive. Body
ze and head size do not scale isomorphically, so it might be that smaller heads
present larger body size. Statues tend to have smaller heads.

Harnad: We are faced with two competing theories: the 'functional' versus the
ecorative' theory of the evolutionary adaptive value of general intelligence. The
nctional theory would be the one that John Maynard Smith articulated before:
at its primary adaptive value has something to do with what intelligence gets you
rectly, and not with how sexy it is for the other gender. The decorative theory
ould be the other way round. One way that I can reconcile this is through the
riginal question I raised at the beginning of this meeting, which was, 'How
uch can we learn from psychometrics about the causal mechanism of
telligence?' My tentative answer was not much. This may be because the causal
echanism of intelligence was determined by the functional value of g, whereas the
ecorative one is what this variation is about. But if this were true, would it not
llow from your prediction that females ought to be better intuitive
sychometricians than males? It should also follow that people as a whole would

be better on-line intuitive psychometricians than the lousy off-line laboratory kin
of psychometrician.

Miller: Indeed, I think that people are pretty good intuitive psychometricians

Harnad: Then why are we bothering to construct tests? We should just be doin
interviews.

Miller: We use tests because interviews can be biased by other factors. Peopl
sometimes say why didn't we just give each other the equivalent of Raven
matrices in the Pleistocene? If any intelligence test that our ancestors might hav
used was too specific like that, people would have simply evolved a specia
adaptation to do that particular task that would not have a very high *g*-loading:
would just be a special purpose adaptation. What is required for an evolutionaril
stable intelligence indicator is something that is really complicated, lik
conversational ability over a span of weeks. It might not be as good as
psychometric test that has been developed specifically to measure contemporar
variation, but such a test would not have proven evolutionarily stable.

Jensen: The assortative mating coefficient is pretty close to 0.5, which is not muc
lower than, for example, the predictive validity of our best tests for scholasti
achievement.

Harnad: I know that, but I am curious. Should it be the case, then, that three t
four weeks of conversation ought to be able to beat the best psychometri
measure?

Deary: That is what Spearman started with. It was later scientists that criticize
him for not using tests. He used teachers' estimates in his first study, and he aske
the children in the playground which were the smartest fellow pupils. These a
correlated quite highly, so they were quite good lay psychometricians. Ther
Cyril Burt used interviews with people to estimate their intelligence, and look a
the trouble he got himself into!

Whiten: You cited the Buss study as one item in favour of your arguments: whe
you ask men and women to rank their preferred characteristics for mate
'intelligence' comes in as second. But I noticed that the *first* preference in bot
men and women is 'kindness and understanding'. This may overlap highly wit
what some of us are calling 'social intelligence', particularly when this is linke
with what Sternberg found out about what people's everyday conceptions abou
the scope of intelligence, i.e. it includes social intelligence. So perhaps Buss's dat
support your hypothesis even more strongly than you have indicated. This migh
also create an interesting link between what are otherwise two competing theorie
for the evolution of hominid intelligence: sexual selection and Machiavellia
intelligence. Finally, relating your work to the question that Stevan Harnad wa
raising about whether women should be better psychometricians than men, the
are so, apparently, with respect to 'kindness and understanding'. I don't know th
paper Stevan referred to, so I don't know what 'understanding' really did mean i

his context, but it sounds as if it has the potential to mean something akin to social ntelligence.

Miller: Two things about social intelligence: first, fitness indicators are not just useful in courtship. They are also useful in many other kinds of social interactions, such as discriminative investment in offspring (choosing which offspring deserve full attention and investment, and which don't), choosing allies and trading partners, and all sorts of similar social judgement tasks. Second, it is quite interesting that social sensitivity might be a particularly good intelligence indicator that is highly sexually valued. Here again, we would like to know what he g-loading is of highly challenging social inference tasks.

Brody: Some of the behaviour genetics literature I have seen suggests that assortative mating is not heritable at all. That is, it comes about simply because people with a certain level of intelligence tend to congregate together. Once you take out these effects there is no evidence of assortative mating because people are genetically similar. Assuming this is a correct inference from the literature, does his have any implications for your theory?

Miller: My whole theory can work even if there is not currently any heritable variation in mate preferences. Possibly we could all have exactly the same mate preferences and the same rank order of sexually desired cues we pay attention to, and we would still end up assortatively mating for intelligence, valuing intelligence highly and favouring intelligent males.

Brody: So your argument is that there is no variation, but the preference for an intelligent mate is not itself heritable.

Miller: For my argument to work, there doesn't have to be variation in the sexual preference for intelligence, but I suspect there is variation, and I frankly would like to see more replications of the studies that find no heritable variation in human mate preferences.

Brody: Reynolds et al (1996) studied the behaviour genetics of assortative mating. The paper indicates that assortative mating occurs as a result of social homogamy.

Houle: I have some sympathy for Geoffrey's thesis here, but I want to try to craft an alternative hypothesis to think about, which is that instead of thinking of mating as a genetic transaction, which is really the basis for Geoffrey's model, we think about it as an economic transaction and reverse the causality. Whatever makes one successful in society is what mates then prefer. This would explain a world where we have attention paid to g, but it wouldn't necessarily have had anything to do with the evolution of g. The question about the cause of assortative mating is relevant to this. Presumably a great deal of current assortative mating is because of the stratification that accompanies education. In a hunter-gatherer society, there would have been essentially no opportunity for such things. The group size was small, so there would be few available mates, and the environment would have been more homogeneous.

Humphrey: Stevan Harnad contrasted what he called the 'functional' view of intelligence and the 'decorative' view, and he seems to be attributing the decorative view to Geoffrey Miller. I think this is a misleading representation of Geoffrey's position as it is now. However, there was a time when Geoffrey suggested that g evolved as a result of runaway sexual selection of the non functional kind. The position he is coming from now is that g is a genuine indicator of fitness and not merely a decoration.

Harnad: Variation in g would be decorative; g itself would be functional.

Humphrey: No, variation in the displays of g would be decorative, and this is where one would expect the sexual dimorphism. But the fact that there seems to be no sexual dimorphism in g itself suggests that it is a fitness indicator and not a consequence of runaway sexual selection.

Miller: That is mostly right. The model I am arguing against is one in which *Homo erectus* has an IQ of about 20 and then there is an increase in g itself. This is a nonsensical model, in the same way that it's silly to think of evolution increasing average fitness in a population over the long term. Fitness tries to be as close to optimum as possible and keeps getting knocked back by mutation: I suspect that the same is true for g. What did evolve are the behavioural and cognitive indicators of g, which are a large suite of these psychological adaptations, many of which our early ancestors didn't have at all.

Harnad: I want to raise a question about the symmetry of male and female IQ. I don't subscribe to Geoffrey Miller's hypothesis, but if I did, I would want to argue that symmetry would be all the more important if females have to judge male fitness. It takes one to know one: if you are dumb, your discriminating capacity will be lower.

Miller: This might be where David Houle's point comes in. There are direct and indirect ways of assessing g. A direct way is through conversation. To follow someone who is really bright, you have to be reasonably bright yourself. The second way is through the proxy of social status. If you hear that someone has won a Fields Medal in mathematics, you may understand that is somehow a good thing, and it is possible to be attracted to them without having the slightest comprehension of what mathematical breakthrough they actually made.

Harnad: Do you have a Pleistocene counterpart for that?

Miller: Achieving high social status as a good hunter, or a good orator or someone with political influence.

Dunbar: Barry Keverne published a paper a few years ago showing that there is genomic imprinting on maternal genes for the neocortex, and there is paternal imprinting for genes that set up the limbic system. How might this fit in? And should we still believe this?

Pomiankowski: We should believe it in as much as the evidence says it is true. There is no explanation of this in terms of evolutionary biology.

Dunbar: What would be the implications of these results for some of the issues that we have been discussing, such as potential sex differences in g? Does this affect that argument?

Pomiankowski: I think it does, but I am reticent to say any more, because no one has published anything on this

Humphrey: Barry Keverne's discovery was with mice, so is there any reason to assume that this is also true of humans?

Pomiankowski: If it works in mice, it is probably true for humans. Mice are a proxy for humans at the level of gene expression.

References

Kranzler JH, Rosenbloom AL, Martinez V, Guevara-Aguire J 1998 Normal intelligence with severe insulin-like growth factor I deficiency due to growth hormone receptor deficiency: a controlled study in a genetically homogeneous population. J Clin Endocrinol Metab 83:1953–1958

Reynolds CA, Baker LA, Pedersen NL 1996 Models of spouse similarity. Application to fluid ability measured in twins and their spouses. Behav Genet 26:73–88

Final general discussion

Rutter: Let me start the wrap-up process by posing two questions. In the original proposal for this symposium, the suggestion was that the bringing together of evolutionary psychology and behaviour genetics would be informative for our understanding of the nature of intelligence. In the course of our discussions, no one has questioned the value of evolutionary studies of various kinds. What is not quite so clear, however, is what the value of these are for the understanding of the nature of intelligence, and also whether the conjunction with behaviour genetics adds anything.

Miller: If one is aware of certain aspects of evolutionary theory, such as mutation–selection balance and strategic polymorphisms, they provide interesting competing accounts of why *g* is so heritable and variable. Many of the measures of fitness and variance in animal species that have been developed provide interesting analogues of psychometric tests, and they might be mutually illuminating. They have been in this symposium.

Rutter: I accept that, as I suspect most of us would. But let us look ahead 30 years, if evolutionary psychology has developed in the way that you and others would like it to develop, what will we have learned about the nature of intelligence?

Miller: In my paper in particular, what I am striving for is a theory of *g*-loadings. I want to explain why some mental adaptations are so much more dependent on *g* than others, and why some are more variable and heritable. If we can have a predictive theory which says which mental adaptations are and aren't, this is a step forward in understanding intelligence.

Mackintosh: Do we know now which of these indicators are or aren't more *g* loaded?

Miller: No; that is why I am making this as a prediction. If I waited until the data were in, people would say that I am simply telling you a 'just so' story.

Mackintosh: To an experimental or cognitive psychologist, the question 'What is the nature of intelligence?' is not being addressed by your work. You are answering a quite different question. The experimental psychologist wants to know: what are the proximal cognitive reasons for this continued variation in human cognitive ability? What does it mean for someone to be more intelligent? What can they do that someone who is less intelligent can't? I wouldn't have thought that we had got very much further by this marriage of evolutionary psychology and psychometrics.

Rutter: Throughout the whole of the meeting no one has questioned the value of either quantitative or molecular behaviour genetics. What will either tell us about the nature of intelligence, however, and does the conjunction of evolutionary psychology add to this?

McGuffin: I tend to agree with Nick Humphrey that behaviour genetics is 'agnostic'. Inevitably, what behaviour genetics will tell us, moving on from quantitative and positional cloning, is what the substrate is of whatever it is that varies in the population. I don't think it will tell us much about why intelligence varies and why it continues to vary, but it will tell us about the nuts and bolts of intelligence.

Rutter: Supposing that your molecular genetics approach does work out, how do you see that leading to a greater understanding of intelligence? There will be the problem of a whole host of genes, and the problem of sorting out what each of those actually does in terms of a gene product and how that gene product actually leads to intelligence functioning. Do you see this leading to a coherent story?

McGuffin: Broadly speaking, we will uncover three sets of genes: those involved in neural development and the organization of the cortex, those involved in neurotransmission and those that we haven't got a clue about.

Brody: One of the long-term pay-offs of defining intelligence molecularly is that we will be able to understand the environment in a way that we have never been able to in the past. Currently, if you want to infer the genotype, all you have is the phenotype. If we had an independent measure of the genotype, we could begin to look at genotype–phenotype discrepancies, and begin to ask questions about why those discrepancies exist. We could then think more critically about modifying the environment in ways that would allow people to actualize whatever potentials they did in fact possess.

Humphrey: On the question of what evolutionary psychology can contribute to understanding human intelligence, one can compare the question of what evolutionary psychology can contribute to understanding language. Evolutionary psychology has a strong story to tell about the conditions under which language would have been adaptive and how it evolved, and how language now develops in the individual under the influence of learning and genes. But it wouldn't of course pretend to answer the question of what we can now do with language, because we can do many things with language which are completely open-ended and never played a part in evolution. In just the same way, an evolutionary approach to intelligence can say interesting things about the conditions under which human beings acquired the levels of intelligence they now have, and about how intelligence develops during childhood. But no one should expect it to answer the question of what people can now do with their intelligence. Evolution gave us capacities which can now be applied in a host of different ways that impact our present day lives, but about which evolutionary psychology can't even begin to comment.

Gangestad: On the first day of this meeting it was pointed out that there are a couple of separate issues being discussed here. One is, 'What is the nature of intelligence as you can learn by studying an $n=1$?' and then the other is, 'Why is there variation, and what is the nature of g?' There is an evolutionary story that could underlie each of those issues. I think it was David Houle who first pointed out that these stories may be very different. The genes that account for what we call 'intelligence' and that we can understand from an $n=1$ may be more or less fixed in the population, with some variations that are not functionally consequential. What accounts for the variation? Perhaps factors that are not specific to understanding intelligence. In some species, genes have been found to affect learning, but in general these genes disrupt the development of the organism in all sorts of ways including screwing up learning. The evolutionary perspective is useful in understanding at least that point.

Houle: I'm struck by the distinction between within-species g and among-species g. Human g is a creature of the variation of mental abilities, not of mental abilities themselves. Psychometricians are very concerned with which traits g loads on more. It would be absurd to try to define g in another species based on the direction of a vector in a space defined by variation in human abilities. The space of variation in rats is a different space from that in humans. There is another level of variation among species that we haven't talked about much. That is, why are we different from chimpanzees? One way to get at that from a genetic direction is to sequence the chimpanzee genome as well as the human genome. Then you can ask the question about what it is that is different between these two species, try to assign functional significance to these differences, and then ask about whether there is any relationship between the genes that cause us to be different from chimpanzees and those that cause us to be different from each other. I suspect that there will not, but that is an interesting question.

Nesse: The tension that we have been flirting with throughout this meeting is between variation within the species and between species. The other latent question is what evolutionary forces are responsible for shaping high intelligence in humans? Geoffrey Miller's hypothesis takes its place as a viable competitor in that particular constellation, but there are several others. We need to lay them out together and see what differential predictions they make. Nick Humphrey has been instrumental in talking about social complexity as a potential selective force; other people have talked about language and thought *per se*; some have talked about group hunting. We also need to distinguish between the runaway sexual selection model, and the sexual selection model having more to do with quality: it would be very interesting to try to tease these apart. Just to go back to where David was, if in fact we can identify these genes that differentiate the development of cognitive architecture in humans from chimps, it will be interesting to see if those genes do contribute to variation in *g*, which is a very different idea than the one that it is just 30 miscellaneous deleterious mutations that are being trapped by *g*.

Maynard Smith: I want to introduce a point of view that has hardly arisen during the last few days. For the last 50 years people have been saying, 'If only we understood development, that would completely transform our understanding of evolution', and I have said this myself. Only during the last 15 years have molecular techniques enabled us to use genetic tools to discover how development does work: it is much the most important thing that is happening in biology right now. We are now at last beginning to understand how development works by identifying particular genes. I suspect that partly by comparisons between humans and chimps and partly by identifying genes which, when they go wrong, produce serious changes in mental function, we might be able to do to brain function what at the moment is being done to the development of the embryo — namely find out how it works. The trouble is that the techniques which we are using for disentangling the developmental recipe are not easily applicable to the development of human intelligence, for perfectly good moral reasons. We can't do human gene knockouts. I am left with the feeling from these discussions that an approach which is centred on the study of variation of intelligence between more or less normal individuals is not a very helpful way of understanding how the machine that is varying works. If you want to know how the brain works, this technique is not telling us much.

Rutter: So you are arguing for a developmental approach.

Maynard Smith: I'm not sure. If I were a young person just starting, I would go for genes with major effects on specific cognitive abilities, such as language or music.

Harnad: I agree, and all I wish to add is a little nomenclature on top of what you have said. Let's make a distinction between cardiology and cardiometry: cardiometry is the study of the individual differences in heart rate and heart performance, and cardiology would be understanding the heart and how it works. I wouldn't put developmental biology in the place of real 'cardiology': I would say cognitive modelling is what is going to tell us about the nature of intelligence. We have to model the causal mechanisms that generates the function. The cardiometry is just talking about the variation in the 'decorative' functions of the heart.

Deary: Just in case the last two speakers think that differential psychologists agree with that, they do: it has been a long time since anyone has seriously thought that individual-differences psychology tells us the structure of mind. We are waiting at the table of the cognitive psychologists to receive the cognitive architecture, for them to tell us about the modal structure of the mind so we can pick off some individual parameters, find individual differences of these and see whether they account for variance in individual differences in psychometric test scores. Before I came here I made a point of looking at an edition of *Intelligence* in the late 1970s where they guessed what intelligence would look like in the year 2000. It is poignant reading. One view was that someone called 'factor-man' was going to change into someone called 'component-man': that is, the cognitive structure of mind was going to be worked out and provide a better-validated account of intelligence individual differences. It hasn't happened yet.

Humphrey: Let me take up John Maynard Smith's point that if he were a young researcher he would be looking for genes that have major direct effects on cognitive abilities. What I understand from Geoffrey Miller's model is that there probably are no such genes varying in the normal population. Those genes which do in fact have a major role in providing cognitive abilities have all gone to fixation, so that almost all humans now have them in full measure; but unfortunately in most people they can't function optimally because of the mutation load. If this is right, then it suggests that Peter McGuffin's programme of looking at the high end is not going to find any interesting genes affecting major components of intelligence. Annette Karmiloff-Smith's programme is more likely to work because it is only at the low end, in pathological cases, that we're likely to find variation in the crucial genes.

McGuffin: I emphasized the study of ability rather than disability in my paper because that was my brief, but we are actually backing multiple horses. I am peripherally involved in a study of reading disability, and this is an area where quite a lot of progress is being made and it looks like there are some replications and the genes are being mapped. There are genes on chromosome 6p and 15q that contribute to reading disability. As far as we know from the quantitative genetics, it is probably the same set of genes that contribute to reading ability in the middle of the range. We can do both things.

Jensen: We have been discussing extensively two different avenues for understanding the nature of intelligence and of *g*. These have been the analysis of the genome and the evolutionary approach. We haven't considered whether there is any value in studying the brain directly. I wouldn't know, but there may be people here who could comment on whether this is a hopeless task or not.

Harnad: I think it is a hopeless task. It is the wrong methodology. If before the days of aeronautical engineering, aeroplanes grew on trees and we were trying to reverse-engineer the functional capacity of aeroplanes rather than the functional capacity of human beings, 'neuroaeroscience' (planes' 'anatomy' and 'physiology') would do us no good. We would need to have some models that would try to *do* what planes do, and then confirm this with the peeking and the poking.

Closing remarks

Michael Rutter

Social, Genetic and Developmental Psychiatry Research Centre, Institute of Psychiatry, De
Crespigny Park, Denmark Hill, London SE5 8AF, UK

My aim in reflecting on our discussions over the last three days is to consider how the bringing together of different research traditions, paradigms and ideas has informed us about the nature of intelligence. Geoffrey Miller's focus in proposing this symposium was on evolutionary psychology and behavioural genetics but the papers covered a broader range, so let me start by noting some of their messages. Britt Anderson was persuasive in arguing that intelligence is an attribute that can be observed in a wide range of animal species and that, in all of them (as in humans), there is marked individual variation. Experimental studies in animals have been informative in showing that interferences with brain structure affect cognitive performance. Recombinant inbred strains, too, can be of value in identifying gene loci with effects on intelligence. The potential of animal studies is clear, although it has to be said that the findings so far remain at a rather general level and have shed only limited light on the nature of intelligence.

Ian Deary brought together a range of research strategies, all of which were designed to relate aspects of brain function to cognitive performance. Again, it is evident that the potential is rich but the harvest so far has been relatively modest. There is a group of replicated findings but in all cases the effect sizes are rather small. At least on the evidence so far, it appears unlikely that the biological basis of intelligence will prove to be a single process, although we remain rather ignorant about how different mechanisms work together.

Andrew Whiten drew attention to the social components that are involved in cognitive performance, asking questions on the extent to which social intelligence (meaning skills in reading and responding to social situations) is the same as abstract logical reasoning skills.

James Flynn took a quite different approach in alerting us to the major rise in measured intelligence that has taken place over time. His findings are convincing in their inference that the rise has been real and not just an artefact of IQ test familiarity. It is evident that some sort of environmental influences must be responsible for the rise, although uncertainty remains on quite what such influences may be.

All four papers served to make us think about the concepts and ideas of sever
key people who were unable to attend the meeting. Let me speculate on what som
of them might have said, if they had been present. Endel Tulving (1983) or Ala
Baddeley (1990) undoubtedly would have followed Annette Karmiloff-Smith'
lead in highlighting the value of studying abnormal groups of one kind c
another. Research in that tradition has been hugely informative in demonstratin
crucial differences between the various forms of memory. The same value applies t
the dissection of variations among cognitive skills. The findings do not necessaril
run counter to the concept of *g* but they definitely underline (the dangers) c
assuming that just because tests intercorrelate they necessarily reflect the sam
underlying function. We need to use research strategies that pull apart differer
cognitive skills, as well as those that put them together, in order to see if thei
external correlates are different.

Chris Frith or Michael Posner, similarly, would have followed Ian Deary's lea
in pointing to the understanding of cognitive function that can stem fror
functional brain imaging (Posner & Raichle 1994, Fletcher et al 1995, Rug
1997). It can be informative in several different ways, but let me mention jus
two. First, by showing that different areas of the brain are involved in differer
cognitive functions (or, alternatively, that the same area subserves sever.
supposedly different functions), it can both dissect apart and group togethe
cognitive skills. Second, by comparing normal and abnormal groups, it can te:
whether the two deal with the same cognitive tasks through different brai
processes. Again, the implication is the need to consider the role of differer
cognitive processes and to appreciate that the same task may be dealt with b
more than one cognitive strategy.

Steve Ceci (Ceci et al 1994a,b) would have reminded us, too, of the importance c
the ways in which intellectual performance is affected by social context. Studies c
cognitive functioning have reflected two contrasting paradigms; on the one han
the Ebbinghaus tradition of investigating cognition through disembodied task
and, on the other hand, the Bartlett tradition of studying performance withi
particular social and substantive contexts. From the late 1960s onwards there ha
been an integration of the two approaches that both recognizes the predictiv
power of IQ tests and emphasizes the role of context as an influence on everyda
cognitive performance. I doubt that he would disagree with any of the main point
that have come out of this meeting but he would urge the value of a developmenta
perspective that appreciates the multiplicity of cognitive resources, and tha
accepts that these include non-intellectual as well as intellectual features.

Let me return to the topic of *g*, as considered from several different perspective
in the papers by David Lubinski, Arthur Jensen, Nathan Brody and Dougla
Detterman. All of us accept its reality. It is not merely a statistical artefact; rathe:
it really does represent something that is biologically important. Equally, it seem

that all of us recognize the reality and importance in some circumstances of special skills. Whether or not they come at the top or bottom of anyone's list of priorities is crucially dependent on the questions being investigated. Special skills and g both contribute to our understanding of cognitive processes.

We also had some useful discussion about the fact that the presence of a special skill does not necessarily imply a rigid modularity. Moreover, the point was made that, in the study of special groups (whether they be individuals with Williams syndrome or autism or severe language delay), the findings have often led to an appreciation that the special skills or deficits are often rather broader than expected on the basis of the traditional concepts as they applied a generation ago.

Conversely, we have also agreed that an acceptance that g is real and has a biological basis does not mean that it is unitary in either the neural functions that it represents or the causal processes that lead to its development. We have varied somewhat in our optimism with respect to what the biological correlates findings have demonstrated but we are largely agreed on the need to investigate a range of neural mechanisms. Currently, we have some limited understanding of the biological basis of cognitive functioning but there is a great deal more to learn. The main question for us has been the extent to which a bringing together of behaviour genetics and evolutionary psychology is likely to aid the gaining of that understanding.

The utility of quantitative genetics for the study of the interplay between genes and environment in the development of individual differences in cognitive skills was accepted by all participants at the symposium. As noted by both Michael Bailey and Peter McGuffin, the findings are consistent in showing that intelligence, like many other traits, shows a moderately strong heritability. Estimates vary across the range of 30% to 80% but there are no important implications of just where in that range it really is. Whatever the figure, genetic influences are substantial. The real value of quantitative genetics does not, and cannot, lie in more precise estimates of the 'true' heritability, if only because heritability figures are population-specific. Instead, the informativeness is to be found in the specifics. Thus, we noted the evidence that the genetic contribution may vary according to the level of cognitive functioning, apparently being greater at the upper end. We also discussed the new evidence (Rowe et al 1999) that environmental factors may be more influential when there is social disadvantage. It was generally accepted that the findings on within-group heritability cannot be extrapolated to the reasons for between-group differences in mean IQ.

Much the same applies to the rise in IQ levels over time — the so-called Flynn effect. Clearly, it is implausible that this has a genetic origin — the gene pool cannot change that quickly. However, we remain in doubt over just which aspects of the environment have been responsible. Turkheimer (1991) made the point that it is a mistake to assume that effects on the level of a trait are necessarily different from effects on individual differences. But, equally, it cannot be assumed that they are the same (Rutter & Smith 1995). The connections between the two require empirical study.

Much the same applies to the distinction between shared and nonshared environmental effects — in other words, the extent to which environmental factors make siblings in the same family similar or different. As both Rutter (2000, Rutter et al 1999) and Turkheimer & Waldron (2000) have pointed out, the behaviour genetic arguments on this topic are rather misleading. Family-wide influences *are* important but often they impinge on individual children in the same family in different ways. Perhaps, the more crucial question is whether environmental influences mainly operate as moderators of genetic liability or as specific causal influences determining the growth of intelligence or the particular pattern of cognitive skills. The evidence is clear that experiences *do* influence cognitive development but, at least so far, the findings do not suggest that they shape the basic pattern of cognitive function.

By contrast, the evidence suggests that, on the whole, the genetic liability underlying specific cognitive skills overlaps greatly with that underlying general intelligence (Cardon & Fulker 1993, Casto et al 1995). That does not necessarily mean that there are no genetic effects or specific cognitive skills or deficits in unusual groups but it does suggest that, in the general population, there is validity to the notion that, to a considerable extent, the same underlying liability applies to both general and specific cognitive skills. It is also relevant that, for the most part, the same genes affect cognitive performance throughout the period of development (Cherny et al 1997).

Peter McGuffin outlined the potential of molecular genetics. There is no doubt that findings on specific susceptibility genes will be informative in a host of different ways (Plomin et al 1997, Rutter & Plomin 1997, Plomin & Rutter 1998). However, the extent to which they will be so in the field of intelligence is perhaps rather more uncertain. Interestingly, in view of the controversies that surround the topic, there was more discussion on the issues in the informal meetings between sessions than in the recorded exchanges during the symposium. Insofar as there was scepticism, it centred on a realization that the positive finding that has been published did not take account of possible stratification biases and has yet to be replicated by other research groups; and that it is dubious whether the findings will lead to an understanding of any unifying causal processes. They may do so but the excitement over this approach to the study of the nature of intelligence is far from universally shared.

In their different ways, David Houle, Randy Nesse, Andrew Pomiankowski and Geoffrey Miller each demonstrated the strength and value of evolutionary psychology research strategies. Sometimes, popularizers of evolutionary approaches are open to the criticism that they are simply telling 'just so ories — explaining what might be the case rather than testing competing ypotheses (Ketelaar & Ellis 2000). The papers in this symposium vividly emonstrate that this is not so with the best of this field of research. On the other and, the findings also raise basic questions about the assumptions underlying isher's fundamental theorem. In a general sense, it may well be true that volutionary influences on adaptive traits will result in the elimination of ubstantial genetic variation between individuals once evolutionary equilibrium as been achieved. It is in this way that features such as a potential for language ecome a universal part of human functioning determined by non-segregating enes shared by everyone rather than segregating genes that bring about ndividual differences. But this apparently straightforward notion raises a host of uestions. To begin with, how can one tell when equilibrium is achieved? Does volution prepare organisms for a particular environment or a range of different nvironments with quite different challenges? To what extent is there evolutionary election for variance rather than for particular levels of traits? Are effects ondition-dependent to a considerable degree? The inescapable conclusion is that he supposed paradox that constituted the basis for this symposium does not exist. volution, as it applies to strongly selected characteristics, does not necessarily esult in the elimination of additive genetic variance. Intelligence is not an xception to a general rule; to the contrary, the findings fit in well with those that pply to a whole series of other traits.

With respect to the general concept of evolutionary fitness, we have rejected the dea that the widely established, but relatively modest, correlation between IQ and ocial success has anything to do with evolutionary fitness. Fitness concerns the umber of surviving well-functioning offspring produced by an individual over lifetime and not the person's social success as measured in other ways. Nevertheless, we heard arguments that the latter may have implications for the ormer. We spent some time considering the ways in which changing conditions n the world may have implications for the manner in which evolutionary forces perate in contemporary society. Not only is it likely that the situation will be hanged by factors such as birth control and assisted reproduction but also the hanging social situations may have implications for the ways in which ndividual differences operate.

I have been puzzled by the contrasting views among us in our concept of the ways in which individual differences within the normal range are due to normal llelic variations or to the accumulation of minor pathological mutations. In a eal sense, all allelic variations have to start as mutations so it may be that we are sing different words to mean the same thing, but that does not seem to be the omplete explanation. For me, at least, that remains an unresolved issue that equires more penetrating discussion than we have been able to have in this ymposium, given that the question is a bit peripheral to our main focus.

Nevertheless, perhaps it does warrant more debate because I remain uncertai
whether the differences in concept amongst us are real.

It would be foolhardy of me to attempt any kind of 'bottom line' message fror
the meeting. Even so, I am sure that we are agreed on the value of botl
evolutionary psychology and behavioural genetics. Both must constitute parts o
the overall research portfolio to be brought to bear on the question of the nature o
intelligence but there is some scepticism on the extent to which, on their own or ir
combination, they provide the best means of tackling the problem. The implici
conclusion throughout our discussion has been the need to use these strategies ir
conjunction with other approaches.

References

Baddeley A 1990 Human memory: theory and practice. Lawrence Erlbaum Associates, Hove

Cardon LR, Fulker DW 1993 Genetics of specific cognitive abilities. In: Plomin R, McClearn GI
   (eds) Nature, nurture, and psychology. American Psychological Association, Washingtor
   DC, p 99–120

Casto SD, DeFries JC, Fulker DW 1995 Multivariate genetic analysis of Wechsler Intelligenc
   Scale for Children — Revised (WISC-R) factors. Behav Genet 25:25–32

Ceci SJ, Baker-Sennett JG, Bronfenbrenner U 1994a Psychometric and everyday intelligence
   synonyms, antonyms and anonyms. In: Rutter M, Hay D (eds) Development through life:
   handbook for clinicians. Blackwell Scientific, Oxford, p 260–283

Ceci SJ, Bronfenbrenner U, Baker-Sennett JG 1994b Cognition in and out of context: a tale o
   two paradigms. In: Rutter M, Hay D (eds) Development through life: a handbook fo
   clinicians. Blackwell Scientific, Oxford, p 239–259

Cherny SS, Fulker DW, Hewitt JK 1997 Cognitive development from infancy to middl
   childhood. In: Sternberg RJ, Grigorenko E (eds) Intelligence, heredity, and environmeni
   Cambridge University Press, New York, p 463–482

Fletcher P, Happé F, Frith U et al 1995 Other minds in the brain: a functional imaging study o
   'theory of mind' in story comprehension. Cognition 57:109–128

Ketelaar T, Ellis BJ 2000 Are evolutionary explanations falsifiable? Evolutionary psycholog
   and the Lakotosian philosophy of science. Psychol Inquiry 11:1–68

Plomin R, Rutter M 1998 Child development, molecular genetics and what to do with genes onc
   they are found. Child Dev 69:1223–1242

Plomin R, DeFries JC, McClearn GE, Rutter M 1997 Behavioral genetics. WH Freeman, Nev
   York

Posner M, Raichle M 1994 Images of mind. Scientific American Library, New York

Rowe DC, Jacobson KC, van den Ooord JCG 1999 Genetic and environmental influences oi
   vocabulary IQ: parental education level as a moderator. Child Dev 70:1151–1162

Rugg MD (ed) 1997 Cognitive neuroscience. Psychology Press, Hove

Rutter M 2000 Psychosocial influences: critiques, findings and research needs. Dev Psychopathc
   12:375–405

Rutter M, Plomin R 1997 Opportunities for psychiatry from genetic findings. Br J Psychiatr
   171:209–219

Rutter M, Smith DJ (eds) 1995 Psychosocial disorders in young people: time trends and thei
   causes. Wiley, Chichester

Rutter M, Silberg J, O'Connor T, Simonoff E 1999 Genetics & child psychiatry: I. Advances ii
   quantitative and molecular genetics. J Child Psychol Psychiatry 40:3–18

Turkheimer E 1991 Individual and group differences in adoption studies of IQ. Psychol Bull 110:392–405

Turkheimer E, Waldron M 2000 Nonshared environment: a theoretical, methodological, and quantitative review. Psychol Bull 126:78–108

Tulving E 1983 Elements of episodic memory. Oxford University Press, London

Index of contributors

Entries in bold indicate papers; other entries refer to discussion contributions.

288

Subject index